THE MACARTHUR NEW TESTAMENT COMMENTARY

1 PETER

John MacArthur Jr.

MOODY PUBLISHERS/CHICAGO

Library of Congress Cataloging-in-Publication Data

MacArthur, John, 1939-
    1 Peter / by John MacArthur, Jr.
        p. cm. — (The MacArthur New Testament commentary)
    ISBN 0-8024-1501-6
    1. Bible. N.T. Peter, 1st—Commentaries. I. Title: First Peter. II. Title.

BS2795.53M23 2004
227'.92077—dc22

2004003857

1 3 5 7 9 10 8 6 4 2

To Louis Herwaldt,
with gratitude for exceptional leadership
and generosity in sharing the vision
and faithfully enduring, through all the years of struggle and sacrifice,
to the present joys of its fulfillment in the outpouring of God's grace on
The Master's College and Seminary. We wouldn't be here without you!

Contents

Preface

It continues to be a rewarding, divine communion for me to preach expositionally through the New Testament. My goal is always to have deep fellowship with the Lord in the understanding of His Word and out of that experience to explain to His people what a passage means. In the words of Nehemiah 8:8, I strive "to give the sense" of it so they may truly hear God speak and, in so doing, may respond to Him.

Obviously, God's people need to understand Him, which demands knowing His Word of Truth (2 Tim. 2:15) and allowing that Word to dwell in them richly (Col. 3:16). The dominant thrust of my ministry, therefore, is to help make God's living Word alive to His people. It is a refreshing adventure.

This New Testament commentary series reflects this objective of explaining and applying Scripture. Some commentaries are primarily linguistic, others are mostly theological, and some are mainly homiletical. This one is basically explanatory, or expository. It is not linguistically technical but deals with linguistics when that seems helpful to proper interpretation. It is not theologically expansive but focuses on the major doctrines in each text and how they relate to the whole of Scripture. It is not primarily homiletical, although each unit of thought is generally treated as one chapter, with a clear outline and logical flow of thought.

Most truths are illustrated and applied with other Scripture. After establishing the context of a passage, I have tried to follow closely the writer's development and reasoning.

My prayer is that each reader will fully understand what the Holy Spirit is saying through this part of His Word, so that His revelation may lodge in the mind of believers and bring greater obedience and faithfulness—to the glory of our great God.

Introduction to 1 Peter

Throughout the nearly two millennia of its existence, the church of Jesus Christ has been no stranger to suffering. The clash of truth with error, of the kingdom of light with the kingdom of darkness, and of the children of God with the children of the devil inevitably results in severe conflict. Opposition, rejection, ostracism, scorn, contempt, persecution, even martyrdom have been the lot of believers through the centuries. That the evil world system vents its fury on the church should surprise no one, for that is how it treated the Lord Jesus Christ. Describing the persecution His followers would experience, Jesus pointed out the axiomatic truth, "A disciple is not above his teacher, nor a slave above his master. It is enough for the disciple that he become like his teacher, and the slave like his master. If they have called the head of the house Beelzebul, how much more will they malign the members of his household!" (Matt. 10:24–25).

Centuries before His birth, Isaiah predicted that Christ would be "despised and forsaken of men, a man of sorrows and acquainted with grief" (Isa. 53:3). The apostle John noted His rejection by the sinful world: "He was in the world, and the world was made through Him, and the world did not know Him. He came to His own, and those who were His own did not receive Him" (John 1:10–11). Jesus plainly told the disciples that He was going to suffer and be killed. Matthew 16:21 records that "Jesus began to show His disciples that He must go to Jerusalem, and suffer many things from the elders and chief priests and scribes, and be killed, and be raised up on the third day" (cf. 17:12; Mark 8:31; 9:12; Luke 9:22; 17:25; 22:15; 24:26, 46; Acts 1:3; 3:18; 17:3; 26:23; Heb. 2:10, 18; 5:8; 13:12; 1 Peter 1:11; 2:21, 23; 4:1; 5:1).

Unable to attack Jesus after His ascension, the enemies of the truth assaulted His followers. Stung by its phenomenal growth, the Jewish authorities desperately and futilely tried to stamp out the newly formed church. Acts 4:1–3 records that

> as [Peter and John] were speaking to the people, the priests and the captain of the temple guard and the Sadducees came up to them, being greatly disturbed because they were teaching the people and proclaiming in Jesus the resurrection from the dead. And they laid hands on them and put them in jail until the next day, for it was already evening.

The next day the Sanhedrin ordered them to stop preaching in the name of Jesus (4:5–21). Undaunted, the apostles continued to preach the gospel, and as a result, "the high priest rose up, along with all his associates (that is the sect of the Sadducees), and they were filled with jealousy. They laid hands on the apostles and put them in a public jail" (5:17–18). Miraculously released from the jail, they went to the temple and resumed preaching the gospel (5:19–25). Hauled before the Sanhedrin a second time, the apostles were once again ordered to stop preaching in the name of Jesus—a threat punctuated this time with a beating (5:26–40). The bold, powerful preacher Stephen faced opposition (6:9–11), arrest, trial before the Sanhedrin (6:12–7:56), and martyrdom (7:57–60). The first persecution aimed at the church as a whole broke out following Stephen's martyrdom (8:1–4; 9:1–2; 11:19). It was spearheaded by the young Jewish firebrand, Saul of Tarsus, who would become the apostle Paul. Later the wicked King Herod killed James the brother of John and arrested Peter—only to see the latter miraculously freed from jail by an angel (12:1–11).

Following his dramatic conversion while en route to Damascus (9:3–18), Paul, once the church's most vicious persecutor, became its most zealous missionary. The Lord set the course of his ministry when He told Ananias, "I will show him how much he must suffer for My name's sake" (Acts 9:16). And suffer he did, almost from the very moment of his conversion (cf. Acts 9:20–25). As he traveled throughout the Roman Empire boldly proclaiming the faith he had once tried to destroy (Gal. 1:23), Paul faced continual affliction and unrelenting opposition (Acts

14:5–6, 19–20; 16:16–40; 17:5–9, 13–14, 18, 32; 18:12–17; 19:9, 21–41; 20:3, 22–23; 21:27–36; 23:12–24:9; 25:10–11; 27:1–28:28; cf. 1 Thess. 2:2; 2 Tim. 1:12; 2:9–10; 3:11). Not surprisingly, suffering is a major theme in his epistles (e.g., Rom. 8:17–18; 2 Cor. 1:5–7; Phil. 1:29; 3:8–10; 1 Thess. 2:14; 2 Thess. 1:5; 2 Tim. 1:8; 2:3).

As time went on, the persecution of the church became more organized, widespread, and barbaric. What began as the isolated acts of the Jewish authorities, or Jewish and Gentile mobs, gradually evolved into the official policy of the Roman government, which saw the refusal of Christians to participate in the state religion as a form of rebellion. Three centuries of increasingly savage and widespread persecutions culminated early in the fourth century in Emperor Diocletian's all-out effort to stamp out the church. In a startling reversal of this, Emperor Constantine in A.D. 313, along with the ruler of the eastern part of the Empire, Licinius, issued the edict of Milan, which granted full toleration to the Christian faith.

Under the Roman Catholic Church, which replaced Imperial Rome as the dominant power during the Middle Ages, persecution broke out anew. The horrors of the Inquisition, the St. Bartholomew's Day Massacre, and the martyrdoms of men like Jan Hus, Hugh Latimer, Nicholas Ridley, Thomas Cranmer, and William Tyndale epitomized the Roman Church's effort to exterminate the gospel of Jesus Christ. More recently, Christians have been brutally repressed by communist and Islamic regimes all over the world.

As Peter penned this epistle, the dark clouds of the first great outbreak of official persecution, instigated by the insane Emperor Nero, were already gathering on the horizon. Seeking scapegoats to divert the public's suspicion that he had started the great fire of July, A.D. 64 that devastated Rome, Nero pinned the blame on the Christians, whom he already perceived as enemies of Rome because they would worship none but Christ. As a result, they were encased in wax and burned at the stake to light his gardens, crucified, and thrown to wild beasts. Though the official persecution apparently was confined to the vicinity of Rome, attacks on Christians undoubtedly spread unchecked by the authorities to other parts of the Empire. It was as a result of Nero's persecution that both Peter and Paul were martyred. But before he died, Peter wrote this magnificent epistle to believers whose suffering would soon intensify. Throughout the centuries, beleaguered Christians have benefited from the apostle's wise counsel and gentle, encouraging words of comfort.

AUTHOR

Peter was the acknowledged leader and spokesman of the Twelve; his name heads all four New Testament lists of the apostles (Matt. 10:2–4; Mark 3:16–19; Luke 6:13–16; Acts 1:13). Peter and his brother Andrew (who introduced him to Jesus [John 1:40–42]) ran a fishing business on the Sea of Galilee (Matt. 4:18; Luke 5:1–3). They were originally from the village of Bethsaida (John 1:44), but later moved to the larger nearby town of Capernaum (Mark 1:21,29). The brothers' business was a successful one, which allowed them to own a spacious house in Capernaum (Mark 1:29, 32–33; Luke 4:38). Peter was married; Jesus healed his mother-in-law (Luke 4:38–39); and his wife accompanied him on his missionary travels (1 Cor. 9:5).

Peter's birth name was Simon, a common name in first-century Palestine. (There are eight other Simons mentioned in the New Testament: Simon the Zealot [Matt. 10:4]; Simon the half brother of the Lord [Matt. 13:55]; Simon the leper [Matt. 26:6]; Simon of Cyrene, who was drafted to carry Jesus' cross [Matt. 27:32], Simon the Pharisee, at whose home Jesus ate a meal [Luke 7:36–40]; Simon, the father of Judas Iscariot [John 6:71]; Simon the magician [Acts 8:9–24]; and Simon the tanner, with whom Peter stayed in Joppa [Acts 9:43].) Peter's full name was Simon Barjona (Matt. 16:17), literally "Simon son of Jonas" (or John; cf. John 1:42). At their first meeting, Jesus named him Cephas (John 1:42; cf. 1 Cor. 1:12; 3:22; 9:5; 15:5; Gal. 1:18; 2:9, 11, 14), which is Aramaic for "rock"; "Peter" is its Greek equivalent (John 1:42).

Peter was sometimes called "Simon" in secular or neutral settings (e.g., in reference to his house [Mark 1:29; Luke 4:38], his mother-in-law [Mark 1:30; Luke 4:38], or his business [Luke 5:3, 10]). At such times, the use of the name had no spiritual implications. But more significantly, Peter was called "Simon" to mark the key failures in his life—those times when he was acting like his unregenerate self.

In Matthew 17:24–25 he confidently assured the tax collectors that Jesus would pay the two-drachma tax levied for the upkeep of the temple. Reminding him that as God's Son, He was exempt from paying the tax, Jesus addressed Peter as "Simon" (v. 25). Grieved at Peter's inability to stay awake with Him during His agony in Gethsemane, Jesus said to him, "Simon, are you asleep? Could you not keep watch for one hour?" (Mark 14:37). After using his fishing boat as a platform from which to teach the crowds, Jesus said to Peter, "Put out into the deep water and let down your nets for a catch" (Luke 5:4). Peter was skeptical and hesitant to follow the Lord's advice; after all, Jesus was a rabbi, not a fisherman. No doubt somewhat exasperated, "Simon answered and said, 'Master, we worked hard all night and caught nothing, but I will do as You say and let down the nets'" (v. 5). The staggering haul of fish that resulted from his obedience (vv. 6–7) opened Simon's eyes to the reality of Jesus' deity, so Luke called him by his new name: "Simon Peter . . . fell down at Jesus' feet, saying, 'Go away from me Lord, for I am a sinful man, O Lord!'" (v. 8). Following a heated debate among the Twelve as to which of them was the greatest, Jesus warned proud, overconfident Peter of his impending betrayal: "Simon, Simon, behold, Satan has demanded permission to sift you like wheat" (Luke 22:31).

After the resurrection, Jesus called Peter "Simon" for the last time. Tired of waiting for the Lord to appear (Matt. 28:7), Peter impulsively announced, "I am going fishing" (John 21:3). Dutifully following their leader, the rest of the disciples "said to him, 'We will also come with you'" (v. 3). But those whom Jesus called to be fishers of men (Matt. 4:19) were not allowed to revert to being catchers of fish, "and that night they caught nothing" (John 21:3). The next morning Jesus met the unsuccessful crew on the shore, where He prepared breakfast for them. Afterward, Jesus asked Peter three times, "Simon, son of John, do you love Me?" (John 21:15–17), and three times he affirmed his love for the Lord.

A few weeks later, the Holy Spirit descended on Peter and the rest of the apostles, and from then on the "Rock" lived up to his name. He took the lead in finding a replacement for Judas Iscariot (Acts 1:15–26), fearlessly preached the gospel (2:14–40; 3:12–26), performed miraculous healings (3:1–9; 5:12–16), boldly confronted the Jewish authorities (4:8–20), and unhesitatingly disciplined sinning church members (5:1–11). It was Peter who confronted Simon the magician, bluntly telling him, "May your silver perish with you, because you thought you could obtain the gift of God with money!" (Acts 8:20). It was through Peter's ministry that the doors of the church were thrown open to the Gentiles (Acts 10:1–11:18).

After his appearance at the Jerusalem Council (Acts 15:7–12), Peter all but disappears from the historical record of the New Testament until he wrote his epistles. From Paul's account of their confrontation, it is evident that Peter visited Antioch (Gal. 2:11–21), and the reference to the Peter faction at Corinth (1 Cor. 1:12) suggests he may have visited that city as well. As noted above, Paul alluded to Peter's missionary travels in 1 Corinthians 9:5, but the extent of those travels is not known. That the apostle addressed 1 Peter to churches in specific regions of Asia Minor (see the discussion below under "Destination and Readers") may indicate that he had preached in those regions.

The strong tradition of the early church places Peter in Rome at the close of his life. He evidently was not there when Paul wrote Romans (c. A.D. 57), since his name does not appear in the list of people Paul greeted (Rom. 16:1–15). Nor is it likely that Peter was in Rome during

Paul's first imprisonment, since he is not mentioned in the Prison Epistles (Ephesians, Philippians, Colossians, Philemon), which were written at that time. Peter most likely arrived in Rome after Paul's release from his first Roman imprisonment. It was there that he, like Paul, suffered martyrdom in connection with Nero's persecution. Since Nero died in A.D. 68, Peter's crucifixion upside down, as tradition holds, undoubtedly occurred before that date.

Despite the circulation of forgeries purporting to be written by Peter (e.g., the Gospel of Peter, the Acts of Peter, and the Apocalypse of Peter), the early church never doubted that the apostle penned 1 Peter. The earliest affirmation of that comes in 2 Peter, which Peter himself described as the second letter he had addressed to his readers (2 Peter 3:1). There are echoes of 1 Peter's words and phrases in such late first- and early second-century writings as the Epistle of Barnabas, the First Epistle of Clement (which uses several Greek words found nowhere in the New Testament except 1 Peter), the Shepherd of Hermas, and the Letters of Ignatius. The earliest extant work that actually quotes from 1 Peter is Polycarp's Epistle to the Philippians, likely written in the second decade of the second century. In the middle of the second century, Justin Martyr may have known of 1 Peter; in the late second and early third centuries, Irenaeus, Tertullian, and Clement of Alexandria definitely attributed 1 Peter to the apostle Peter. Summarizing the early church's view of 1 Peter's authenticity, the fourth-century church historian Eusebius of Caesarea wrote, "As to the writings of Peter, one of his epistles called the first is acknowledged as genuine. For this was anciently used by the ancient fathers in their writings, as an undoubted work of the apostle" (*Ecclesiastical History* 3.3).

But despite the clear testimony of the early church, modern unbelieving skeptics, as they do with most of the rest of the New Testament books, deny the authenticity of 1 Peter. Some see in it a slavish dependence on the writings of Paul, and argue that could not have characterized a genuine writing of Peter, who was himself an eminent apostle. It is true that Peter was familiar with at least some of Paul's writings, since he refers to them in 2 Peter 3:16. Yet the similarities between 1 Peter and Paul's epistles are not so great as to demand literary dependence, especially between two men who taught the same apostolic truth (cf. Acts 2:42). E. G. Selwyn wisely cautions,

> The vocabulary of the N. T. is not a very wide one; and the number of words which are available for the expression of a particular idea is not unlimited. Verbal parallels, therefore, often have no other reason than the fact that the word in question was the obvious and natural word to use in the circumstances. Nor are the ideas themselves infinitely numerous; for they form part of, or derive from, a definite Gospel . . .

which was the *raison d'être* of the Christian Church and its faith. (*The First Epistle of St. Peter* [London: Macmillan, 1961], 8)

Others argue that Peter, a companion of Jesus, would have included more personal reminiscences of the Lord in his epistle. But it is precisely the *presence* of such reminiscences in 2 Peter that causes critics to reject its authenticity (cf. 2 Peter 1:16–18; 3:2). They cannot have it both ways. Nor are such reminiscences entirely lacking in 1 Peter (5:1; cf. 5:2 with John 21:16; 5:5 with John 13:3–5). In a related theme, 1 Peter contains striking parallels to Peter's sermons recorded in Acts (cf. 1:10–12 with Acts 3:18; 1:17 with Acts 10:34; 1:20 with Acts 2:23; 1:21 with Acts 2:32; 2:4, 7 with Acts 4:11; 3:22 with Acts 2:33; 4:5 with Acts 10:42; the use of *xulon* ["cross"; lit., "wood"] in 2:24 and Acts 5:30 and 10:39).

Another argument advanced by those who reject Petrine authorship is that the persecution in view in 1 Peter took place under the Emperor Trajan (A.D. 98–117). That, of course, was well after Peter's lifetime, and thus he could not be the author of this epistle. They note that Pliny, Roman governor of Bithynia, wrote to Emperor Trajan, asking in part "whether the name [Christian] itself, even if innocent of crime, should be punished, or only the crimes attaching to that name" (cited in Henry Bettenson, *Documents of the Christian Church* [London: Oxford Univ., 1967], 3). They see that as the background for Peter's admonition, "but if anyone suffers as a Christian, he is not to be ashamed, but is to glorify God in this name" (4:16). But the concept of suffering for the name of Christ was not new to 1 Peter; it was introduced by Jesus Himself. In Mark 13:13 He warned His followers, "You will be hated by all because of My name." After being beaten by the Sanhedrin, the apostles "went on their way from the presence of the Council, rejoicing that they had been considered worthy to suffer shame for His name" (Acts 5:41; cf. 9:16; Matt. 5:11; 10:22; 24:9).

But the most telling argument for those who reject 1 Peter's authenticity is the linguistic one. A simple Galilean fisherman whose native language was Aramaic, they insist, could not have written the smooth, polished Greek of 1 Peter—especially a man described in Acts 4:13 as "uneducated and untrained." A corollary argument is that Peter, not a native speaker of Greek, would not have quoted from the Septuagint, as the writer of 1 Peter does.

There are good responses to each of those allegations. First, some have exaggerated the classical affinities of the Greek of 1 Peter. Second, the epistle contains Semitic expressions consistent with Peter's Jewish background. Third, Peter was from Galilee, which even in Isaiah's day was known as "Galilee of the Gentiles" (Isa. 9:1). Greek, along with Aramaic and Hebrew, was commonly spoken throughout Palestine

(Robert L. Thomas and Stanley N. Gundry, *A Harmony of the Gospels* [Chicago: Moody, 1979], 309ff.). That was especially true in Galilee, where Hellenistic influence was strong, and which area was near the Gentile region known as the Decapolis. As a businessman in Galilee, Peter would almost certainly have been fluent in Greek. In addition, Peter (Acts 15:14) and his fellow Galileans Andrew and Philip had Greek names. Matthew and James, also Galileans, wrote New Testament books in excellent Greek. Fourth, Peter penned this epistle after three decades of traveling and ministering among largely Greek-speaking people, which would have given him even greater proficiency in Greek. Fifth, it was only natural for Peter to quote the Septuagint, since that was the version most of his readers were familiar with. Sixth, the phrase "uneducated and untrained" in Acts 4:13 does not mean that Peter was illiterate, but rather that he was a layman, with no rabbinic training (cf. John 7:15). Nor are scholars the only ones capable of producing literary masterpieces; for example, John Bunyan, author of one of the greatest works in the English language, *Pilgrim's Progress*, was a humble tinker (one who repaired household utensils). Finally, it was common for ancient writers to use an amanuensis, or secretary, to assist them in writing their books. Though he was a highly educated scholar (Acts 26:24), Paul made use of such an amanuensis (Rom. 16:22; cf. 1 Cor. 16:21; Col. 4:18; 2 Thess. 3:17). Peter also used one in writing 1 Peter, dictating his letter to Silvanus (5:12), who may have, under Peter's supervision, smoothed out the apostle's literary style.

Those who deny Peter's authorship allege that 1 Peter was either an anonymous letter that his name somehow became attached to, or else the pseudepigraphical work of a "pious forger," who attached Peter's name to his letter in an attempt to invest it with apostolic authority. But such specious claims are fraught with overwhelming difficulties. Those who claim the letter was originally anonymous argue that its introduction and conclusion were added later to make it appear as if Peter had written it. But it is hard to imagine how a letter that had been circulating anonymously could suddenly have had Peter's name added to it without raising suspicions in the churches to which it was addressed. Nor is there any ancient manuscript evidence that 1 Peter ever circulated without its introduction and conclusion.

Another version of the "pious forger" view holds that an individual used Peter's name, not to deceive, but as a harmless literary device his readers would have understood. But that theory fares no better, as Donald Guthrie notes:

> It is impossible to make out an intelligible case for the use of pseudonymity in 1 Peter. The fact that the author's purpose is encouragement means that personal relations between readers and writer would play a much more important part than apostolic authority. Why did not the

author, if not Peter, publish his encouragements in his own name? There seems to be no satisfactory answer to this question. The epistle deals with no heresy which might have required apostolic authority to refute it. Moreover, the mention of Silas and Mark cannot be regarded as part of the pseudepigraphical machinery, for a pseudo-Peter would surely avoid associating so closely with Peter those who, according to Acts and the Pauline epistles, were associates of Paul. (*New Testament Introduction* [4th rev. ed.; Downers Grove, Ill.: InterVarsity, 1990], 778)

The claim that pseudonymity was an accepted literary device is also false; the early church did not approve of so-called pious forgeries. Paul warned of false letters purporting to come from him (2 Thess. 2:2), and he took steps to authenticate his letters (1 Cor. 16:21; Col. 4:18cf.; 2 Thess. 3:17). The church father Tertullian wrote of a church leader who was removed from office for forging a document in Paul's name, although he did it out of love for Paul (*On Baptism, XVII; The Ante-Nicene Fathers* [reprint; Grand Rapids: Eerdmans, 1973], 3:677). D. A. Carson, Douglas J. Moo, and Leon Morris caution that "we should not approach the New Testament epistles as though it were common for the early Christians to write letters in a name not their own. As far as our knowledge goes, there is not one such letter emanating from the Christians from anywhere near the New Testament period" (*An Introduction to the New Testament* [Grand Rapids: Zondervan, 1992], 368. For a thorough discussion of the issue of pseudonymity, see pp. 367–71; see also Thomas R. Schreiner, *1, 2 Peter, Jude,* The New American Commentary [Nashville: Broadman & Holman, 2003], 270–73).

Despite the cavils of the critics, the evidence strongly supports the letter's own claim to have been written by "Peter, an apostle of Jesus Christ" (1:1).

DESTINATION AND READERS

Peter addressed his epistle to Christians residing in "Pontus, Galatia, Cappadocia, Asia, and Bithynia" (1:1), regions within the Roman Empire that are now part of Turkey. The order in which they are named may reflect the route the bearer of the letter (Silvanus; 5:12) took when he delivered it. It is not known for certain how the gospel spread to those regions. Paul ministered in at least part of Galatia and Asia, but there is no record of his evangelistic work in Pontus, Cappadocia, or Bithynia. In fact, he was forbidden by the Holy Spirit from entering Bithynia (Acts 16:7). It may be that Paul's converts founded some of the churches (cf. Acts 19:10, 26). And others may have been founded by those who were converted on the day of Pentecost (cf. Acts 2:9). Peter also may have ministered in those regions, though there is no record of that in Acts. The congregations consisted primarily of Gentiles (cf. 1:14, 18; 2:9–10; 4:3–4), but undoubtedly included some Jewish Christians as well.

DATE AND PLACE OF WRITING

Three possible locations have been suggested for the "Babylon" from which Peter wrote (5:13). Some argue for the ancient city of Babylon in Mesopotamia, but that region was sparsely populated in Peter's day. It is unlikely that he, Mark, and Silvanus would all have been there at the same time. Others point to a Babylon on the Nile River in Egypt. It, however, was little more than a Roman military outpost, and again it is highly improbable that Peter (along with Mark and Silvanus) would have taken up residence there. "Babylon" is most likely a cryptic name for Rome, chosen because of the Imperial capital's debauchery and idolatry (which will characterize the Babylon of the end times; cf. Rev. 17, 18). With persecution looming on the horizon, Peter took care not to endanger the Christians in Rome, who might have faced further difficulties if his letter had been discovered by the Roman authorities. The strong association of Peter with Rome in early tradition further supports the view that the apostle wrote 1 Peter from Rome.

The most probable date for 1 Peter is just before Nero's persecution, which followed the great fire that ravaged Rome in the summer of A.D. 64. The absence of any reference to martyrdom makes it less likely that the epistle was written after the persecution began, since numerous Christians would by then have been put to death.

THEME AND PURPOSE

Peter's expressed purpose in writing his epistle was that his readers would stand firm in the true grace of God (5:12) in the face of escalating persecution and suffering. To that end he reminded them of their election and the sure hope of their heavenly inheritance, delineated the privileges and blessings of knowing Christ, gave them instruction on how to conduct themselves in a hostile world, and pointed them to the example of Christ's suffering. Peter wanted his readers to live triumphantly in the midst of hostility without abandoning hope, becoming bitter, losing faith in Christ, or forgetting His second coming. When they are obedient to God's Word despite the world's antagonism, Christians' lives will testify to the truth of the gospel (2:12; 3:1, 13–17).

OUTLINE

Salutation (1:1–2)

I. Suffering Christians Should Remember Their Great Salvation (1:3–2:10)
  A. The Certainty of Their Salvation (1:3–12)
    1. It is preserved by the power of God (1:3–5)
    2. It is proven by the trials from God (1:6–9)
    3. It was predicted by the prophets of God (1:10–12)
  B. The Consequences of Their Salvation (1:13–2:10)
    1. The priority of holiness (1:13–23)
    2. The power of the Word (1:24–2:3)
    3. The priesthood of believers (2:4–10)

II. Suffering Christians Should Remember Their Example Before Men (2:11–4:6)
  A. Living Honorably Before Unbelievers (2:11–3:7)
    1. Submission in the civic realm (2:11–17)
    2. Submission in the workplace (2:18–25)
    3. Submission in the family (3:1–7)
  B. Living Honorably Before Believers (3:8–12)
  C. Living Honorably in the Midst of Suffering (3:13–4:6)
    1. The principle of suffering for righteousness (3:13–17)
    2. The paragon of suffering for righteousness (3:18–22)
    3. The purpose of suffering for righteousness (4:1–6)

III. Suffering Christians Should Remember Their Lord Will Return (4:7–5:11)
  A. The Responsibilities of Christian Living (4:7–11)
  B. The Reality of Christian Suffering (4:12–19)
  C. The Requirements for Christian Leadership (5:1–4)
  D. The Realization of Christian Victory (5:5–11)

Conclusion (5:12–14)

The Elements of Election (1 Peter 1:1–2)

Peter, an apostle of Jesus Christ, To those who reside as aliens, scattered throughout Pontus, Galatia, Cappadocia, Asia, and Bithynia, who are chosen according to the foreknowledge of God the Father, by the sanctifying work of the Spirit, to obey Jesus Christ and be sprinkled with His blood: May grace and peace be yours in the fullest measure. (1:1–2)

Even though it is the starting point of redemptive history, it may seem startling to begin an epistle with reference to the doctrine of election, yet that is exactly what the apostle Peter does (cf. Eph. 1:1–5 and Titus 1:1–2, where Paul begins the same way). And he does so unhesitatingly, after the opening identifications, with the phrase **who are chosen** (v. 1). He thus opens his letter by writing of one of the most controversial and hated doctrines and doing so with no self-consciousness, no apology, no effort to palliate, and no explanation of or deferral to opposing arguments. He states this truth of sovereign election for what it is, a reality recognized and believed among the apostles and in the church. Still, today this unquestionably true doctrine is questioned by many and despised by many others. Arthur W. Pink, the British-born Bible teacher and prolific theological writer who died in 1952, wrote this about people's views of God's sovereignty and, by implication, the subsidiary doctrine of divine election:

> We are well aware that what we have written is in open opposition to much of the teaching that is current both in religious literature and in the representative pulpits of the land. We freely grant that the postulate of God's Sovereignty with all its corollaries is at direct variance with the opinions and thoughts of the natural man, but the truth is, the natural man is quite *unable* to think upon these matters: he is not competent to form a proper estimate of God's character and ways, and it is because of this that God has given us a revelation of *His* mind, and in that revelation He plainly declares, "My thoughts are not your thoughts, neither are your ways My ways, saith the Lord. For as the heavens are higher than the earth, so are My ways higher than your ways, and My thoughts than your thoughts" (Isa. 55: 8, 9). In view of this scripture, it is only to be expected that much of the contents of the Bible *conflicts* with the sentiments of the carnal mind, which is *enmity* against God. Our appeal then is not to the popular beliefs of the day, nor to the creeds of the churches, but to the Law and Testimony of Jehovah. All that we ask for is an impartial and attentive examination of what we have written, and that, made prayerfully in the light of the Lamp of Truth. (*The Sovereignty of God,* rev. ed. [Edinburgh: Banner of Truth, 1961], 19; italics in original)

As Pink's still-relevant analysis reveals, it is imperative that Christians fully understand and appreciate this most vital and crucial teaching. Peter unfolds the theological and practical implications of divine election under seven headings: the condition of election, the nature of election, the source of election, the sphere of election, the effect of election, the security of election, and the advantages of election.

THE CONDITION OF ELECTION

Peter, an apostle of Jesus Christ, To those who reside as aliens, scattered throughout Pontus, Galatia, Cappadocia, Asia, and Bithynia, (1:1*a*)

Peter, the inspired author, identifies himself as **an apostle of Jesus Christ.** Other New Testament verses also identify Peter as an apostle and furthermore, by placing his name at the head of each list of Jesus' apostles (Matt. 10:2; Mark 3:16; Luke 6:14; Acts 1:13), emphasize that he was the leader of the Twelve.

Peter's intention in this first part of his salutation was not only to identify his readers as to their heavenly origin, as the elect of God, but also in relation to their condition as earthly residents. The apostle describes his readers in their earthly condition as **aliens.** *Parepidēmois* (**aliens**) can denote those who are temporary residents, or who are foreigners or refugees (cf. Gen. 23:4; Ex. 2:22; 22:21; Ps. 119:19; Acts 7:29; Heb. 11:13). The apostle further identifies them as people who were **scattered throughout** various locales. **Scattered** translates *diaspora,* from which root another English term, *dispersion,* derives. Commentaries, theological works, and works on Bible history often transliterate *diaspora* and use it interchangeably with dispersion. In its other two New Testament appearances, *diaspora* is a technical term referring to the dispersing of the Jews throughout the world by the Assyrian and Babylonian captivities. Both times the word has the definite article (John 7:35; James 1:1). However here Peter does not include the definite article; therefore it is best to interpret the term as a non-technical reference to believers widely distributed geographically.

Though God called Peter to be the **apostle** to the Jews (Gal. 2:7), the absence of the definite article with *diaspora* argues that Peter was not addressing Jews as such in his salutation. Another passage supports that interpretation. In 2:11 he identifies his readers, not racially or nationally, but spiritually: "Beloved, I urge you as aliens and strangers to abstain from fleshly lusts which wage war against the soul." Thus the apostle addressed not only Jews who were dispersed from their native land, but Gentile believers, both of whom spiritually were **aliens** in the world.

The church is composed of strangers and pilgrims **scattered throughout** the earth, away from their true home in heaven (cf. Phil. 3:20; Heb. 11:13–16; 13:14). Specifically, he was addressing the church in **Pontus, Galatia, Cappadocia, Asia, and Bithynia,** all provinces in Asia Minor (modern Turkey) at the time. **Pontus** was in the far north, and Jewish pilgrims from there were in Jerusalem during the extraordinary events of Pentecost (Acts 2:9). The province was also the home of Aquila (Acts 18:2), the Jew who with his wife Priscilla became Christians in Rome and subsequently ministered with Paul (Acts 18:18). **Galatia** was in central Asia Minor and contained the towns of Derbe, Lystra, and Iconium where Paul ministered several times (Acts 14:1–13; 16:1–5; 18:23). **Cappadocia** was located in the east portion of Asia Minor, north of Cilicia, and is also mentioned in connection with the Acts 2:9 pilgrims. **Asia** included most of western Asia Minor and contained such subdivisions as Mysia, Lydia, Caria, and much of Phrygia. The province was the site of extensive ministry by Paul on his third journey: "all who lived in Asia heard the word of the Lord, both Jews and Greeks" (Acts 19:10) and is mentioned twelve other places in Acts. **Bithynia** was located in northwest Asia Minor near the Bosphorus, the strait separating the European

and Asian sections of modern Turkey. This province is mentioned only
one other place in the New Testament, when the Holy Spirit, during Paul's
second missionary journey, forbade him from entering it (Acts 16:7).

As the geographical areas Peter mentioned in his salutation indicate, this letter had a very wide circulation. No doubt, in each of those
areas, churches received and read the letter. For example, there were at
least seven churches in Asia Minor (Ephesus, Smyrna, Pergamum, Thyatira, Sardis, Philadelphia, and Laodicea) that thirty years later received special revelation from the risen Christ Himself (Rev. 1:11; chaps. 2–3). And
there were other notable places in Asia Minor, such as Colossae, that
Peter did not even mention. So he was writing to a large number of
believers scattered as spiritual aliens throughout a hostile, pagan region.

Peter addressed such a wide audience because the Roman persecution of Christians had swept across the Empire. Believers in every
place were going to suffer (cf. Luke 21:12; Phil. 1:29; James 1:1–3). The
apostle wanted those believers to remember that, in the midst of poten-
tially great suffering and hardship, they were still the chosen of God, and
that as such they could face persecution in triumphant hope (cf. 4:13, 16,
19; Rom. 8:35–39; 2 Tim. 3:11; Heb. 10:34–36).

THE NATURE OF ELECTION

who are chosen (1:1b)

As spiritual aliens, the most important thing for Peter's readers
was not their relationship to earth but their relationship to heaven.
Describing Abraham's hope, the writer of Hebrews said, "He was looking
for the city which has foundations, whose architect and builder is God"
(11:10; cf. vv. 13–16; John 14:1–3; Phil. 3:20).

Understanding that truth, Peter identifies his audience as those
who are chosen (*eklektos*). The apostle reiterates this concept in 2:9,
"You are a chosen race, a royal priesthood, a holy nation, a people for
God's own possession, so that you may proclaim the excellencies of Him
who has called you out of darkness into His marvelous light." Peter's Old
Testament allusions in that verse make it plain that he knew God had
sovereignly chosen Israel: "For you are a holy people to the Lord your
God; the Lord your God has chosen you to be a people for His own possession out of all the peoples who are on the face of the earth" (Deut. 7:6;
cf. 14:2; Pss. 105:43; 135:4).

God's sovereign love also prompted His choice of the church.
The apostle Paul told the church at Ephesus, "We have obtained an inheritance, having been predestined according to His purpose who works all

things after the counsel of His will" (Eph. 1:11). He told the Thessalonians, "But we should always give thanks to God for you, brethren beloved by the Lord, because God has chosen you from the beginning for salvation through sanctification by the Spirit and faith in the truth" (2 Thess. 2:13; cf. John 15:16; Rom. 8:29–30; 1 Cor. 1: 27; Eph. 1:4–5; 2:10; Col. 3:12; 1 Thess. 1:4; Titus 1:1).

Jesus also did not hesitate to unambiguously and unapologetically teach the truth of election: "'No one can come to Me unless the Father who sent Me draws him; and I will raise him up on the last day'" (John 6:44); "'I do not speak of all of you. I know the ones I have chosen'" (13:18; cf. Luke 10:20; 18:7; John 17:6, 9). The Lord assumed the truth of divine election in His Olivet Discourse, making indirect reference to it three times: "'Unless those days had been cut short, no life would have been saved; but for the sake of the elect those days will be cut short'" (Matt. 24:22; see also vv. 24, 31; Mark 13:20).

God has chosen people out of all the world (Rev. 5:9; 7:9; cf. John 10:16; Acts 15:14) to belong to Him, and the church is that people (cf. Rom. 8:29; Eph. 5:27). Throughout the New Testament this critical truth of election is clearly presented (2:8–9; Matt. 24:22, 24, 31; Luke 18:7; Col. 3:12; Titus 1:1–2; James 2:5). The apostle John repeatedly quotes Jesus saying that the Father gives whomever He chooses to the Son:

> "All that the Father gives Me will come to Me, and the one who comes to Me I will certainly not cast out. For I have come down from heaven, not to do My own will, but the will of Him who sent Me. This is the will of Him who sent Me, that of all that He has given Me I lose nothing, but raise it up on the last day. For this is the will of My Father, that everyone who beholds the Son and believes in Him will have eternal life, and I Myself will raise him up on the last day." Therefore the Jews were grumbling about Him, because He said, "I am the bread that came down out of heaven." They were saying, "Is not this Jesus, the son of Joseph, whose father and mother we know? How does He now say, 'I have come down out of heaven'?" Jesus answered and said to them, "Do not grumble among yourselves. No one can come to Me unless the Father who sent Me draws him; and I will raise him up on the last day. It is written in the prophets, 'And they shall all be taught of God.' Everyone who has heard and learned from the Father, comes to Me. (John 6:37–45)

> I have manifested Your name to the men whom You gave Me out of the world; they were Yours and You gave them to Me, and they have kept Your word. . . . While I was with them, I was keeping them in Your name which You have given Me; and I guarded them and not one of them perished but the son of perdition, so that the Scripture would be fulfilled. . . . Father, I desire that they also, whom You have given Me, be with Me

where I am, so that they may see My glory which You have given Me, for You loved Me before the foundation of the world. (17:6, 12, 24)

The chosen are expressions of the Father's love for the Son. All whom the Father gives, the Son receives; and the Son keeps them and raises them to eternal life. In principle, Jesus revealed it to His disciples in the Upper Room: "'You did not choose Me but I chose you, and appointed you that you would go and bear fruit, and that your fruit would remain, so that whatever you ask of the Father in My name He may give to you'" (John 15:16). John 5:21 says, "For just as the Father raises the dead and gives them life, even so the Son also gives life to whom He wishes." Luke chronicled God's sovereign election of the church in Pisidian Antioch during Paul's first missionary journey:

> Paul and Barnabas spoke out boldly and said, "It was necessary that the word of God be spoken to you [Jews] first; since you repudiate it and judge yourselves unworthy of eternal life, behold, we are turning to the Gentiles. For so the Lord has commanded us, 'I have placed You as a light for the Gentiles, that you may bring salvation to the end of the earth.'" When the Gentiles heard this, they began rejoicing and glorifying the word of the Lord; and as many as had been appointed to eternal life believed. And the word of the Lord was being spread through the whole region. (Acts 13:46–49)

Paul wrote clearly the truth that election is completely the result of God's sovereign purpose and grace: "who [the Lord] has saved us and called us with a holy calling, not according to our works, but according to His own purpose and grace which was granted us in Christ Jesus from all eternity" (2 Tim. 1:9). The great apostle further defines this truth in Romans 8:28–30,

> And we know that God causes all things to work together for good to those who love God, to those who are called according to His purpose. For those whom He foreknew, He also predestined to become conformed to the image of His Son, so that He would be the firstborn among many brethren; and these whom He predestined, He also called; and these whom He called, He also justified; and these whom He justified, He also glorified.

John further emphasizes the eternality of election at the end of the New Testament when he notes that the Book of Life existed before the foundation of the world (Rev. 13:8; 17:8; cf. 3:5; 20:12, 15; 21:27). From eternity past, God has had a large body of believers in mind whom He chose to love (1 John 4:10; cf. Rom. 10:20), to save from their sin (Eph. 2:1–5; Col. 2:13), and conform to the image of His Son (Rom. 8:29; 1 Cor. 1:7–9; 2 Cor.

3:18; Jude 24–25). And each one of those names, from every nationality and every era of history, God specifically secured in eternal purpose before the world began.

THE SOURCE OF ELECTION

according to the foreknowledge of God the Father, (1:2a)

One popular explanation for election by those who cannot accept God's sovereign choice based on nothing but His own will stems from a faulty understanding of **foreknowledge.** According to that understanding, the term merely means foresight or supernatural knowledge of the future. Proponents say that God in His omniscience looked down the corridors of time and saw who would believe the gospel and who would not. He then chose for salvation all those He knew would choose to believe and guaranteed that they would reach heaven. But there are at least three reasons such an interpretation of **foreknowledge** is unscriptural. First of all, it makes man sovereign in salvation instead of God, though Jesus affirmed His and the Father's sovereignty when He told the disciples, "You did not choose Me but I chose you" (John 15:16; cf. Rom. 9:11–13, 16). Second, it gives man undue credit for his own salvation, allowing him to share the glory that belongs to God alone. The familiar salvation passage, Ephesians 2:8–9, shatters that notion: "For by grace you have been saved through faith; and that not of yourselves, it is the *gift* of God; not as a result of works, so that *no one may boast*" (italics added; cf. 1 Cor. 1:29, 31). Third, it assumes fallen man can seek after God. Romans 3:11, quoting from Psalms 14:1–3 and 53:1–3, clearly states, "There is none who understands, there is none who seeks for God" (cf. Eph. 2:1). The apostle John accurately defines God's saving initiative this way: "In this is love, not that we loved God, but that He loved us and sent His Son to be the propitiation for our sins" (1 John 4:10; cf. Rom. 5:8).

Any sort of man-centered definition of foreknowledge is incompatible with God's absolute sovereignty over all things: "Remember the former things long past, for I am God, and there is no other; I am God, and there is no one like Me, declaring the end from the beginning, and from ancient times things which have not been done, saying, 'My purpose will be established, and I will accomplish all My good pleasure'" (Isa. 46:9–10; cf. 14:24, 27; Job 42:1–2; Pss. 115:3; 135:6; Jer. 32:17).

The usage of the Greek word rendered **foreknowledge** in verse 2 also proves it cannot mean simply knowledge of future events and attitudes. *Prognōsis* (**foreknowledge**) refers to God's eternal, predetermined, loving, and saving intention. In 1:20, Peter used the related verb "was fore-known," a form of *proginōskō*, in reference to God's knowledge from eternity past that He would send His Son to redeem sinners. Usage of this verb cannot mean He looked into future history and saw that Jesus would choose to die, so He made Him the Savior. In the same way that God the Father foreknew His plan for Christ's crucifixion from before the foundation of the world (Acts 2:23; cf. 1 Peter 2:6), He foreknew the elect. In neither case was it a matter of mere prior information about what would happen. Therefore **foreknowledge** involves God's predetermining to have a relationship with some individuals, based on His eternal plan. It is the divine purpose that brings salvation for sinners to fulfillment, as accomplished by Jesus Christ's death on the cross, not merely an advance knowledge that observes how people will respond to God's offer of redemption.

In the Old Testament, "knowing" someone could indicate a sexual relationship (Num. 31:18, 35; Judg. 21:12; cf. Gen. 19:8). Long before Peter articulated the nature of God's foreknowledge, "The Lord said to Moses, 'I will do this thing of which you have spoken; for you have found favor in My sight and I have known you by name'" (Ex. 33:17). Regarding Christ the Servant, Isaiah 49:1–2 declares, "Listen to Me, O islands, and pay attention, you peoples from afar. The Lord called Me from the womb; from the body of My mother He named Me. He has made My mouth like a sharp sword, in the shadow of His hand He has concealed Me; and He has also made Me a select arrow, He has hidden Me in His quiver." God had a predetermined relationship with the prophet Jeremiah: "Before I formed you in the womb I knew you, and before you were born I consecrated you; I have appointed you a prophet to the nations" (Jer. 1:5). Amos wrote about God's foreknowledge of Israel: "You only have I known of all the families of the earth" (Amos 3:2, NKJV). With all of the foregoing references, the point is not simply God's having information *about* someone, but His establishing an intimate relationship *with* someone. And **foreknowledge** was God establishing that by divine decree before time began.

In accord with the continuity of Scripture, the Old Testament's understanding of foreknowledge appears again in the Gospels. Jesus, in making clear the true nature of salvation in His Sermon on the Mount, declared this about the pseudo-elect: "Many will say to Me on that day, 'Lord, Lord, did we not prophesy in Your name, and in Your name cast out demons, and in Your name perform many miracles?' And then I will declare to them, 'I never knew you; depart from Me, you who practice lawlessness'" (Matt. 7:22–23). Certainly, Jesus knew who such people were, but He never "knew" them in the sense that He had predetermined a saving relationship with them. That sort of relationship is reserved for

His sheep: "I am the good shepherd, and I know My own and My own know Me" (John 10:14; cf. vv. 16, 26–28; 17:9–10, 20–21). Salvation **fore- knowledge,** then, involves God predetermining to know someone by having an intimate, saving relationship, so choosing them from eternity past to receive His redeeming love.

THE SPHERE OF ELECTION

by the sanctifying work of the Spirit (1:2b)

The outworking of God's choice of the elect made in eternity past begins in time **by the sanctifying work of the Spirit. The sancti- fying work** encompasses all that **the Spirit** produces in salvation: faith (Eph. 2:8), repentance (Acts 11:15–18), regeneration (Titus 3:5), and adoption (Rom. 8:16–17). Thus election, the plan of God, becomes a real- ity in the life of the believer through salvation, the work of God, which the Holy Spirit carries out.

Sanctifying work (*hagiasmō*) refers to separation, consecra- tion, and holiness. First Peter 2:9–10 illustrates the principle: "But you are a chosen race, a royal priesthood, a holy nation, a people for God's own pos- session, so that you may proclaim the excellencies of Him who has called you out of darkness into His marvelous light; for you once were not a peo- ple, but now you are the people of God; you had not received mercy, but now you have received mercy." At salvation **the sanctifying work of the Spirit** sets believers apart from sin to God, separates them from darkness to light, sets them apart from unbelief to faith, and mercifully separates them from a love of sin and brings them to a love of righteousness (John 3:3–8; Rom. 8:2; 2 Cor. 5:17; cf. 1 Cor. 2:10–16; Eph. 2:1–5; 5:8; Col. 2:13).

Years earlier, at the Jerusalem Council, Peter expressed the same principle:

> After there had been much debate, Peter stood up and said to them, "Brethren, you know that in the early days God made a choice among you, that by my mouth the Gentiles would hear the word of the gospel and believe. And God, who knows the heart, testified to them giving them the Holy Spirit, just as He also did to us; and He made no dis- tinction between us and them, cleansing their hearts by faith." (Acts 15:7–9)

The Holy Spirit by faith cleansed the hearts of the Gentile converts. That underscores again that salvation is the Spirit's work (John 3:3–8; cf. Rom. 15:16; 1 Cor. 6:11; 1 Thess. 1:4–6; 2 Thess. 2:13; Titus 3:5).

Once the Holy Spirit at salvation separates believers from sin, He continues to make them more and more holy (cf. Phil. 1:6) in the life-long, progressive separation process of sanctification (Rom. 12:1–2; 2 Cor. 7:1; 1 Thess. 5:23–24; Heb. 12:14; cf. Eph. 4:24, 30; 2 Tim. 4:18). Paul says that God chose believers "that [they] would be holy and blameless before Him" (Eph. 1:4). That begins at salvation and is completed at glori-fication. The sanctifying process is the working out of God's elective pur-pose in the earthly lives of Christians (cf. Rom. 6:22; Gal. 4:6; Phil. 2:12–13; 2 Thess. 2:13; Heb. 12:14).

THE EFFECT OF ELECTION

to obey Jesus Christ (1:2c)

Obedience to Jesus Christ is the effect or by-product of divine election. Ephesians 2:10 says, "For we are His workmanship, created in Christ Jesus for good works, which God prepared beforehand so that we would walk in them." For one **to obey Jesus Christ,** then, is the equiva-lent of being saved. Paul called it "the obedience of faith" (Rom. 1:5). Believers do not obey perfectly or completely (1 John 1:8–10; cf. Rom. 7:14–25), but nonetheless there is a pattern of obedience in their lives as they through Christ become servants of righteousness (Rom. 6:17–18; cf. Rom. 8:1–2; 2 Cor. 10:5b).

Paul was thankful for the believing Thessalonians because he saw in their lives many examples of obedience to Christ.

We give thanks to God always for all of you, making mention of you in our prayers; constantly bearing in mind your work of faith and labor of love and steadfastness of hope in our Lord Jesus Christ in the presence of our God and Father, knowing, brethren beloved by God, His choice of you; for our gospel did not come to you in word only, but also in power and in the Holy Spirit and with full conviction; just as you know what kind of men we proved to be among you for your sake. You also became imitators of us and of the Lord, having received the word in much tribulation with the joy of the Holy Spirit, so that you became an example to all the believers in Macedonia and in Achaia. For the word of the Lord has sounded forth from you, not only in Macedonia and Achaia, but also in every place your faith toward God has gone forth, so that we have no need to say anything. For they themselves report about us what kind of a reception we had with you, and how you turned to God from idols to serve a living and true God, and to wait for His Son from heaven, whom He raised from the dead, that is Jesus, who rescues us from the wrath to come. (1 Thess. 1:2–10)

All of those examples—their faith, love, and hope in Christ; their imitation of Paul and the Lord; their exemplary behavior before others; their proclamation of the Word; their turning from idols; their waiting for Christ—demonstrated their genuine regeneration. (John's first epistle makes an even more extensive case for true salvation resulting in obedience to Christ [2:3–5; 3:6–10, 24; 5:2–3].)

In glorification comes the realization of the purpose of election and of the ultimate work of sanctification, when believers become completely conformed to Christ (Rom. 8:29; 1 John 3:2). Until then, obedience is the effect of election.

THE SECURITY OF ELECTION

and be sprinkled with His blood: (1:2*d*)

Another profoundly important, practical component of election is security for the believer. That is affirmed in the passage quoted earlier (John 6:37–40), in which Jesus said He would not cast out or lose those who genuinely trust in Him, but raise them all on the final day. God indicates that security in that the elect are **sprinkled with His** [Christ's] **blood.** Peter's metaphor here looks back to the time in the Old Testament when blood was sprinkled on the people of Israel. That event is significant enough that the letter to the Hebrews mentions it once specifically and once by allusion (9:19–20; 12:24). The following passage in Exodus describes the remarkable event:

> Then Moses came and recounted to the people all the words of the Lord and all the ordinances; and all the people answered with one voice and said, "All the words which the Lord has spoken we will do!" Moses wrote down all the words of the Lord. Then he arose early in the morning, and built an altar at the foot of the mountain with twelve pillars for the twelve tribes of Israel. He sent young men of the sons of Israel, and they offered burnt offerings and sacrificed young bulls as peace offerings to the Lord. Moses took half of the blood and put it in basins, and the other half of the blood he sprinkled on the altar. Then he took the book of the covenant and read it in the hearing of the people; and they said, "All that the Lord has spoken we will do, and we will be obedient!" So Moses took the blood and sprinkled it on the people, and said, "Behold the blood of the covenant, which the Lord has made with you in accordance with all these words." (24:3–8)

Moses had just returned from Mount Sinai and orally reviewed to the people God's law received there. As the text says, they responded very dutifully by pledging to obey all God required. This began the covenant-making agreement between God and His people (cf. Ex. 19:3–20:17). Under the Spirit's inspiration, Moses recorded all the words of the law just recited. When he finished the next morning, he built an altar at the foot of the mountain to symbolize the sealing of the covenant between God and the people. To represent the entire nation's involvement, the altar consisted of twelve stacks of stones (pillars), one for each of the twelve tribes. To further provide the people an opportunity to express their determination to obey the Law, Moses offered burnt offerings and peace offerings of young bulls. Moses placed half the blood from the slain sacrificial animals in large basins, and the other half he splashed on God's altar. Then Moses read for the people the words of the Law he had recorded the previous night and they again pledged their obedience. After that, Moses splattered the people with the remaining blood from the basins, thereby visually and ceremonially making the people's obedience promise and pledge to God official. Shed blood was a tangible demonstration that two parties had made a binding commitment (cf. Gen. 15:9–18; Jer. 34:18–19). Israel made a promise of obedience to God, mediated through sacrifice. The blood splattered on the altar represented God's agreement to reveal His law, and the blood sprinkled on the people signified their consent to obey.

The Holy Spirit compares that unique pledge to the inherent covenant in saving faith in Jesus Christ, which entails a similar promise to obey the Word of the Lord. When believers trust in Christ's atoning sacrifice for them, they are not just accepting the benefit of His death on their behalf. They are also submitting to His sovereign lordship (cf. Matt. 7:24–27; 1 Thess. 1:9; 2:13; James 1:21–23). And Christ's blood, shed at the cross, acts like a seal to that covenant. In fact, the night before He died, when He instituted the Lord's Supper, Jesus echoed Moses' words in Exodus 24:8, "And when He had taken a cup and given thanks, He gave it to them, saying, 'Drink from it, all of you; for this is My blood of the covenant, which is poured out for many for forgiveness of sins'" (Matt. 26:27–28). Inherent in the New Covenant was the promise that the Lord would come and redeem sinners and they would respond by keeping His Word.

Peter states that when believers were spiritually **sprinkled with** Christ's **blood,** they entered into a covenant of obedience. Years earlier, Peter and the other apostles referred to the truth of obedience when they told the Jewish leaders, "He is the one whom God exalted to His right hand as a Prince and a Savior, to grant repentance to Israel, and forgiveness of sins. And we are witnesses of these things; and so is the Holy Spirit, whom God has given to those who obey Him" (Acts 5:31–32).

To recapitulate the Old Testament analogy: the blood sprinkled on God's altar symbolized His commitment to forgiveness (fully realized in the sacrificial death of Christ), and the blood sprinkled on the people symbolized their intention to obey God's law (more fully realized when Christians walk in the Spirit and obey the Word). First John 2:3–6 is unambiguous about this submission:

> By this we know that we have come to know Him, if we keep His commandments. The one who says, "I have come to know Him," and does not keep His commandments, is a liar, and the truth is not in him; but whoever keeps His word, in him the love of God has truly been perfected. By this we know that we are in Him: the one who says he abides in Him ought himself to walk in the same manner as He walked.

As a coin has two sides, the new covenant has two sides: salvation and obedience. As a result of divine election, God's children are saved from sin and given the desire to obey Him, and He promises to forgive them when they do not do so. The same blood of Jesus Christ that sealed the new covenant keeps on spiritually cleansing the sins of Christians when they disobey (cf. Heb. 7:25; 9:11–15; 10:12–18; 1 John 1:7).

The Advantages of Election

May grace and peace be yours in the fullest measure. (1:2*e*)

The salutations of many other New Testament epistles (e.g., Rom. 1:7; 1 Cor. 1:3; Gal. 1:3; Phil. 1:2; 2 Thess. 1:2; Titus 1:4; Rev. 1:4) repeat Peter's wish for his readers. That idea of wishing here derives from the optative mood of the verb *plēthuntheiē*, **may . . . be . . . in the fullest measure.** The apostle wished for his audience God's **grace** and its resultant **peace** (Rom. 5:1) in maximum allotment or quantity. He wished for them all the best that God can offer believers, and that it would repeatedly increase to their advantage.

Peter wanted the recipients of his letter to experience all the rich and varied blessings of being God's elect. Today, however, the tendency is usually to avoid election's profound implications. Christians often justify such an attitude by claiming the doctrine is too deep, too confusing, and too divisive. But believers ought to rejoice over the glorious advantages that an understanding of election provides, and this verse points toward a few of those.

First of all, the doctrine of election is the most humbling truth in all of Scripture. For believers it is most sobering to realize they had absolutely nothing to do with God's choice of them (John 1:12–13; Rom.

9:16). When properly understood, election crushes one's moral and religious pride, which is a blessing because God gives grace to the humble (5:5; Prov. 3:34).

Second, election is a God-exalting, worship-enhancing doctrine because it gives all the glory to Him. Election makes it clear that the sinner's faith, repentance, and ability to obey God come from Him (cf. Ps. 110:3, KJV; Eph. 2:8–9). Only God can grant forgiveness to His people when they sin (Prov. 20:9; Mic. 6:7; Eph. 1:7; 1 John 1:7; 3:5). The psalmist declares, "Not to us, O Lord, not to us, but to Your name give glory because of your lovingkindness, because of Your truth" (Ps. 115:1).

A third advantage of election is that it produces ultimate joy. Those whom God chooses rejoice because they know they would have no hope for salvation apart from His electing grace (John 6:44; Acts 4:12; 1 Tim. 2:5–6). The elect would ultimately perish forever like all other sinners if God had not chosen them (cf. Rom. 9:29). Psalm 65:4 says in part, "How blessed is the one whom You choose and bring near to You to dwell in Your courts." It is a supreme joy for the elect to consider that the Lord has loved them with an everlasting love (cf. Luke 10:20), from before the foundation of the world and on into eternity future.

Fourth, election is advantageous because it promises Christians an eternity of spiritual privileges. The apostle Paul's prayerful expression of praise and gratitude to God, which opens his letter to the Ephesians, is a fitting summary of many of those privileges.

> Blessed be the God and Father of our Lord Jesus Christ, who has blessed us with every spiritual blessing in the heavenly places in Christ, just as He chose us in Him before the foundation of the world, that we would be holy and blameless before Him. In love He predestined us to adoption as sons through Jesus Christ to Himself, according to the kind intention of His will, to the praise of the glory of His grace, which He freely bestowed on us in the Beloved. In Him we have redemption through His blood, the forgiveness of our trespasses, according to the riches of His grace which He lavished on us. In all wisdom and insight He made known to us the mystery of His will, according to His kind intention which He purposed in Him with a view to an administration suitable to the fullness of the times, that is, the summing up of all things in Christ, things in the heavens and things on the earth. In Him also we have obtained an inheritance, having been predestined according to His purpose who works all things after the counsel of His will, to the end that we who were the first to hope in Christ would be to the praise of His glory. In Him, you also, after listening to the message of truth, the gospel of your salvation—having also believed, you were sealed in Him with the Holy Spirit of promise, who is given as a pledge of our inheritance, with a view to the redemption of God's own possession, to the praise of His glory. (Eph. 1:3–14; cf. 1 Peter 2:9–10)

Finally, the doctrine of election is a powerful incentive to holy living. Knowing God has set them apart because of His own special love for them is a most effective motivation for believers to live to the glory of God. That principle was undoubtedly on Paul's mind when he exhorted the Colossians, "So, as those who have been chosen of God, holy and beloved, put on a heart of compassion, kindness, humility, gentleness and patience; bearing with one another, and forgiving each other, whoever has a complaint against anyone; just as the Lord forgave you, so also should you" (Col. 3:12–13). Their gratitude to God for His election of them should compel believers to a life of obedience and holiness.

If Christians ignore the doctrine of election, they fail to understand the glories of redemption, they fail to honor the sovereignty of God and Christ, and they fail to appreciate the immense spiritual privileges that are theirs. Present-day believers, just as those in Peter's time, need not be ignorant of election, because God wants them to know what His grace has provided, and because every scriptural teaching is cause to offer Him the praise He deserves (cf. Pss. 19:7–9; 119:7, 14–16).

Election is such a powerful truth that when Christians understand it, the practical ramifications of election will transform the way they live their daily lives. Knowing the condition of their election (they reside on earth as spiritual aliens to reach those around them), the nature of their election (it is completely the result of God's sovereign choice), the source of their election (God set His love on them from eternity past), the sphere of their election (it becomes a reality by the Holy Spirit's sanctifying work), the effect of their election (loving obedience to Jesus Christ), the security of their election (the covenant of obedience, which ensures divine forgiveness), and the advantages of their election (the many spiritual blessings and privileges available) produces power in believers' lives that they would otherwise never be able to fully appreciate.

The Believer's Eternal Inheritance (1 Peter 1:3–5)

Blessed be the God and Father of our Lord Jesus Christ, who according to His great mercy has caused us to be born again to a living hope through the resurrection of Jesus Christ from the dead, to obtain an inheritance which is imperishable and undefiled and will not fade away, reserved in heaven for you, who are protected by the power of God through faith for a salvation ready to be revealed in the last time. (1:3–5)

The apostle Peter follows the introduction of his first letter with a sweeping doxology regarding the wonder of salvation. He considered it essential to begin the body of the letter with this joyous paean of praise inasmuch as the believers he addressed faced severe persecution from Rome. The passage is a hymn of worship designed to encourage Christians living in a hostile world to look past their temporal troubles and rejoice in their eternal inheritance.

Peter's doxology has components that help all believers praise God more intelligently. To help the church grasp its eternal inheritance and bless and worship God more fully, Peter sets forth five relevant features: the source, motive, appropriation, nature, and security of the believer's inheritance.

THE SOURCE OF THE BELIEVER'S INHERITANCE

Blessed be the God and Father of our Lord Jesus Christ, (1:3*a*)

Peter assumes it is necessary for believers to bless **God.** The intention is so implicit that the Greek text omits the word **be,** which the translators added. (In the original, the sentence literally begins, "Blessed the God," which conveys Peter's expectation that his audience "bless God" as the source of all spiritual inheritance.) The apostle adores God and implores others to do the same.

Peter further calls Him **the God and Father of our Lord Jesus Christ,** a phrase that identified God in a distinctly Christian way. Historically the Jews had blessed God as their creator and redeemer from Egypt. His creation emphasized His sovereign power at work and His redemption of Israel from Egypt His saving power at work. But those who became Christians were to bless **God** as the **Father of** their **Lord Jesus Christ.**

With one exception (when the Father forsook Him on the cross, Matthew 27:46), every time the Gospels record that Jesus addressed God, He called Him "Father" or "My Father." In so doing, Jesus was breaking with the Jewish tradition that seldom called God Father, and always in a collective rather than personal sense (e.g., Deut. 32:6; Isa. 63:16; 64:8; Jer. 3:19; 31:9; Mal. 1:6; 2:10). Furthermore, in calling God His **Father,** Jesus was claiming to share His nature. While speaking with the Jews at an observance of the Feast of the Dedication, Christ declared, "I and the Father are one" (John 10:30). Later, in response to Philip's request that He reveal the Father, Jesus said, "He who has seen Me has seen the Father" (John 14:9; cf. vv. 8, 10–13). Jesus affirmed that He and the Father possess the same divine nature—that He is fully God (cf. John 17:1, 5). The Father and the Son mutually share the same life—one is intimately and eternally equal to the other—and no one can truly know one without truly knowing the other (cf. Matt. 11:27; Luke 10:22). No person can claim to know God unless he knows Him as the One revealed in Jesus Christ, His Son. Jesus Himself said, "I am the way, and the truth, and the life; no one comes to the Father but through Me. If you had known Me, you would have known My Father also; from now on you know Him, and have seen Him" (John 14:6–7).

In his writings, the apostle Paul also declared the Father and the Son to be of the same essence: "Blessed be the God and Father of our Lord Jesus Christ" (2 Cor. 1:3; cf. Eph. 1:3, 17). Likewise, John wrote in his second epistle: "Grace, mercy and peace will be with us, from God the Father and from Jesus Christ, the Son of the Father, in truth and love" (2 John 3). Whenever the New Testament calls God Father, it primarily denotes that He is the **Father of** the **Lord Jesus Christ** (Matt. 7:21; 10:32; 11:25–27; 16:27; 25:34; 26:39; Mark 14:36; Luke 10:21–22; 22:29; 23:34; John 3:35; 5:17–23; 6:32, 37, 44; 8:54; 10:36; 12:28; 15:9; 17:1; Rom. 15:6; 2 Cor. 11:31; cf. John 14:23; 15:16; 16:23; 1 John 4:14; Rev. 1:6). God is also the Father of all believers (Matt. 5:16, 45, 48; 6:1, 9; 10:20; 13:43; 23:9; Mark 11:25; Luke 12:30, 32; John 20:17; Rom. 1:7; 8:15; Gal. 4:6; Eph. 2:18; 4:6; Phil. 4:20; Heb. 12:9; James 1:27; 1 John 2:13; 3:1).

One commentator calls Peter's use in verse 3 of Christ's full redemptive name "a concentrated confession." All that the Bible reveals about the Savior appears in that title: **Lord** identifies Him as sovereign Ruler; **Jesus** as incarnate Son; and **Christ** as anointed Messiah-King. The apostle personalizes that magnificent title with the simple inclusion of the pronoun **our.** The divine **Lord** of the universe belongs to all believers, as does the **Jesus** who lived, died, and rose again for them, and as does the **Christ,** the Messiah whom God anointed to be their eternal King who will grant them their glorious inheritance.

THE MOTIVE FOR THE BELIEVER'S INHERITANCE

who according to His great mercy (1:3*b*)

His great mercy was the motive behind God's granting believers eternal life—sharing the very life of the Father, Son, and Spirit. Ephesians 2:4–5 also expresses this divine generosity, "But God, being rich in mercy, because of His great love with which He loved us, even when we were dead in our transgressions, made us alive together with Christ (by grace you have been saved)" (cf. Titus 3:5). Both here and in Ephesians, the apostolic writer added an enlarging adjective (**great** and "rich").

Mercy focuses on the sinner's miserable, pitiful condition. The gospel is prompted by God's compassion toward those who were dead in their trespasses and sins (Eph. 2:1–3). All believers were once in that wretched, helpless condition, compounded by a deceitful heart (Gen. 6:5; 8:21; Eccl. 9:3; Jer. 17:9; Mark 7:21–23), corrupt mind (Rom. 8:7–8; 1 Cor. 2:14), and wicked desires (Eph. 4:17–19; 5:8; Titus 1:15) that made them slaves to sin, headed for just punishment in hell. Therefore they needed God, in **mercy,** to show compassion toward their desperate, lost condition and remedy it (cf. Isa. 63:9; Hab. 3:2; Matt. 9:27; Mark 5:19; Luke 1:78; Rom. 9:15–16, 18; 11:30–32; 1 Tim. 1:13; 1 Peter 2:10).

Mercy is not the same as grace. Mercy concerns an individual's miserable condition, whereas grace concerns his guilt, which caused that condition. Divine mercy takes the sinner from misery to glory (a change of condition), and divine grace takes him from guilt to acquittal (a change of position; see Rom. 3:24; Eph. 1:7). The Lord grieves over the unredeemed sinner's condition of gloom and despair (Ezek. 18:23, 32; Matt. 23:37–39). That is manifest clearly during His incarnation as Jesus healed people's diseases (Matt. 4:23–24; 14:14; 15:30; Mark 1:34; Luke 6:17–19). He could have demonstrated His deity in many other ways, but He chose healings because they best illustrated the compassionate, merciful heart of God toward sinners suffering the temporal misery of their fallen condition (cf. Matt. 9:5–13; Mark 2:3–12). Jesus' healing miracles, which nearly banished illness from Israel, were proof that what the Old Testament said about God the Father being merciful (Ex. 34:6; Ps. 108:4; Lam. 3:22; Mic. 7:18) was true.

Apart from even the possibility of any merit or worthiness on the sinner's part, God grants mercy to whomever He will: "For He [God] says to Moses, 'I will have mercy on whom I have mercy, and I will have compassion on whom I have compassion.' So then it does not depend on the man who wills or the man who runs, but on God who has mercy" (Rom. 9:15–16). Out of His infinite compassion and free, abundant, and limitless **mercy,** He chose to grant eternal life—it was not because of anything sinners could do or deserve (Ex. 33:19; Rom. 9:11–13; 10:20; 2 Tim. 1:9). It is completely understandable that Paul called God "the Father of mercies" (2 Cor. 1:3).

THE APPROPRIATION OF THE BELIEVER'S INHERITANCE

has caused us to be born again to a living hope through the resurrection of Jesus Christ from the dead, (1:3c)

The prophet Jeremiah once asked the rhetorical question, "Can the Ethiopian change his skin or the leopard his spots?" (Jer. 13:23). His graphic analogy implied a negative answer to the question of whether or not sinners could change their natures (cf. 17:9). Humanity's sinful nature needs changing (Mark 1:14–15; John 3:7, 17–21, 36; cf. Gen. 6:5; Jer. 2:22; 17:9–10; Rom. 1:18–2:2; 3:10–18), but only God, working through His Holy Spirit, can transform the sinful human heart (Jer. 31:31–34; John 3:5–6, 8; Acts 2:38–39; cf. Ezek. 37:14; Acts 15:8; Rom. 8:11; 1 John 5:4). In order for sinners to receive an eternal inheritance from God, they must experience His means of spiritual transformation, the new birth. Peter affirms that truth in this last portion of verse 3, when he says God **has caused** believers **to be born again** (see discussion on 1:23–25 in chapter 7 of this volume; cf. 2 Cor. 5:17).

Jesus effectively explained the necessity of regeneration—the new birth—to Nicodemus, a prominent Jewish teacher.

Now there was a man of the Pharisees, named Nicodemus, a ruler of the Jews; this man came to Jesus by night and said to Him, "Rabbi, we know that You have come from God as a teacher; for no one can do these signs that You do unless God is with him." Jesus answered and said to him, "Truly, truly, I say to you, unless one is born again he cannot see the kingdom of God." Nicodemus said to Him, "How can a man be born when he is old? He cannot enter a second time into his mother's womb and be born, can he?" Jesus answered, "Truly, truly, I say to you, unless one is born of water and the Spirit he cannot enter into the kingdom of God. That which is born of the flesh is flesh, and that which is born of the Spirit is spirit. Do not be amazed that I said to you, 'You must be born again.' The wind blows where it wishes and you hear the sound of it, but do not know where it comes from and where it is going; so is everyone who is born of the Spirit." Nicodemus said to Him, "How can these things be?" Jesus answered and said to him, "Are you the teacher of Israel and do not understand these things? Truly, truly, I say to you, we speak of what we know and testify of what we have seen, and you do not accept our testimony. If I told you earthly things and you do not believe, how will you believe if I tell you heavenly things? No one has ascended into heaven, but He who descended from heaven: the Son of Man. As Moses lifted up the serpent in the wilderness, even so must the Son of Man be lifted up; so that whoever believes will in Him have eternal life. (John 3:1–15)

To illustrate the means of the new birth, Jesus referred to the episode of the bronze serpent (Num. 21:4–9), an Old Testament narrative Nicodemus would have known well. When the snake-bitten Israelites in the wilderness acknowledged their sin and God's judgment on them for it and looked to the means He provided to deliver them (a bronze snake on a pole), they received physical healing from their poisonous bites. By analogy, if sinners would experience spiritual deliverance, they must recognize their spiritual condition as poisoned by their sin and experience salvation from spiritual and eternal death by looking to the Son of God and trusting in Him as their Savior. Jesus cut to the core of Nicodemus's self-righteousness and told him what all sinners need to hear, that they are spiritually regenerated only by faith in Jesus Christ (cf. John 1:12–13; Titus 3:5; James 1:18).

Peter goes on to declare that regeneration results in believers receiving **a living hope.** The unbelieving world knows only dying hopes (Job 8:13; Prov. 10:28; Eph. 2:12), but believers have a living, undying hope (Pss. 33:18; 39:7; Rom. 5:5; Eph. 4:4; Titus 2:13; Heb. 6:19) that will come to a complete, final, and glorious fulfillment (Rom. 5:2; Col. 1:27). It is a hope that Peter later described when he wrote, "according to His promise we are looking for new heavens and a new earth, in which righteousness dwells" (2 Peter 3:13). This hope is what prompted Paul to tell the Philippians, "For to me, to live is Christ and to die is gain" (Phil. 1:21). At death believers' hope becomes reality as they enter the glorious presence of God and the full, unhindered, joyous fellowship with the Trinity, the angels, and other saints (Rom. 5:1–2; Gal. 5:5).

The means of Christians' appropriating this living hope and eternal inheritance is spiritual birth, and the power for that appropriation was demonstrated by **the resurrection of Jesus Christ from the dead.** Jesus told Martha, just prior to the raising of her brother Lazarus from the grave, "I am the resurrection and the life; he who believes in Me will live even if he dies, and everyone who lives and believes in Me will never die" (John 11:25–26; cf. 14:19). Paul instructed the Corinthians concerning the vital ramifications of the resurrection, "If Christ has not been raised, your faith is worthless; you are still in your sins" (1 Cor. 15:17). Even if one hoped in Christ in this life, but not beyond it, he would be lost (v. 19). However, Christ rose from the dead, forever securing the believer's living hope in heaven by finally conquering death (vv. 20–28, 47–49, 54–57).

The Nature of the Believer's Inheritance

to obtain an inheritance which is imperishable and undefiled and will not fade away, (1:4*a*)

The key word of this entire passage is **inheritance,** which is wealth passed down, or a legacy one receives as a member of a family. The concept had roots in the Old Testament, which the Jewish Christians in Peter's audience would have easily identified with. In fact, the same Greek root (*klēronomia*), rendered **inheritance** here, is used in the Septuagint to speak of the portions of Canaan allotted by God to each tribe in Israel except Levi (cf. Num. 18:20–24; Josh. 13:32–33). See Numbers 26:54, 56 (the verb form appears in vv. 53, 55); 34:2 (where it is used of the entire Promised Land as Israel's collective inheritance; cf. Deut. 12:9); Joshua 11:23; Deuteronomy 3:20 (of the Transjordan tribes' portion of land). The word is also used numerous times of other kinds of inheritance (e.g., the individual inheritance of the daughters of Zelophehad [Num. 27:7–11]). *Klēronomia* is often translated "possession" in English translations of the Old Testament.

The Old Testament repeatedly affirms that under the old covenant the people of God, the nation of Israel, received an inheritance (Num. 26:53–56; 34:2, 29; Deut. 3:28; 26:1; 31:7; Josh. 11:23; 14:1; 1 Kings 8:36; 1 Chron. 16:18; Ps. 105:11; cf. Ps. 78:55). Peter told his readers that just as Israel received an earthly inheritance, the land of Canaan, so the church receives a spiritual inheritance in heaven (Acts 20:32; 26:18; Eph. 1:11, 18; Col. 1:12; 3:24; Heb. 9:15). The apostle reminded them that in the midst of their persecution they ought to praise God and patiently wait for His promised eternal **inheritance** (4:13; Matt. 24:13; Heb. 12:2–3; cf. Rom. 6:18; 8:18; 12:12). Therefore he wanted to increase their knowledge (and that of all believers) of the eternal blessing that is already theirs by promise in Christ (cf. Rom. 8:16–17; 1 John 3:2–3). Until then, God is in the process of maturing His children and conforming their behavior so that it is increasingly consistent with their spiritual inheritance (cf. 4:12–13, 19; 5:10; Heb. 12:5–12; James 1:2–4; 5:11). Peter's words remind of Paul's exhortation to the Colossians to focus on that inheritance: "Therefore if you have been raised up with Christ, keep seeking the things above, where Christ is, seated at the right hand of God. Set your mind on the things above, not on the things that are on earth" (Col. 3:1–2; cf. Matt. 6:33; 1 John 2:15–17).

Peter adds three descriptive terms to further define the kind of inheritance believers obtain: it **is imperishable and undefiled and will not fade away. Imperishable** (*aphtharton*) refers to what is not corruptible, not liable to death, or not subject to destruction. Unlike the Israelites' earthly inheritance that came and went because of their sins, believers' spiritual inheritance will never be subject to destruction. Believers' inheritance in heaven, yet to be revealed in the future, is a glorious treasure that will never be lost.

Undefiled (*amianton*) describes things that are unstained or unpolluted. Everything in the fallen creation is stained and polluted by sin (Rom. 8:20–22; 1 John 5:19), and therefore it is all flawed. That is what the apostle Paul referred to when he wrote, "For we know that the whole creation groans and suffers the pains of childbirth together until now" (Rom. 8:22). All earthly inheritance is defiled, but not the **undefiled** inheritance believers have in Jesus Christ (cf. Phil. 3:7–9; Col. 1:12). It is flawless and perfect.

Finally, the believer's inheritance **will not fade away.** That phrase translates the word *amaranton,* which was used in secular Greek to describe a flower that did not wither or die. The term in this context suggests that believers have an inheritance that will never lose its magnificence. None of the decaying elements of the world can affect the kingdom of heaven (Luke 12:33; cf. Rev. 21:27; 22:15). None of the ravages of time or the evils of sin can touch the believer's inheritance because it is in a timeless, sinless realm (cf. Deut. 26:15; Ps. 89:29; 2 Cor. 5:1). Later in this letter, Peter reiterates the unfading nature of the church's inheritance: "And when the Chief Shepherd appears, you will receive the unfading crown of glory" (5:4).

The Security of the Believer's Inheritance

reserved in heaven for you, who are protected by the power of God through faith for a salvation ready to be revealed in the last time. (1:4*b*–5)

Having pledged that the believer's spiritual inheritance was permanent in nature, Peter adds to his readers' security by declaring that the believer's inheritance is **reserved in heaven.** Its nature is fixed and unalterable and so is its place. **Reserved** (*tetērēmenēn*) means "guarded" or "watched over." The perfect passive participle conveys the idea of the already existing inheritance being carefully guarded **in heaven** for all those who trust in Christ. Not only will that inheritance not change, but no one will plunder it. The reality of a guarded and imperishable eternal inheritance is precisely what Jesus referred to when He said,

> Do not store up for yourselves treasures on earth, where moth and rust destroy, and where thieves break in and steal. But store up for yourselves treasures in heaven, where neither moth nor rust destroys, and where thieves do not break in or steal; for where your treasure is, there your heart will be also. (Matt. 6:19–21)

Heaven is the securest place in all the universe. The apostle John characterizes it as a place where "nothing unclean, and no one who practices abomination and lying, shall ever come into it, but only those whose names are written in the Lamb's book of life" (Rev. 21:27; cf. 22:14–15).

Not only is the inheritance divinely guarded, those who possess it **are** also **protected by the power of God** from doing anything to forfeit it or be severed from it. God's **power** is His sovereign omnipotence that continuously protects His elect. If God is for believers, no one can successfully oppose them (Rom. 8:31–39; Jude 24). All the details of this promise are to provide the believer with an undying hope of heaven, so as to provide joy and endurance.

The Christian's continued **faith** in God is evidence of His keeping and protecting work (John 8:31; Col. 1:21–23; Heb. 3:6, 14; James 2:17, 20–26; 1 John 5:4, 11–13). At conversion, God energizes faith in believers' hearts, and as He keeps them He continues to energize their faith (Ps. 37:24; John 10:28; Phil. 1:6). By His grace, God's omnipotent, protecting power and the believer's perseverance of faith always work hand in hand (cf. Dan. 6:1–23).

This security for the believer and his inheritance both look beyond this life and human history **for a salvation ready to be re-**

vealed in the last time. Salvation (*sōtērian*) means "rescue" or "deliverance," and here it denotes the full, final, eternal life God has not yet consummated. The New Testament implicitly reveals a threefold chronology for salvation. The past aspect of salvation is justification; it comes when one believes in Christ (Rom. 10:9–10, 14–17) and is delivered from the penalty of sin. The present aspect of salvation is sanctification. Believers are continually being delivered from the power of sin (1 John 1:9). Ephesians 2:8 declares, "For by grace you have been saved." The Greek literally says, "you are having been saved." Salvation thus is a past occurrence with continuing results in the present. Third, salvation also has a future aspect, glorification (cf. Rom. 13:11). Whenever a believer dies, God completely and finally delivers him from the presence of sin (cf. Heb. 9:28) and instantly brings him into his eternal inheritance in His heavenly presence. Paul eloquently expressed to Timothy his personal confidence in the certainty of his future inheritance: "The Lord will rescue me from every evil deed, and will bring me safely to His heavenly kingdom; to Him be the glory forever and ever. Amen" (2 Tim. 4:18; cf. Acts 26:18; Eph. 1:11, 14, 18; Col. 1:12).

The book of Hebrews has much to say about the believer's future inheritance. In reference to angels, the writer rhetorically asks, "Are they not all ministering spirits, sent out to render service for the sake of those who will inherit salvation?" (1:14). Later on the writer says this concerning Christ and the new covenant: "For this reason He is the mediator of a new covenant, so that, since a death has taken place for the redemption of the transgressions that were committed under the first covenant, those who have been called may receive the promise of the eternal inheritance" (9:15; cf. v. 28).

The future aspect of salvation is particularly said to be **ready,** that is, complete and already awaiting the believer's arrival. But future salvation is also connected to the end of human history. Peter says it is **to be revealed in the last time.** God will not make believers' inheritance fully complete until the last episode of redemptive history, namely the return of Jesus Christ (cf. Matt. 25:34). After the rapture, all believers receive rewards at the judgment seat of Christ:

> For no man can lay a foundation other than the one which is laid, which is Jesus Christ. Now if any man builds on the foundation with gold, silver, precious stones, wood, hay, straw, each man's work will become evident; for the day will show it because it is to be revealed with fire, and the fire itself will test the quality of each man's work. If any man's work which he has built on it remains, he will receive a reward. (1 Cor. 3:11–14; cf. 2 Cor. 5:10; 2 Tim. 4:1, 8)

And the fullness of the Christian's eternal inheritance will be realized at the end of the millennial kingdom when God creates the new heaven and new earth (Rev. 21:1–27):

> Then he showed me a river of the water of life, clear as crystal, coming from the throne of God and of the Lamb, in the middle of its street. On either side of the river was the tree of life, bearing twelve kinds of fruit, yielding its fruit every month; and the leaves of the tree were for the healing of the nations. There will no longer be any curse; and the throne of God and of the Lamb will be in it, and His bond-servants will serve Him; they will see His face, and His name will be on their foreheads. And there will no longer be any night; and they will not have need of the light of a lamp nor the light of the sun, because the Lord God will illumine them; and they will reign forever and ever. (Rev. 22:1–5)

Just as originally the Lord Himself was the inheritance of the Levites (Josh. 13:33), the priestly tribe of Israel, so He also is the inheritance of the royal priesthood of Christ (1 Peter 2:9). The psalmist knew with certainty that he would inherit God: "The Lord is the portion of my inheritance and my cup; You support my lot. The lines have fallen to me in pleasant places; indeed, my heritage is beautiful to me" (Ps. 16:5–6; cf. 73:23–26). The prophet Jeremiah, even in the midst of the most difficult times, firmly grasped the same concept: "'The Lord is my portion,' says my soul, 'Therefore I have hope in Him'" (Lam. 3:24). Christians are also heirs of God with Christ: "The Spirit Himself testifies with our spirit that we are children of God, and if children, heirs also, heirs of God and fellow heirs with Christ" (Rom. 8:16–17).

Christians possess some of the benefits of salvation in this life, but the great fullness of redemption is yet to come. God has promised unfathomable glories in the eternal perfection of heaven that will one day be the conscious experience of every believer. He is the source of the believer's inheritance; it came because of His mercy and by the gracious means of the new birth; and it remains perfect and eternally secure, a reality all believers can fix their hope on.

Salvation Joy
(1 Peter 1:6–9)

3

In this you greatly rejoice, even though now for a little while, if necessary, you have been distressed by various trials, so that the proof of your faith, being more precious than gold which is perishable, even though tested by fire, may be found to result in praise and glory and honor at the revelation of Jesus Christ; and though you have not seen Him, you love Him, and though you do not see Him now, but believe in Him, you greatly rejoice with joy inexpressible and full of glory, obtaining as the outcome of your faith the salvation of your souls. (1:6–9)

One of the most treasured chapters in all of the Gospels is Luke 15. There Christ tells three memorable parables: the story of the lost sheep (vv. 4–7), the story of the lost coin (vv. 8–10), and the story of the lost (prodigal) son (vv. 11–32). Each parable represents salvation—each portrays a lost soul forgiven and reconciled to God. And each parable concludes with a celebration of tremendous joy at the recovery of that which was lost, illustrating heaven's response to the salvation of a sinner (15:6,9,32).

Genuine salvation and true joy belong together and are not limited to heavenly inhabitants. Peter's goal in this text is to have believers understand the joy that should be their own constant expression in light of eternal salvation. This joy reflects what Peter certainly knew from Old Testament revelation. The psalmist had much to say about joy and the believer: "O send out Your light and Your truth, let them lead me; let them bring me to Your holy hill and to Your dwelling places. Then I will go to the altar of God, to God my exceeding joy; and upon the lyre I shall praise You, O God, my God" (Ps. 43:3–4; cf. 4:7; 5:11; 9:2; 32:11; 37:4; 51:12). The prophet Isaiah wrote, "And the ransomed of the Lord will return and come with joyful shouting to Zion, with everlasting joy upon their heads. They will find gladness and joy, and sorrow and sighing will flee away" (Isa. 35:10; cf. 61:10). The gospel of Luke calls word of Christ's birth "good news of great joy" (2:10), and Paul commended the Thessalonian believers for receiving his evangelistic message "with the joy of the Holy Spirit" (1 Thess. 1:6; cf. Phil. 4:4; 1 Thess. 5:16).

Peter wrote early on the subject of joy and the believer because his readers needed the reminder and the encouragement as they faced severe persecution. Later, in 2:12, he exhorted them, "Keep your behavior excellent among the Gentiles, so that in the thing in which they slander you as evildoers, they may because of your good deeds, as they observe them, glorify God." The clear implication is that though the recipients of this letter were suffering unjustly, they should expect such mistreatment and endure it with joy and patience (cf. 2:18–21; 3:9, 14–15, 17; 4:1, 12, 14, 16, 19; 5:10). In light of the blessedness of salvation, no earthly difficulties should have diminished their joy (cf. Hab. 3:17–18; Matt. 5:11–12; James 1:2).

Salvation joy is not some brief, shallow, circumstantial emotion, but rather something permanent and profound (Rom. 5:11; 14:17; Gal. 5:22; Phil. 1:25; 4:4; cf. 1 Chron. 16:27; 29:17; Ezra 3:12; Neh. 8:10; Job 8:19; Pss. 5:11; 16:11; 43:4; Isa. 35:10; 51:11; Matt. 13:44; 25:21; Luke 24:52; John 16:24; Acts 13:52; Jude 24), tied closely to the spiritual blessings of faith, hope, and love (cf. Rom. 5:2; 12:12; 15:13; Heb. 12:2) and given by God through His Son and the Holy Spirit (Luke 2:10–11, 29–32, 38; 24:52; John 15:11; 16:22; 17:13; 1 Thess. 1:6; cf. John 10:10; 14:26–27; 16:33). Mere happiness comes from positive external events, but salvation joy results from the deep-rooted confidence that one possesses eternal life from the living God through the crucified and risen Christ (cf. Phil. 3:7–11; Heb. 6:19–20; 10:19–22; 1 John 5:13–14), which joy will be fully realized in the glory of heaven.

Peter gives five perspectives on joy so that believers may triumph even in the most adverse circumstances. He highlights the reality that joy derives from confidence in a protected inheritance, in a proven faith, in a promised honor, in a personal fellowship with Christ, and in a present deliverance.

CONFIDENCE IN A PROTECTED INHERITANCE

In this you greatly rejoice, (1:6a)

In this refers back to the preceding passage (1:3–5), which detailed the first great truth that brings Christians joy, namely their protected eternal inheritance. **Greatly rejoice** (from *agalliaō*) is an intense, expressive term that means to be supremely and abundantly happy—a happiness that is not tentative nor based on circumstances or superficial feelings. Jesus used it in Matthew 5:12 in addition to the more ordinary word for **rejoice** (*chairō*). With that usage, He intensified the meaning of His command to His disciples. In fact, in that verse the King James translators rendered the word "be exceeding glad." In the New Testament, *agalliaō* always refers to spiritual rather than temporal joy, and it usually has reference to a relationship with God (cf. 1:8; 4:13; Luke 1:47; 10:21; Acts 2:26; 16:34; Rev. 19:7). Furthermore, since Peter put it in the present tense, it conveys the notion of *continual* joy and happiness.

As discussed in the previous chapter of this volume, God has reserved and securely protected an eternal inheritance in heaven for every believer. That is why the apostle Paul urged believers to focus "on the things above, not on the things that are on earth" (Col. 3:2). There was a time when that joy seemed elusive to Christ's disciples. Jesus told them in the Upper Room, "Truly, truly, I say to you, that you will weep and lament, but the world will rejoice; you will grieve, but your grief will be turned into joy" (John 16:20). For a short time, unbelievers would rejoice and the disciples would grieve as a result of the Savior's death (cf. Matt. 27:39, 44; Mark 14:27; 16:10–11, 14; Luke 24:17, 36–39). But when He arose from the grave and the disciples saw Him, their sorrow turned to joy (Luke 24:12, 32, 52–53; cf. John 21:7) and His promise of life after death for believers (cf. John 11:25–26; 14:1–4) became credible.

All believers have the indwelling Holy Spirit (John 14:16–17; Acts 1:8; Rom. 8:9; 1 Cor. 6:19; 12:13; Gal. 3:14; 1 John 2:27; 3:24; 4:13; cf. John 14:26; 16:13; Acts 6:5; 2 Cor. 6:16), who serves as a pledge or seal to guarantee their eternal inheritance:

> In Him, you also, after listening to the message of truth, the gospel of your salvation—having also believed, you were sealed in Him with the Holy Spirit of promise, who is given as a pledge of our inheritance, with a view to the redemption of God's own possession, to the praise of His glory. (Eph. 1:13–14; cf. 4:30)

The author of Hebrews also focuses on the believer's protected spiritual inheritance (4:1–10; 6:9–12, 19–20; 9:11–15; 11:13–16) and encourages his Jewish readers to do likewise in the midst of suffering:

But remember the former days, when, after being enlightened, you endured a great conflict of sufferings, partly by being made a public spectacle through reproaches and tribulations, and partly by becoming sharers with those who were so treated. For you showed sympathy to the prisoners and accepted joyfully the seizure of your property, knowing that you have for yourselves a better possession and a lasting one. Therefore, do not throw away your confidence, which has a great reward. For you have need of endurance, so that when you have done the will of God, you may receive what was promised. (10:32–36)

No matter what difficult circumstances and persecutions they face, the faithful **greatly rejoice** because of the future hope that derives from Christ's resurrection (1:3; 1 Cor. 15:51–57; cf. Rom. 5:2; 12:12) and the present reality of the indwelling Spirit (1:2), securing a protected, eternal inheritance (cf. Heb. 10:32–36).

CONFIDENCE IN A PROVEN FAITH

even though now for a little while, if necessary, you have been distressed by various trials, so that the proof of your faith, being more precious than gold which is perishable, even though tested by fire, (1:6b–7a)

Peter next turns to a source of joy that has immense practical ramifications for believers—confidence in a proven faith. Rather than allow severe trials and persecutions to steal their joy and spoil their anticipation of future blessing in heaven, genuine believers with a biblical perspective know that such sufferings actually can add to their joy as they experience grace and anticipate the future.

In the remainder of verse 6 the apostle lists four concise features of the trouble God uses to prove believers' faith. First he declares that their troubles are **now for a little while.** They are transitory (cf. Ps. 30:5; Isa. 54:7–8; Rom. 8:18), literally "for a season," which means they will pass quickly, as does one's time on earth. Paul calls them "momentary, light affliction" (2 Cor. 4:17), relative to the "eternal weight of glory."

Second, troubles come **if necessary;** that is, when they serve a purpose in believers' lives (cf. Job 5:6–7; Acts 14:22; 1 Thess. 3:3). God uses troubles to humble believers (Deut. 8:3; 2 Cor. 12:7–10), wean them away from worldly things and point them toward heaven (John 16:33; Rev. 14:13; cf. Job 19:25–26), teach them to value God's blessing as opposed to life's pain (4:13; Rom. 8:17–18), enable them to help others (2 Cor. 1:3–7; Heb. 13:3), chasten them for their sins (1 Cor. 11:30; cf. Job 5:17; Luke 15:16–18; Heb. 12:5–12), and to help strengthen spiritual character (Rom. 5:3; 2 Thess. 1:4–6; James 1:2–4; 5:11). Later in this letter Peter sums up troubles' benefit, "After you have suffered for a little while, the God of all grace, who called you to His eternal glory in Christ, will Himself perfect, confirm, strengthen and establish you" (5:10).

Third, Peter with the term **been distressed** acknowledges that trouble undeniably brings pain (cf. Gen. 3:16–19; Pss. 42:7; 66:12; 89:30–32). **Distressed** refers not only to physical pain, but also to mental anguish, including sadness, sorrow, disappointment, and anxiety. By God's design, trouble needs to be painful in order to refine believers for greater spiritual usefulness (cf. Pss. 34:19; 78:34; 119:71; John 9:1–3; 11:3–4; 2 Cor. 12:10).

Fourth, the apostle notes in verse 6 that Christians experience **various trials;** troubles come in many forms (James 1:2). The Greek word rendered **various** is *poikilos,* which means "many colored." Later Peter uses the same word (rendered "manifold" in the NASB and KJV) to describe the diverse grace of God (4:10). Just as trouble is diverse, God's sufficient grace for believers is equally diverse. There is no form of trouble that some facet of divine grace cannot supersede (cf. 1 Cor. 10:13). God's grace is sufficient for every human trial.

Those simply stated elements implicitly reiterate why trouble should not diminish believers' joy, and the first half of verse 7 states the reason explicitly: they rejoice **so that the proof of** [their] **faith, being more precious than gold which is perishable, even though tested by fire.** This perspective on trouble not only does not diminish joy but actually produces triumphant joy, since the experience validates Christians' faith. **Proof** (*dokimion*) was used to describe the assaying of metal. The assaying process discovers a metal's purity and determines its true content and worth after all impurities have been smelted away (Num. 31:22–23; cf. Prov. 17:3; Zech. 13:9). By analogy, God tests the believer's faith to reveal its genuineness (cf. Job 23:10). (He does this not because He needs to discover who is a true believer, but so that believers will gain joy and confidence in their proven faith [cf. Abraham in Gen. 22:1–19, and the example of the seeds in shallow and thorny soils in Matt. 13:5–7].) The adjectival phrase **proof of your faith,** more accurately "the tested residue of your faith," captures the essence of the spiritual assaying process.

In addition to Abraham, the Old Testament contains several other examples of how God put the faith of His people to the test. Exodus 16:4 says, "Then the Lord said to Moses, 'Behold, I will rain bread from heaven for you; and the people shall go out and gather a day's portion every day, that I may test them, whether or not they will walk in My instruction.'" In Deuteronomy 8:2 Moses commanded the Israelites, "You shall remember all the way which the Lord your God has led you in the wilderness these forty years, that He might humble you, testing you, to know what was in your heart, whether you would keep His command- ments or not." But the entire book of Job is the classic example of God's putting a believer to the test. No matter what Satan, with God's permis- sion, threw at Job, Job never stopped trusting the Lord (Job 1:6–2:10). In spite of his friends' terribly misplaced efforts at consoling and advising him, and their constantly misjudging him—in addition to his faithless wife's demand that he curse God and die—Job remained steady and his faith proved real (27:1–6) and was greatly strengthened (42:1–6, 10–17).

Peter used **gold** in his analogy because it was the most precious and highly prized of all metals (Ezra 8:27; Job 28:15–16; Ps. 19:10; cf. 2 Kings 23:35; Matt. 2:11), and in ancient times it was the basis for most monetary transactions (cf. Ezek. 27:22; Matt. 10:9). Just as **fire** separates gold from useless dross, so God uses suffering and trials to separate true faith from superficial profession. But even though gold can be purified when **tested by fire,** it is **perishable** (cf. James 5:3). However, proven faith is eternal, making it **more precious than gold.**

The apostles, ministering in the aftermath of Pentecost, are excel- lent examples of those who went through difficult trials and thus became confident in their proven faith. After the Jewish leaders flogged them for continuing to preach the gospel, "they went on their way from the presence of the Council, rejoicing that they had been considered worthy to suffer shame for His name" (Acts 5:41; cf. 4:13–21; 5:17–29, 40–41). They rejoiced not only because God deemed them worthy to suf- fer for righteousness' sake, but also undoubtedly because of the confi- dence they gained in passing the test. They had come a long way since the days when Jesus admonished them for their "little faith" (Matt. 8:26; cf. 16:8; 17:20; Luke 8:25; 17:5), when they forsook Him and fled prior to His crucifixion (Mark 14:27, 50–52), and when Peter denied Him three times (Luke 22:54–62).

CONFIDENCE IN A PROMISED HONOR

may be found to result in praise and glory and honor at the reve- lation of Jesus Christ; (1:7*b*)

The apostle's discussion of proven faith in the first part of verse 7 actually leads into his main point in the latter half, namely that believers would rejoice in the prospect of a promised honor. True faith will ulti- mately come through all of life's troubles and trials and obtain eternal honor from God.

Peter's focus is not on Christians' honoring God (though they will, cf. Matt. 28:16–17; John 4:23; 9:38; Rev. 4:10–11), but on His commendation of them. God will grant believers **praise and glory and honor at the revelation of Jesus Christ.** Incredibly, believers, who in this life are called to give honor to the Lord always, can by their faithfulness in trials elicit **praise** from the Lord in the life to come (cf. 1 Sam. 2:26; Pss. 41:11; 106:4; Prov. 8:35; 12:2; Acts 7:46). Near the conclusion of His parable of the talents, Jesus told the disciples,

> His master said to him, "Well done, good and faithful slave. You were faithful with a few things, I will put you in charge of many things; enter into the joy of your master." Also the one who had received the two talents came up and said, "Master, you entrusted two talents to me. See, I have gained two more talents." His master said to him, "Well done, good and faithful slave. You were faithful with a few things, I will put you in charge of many things; enter into the joy of your master." (Matt. 25:21–23; cf. 24:47; 25:34; Luke 22:29; 2 Tim. 4:8)

True saving faith and its resultant good works always receive divine commendation. "But he is a Jew who is one inwardly; and circumcision is that which is of the heart, by the Spirit, not by the letter; and his praise is not from men, but from God" (Rom. 2:29). That God would praise saving faith and genuine faithfulness in difficulty is truly amazing, inasmuch as both are gifts of His grace and power in the first place (Eph. 2:8; Phil. 1:29). Such praise for believers demonstrates His supreme generosity (cf. Ex. 34:6; Pss. 33:5; 104:24; 2 Cor. 8:9).

Peter also uses the term **glory,** which, like **praise,** refers to that which believers receive from God. This echoes the apostle Paul's teaching: "[God] will render to each person according to his deeds: to those [believers] who by perseverance in doing good seek for glory and honor and immortality, eternal life . . . glory and honor and peace to everyone who does good, to the Jew first and also to the Greek" (Rom. 2:6–7, 10). **Glory** may relate best to the Christlikeness God will endow every believer with (John 17:22; Rom. 9:23; 1 Cor. 15:42–44; 2 Cor. 3:18; Phil. 3:21; Col. 3:4; 2 Thess. 2:14; 1 John 3:2). Jesus Christ was God incarnate (John 1:14), and the apostle John says, "We know that when He appears, we will be like Him, because we will see Him just as He is" (1 John 3:2).

Honor likely refers to the rewards God will give to believers because of their service to Him. Paul explains this in more detail in 1 Corinthians 3:10–15.

> According to the grace of God which was given to me, like a wise master builder I laid a foundation, and another is building on it. But each man must be careful how he builds on it. For no man can lay a foundation other than the one which is laid, which is Jesus Christ. Now if

any man builds on the foundation with gold, silver, precious stones, wood, hay, straw, each man's work will become evident; for the day will show it because it is to be revealed with fire, and the fire itself will test the quality of each man's work. If any man's work which he has built on it remains, he will receive a reward. If any man's work is burned up, he will suffer loss; but he himself will be saved, yet so as through fire. (cf. 9:25; 2 Cor. 5:10; Col. 3:24; James 1:12; 1 Peter 5:4; 2 John 8; Rev. 21:7; 22:12)

This threefold tribute (**praise and glory and honor**) occurs **at the revelation of Jesus Christ. Revelation** (*apokalupsei*) refers to the second coming of Christ and particularly focuses on the time when He returns to reward His redeemed people. Later in this same chapter Peter again directs his audience to these realities: "Therefore, prepare your minds for action, keep sober in spirit, fix your hope completely on the grace to be brought to you at the revelation of Jesus Christ" (1:13; cf. 4:13; Rom. 8:18; 1 Cor. 1:7–8; 2 Thess. 1:5). In His parable of the expectant steward, Jesus spoke of such eager anticipation of eternal reward:

Be dressed in readiness, and keep your lamps lit. Be like men who are waiting for their master when he returns from the wedding feast, so that they may immediately open the door to him when he comes and knocks. Blessed are those slaves whom the master will find on the alert when he comes; truly I say to you, that he will gird himself to serve, and have them recline at the table, and will come up and wait on them. (Luke 12:35–37)

None of these passages, however, indicate that believers have to wait until Christ's return before He finds their faith genuine. The reality of their faith is already validated by their faithful enduring of trials and testings. It is an amazing truth that when Jesus returns for His own, not only will they joyfully serve Him, but also He will graciously serve and honor them.

CONFIDENCE IN A PERSONAL FELLOWSHIP WITH CHRIST

and though you have not seen Him, you love Him, and though you do not see Him now, but believe in Him, you greatly rejoice with joy inexpressible and full of glory, (1:8)

Love and trust are the two crucial ingredients in any meaningful relationship. In this verse, the apostle exalts those two aspects as essential to believers' relationship with Christ and vital to the joy that results.

He also reflects genuine pathos and personal humility with these words, based on his past, personal experience as one of the Twelve.

Excluding Judas Iscariot (Matt. 26:14, 16; Luke 22:47–48), Peter was the one disciple who exhibited the most egregious breach of faith and trust in his Lord. Not long after Peter's three-time denial of Christ (Luke 22:54–62), Jesus confronted him and three times asked him, "Do you love Me?" (John 21:15–22). In humble fashion he reflected on that time and by implication commended his persecuted readers for their relationship to Christ. Peter, even though he was the leader of the apostles and lived with Jesus for three years, in a crucial time failed to sustain his love and trust in Him. In marked contrast, his readers, **though** they had **not seen Him,** maintained a true love for and strong trust in Jesus in the midst of threatening persecution and sufferings.

The word **love** (*agapate*) is the love of the will, the noblest form of love. The present tense indicates that Peter's audience constantly loved their Lord, which **love** defines the essence of being a Christian. Peter underscores this fact later in the letter, "Unto you therefore which believe he [Christ] is precious" (2:7, KJV; cf. 1 Cor. 16:22; Eph. 6:24; 1 John 4:19). Real joy flows from a love for the unseen Master, the One whom believers also obey (cf. John 14:21).

Peter next commends his readers' faith and trust in Christ. Obviously to **believe in Him** goes hand in hand with loving Him. The soul that loves Christ cannot help but believe in Him, and the soul that believes cannot help but love. **Though** Christians **do not see Him now,** still they **believe in Him.** Jesus told Thomas, "Because you have seen Me, have you believed? Blessed are they who did not see, and yet believed" (John 20:29; cf. Heb. 11:1). Faith accepts the revealed, written record of Jesus Christ (the Gospels; 2 Tim. 3:15; cf. 2 Chron. 20:20; Acts 24:14), which portrays Him in all His glory and leads believers to love Him (cf. Heb. 11:6). The more faith can know of Christ, and the more such knowledge possesses the heart, the stronger believers' love for Him becomes (cf. 2 Cor. 8:7; Gal. 5:6; 1 Tim. 1:5; 1 John 2:5) and the more joy they exhibit (cf. Pss. 5:11; 16:11). Thus love and trust are the two elements that bind believers to a living fellowship with Jesus Christ.

That wondrous relationship caused Peter's readers to **greatly rejoice with joy inexpressible and full of glory. Inexpressible** (*aneklalētō*) literally means "higher than speech." Those who live in personal communion with Christ experience a **joy** so divine that they cannot communicate it; humanly speaking, such joy is beyond the reach of speech and expression. And that joy is also **full of glory** (*doxazō*), meaning "to render highest praise" and from which *doxology* derives. In their fellowship with the Lord, believers have both a supernatural love (cf. Gal. 5:22; 2 Thess. 3:5; 1 John 4:19) and a transcendant **joy** (cf. Eccl. 2:26; Pss. 4:7; 21:6; 68:3; 97:11; Jude 24).

CONFIDENCE IN A PRESENT DELIVERANCE

obtaining as the outcome of your faith the salvation of your souls.
(1:9)

Peter is not looking at the future but at the here and now; one could literally render **obtaining** (*komizomenoi*), "presently receiving for yourselves." The root, *komizō*, means "to receive what is deserved." Flowing out of believers' personal fellowship with Christ is the result due them, **the** present **outcome of** their **faith,** namely **the salvation of** their **souls. Salvation** refers to believers' constant, present deliverance from the penalty and power of sin—from its guilt (Rom. 6:18; Eph. 1:7; Col. 2:13–14), condemnation (Rom. 8:1), wrath (Rom. 5:9; 1 Thess. 1:10), ignorance (Rom. 10:3; Gal. 4:8; 1 Tim. 1:13), distress, confusion, hopelessness (1 Cor. 15:17; 1 Peter 1:3), and dominion (Rom. 6:10–12).

There is really no reason for believers to lose their joy when they can tap into all the present and future spiritual realities mentioned in this passage—present proven faith, fellowship with Christ, and deliverance; and a protected future inheritance and promised honor. As Jesus assured the apostles, "These things I have spoken to you so that My joy may be in you, and that your joy may be made full" (John 15:11).

Salvation's Greatness (1 Peter 1:10–12)

4

As to this salvation, the prophets who prophesied of the grace that would come to you made careful searches and inquiries, seeking to know what person or time the Spirit of Christ within them was indicating as He predicted the sufferings of Christ and the glories to follow. It was revealed to them that they were not serving themselves, but you, in these things which now have been announced to you through those who preached the gospel to you by the Holy Spirit sent from heaven—things into which angels long to look. (1:10–12)

The story began one summer's day toward the end of the nineteenth century when an English city boy was on a visit to rural Scotland. That afternoon the boy went swimming in a small countryside lake. After swimming quite a distance from shore, a severe cramp seized him so that he could not continue swimming. He was in great pain and soon cried out at the top of his voice for help. A farm boy working in a nearby field heard the city boy's screams and ran as fast as he could to the lake. There the farm boy threw off his shirt, dived into the water, swam to the imperiled city boy, and brought him safely to the shore.

Several years later the two boys met again. The city boy, still filled with gratitude that the other boy had saved his life, was thrilled to see the farm boy again and asked him what career the boy had decided to pursue. The farm boy said he had chosen a career in medicine. Since the city boy's parents were quite wealthy and were greatly indebted to the other boy for saving their son's life, upon hearing of the farm boy's career choice they immediately promised to pay for his medical education. They followed through on their promise and the young man went on to have a brilliant career in scientific investigation.

In 1928 that farm boy, then both a physician and bacteriologist, discovered the famous wonder drug penicillin. In 1945 he shared the Nobel prize with two other scientists for the discovery and development of that antibiotic. That Scottish farm boy turned scientific researcher, who died in 1955, was Alexander Fleming.

The rescued city boy also gained great renown. During World War II he contracted a life-threatening case of pneumonia. He recovered at a hospital after receiving penicillin, which meant that indirectly the one-time farm boy Alexander Fleming had saved his life twice. The city boy's name was Winston Churchill, the famous wartime British prime minister and world statesman. Interestingly, just like Fleming, Churchill won a Nobel prize. But in his instance, he won the 1953 award in literature for his incisive writings on the history of the Second World War.

It is wonderful to save a life, and even more wonderful to save someone's life twice, especially when the one saved was such an influential person as Winston Churchill. But the hard-working, selfless contributions of Alexander Fleming are nothing compared to the greatness of saving people's eternal souls. That great salvation is the heart of the apostle Peter's concern in this passage. He wanted his believing audience to focus on that full, final rescue from sin, Satan, death, and hell that God so graciously chose to give them through faith in His Son, Jesus Christ. Peter celebrates salvation's greatness by reminding his readers that no matter how difficult the circumstances or how severe the persecution, they can confidently hold to the hope of eternal salvation.

There is hardly another word as blessed, hopeful, comforting, or assuring as *salvation*. The message of the Bible is that even though man cannot save himself from the eternal, damning consequences of his sin (Gen. 2:17; Jer. 2:22; 18:12; John 3:19; Rom. 6:23; Eph. 2:1–3; Col. 2:13; 2 Tim. 2:25–26), God can and will rescue from condemnation all those who trust in Him and believe His Word (Matt. 11:28–30; Luke 19:10; John 1:12–13, 29; 3:14–17; Acts 10:43; Eph. 1:7; 1 Thess. 5:9; 2 Tim. 1:9; Heb. 7:25; James 1:18). The apostle Paul wrote, "But God demonstrates His own love toward us, in that while we were yet sinners, Christ died for us" (Rom. 5:8). Not only does God love sinners, but He alone is able to rescue them since "salvation belongs to the Lord" (Ps. 3:8). Furthermore, God is willing to rescue sinners; He "desires all men to be saved and to come to the knowledge of the truth" (1 Tim. 2:4).

Above all, salvation is according to God's sovereign plan and purpose (Rom. 8:28–30; 2 Thess. 2:13–14; Rev. 13:8). Paul reminded Timothy that God "has saved us and called us with a holy calling, not according to our works, but according to His own purpose and grace which was granted us in Christ Jesus from all eternity" (2 Tim. 1:9). That statement also indicates that God designated His Son to be the means of salvation (cf. 2:6; Isa. 53:6, 10; Matt. 20:18–19; John 1:17; Acts 2:22–24; 13:23–32). Paul earlier declared to the Roman believers, "For I am not ashamed of the gospel, for it is the power of God for salvation to everyone who believes" (Rom. 1:16). And God was faithful to ordain preachers to announce that the work of Jesus Christ is the only means of rescuing sinners (cf. Acts 13:1–3; Rom. 10:14–17; 1 Cor. 1:21–25). As discussed in the previous chapter of this volume, Peter noted the joy of the church in the glorious gift of salvation (1:6–9). No matter how adverse their circumstances, Christians should never stop rejoicing over the greatness of their salvation: "Sing to the Lord, bless His name; proclaim good tidings of His salvation from day to day" (Ps. 96:2; cf. Pss. 9:14; 21:1; 40:16; 71:23; 1 Chron. 16:23; Isa. 25:9; 35:10; 1 Cor. 6:20; 1 Thess. 5:16; Rev. 5:9).

Peter's theme in the opening chapter of this letter is the blessedness or greatness of salvation. Here he examines it from the viewpoint of four divine agents who were involved with the message of salvation: the Old Testament prophets who studied it, the Holy Spirit who inspired it, the New Testament apostles who preached it, and the angels who examined it.

SALVATION WAS THE THEME OF THE PROPHETS' STUDY

As to this salvation, the prophets who prophesied of the grace that would come to you made careful searches and inquiries, seeking to know what person or time (1:10–11a)

The apostle first draws attention to the **salvation** referred to in verse 9 from the viewpoint of **the prophets.** They were God's Old Testament spokesmen **who prophesied of the grace that would come.** They then pursued the meaning of their own prophetic writings to know all they could about God's promised salvation. Of all the truth the prophets received through divine revelation (cf. Hos. 12:10; Amos 3:7; Heb. 1:1; James 5:10), the truth of salvation was their greatest passion. From Moses to Malachi, all of the Old Testament prophets were fascinated by the promises of salvation. However, they did not merely *wish* to receive that salvation; they *actually* obtained it. But they received the gift of God's salvation without seeing its full accomplishment (cf. Heb. 11:39–40), without seeing Jesus Christ or having a relationship with Him. Though the prophets wrote of Messiah, they never fully comprehended all that was involved in Christ's life, death, and resurrection.

The focus of the prophets' intense study in trying to comprehend the person and work of Christ was centered on **the grace that would come** to sinners through Him. Salvation concerns primarily the divine act of saving sinners (cf. Matt. 20:28; Luke 24:46–47; John 12:32–33; Titus 3:7; Heb. 9:24–28), whereas grace encompasses the entire motive behind God's saving work (cf. Acts 20:32; Rom. 5:15; Eph. 2:5, 8–10; 2 Thess. 1:11–12). The prophets sought to understand God's **grace** and mercy in Christ, His forgiveness, goodness, unmerited favor, and blessing lavished on undeserving sinners. They knew that God's promise of a salvation by **the grace that would come** extended far beyond Israel to include people from every nation on earth (Isa. 45:22; 49:6; 52:10; cf. John 10:16; Rom. 15:9–12; 1 John 2:2; Rev. 4:8–10; 7:9).

It is crucial to emphasize that the phrase **prophesied of the grace that would come** does not indicate that the prophets looked forward to a saving grace that did not exist at all in Old Testament times. By nature God has always been an unchangeably gracious God (Ex. 34:6; Pss. 102:26–27; 116:5; James 1:17). In the Old Testament, He was gracious to those who believed before Christ came (cf. Ps. 84:11), and since then He is gracious to all who believe (John 1:14).

Noah received grace from the Lord (Gen. 6:8). Moses was fully aware of that grace when he first recorded the moral and property right principles of God's law, as Exodus 22:26–27 demonstrates: "If you ever take your neighbor's cloak as a pledge, you are to return it to him before the sun sets, for that is his only covering; it is his cloak for his body. What else shall he sleep in? And it shall come about that when he cries out to Me, I will hear him, for I am gracious" (cf. 33:19; Gen. 43:29). The prophet Jonah, even as he struggled to accept the Ninevites' repentance, acknowledged God's grace: "He prayed to the Lord and said, 'Please Lord, was not this what I said while I was still in my own country? Therefore in order to forestall this I fled to Tarshish, for I knew that You are a gracious and compassionate God, slow to anger and abundant in lovingkindness, and one who relents concerning calamity'" (Jonah 4:2).

Salvation has always been available to sinners (Deut. 32:15; Pss. 3:8; 27:1; Isa. 55:1–2, 6–7; Jonah 2:9) and always and only by grace. So there was never any question during the Old Testament whether or not God was gracious, but the great manifestation of His grace **would come** with the arrival of His Son. Isaiah prophesied of it:

Gather yourselves and come; draw near together, you fugitives of the nations; they have no knowledge, who carry about their wooden idol and pray to a god who cannot save. Declare and set forth your case; indeed, let them consult together. Who has announced this from of old? Who has long since declared it? Is it not I, the Lord? And there is no other God besides Me, a righteous God and a Savior; there is none except Me. Turn to Me and be saved, all the ends of the earth; for I am God, and there is no other. I have sworn by Myself, the word has gone forth from My mouth in righteousness and will not turn back, that to Me every knee will bow, every tongue will swear allegiance. They will say of Me, "Only in the Lord are righteousness and strength." Men will come to Him. (Isa. 45:20–24)

The prophet reveals God's provision of salvation for all the nations. Isaiah and the other prophets did not see that Gentile salvation realized (cf. Rom. 15:8–12; Eph. 3:4–7), but they knew Messiah would effect it (Isa. 53:4–5). They wrote about a salvation grace that was far more extensive than anything they had observed (cf. Deut. 32:43; 2 Sam. 22:50; Pss. 18:49; 117:1; 118:22; Isa. 8:14; 11:1–5, 10; 28:16; 65:1–2; Jer. 17:7; Hos. 1:10; 2:23), and those prophecies contained several basic facts, some of which were later quoted by New Testament writers such as the apostle Paul (e.g., Rom. 9:25–26, 33; 10:11–13, 20; 15:8–12, 20–21). First, the prophecies declared that Messiah would suffer. Psalm 22 describes His crucifixion, and Isaiah 53 describes other details of His suffering. Second, the Old Testament writers prophesied that Messiah would triumph. The psalmist says God will set His King, Jesus Christ, on His holy hill, where Christ will then rule with a rod of iron (Ps. 2:6–9). Psalm 16:10 says God will not allow His Holy One to undergo decay—and Christ did rise from the grave and ascend to heaven forty days later (Luke 24:1–12; Acts 1:2–9). The prophet Isaiah wrote that the government would be on Messiah's shoulders and He would be a mighty God, reigning from the throne of David (Isa. 9:6–7). Third, the prophets foresaw a Messiah who would save. Isaiah gave the Messiah's mandate: "The Spirit of the Lord God is upon me, because the Lord has anointed me to bring good news to the afflicted; He has sent me to bind up the brokenhearted, to proclaim liberty to captives and freedom to prisoners; to proclaim the favorable year of the Lord" (Isa. 61:1–2). Jesus read those words to the congregation in His hometown synagogue and proclaimed Himself the fulfillment of them (Luke 4:16–21).

Though the Old Testament prophets knew that their writings described a future manifestation of salvation grace, their desire to understand those prophecies was still so compelling and pervasive that they **made careful searches and inquiries** into their own writings. Those two terms emphasize the intensity with which the prophets had delved into their prophecies and the diligence with which they had investigated them to better understand the magnitude of salvation grace.

As Jesus told His disciples, "For truly I say to you that many prophets and righteous men desired to see what you see, and did not see it, and to hear what you hear, and did not hear it" (Matt. 13:17; cf. Isa. 6:11; Hab. 1:2). Because the Old Testament prophets, including the last one, John the Baptist, were limited, they were all the more intent on studying their own writings to see the Messiah and comprehend the salvation He would bring.

Some commentators have suggested that Peter here reflects upon the prophets' attitude *before* God gave them any prophecies. According to this view, the prophets desired so strongly to comprehend salvation's full significance that they carefully looked into truth that was as yet unrevealed. As a result, God gave them prophecies about Messiah so they would better understand His salvation. However, that makes no sense because the prophets first needed divine revelation about salvation, otherwise they would have had no basis upon which to make their **careful searches and inquiries.** If the prophets had had no revelation about a future grace brought by Messiah, they would not have sought further information about it, because one does not ask questions about something he is unaware of. Furthermore, God did not give revelation to men simply because they begged for it, were curious about it, or had an intense desire to know something—He sovereignly chose His prophets and spokesmen and the message He would inspire them to write (cf. Ex. 3:1–10; 1 Sam. 3; Isa. 6; Jer. 1:4–5).

Peter further indicates that the Old Testament prophets were not interested in just the general doctrine of salvation or the general teaching about Messiah. They sought to know more precisely **what person** would come as savior, judge, prophet, priest, and king, and during what season or era (**time**) that coming would occur. The queries were about who and when. (It should be noted here that today's believers regularly face the same questions regarding New Testament prophecies of the future. They can know the events revealed in Scripture, but the exact identities of key persons involved and when precisely certain events will occur is an ongoing course of study for all interested in eschatology.) John the Baptist, the last Old Testament prophet and forerunner of Christ, provides a classic illustration of this searching inquisitiveness among the prophets. John's disciples already knew about Jesus' ministry (cf. Matt. 9:14) and had reported to him about it (Luke 7:18). Yet John wanted to know for sure if Jesus was the predicted Messiah:

> When Jesus had finished giving instructions to His twelve disciples, He departed from there to teach and preach in their cities. Now when John, while imprisoned, heard of the works of Christ, he sent word by

his disciples and said to Him, "Are You the Expected One, or shall we look for someone else?" (Matt. 11:1–3)

In response, Jesus gave His credentials—all of which fulfilled Old Testament prophecy (cf. Isa. 29:18–19; 35:5–10; 61:1) about Messiah: "Jesus answered and said to them, 'Go and report to John what you hear and see: the blind receive sight and the lame walk, the lepers are cleansed and the deaf hear, the dead are raised up, and the poor have the gospel preached to them'" (vv. 4–5). John had earlier pointed to Jesus and prophesied, "Behold, the Lamb of God who takes away the sin of the world!" (John 1:29). Even though the Holy Spirit inspired him to declare that, he still pondered its meaning and wanted to ascertain if indeed Jesus was the Messiah (Luke 7:18–23).

If the greatness of the salvation yet to come was the intense, preoccupying study of all the prophets, then it ought to be just as precious, if not more so, to those believers today who have the full revelation.

SALVATION WAS THE THEME OF THE SPIRIT'S INSPIRATION

the Spirit of Christ within them was indicating as He predicted the sufferings of Christ and the glories to follow. It was revealed to them that they were not serving themselves, but you, (1:11b–12a)

The prophecies the Holy Spirit revealed to the prophets were divinely inspired and recorded under His superintendence (cf. Jer. 1:9; 23:28; Ezek. 2:7; Amos 3:7–8). And the overall theme of those prophecies was twofold: **the sufferings of Christ and the glories to follow.** The Old Testament refers to **the sufferings of Christ** in such passages as Psalm 22:1–31; Isaiah 52:13–53:12; Daniel 9:24–26; and Zechariah 12:10; 13:7 (cf. Ps. 89:24–37; Luke 24:25–27; Rev. 19:10). **The glories to follow,** including such truths as the resurrection, ascension, and enthronement of Christ, appear in passages like Isaiah 9:6–7; Daniel 2:44; 7:13–14; and Zechariah 2:10–13; 14:16–17.

That Peter used the phrase **Spirit of Christ within them** (cf. Rom. 8:9) demonstrates that the eternal Christ, inseparable from the Holy Spirit, worked from within the Old Testament writers to record God's infallible revelation. Hence the apostle wrote in his second letter that "no prophecy was ever made by an act of human will, but men moved by the Holy Spirit spoke from God" (2 Peter 1:21; cf. 2 Tim. 3:16). The Spirit **was indicating** (*edēlou,* "making plain") to them **as He predicted** (*promarturomenon,* "witnessed beforehand") what was coming. He was plainly testifying to the prophets about God's salvation that would be fully accomplished through Jesus Christ (cf. the KJV and NKJV rendering, "testified beforehand").

The Spirit also made it clear that the prophets' searching would never be fully satisfied because the complete gospel message could not be revealed during that time. Peter indicated this reality when he wrote: **it was revealed to them that they were not serving themselves.** In the Pentateuch, Moses prophesies about the coming Prophet, who actually was the Messiah: "The Lord your God will raise up for you a prophet like me from among you, from your countrymen, you shall listen to him" (Deut. 18:15; cf. Num. 24:17). Moses and the other prophets were looking ahead to the culmination of Christ's saving work in a future segment of redemptive history (cf. Heb. 1:1–2). The writer of Hebrews provides additional insight, "All these died in faith, without receiving the promises, but having seen them and having welcomed them from a distance" (Heb. 11:13; cf. vv. 39–40).

Still the prophecies had immense value (cf. Luke 1:70; Acts 3:18; 1 Thess. 5:20; 2 Peter 1:19), though their fulfillment was not for the Old Testament prophets to witness. They instead looked ahead to a time when Messiah's saving work would embrace believers from all nations in new covenant blessings (Pss. 22:27–28; 72:8–17; cf. Isa. 42:6; 60:1–3; 62:1–3, 11–12; 66:12–13). They lived in hope, just as Christians do who anticipate their Lord's Second Coming. Old Testament saints were saved by faith in God based on the fact that Messiah Jesus would in the future bear the full judgment of God for their sins (Isa. 53:4–6). God was always applying the new covenant, always by grace offering forgiveness of sins to those who repented and believed, although the new covenant was not ratified until the cross. Old Testament believers were saved by a future grace, New Testament ones by a past grace—the Cross is the pinnacle of redemption.

SALVATION WAS THE THEME OF THE APOSTLES' PREACHING

in these things which now have been announced to you through those who preached the gospel to you by the Holy Spirit sent from heaven (1:12b)

The Holy Spirit inspired not only the Old Testament prophets, but also the New Testament apostles, who took the fully revealed gospel as the theme of their preaching. **These things** again refers to the salvation grace that was to come, specifically to the person of Christ and the present proclamation of the gospel. Years earlier Peter **announced** these truths in the first recorded apostolic sermon, delivered on Pentecost, "Peter said to them, 'Repent, and each of you be baptized in the name of Jesus Christ for the forgiveness of your sins; and you will receive the Holy Spirit. For the promise is for you and your children and for all who are far off, as many as the Lord our God will call to Himself'" (Acts 2:38–39; cf. 2 Cor. 6:2). In addition to Peter, **those who preached the gospel** included the remainder of the Twelve, Paul, Barnabas, Silas, Timothy, Philip, James the half-brother of Jesus, Jude the half-brother of Jesus, Stephen, and others unnamed. Not all were apostles of Christ in the same sense as Paul and the Twelve (they had not all seen the risen Lord), but they were sent by the church as messengers of the gospel empowered by the **Holy Spirit sent from heaven.**

Paul illustrates well the singular devotion such preachers had to the greatness of the salvation message. He wrote to the Corinthian believers,

> And when I came to you, brethren, I did not come with superiority of speech or of wisdom, proclaiming to you the testimony of God. For I determined to know nothing among you except Jesus Christ, and Him crucified. I was with you in weakness and in fear and in much trembling, and my message and my preaching were not in persuasive words of wisdom, but in demonstration of the Spirit and of power, so that your faith would not rest on the wisdom of men, but on the power of God. (1 Cor. 2:1–5; cf. Rom. 1:16–17)

SALVATION IS THE THEME OF THE ANGELS' EXAMINATION

—things into which angels long to look. (1:12c)

Believers wonder what the angels know and experience in the spiritual and invisible realm. Scripture indicates some of the things angels do (oppose demons, Dan. 10:13; Jude 9; carry messages from God, Dan. 8:16–17; 9:21–23; 10:11; 12:6–7; Matt. 2:13; Luke 1:19, 28; 2:10–14; and perform other divine service, 1 Kings 19:5; Ps. 91:11–12; Matt. 4:11; 13:39–42; Acts 12:7–11; Heb. 1:14). Christians desire to have eternal holiness and experience glory and fellowship with the Trinity as the elect angels do. But conversely the angels wonder what it is like to experience the grace and glory of salvation and God's forgiveness from sin. In fact, Peter says, they are continually looking with fascination into salvation's greatness.

Things denotes the many features of salvation **into which angels long to look. Long** translates *epithumousin*, which describes having a strong desire or overpowering impulse that is not easily satisfied. The term indicates that the angels' interest in salvation is not merely whimsical or an incidental curiosity but a strong passion with them. **Look** (*parakupsai*) literally means to stretch one's head forward or to bend down. Another form of the same word denotes what the apostle John did at Jesus' tomb, "and stooping and looking in, he saw the linen wrappings lying there" (John 20:5; cf. v. 11). The angels, as it were, want to get down close and look deeply into the matters related to salvation. They have a holy curiosity to understand the kind of grace they will never experience. The holy angels do not need to be saved, and the fallen angels cannot be saved. But the holy ones seek to understand salvation so that they might glorify God more fully, which is their primary reason for existence (Job 38:7; Ps. 148:2; Isa. 6:3; Luke 2:13–14; Heb. 1:6; Rev. 5:11–12; 7:11–12; cf. Neh. 9:6; Phil. 2:9–11).

It is not that the angels have been uninvolved in God's plan of salvation. They announced Christ's birth (Luke 1:26–35; 2:10–14), ministered to Him during His times of testing (Matt. 4:11; Luke 22:43), stood by the grave when He arose from the dead (Matt. 28:5–7; Mark 16:4–7; Luke 24:4–7), attended His ascension into heaven (Acts 1:10–11), and now serve Him by ministering to all believers (3:22; Heb. 1:14). God has made His angels witnesses to what occurs in the body of Christ. They rejoice and praise God whenever He saves a sinner (Luke 15:7, 10). They were watching the apostle Paul and the other apostles (1 Cor. 4:9). God continues to put His saving grace on display before the angels "that the manifold wisdom of God might now be made known through the church to the rulers and authorities in the heavenly places" (Eph. 3:10).

Though the angels will never experience redemption, the book of Revelation contains a fascinating portrayal of their interest in it:

> And He [Christ, the Lamb] came and took the book out of the right hand of Him who sat on the throne. When He had taken the book, the four living creatures and the twenty-four elders fell down before the Lamb, each one holding a harp and golden bowls full of incense, which are the prayers of the saints. And they sang a new song, saying, "Worthy are You to take the book and to break its seals; for You were slain, and purchased for God with Your blood men from every tribe and tongue and people and nation. You have made them to be a kingdom and priests to our God; and they will reign upon the earth." Then I looked, and I heard the voice of many angels around the throne and the living creatures and the elders; and the number of them was myriads of myriads, and thousands of thousands, saying with a loud voice, "Worthy is the Lamb that was slain to receive power and riches and wisdom and might and honor and glory and blessing." (Rev. 5:7–12)

The holy angels will join the song of redemption even though they have not experienced salvation. They have been witnesses to the greatness of God's salvation, and they **long to look** further into it so they might praise and glorify Him more.

No matter how difficult life's trials are, Christians can face them triumphantly because of the greatness of God's grace in giving them a salvation the prophets studied, the Holy Spirit inspired, the apostles preached, and the angels continue to investigate.

The Believer's Response to Salvation (1 Peter 1:13–17)

5

Therefore, prepare your minds for action, keep sober in spirit, fix your hope completely on the grace to be brought to you at the revelation of Jesus Christ. As obedient children, do not be conformed to the former lusts which were yours in your ignorance, but like the Holy One who called you, be holy yourselves also in all your behavior; because it is written, "You shall be holy, for I am holy." If you address as Father the One who impartially judges according to each one's work, conduct yourselves in fear during the time of your stay on earth; (1:13–17)

In His parable of the faithful steward, Jesus told His hearers, "From everyone who has been given much, much will be required" (Luke 12:48). That principle surely also relates to Christians' response to their salvation. Since no gift is greater than God's gift of forgiveness and salvation in Jesus Christ, nothing can demand a greater response.

In verses 1–12, the apostle Peter described salvation's supreme place in God's foreordained plan, explained its marvelous promise of eternal inheritance, and proclaimed its intrinsic greatness. Then in verse 13 Peter shifts to the imperative mode. He moves from describing and explaining the nature of salvation to commanding those who have received it concerning the obligations and responsibilities divine salvation places on all who have received it. These obligations can be summarized in three words: hope, holiness, and honor.

BELIEVERS MUST RESPOND WITH HOPE

Therefore, prepare your minds for action, keep sober in spirit, fix your hope completely on the grace to be brought to you at the revelation of Jesus Christ. (1:13)

The transitional conjunction **therefore** moves the reader from statement to application, from fact to inference. It directs believers to the main emphasis of this verse, which is to **fix** their **hope**. *Elpisate* is an aorist active imperative by which Peter exhorts believers in military fashion to a decisive kind of action, to a **hope** that is an obligatory act of the will, not merely an emotional feeling. They are commanded to live expectantly, anticipating with "a living hope" their "inheritance . . . reserved in heaven . . . to be revealed in the last time" (1:3, 4, 5).

Genuine hope is a vital spiritual reality, one of the three supreme virtues of the Christian life (1 Cor. 13:13). Basically defined, **hope** is the Christian's attitude toward the future (Acts 24:15; Titus 1:2; 2:13; 3:7). In its essence, **hope** is equivalent to faith (Rom. 5:1–2; Gal. 5:5; Heb. 11:1); it is trusting God (1 Peter 1:21). The major difference between the two attitudes is that faith involves trusting God in the present (Rom. 1:17; 3:28; 2 Cor. 5:7; Gal. 2:20; 1 Tim. 6:12; James 1:6), whereas hope is future faith, trusting God for what is to come (Heb. 3:6). Faith appropriates what God has already said and done in His revealed Word, and hope anticipates what He will yet do, as promised in Scripture. **Completely** means unreservedly, and could also be rendered "fully" or "perfectly." Christians are not to hope half-heartedly or indecisively, but with finality, without any equivocation or doubt concerning the promises of God (cf. Rom. 8:25; 15:13; Col. 1:23; Heb. 6:19–20).

Believers owe their **hope** exclusively to God's graciousness and faithfulness (Pss. 33:18; 39:7; Titus 1:2; 1 Peter 1:21). He provided the perfect salvation in Christ (Isa. 45:21–22; John 3:14–16; Acts 4:12; Rom. 1:16–17; 2 Tim. 1:10; cf. 1 Tim. 1:1), which resulted in the forgiveness of all their sins—past, present, and future (Matt. 1:21; John 1:29; Eph. 1:7; Col. 2:13–14; 1 John 1:7; 3:5) and their transformation from the kingdom of darkness to the eternal kingdom of light (Col. 1:13). God has been faithful in the past, is being faithful in the present, and will be faithful to all His promises for the future (Pss. 89:33; 119:90; 146:6; Isa. 49:7; 1 Cor. 1:9; 1 Thess. 5:24; cf. 1 Cor. 10:13; 2 Thess. 3:3; 1 John 1:9). Therefore saints live in a settled hope. The Thessalonians illustrated this: "[they] turned to God from idols to serve a living and true God, and to wait for His Son from heaven" (1 Thess. 1:9*b*–10*a*).

But even though hope is beneficial to settle and strengthen saints (cf. Ps. 39:7; Acts 24:15; Rom. 4:18; 1 Thess. 1:3), it is also a form of worship that rests in the faithfulness of God (cf. Job 13:15; Pss. 13:5; 31:14; 65:5; Prov. 14:26) and thus glorifies His name (cf. Pss. 5:11; 33:21). Biblical hope affirms the integrity of God's promise and declares that He is a covenant keeping God (Deut. 7:9; Ps. 111:5). Paul used Abraham to illustrate this hope:

> For this reason it is by faith, in order that it may be in accordance with grace, so that the promise will be guaranteed to all the descendants, not only to those who are of the Law, but also to those who are of the faith of Abraham, who is the father of us all, (as it is written, "A father of many nations have I made you") in the presence of Him whom he believed, even God, who gives life to the dead and calls into being that which does not exist. In hope against hope he believed, so that he might become a father of many nations according to that which had been spoken, "So shall your descendants be." Without becoming weak in faith he contemplated his own body, now as good as dead since he was about a hundred years old, and the deadness of Sarah's womb; yet, with respect to the promise of God, he did not waver in unbelief but grew strong in faith, giving glory to God. (Rom. 4:16–20)

The patriarch hoped in God's promise that He would give him a son, and even though it was "hope against hope" (humanly impossible), his faith grew stronger to the glory of God. God is honored when He is trusted.

The ultimate feature of the believer's **hope** is **the grace to be brought.** Peter used the present participle *pheromenēn*, but the translators express it as future, recognizing the Greek grammatical construction that indicates the absolute assurance of a future event by referring to it as if it were already happening. The context clearly calls for such a use of the present, because the event **to be brought** is the future **revelation** (*apokalupsei*, "unveiling") **of Jesus Christ**—His Second Coming. Peter urged his readers to hope for it as though it were a present reality (see also 1:7; 4:13; cf. 1 Cor. 1:7). This phrase, **the revelation of Jesus Christ,** is the exact phrase that opens the book of Revelation, which unfolds the future culmination of redemptive history, as summarized in Revelation 1:7, "Behold, He is coming with the clouds, and every eye will see Him, even those who pierced Him; and all the tribes of the earth will mourn over Him. So it is to be. Amen." The apocalypse then describes the astonishing, wonderful, and breathtaking visions of Christ associated with His return.

Believers have an obligation to live in view of the Second Coming. In **hope** they look forward to that day when Christ will return for His people and then to reward and glorify them (Rom. 8:23; Phil. 3:20–21; Col. 3:4; 2 Tim. 4:8; 1 John 3:2; Rev. 22:12). Paul refers to this privilege in his letter to Titus:

> For the grace of God has appeared, bringing salvation to all men, instructing us to deny ungodliness and worldly desires and to live sensibly, righteously and godly in the present age, looking for the blessed hope and the appearing of the glory of our great God and Savior, Christ Jesus, who gave Himself for us to redeem us from every lawless deed, and to purify for Himself a people for His own possession, zealous for good deeds. (Titus 2:11–14)

Peter does not command Christians to fix their attention on the amazing phenomena of the Second Coming, as outlined for their understanding in Revelation, the Old Testament prophecies, and the Olivet Discourse (Matt. 24–25). Nor does he here reiterate the rewards they will receive, as previously stated in 1:3–4 (cf. Rev. 22:12). Rather he exhorts them and all believers to view all these things from the standpoint of their utter unworthiness and to see the realization of all these promises in eternal glory as **the grace to be brought to** them. The apostle's point is that just as initial salvation was all of God's **grace** (Eph. 2:5, 8; 2 Tim. 1:9; cf. Acts 15:11), so also will be its culmination in their glorification and eternal life in heaven. Just as they did not deserve their souls' redemption (Eph. 2:9; Titus 3:5), the indwelling of the Holy Spirit (1 Cor. 6:19; Eph. 1:13–14), or the forgiveness of sin (Eph. 1:7; Col. 1:14), they will not deserve the redemption of their sinful bodies (Rom. 8:23; cf. Gal. 1:4), the enjoyment of "an eternal weight of glory" (2 Cor. 4:17), or the privileges of eternal perfection and heavenly bliss and communion with the Father (cf. Rev. 7:16–17). Whatever the elect receives from God always derives from His gracious purpose, not their worth or merit.

At the beginning of verse 13, two modifying participial phrases describe how believers are to fix their hope. First, Peter tells his readers to **prepare** their **minds for action. Prepare** literally means "gird up" and can refer to tightening a belt, cinching up a cord or rope, or tying something down in preparation for a certain action. In ancient times, this concept referred to the gathering up of one's robe (Ex. 12:11; 1 Kings 18:46; 2 Kings 4:29; 9:1; Jer. 1:17). If a person wanted to move quickly and easily, often he would pull the corners of his robe up through his belt or sash to tie those corners in place. Peter metaphorically applies this process to the mind. He urges believers to pull in all the loose ends of their lives, meaning to discipline their thoughts (cf. Rom. 12:2), live according to biblical priorities (cf. Matt. 6:33), disentangle themselves from the world's sinful hindrances (cf. 2 Tim. 2:3–5; Heb. 12:1), and conduct life righteously and godly, in view of the future grace that accompanies Christ's return (cf. Luke 12:35; Col. 3:2–4).

Paul used the same word and metaphor in his passage on the armor of God: "Stand firm therefore, having girded your loins with truth, and having put on the breastplate of righteousness" (Eph. 6:14). Implied in the phrase "having girded your loins with truth" is again the concept of using a belt. In fact, a more literal translation of "truth" would be "belt of truthfulness." The first thing a Roman soldier did prior to heading into battle was put on his belt and tie up his robe so that its loose ends would not hinder his combat effectiveness. When he girded up his robe, it indicated the soldier was serious about preparing for the life and death of hand-to-hand combat. Peter is saying that believers must take the same approach to living the Christian life (cf. James 4:7; 1 Peter 5:8–9).

Peter's second participial phrase commands his audience also to **keep sober in spirit,** literally meaning not to become intoxicated, which is to lose control of thought and action. Metaphorically it means not to lose spiritual control by imbibing the world's sinful system. It connotes the entire realm of spiritual steadfastness or self-control: having clarity of mind and discipline of heart, being in charge of one's priorities and balancing one's life so as not to be subject to the controlling and corrupting influence of the flesh's allurements (cf. Matt. 16:26; 18:7; John 15:18–19; Rom. 12:2; 1 Cor. 1:20–21; 2:12; 3:19; Gal. 4:3; 6:14; Eph. 2:2; Phil. 2:15; Col. 2:8, 20; 1 Tim. 6:20; Titus 2:12; James 1:27; 2 Peter 1:4). Obedience to this charge comes through the work of the Word and the Spirit (Eph. 5:18; Col. 3:16).

If a Christian finds anything more attractive than fellowship with Jesus Christ (2 Tim. 4:10; James 4:4), if he yearns more to enjoy this world than to receive the joys of heaven, then he does not love His appearing. All believers must instead adopt the perspective of the apostle John: "He who testifies to these things says, 'Yes, I am coming quickly.' Amen. Come, Lord Jesus'" (Rev. 22:20). This kind of hope is the right response for those who have received God's great gift of salvation.

BELIEVERS MUST RESPOND IN HOLINESS

As obedient children, do not be conformed to the former lusts which were yours in your ignorance, but like the Holy One who called you, be holy yourselves also in all your behavior; because it is written, "You shall be holy, for I am holy." (1:14–16)

Believers living in anticipation of the return of Christ and considering its full significance will be motivated to live in holiness. The apostle John says, "And everyone who has this hope fixed on Him purifies himself, just as He is pure" (1 John 3:3). Genuine hope results in purity of life, or holiness—the believer's second obligatory response to receiving the gift of salvation.

Peter opens this passage with the significant expression **as obedient children.** The word (*hupakoēs*), translated as the adjective **obedient** by the *New American Standard Bible,* is actually a genitive noun. It means that obedience characterizes every true child of God (John 8:31–32; 14:15, 21; 15:10; Rom. 6:17; Eph. 2:10; 1 John 5:2–3; cf. Luke 6:46) and distinguishes Christians from non-Christians, called the "sons of disobedience" (Eph. 2:2). They are opposites; the basic character of a believer is obedience to God, whereas the basic character of an unbeliever is disobedience (John 3:20; Rom. 1:28–32; 8:7–8; Eph. 2:2; 4:17–18; 2 Tim. 3:2; Titus 1:16; 3:3).

Disobedience, however, sometimes breaks believers' patterns of obedience (cf. Matt. 18:15; Gal. 6:1; Heb. 12:1; 1 John 1:8–10) because their redeemed spirits are incarcerated in fleshly bodies, where sin still dwells (Rom. 7:18, 25; 8:12–13; cf. Mark 14:38). In view of that reality, Peter calls them to be holy. Obedience is an inevitable result of salvation (Eph. 2:10; 4:24; 1 Thess. 4:7; 2 Tim. 1:9), yet the apostle urges believers to live consistent with the longings of the new heart by pursuing holiness (cf. Rom. 6:12–14; 12:1; 2 Cor. 7:1; Eph. 5:1–3, 8; Col. 3:12–13; Heb. 12:14; 2 Peter 3:11).

True holiness has a negative aspect. It is experienced when believers are **not** being **conformed to the former lusts. Conformed** means "to be shaped by" or "fashioned after" (cf. Rom. 12:2; Eph. 4:20–24). The **lusts** that characterized that former life include sinful desires and thoughts, evil longings, uncontrolled appetites, sensual impulses, and all other unrighteous motivations and urges that compel the unregenerate (cf. 1 Cor. 6:9–11; Gal. 5:19–24; Eph. 5:3–5; 1 Thess. 4:4–5). For believers, such **former lusts . . . were** theirs **in ignorance,** before they were saved and when they did not know any better (cf. Acts 26:18; Eph. 2:1), which could be true of both Gentiles (cf. Eph. 4:17–19) and Jews (cf. Rom. 10:2–3). Regeneration creates a new life (2 Cor. 5:17) that has both the desire and the power to live righteously. Paul's inspired words in Colossians 3:1–10 echo Peter's call to holiness:

> Therefore if you have been raised up with Christ, keep seeking the things above, where Christ is, seated at the right hand of God. Set your mind on the things above, not on the things that are on earth. For you have died and your life is hidden with Christ in God. When Christ, who is our life, is revealed, then you also will be revealed with Him in glory. Therefore consider the members of your earthly body as dead to

immorality, impurity, passion, evil desire, and greed, which amounts to idolatry. For it is because of these things that the wrath of God will come upon the sons of disobedience, and in them you also once walked, when you were living in them. But now you also, put them all aside: anger, wrath, malice, slander, and abusive speech from your mouth. Do not lie to one another, since you laid aside the old self with its evil practices, and have put on the new self who is being renewed to a true knowledge according to the image of the One who created him.

Peter then presents the positive standard of holiness as the very perfection of **the Holy One who called** believers, namely God Himself. Negatively, they are to stop living sinfully as they did prior to regeneration; positively, they are to **be holy . . . in all** their **behavior.** In the Sermon on the Mount, Jesus set forth this same standard, "Therefore you are to be perfect, as your heavenly Father is perfect" (Matt. 5:48; cf. Eph. 5:1). In this life believers cannot be sinless (cf. Rom. 7:14–25; 1 John 1:8) as God is, but no less than His holiness is the goal at which they are, equipped by the Word and the Spirit, to aim (Eph. 2:10).

Peter's call to holiness was not new but echoed that of the Old Testament, as he indicates by introducing an Old Testament quote with the common phrase **because it is written** (cf. Mark 1:2; Luke 2:23; John 6:31; Rom. 1:17), followed by the quote, **"You shall be holy, for I am holy,"** derived from Leviticus 11:44; 19:2; and 20:7. God reiterated this command elsewhere in the Mosaic law (cf. Ex. 19:5–6; Deut. 7:6–8). In Leviticus 11:43–45 He also declared,

"Do not render yourselves detestable through any of the swarming things that swarm; and you shall not make yourselves unclean with them so that you become unclean. For I am the Lord your God. Consecrate yourselves therefore, and be holy, for I am holy. And you shall not make yourselves unclean with any of the swarming things that swarm on the earth. For I am the Lord who brought you up from the land of Egypt to be your God; thus you shall be holy, for I am holy."

The dominant, compelling reason for God's people to live in holiness was their relationship with God: "Then the Lord spoke to Moses, saying, 'Speak to all the congregation of the sons of Israel and say to them, "You shall be holy, for I the Lord your God am holy"'" (Lev. 19:1–2; cf. vv. 3, 10, 12, 14, 16, 18, 25, 28, 30–32, 34, 36–37; 18:2, 4–6, 21, 30; 20:7–8, 24, 26; 21:6–8, 12, 15, 23; 22:2, 16, 32–33; 23:22). As the children of Israel were called to love and serve God and to separate themselves from immorality and uncleanness, believers today must heed the sovereign call to bear His image (Col. 3:10; cf. Rom. 8:29; 1 Cor. 15:49; 2 Cor. 3:18) and obey His commands to be holy since the Holy One has identified Himself with them in an eternally glorious work of saving grace.

BELIEVERS MUST RESPOND IN HONOR

If you address as Father the One who impartially judges according to each one's work, conduct yourselves in fear during the time of your stay on earth; (1:17)

Inseparably linked to believers' obligation to respond to salvation in hope and holiness is their responsibility to honor God. The phrase **conduct yourselves in fear,** meaning "reverence," "awe," and "respect" toward God is the command in this sentence. Hope and holiness produce a life of worship, the most foundational of spiritual virtues: "The fear of the Lord is the beginning of wisdom, and the knowledge of the Holy One is understanding" (Prov. 9:10; cf. 14:26–27; 15:33; 19:23; Ex. 18:21; Lev. 25:17; Deut. 5:29; 6:13, 24; 10:12; Josh. 4:24; 1 Sam. 12:14, 24; Pss. 19:9; 25:14; 33:8; 34:9; 103:11; 111:10; 115:11, 13; 118:4; 2 Cor. 5:11; Heb. 12:28–29; 1 Peter 2:17; Rev. 14:7; 19:5).

Peter begins this verse by stating the reason for such conduct— God is the judge. **If you address** [God] **as Father** implies that believers all the time **address** (the present middle voice of *epikaleisthe,* "to call upon" or "appeal to") God that way—and they should. Jesus instructed the disciples to pray, "Our Father who is in heaven" (Matt. 6:9). Paul affirmed the legitimacy of such an intimate form of address when he told the Galatians, "Because you are sons, God has sent forth the Spirit of His Son into our hearts, crying, 'Abba! Father!'" (Gal. 4:6; cf. Rom. 8:15). That is the appropriate manner for saints to call on God.

But Peter did not want believers to forget that though they have an intimate relationship with their heavenly Father, they must **conduct** themselves in holiness **during the time of** their **stay on earth** because God is also **the One who impartially judges according to each one's work** (1 Cor. 3:10–15; 2 Cor. 5:9–10; Heb. 12:5–6; cf. Eph. 6:9).

As long as people live on this earth as believers, God is keeping the record of their works. At the revelation of Jesus Christ, there will be a judgment of all believers. Paul described it to the Corinthians:

> According to the grace of God which was given to me, like a wise master builder I laid a foundation, and another is building on it. But each man must be careful how he builds on it. For no man can lay a foundation other than the one which is laid, which is Jesus Christ. Now if any man builds on the foundation with gold, silver, precious stones,

wood, hay, straw, each man's work will become evident; for the day will show it because it is to be revealed with fire, and the fire itself will test the quality of each man's work. If any man's work which he has built on it remains, he will receive a reward. If any man's work is burned up, he will suffer loss; but he himself will be saved, yet so as through fire. (1 Cor. 3:10–15)

But to me it is a very small thing that I may be examined by you, or by any human court; in fact, I do not even examine myself. For I am conscious of nothing against myself, yet I am not by this acquitted; but the one who examines me is the Lord. Therefore do not go on passing judgment before the time, but wait until the Lord comes who will both bring to light the things hidden in the darkness and disclose the motives of men's hearts; and then each man's praise will come to him from God. (1 Cor. 4:3–5)

Therefore we also have as our ambition, whether at home or absent, to be pleasing to Him. For we must all appear before the judgment seat of Christ, so that each one may be recompensed for his deeds in the body, according to what he has done, whether good or bad. (2 Cor. 5:9–10)

But this warning about God as judge of believers is not limited to their future reward. First Peter 4:17 says, "It is time for judgment to begin with the household of God; and if it begins with us first, what will be the outcome for those who do not obey the gospel of God?" Sometimes this work of God as judge of His church brings His direct discipline, as indicated in Hebrews 12:5–11,

You have forgotten the exhortation which is addressed to you as sons, "My son, do not regard lightly the discipline of the Lord, nor faint when you are reproved by Him; for those whom the Lord loves He disciplines, and He scourges every son whom He receives." It is for discipline that you endure; God deals with you as with sons; for what son is there whom his father does not discipline? But if you are without discipline, of which all have become partakers, then you are illegitimate children and not sons. Furthermore, we had earthly fathers to discipline us, and we respected them; shall we not much rather be subject to the Father of spirits, and live? For they disciplined us for a short time as seemed best to them, but He disciplines us for our good, so that we may share His holiness. All discipline for the moment seems not to be joyful, but sorrowful; yet to those who have been trained by it, afterwards it yields the peaceful fruit of righteousness.

At other times this discipline from God is indirect, carried out by the church, as Jesus instructed the disciples:

If your brother sins, go and show him his fault in private; if he listens to you, you have won your brother. But if he does not listen to you, take one or two more with you, so that by the mouth of two or three witnesses every fact may be confirmed. If he refuses to listen to them, tell it to the church; and if he refuses to listen even to the church, let him be to you as a Gentile and a tax collector. Truly I say to you, whatever you bind on earth shall have been bound in heaven; and whatever you loose on earth shall have been loosed in heaven. Again I say to you, that if two of you agree on earth about anything that they may ask, it shall be done for them by My Father who is in heaven. For where two or three have gathered together in My name, I am there in their midst. (Matt. 18:15–20)

True love and worship to God are marked by understanding that He is the Christian's loving, gracious, and generous Father, but also his holy, disciplining Judge. How believers **conduct** themselves before His omniscient presence matters in both time and eternity. Paul's testimony to the Thessalonian believers is a pattern for all believers:

You are witnesses, and so is God, how devoutly and uprightly and blamelessly we behaved toward you believers; just as you know how we were exhorting and encouraging and imploring each one of you as a father would his own children, so that you would walk in a manner worthy of the God who calls you into His own kingdom and glory. (1 Thess. 2:10–12)

The Wonder
of Redemption
(1 Peter 1:18–21)

6

knowing that you were not redeemed with perishable things like silver or gold from your futile way of life inherited from your forefathers, but with precious blood, as of a lamb unblemished and spotless, the blood of Christ. For He was foreknown before the foundation of the world, but has appeared in these last times for the sake of you who through Him are believers in God, who raised Him from the dead and gave Him glory, so that your faith and hope are in God. (1:18–21)

The Puritan Thomas Watson rightly observed that redemption was God's greatest work: "Great was the work of creation, but greater the work of redemption; it cost more to redeem us than to make us; in the one there was but the speaking of a Word, in the other the shedding of blood. Luke 1:51. The creation was but the work of God's fingers. Psalm 8:3. Redemption is the work of His arm" (*Body of Divinity* [reprint; Grand Rapids: Baker, 1979], 146).

Redemption is a term that describes one of the essential features of salvation. It deals specifically with the cost of salvation and the means by which God received payment. Because all people are helpless slaves to sin and condemned by the law, if they are to be forgiven and reconciled to God, He has to purchase them back from their condition. Only then can He release them from sin's bondage and curse.

Redeemed is the key word in this passage. This term (*lutroō*) means "to purchase release by paying a ransom," or "to deliver by the payment of a price." To the Greeks the word was also a technical term for paying money to buy back a prisoner of war.

Rather than the typical Greek sense of the word, referring to slaves and prisoners, the apostle Peter's imagery describing **redemption** derives from several Old Testament passages. Undoubtedly a primary one was the narrative of the first Passover:

> Now the Lord said to Moses and Aaron in the land of Egypt, "This month shall be the beginning of months for you; it is to be the first month of the year to you. Speak to all the congregation of Israel, saying, 'On the tenth of this month they are each one to take a lamb for themselves, according to their fathers' households, a lamb for each household. Now if the household is too small for a lamb, then he and his neighbor nearest to his house are to take one according to the number of persons in them; according to what each man should eat, you are to divide the lamb. Your lamb shall be an unblemished male a year old; you may take it from the sheep or from the goats. You shall keep it until the fourteenth day of the same month, then the whole assembly of the congregation of Israel is to kill it at twilight. Moreover, they shall take some of the blood and put it on the two doorposts and on the lintel of the houses in which they eat it. They shall eat the flesh that same night, roasted with fire, and they shall eat it with unleavened bread and bitter herbs. Do not eat any of it raw or boiled at all with water, but rather roasted with fire, both its head and its legs along with its entrails. And you shall not leave any of it over until morning, but whatever is left of it until morning, you shall burn with fire. Now you shall eat it in this manner: with your loins girded, your sandals on your feet, and your staff in your hand; and you shall eat it in haste—it is the Lord's Passover. For I will go through the land of Egypt on that night, and will strike down all the firstborn in the land of Egypt, both man and beast; and against all the gods of Egypt I will execute judgments—I am the Lord. The blood shall be a sign for you on the houses where you live; and when I see the blood I will pass over you, and no plague will befall you to destroy you when I strike the land of Egypt.'" (Ex. 12:1–13)

The lamb's life was the price required to spare the life of the Israelite family's firstborn child. The lamb was a divinely ordained illustration, and its sacrifice typified the sacrificial death of an innocent substitute that redeemed those in bondage. This Passover event immediately became the symbol of substitutionary redemption (1 Cor. 5:7–8). God further decreed that Israel annually celebrate Passover to perpetually remind the nation of His powerful deliverance of her from Egypt (Deut. 16:2–3, 5–7) and to point the people toward the true Lamb who would one day die and rise again as the perfect and final substitutionary sacrifice to redeem sinners with His blood (cf. Matt. 26:28; John 1:29; 1 Cor. 11:25–26; Heb. 9:11–12, 28).

The Israelites remembered the first Passover as God's greatest display of redeeming power up to that time: "In Your lovingkindness You have led the people whom You have redeemed" (Ex. 15:13; cf. Deut. 7:8; 2 Sam. 7:23; Pss. 78:35; 106:10–11; Isa. 63:9). But as great as that redemption was, the one about which Peter wrote infinitely surpassed it. As if to reemphasize the greatness of God's salvation (cf. 1:1–12), this passage provides believers with a theology of redemption by answering four crucial questions: What did God redeem believers from? What did He redeem them with? By whom did He redeem them? And, for what did He redeem them?

WHAT DID GOD REDEEM BELIEVERS FROM?

From your futile way of life inherited from your forefathers (1:18*b*)

Scripture makes clear the truth that all believers were once in bondage to sin and wrath, and that only Christ's redemption broke that bondage. Romans 6:6, 17–18 says,

> Knowing this, that our old self was crucified with Him, in order that our body of sin might be done away with, so that we would no longer be slaves to sin. . . . But thanks be to God that though you were slaves of sin, you became obedient from the heart to that form of teaching to which you were committed, and having been freed from sin, you became slaves of righteousness. (cf. vv. 20, 22; Gal. 3:13; Eph. 1:7; Col. 1:13–14; Titus 2:14; 3:5; Heb. 9:15).

In light of that reality, Peter set forth four features that characterize everyone, including the redeemed, prior to their redemption.

The first feature of all unredeemed sinners is what verse 14 of this chapter calls "the former lusts." "Lusts" (*epithumiais*) are compelling, driving passions, usually for what is evil (cf. 4:2–3; Matt. 5:28; Rom. 1:24; Eph. 4:22; 1 Thess. 4:5; Titus 3:3; James 1:14–15; 2 Peter 1:4; 1 John 2:16; Jude 16, 18). The term *imagination,* often used in older Christian literature but seldom in contemporary writings and Bible translations, sheds additional light on the meaning of lust. The King

James Version's rendering of Genesis 6:5, the description of pre-Flood society's gross sinfulness, is an example: "And God saw that the wickedness of man was great in the earth, and that every imagination of the thoughts of his heart was only evil continually." "Thoughts of his heart" clearly refers to the mind, and all sin—especially lust—originates in the mind and its "imagination." James 1:14–15 describes the work of the sinful imagination: "But each one is tempted when he is carried away and enticed by his own lust. Then when lust has conceived, it gives birth to sin; and when sin is accomplished, it brings forth death." Jeremiah 3:17 says, "At that time they shall call Jerusalem the throne of the Lord; and all the nations shall be gathered unto it, to the name of the Lord, to Jerusalem: neither shall they walk any more after the imagination of their evil heart" (KJV; cf. Jer. 7:24; 9:14; 11:8; 13:10; 16:12; 18:12; 23:17 in the KJV).

The flesh controls the imagination of the unredeemed (cf. 1 Cor. 2:14; 2 Cor. 4:3–4), and if not kept in check, it can also affect the believer's imagination (cf. Mark 14:38; Rom. 13:14; Gal. 5:24; Phil. 3:3). When the flesh feeds a sinful thought into the imagination, the imagination concocts a sinful fantasy scenario, that scenario excites lust, lust moves the emotions, the emotions activate the will, and the will initiates sinful conduct (see again James 1:14–15). The sinful imagination consists primarily of lies and distortions about oneself, personal relationships, personal fulfillment, the general nature of things, and God (cf. Jer. 17:9; Mark 7:21–22; Rom. 7:23; 8:6–8). Such false perceptions lead people to all sorts of sinful behavior, which results in miserable guilt feelings. Therefore, since God has redeemed believers from an evil, lustful imagination, then they ought to guard their minds (Pss. 25:20; 39:1; Prov. 4:23; Luke 21:34; 2 John 8) from all the destructive influences that seek to draw them back into such sinful desires. As David concluded his praise for the people's generous offering for construction of the temple, he offered this model prayer:

> Since I know, O my God, that You try the heart and delight in uprightness, I, in the integrity of my heart, have willingly offered all these things; so now with joy I have seen Your people, who are present here, make their offerings willingly to You. O Lord, the God of Abraham, Isaac and Israel, our fathers, preserve this forever in the intentions [imaginations] of the heart of Your people, and direct their heart to You. (1 Chron. 29:17–18)

Verse 14 secondly identifies the unredeemed's bondage as "ignorance," which refers to the absence of spiritual understanding. The Jewish leaders' spiritual ignorance prompted Jesus to rebuke them this way:

> Why do you not understand what I am saying? It is because you cannot hear My word. You are of your father the devil, and you want to do the desires of your father. He was a murderer from the beginning, and does not stand in the truth because there is no truth in him. Whenever he speaks a lie, he speaks from his own nature, for he is a liar and the father of lies. (John 8:43–44; cf. 17:25)

The apostle Paul perhaps best summarized such benightedness in Ephesians 4:18 when he said the unredeemed are "darkened in their understanding, excluded from the life of God because of the ignorance that is in them, because of the hardness of their heart" (cf. 2:1–3, 12; Rom. 1:28; 1 Cor. 2:14; Gal. 4:8). Paul testified to his own former state in that condition: "I was formerly a blasphemer and a persecutor and a violent aggressor. Yet I was shown mercy because I acted ignorantly in unbelief" (1 Tim. 1:13).

The opening verse of this passage refers to the third feature characterizing the unredeemed, their **futile way of life,** which identifies a vain, useless, and worthless existence. No matter what they may think, every unredeemed man or woman is living a **futile life.** Even the grandest accomplishments unbelievers seem to achieve are pointless from eternity's perspective. Jesus made that clear by means of two penetrating questions to His disciples: "For what will it profit a man if he gains the whole world and forfeits his soul? Or what will a man give in exchange for his soul?" (Matt. 16:26).

Paul recognized the futility of the unredeemed life when he forbade the people at Lystra from worshiping Barnabas and him. "Men, why are you doing these things? We are also men of the same nature as you, and preach the gospel to you that you should turn from these vain things to a living God, who made the heaven and the earth and the sea and all that is in them" (Acts 14:15; cf. Rom. 1:21; 6:20–21; 8:20; 1 Cor. 3:20). Paul also exhorted the Ephesian believers to forsake such futile ways: "So this I say, and affirm together with the Lord, that you walk no longer just as the Gentiles also walk, in the futility of their mind" (Eph. 4:17).

Here also is a fourth feature of the unredeemed's lost condition, namely religious tradition, identified as ideas **inherited from** their **forefathers.** The Pharisees and their followers were prime adherents to such worthless tradition, which prompted Jesus' harsh rebuke of them: "You hypocrites, rightly did Isaiah prophesy of you: 'This people honors Me with their lips, but their heart is far away from Me. But in vain do they worship Me, teaching as doctrines the precepts of men'" (Matt. 15:7–9; 23:1–4). Traditional religion, whether it is apostate Judaism or paganism in its multitude of forms, is a feature of sin's bondage (cf. Isa. 29:13; Matt. 15:3, 6; Mark 7:8–9, 13; Gal. 1:14; Col. 2:8) from which people need redemption.

Paul's words to Titus summarize well this total bondage of the unredeemed: "For we also once were foolish ourselves, disobedient, deceived, enslaved to various lusts and pleasures, spending our life in malice and envy, hateful, hating one another" (Titus 3:3; cf. Jer. 2:22; Rom. 1:18–32; Gal. 5:19–21; Eph. 5:5; Col. 3:5–7). From this bondage only God can free souls. Psalm 107 pictures this dramatically:

> There were those who dwelt in darkness and in the shadow of death, prisoners in misery and chains, because they had rebelled against the words of God and spurned the counsel of the Most High. Therefore He humbled their heart with labor; they stumbled and there was none to help. Then they cried out to the Lord in their trouble; He saved them out of their distresses. He brought them out of darkness and the shadow of death and broke their bands apart. Let them give thanks to the Lord for His lovingkindness, and for His wonders to the sons of men! For He has shattered gates of bronze and cut bars of iron asunder. (vv. 10–16; cf. Prov. 20:9; Isa. 43:25; 61:1; Jonah 2:9; Rom. 7:4–6; Gal. 4:3–5; Col. 2:13–14)

WHAT DID GOD REDEEM BELIEVERS WITH?

Knowing that you were not redeemed with perishable things like silver or gold . . . but with precious blood, as of a lamb unblemished and spotless, the blood of Christ. (1:18a, 19)

Psalm 49:7–8 says, "No man can by any means redeem his brother or give to God a ransom for him—for the redemption of his soul is costly, and he should cease trying forever." Indeed the price "for the redemption of [a] soul is costly." Peter appealed to his readers' basic knowledge that there was nothing available to mankind that could meet that price. **Knowing** emphasizes **that** believers know that they **were not redeemed with perishable things.** Redemption's price was not some valuable earthly commodity—**like silver or gold.** But why did Peter in this context even mention those prized metals? In this instance he quite possibly recalled the Old Testament passage about the ransom money God required the Israelites to pay (cf. Ex. 30:13, 15) for the action of numbering all males of military age:

> The Lord also spoke to Moses, saying, "When you take a census of the sons of Israel to number them, then each one of them shall give a ransom for himself to the Lord, when you number them, so that there will be no plague among them when you number them. This is what everyone who is numbered shall give: half a shekel according to the shekel of the sanctuary (the shekel is twenty gerahs), half a shekel as a contribution to the Lord. Everyone who is numbered, from twenty years old

and over, shall give the contribution to the Lord. The rich shall not pay more and the poor shall not pay less than the half shekel, when you give the contribution to the Lord to make atonement for yourselves. You shall take the atonement money from the sons of Israel and shall give it for the service of the tent of meeting, that it may be a memorial for the sons of Israel before the Lord, to make atonement for yourselves." (Ex. 30:11–16)

The taking of a census was a sin and considered as a lack of trust in God. On that one occasion when God ordered a census, He required a purification ceremony for cleansing. By that the Israelites would cancel the punishment implicit in the census. When Israel took a census in direct disobedience to God's command not to do so, signifying an act of sinful distrust in His power, as David did in 1 Chronicles 21, Scripture records that he fell to Satan's temptation to gratify his pride in the nation's military strength. David's failure to trust and obey God in dealing with his enemies incurred the Lord's fury and moved Him to punish Israel with a lethal plague brought by a destroying angel (vv. 11–17).

Peter knew that, unlike the temporal redemption with money that God permitted the Israelites to purchase in Exodus 30, no amount of money could redeem people's souls from the bondage of sin. The prophet Isaiah saw the true nature of God's ultimate redemption of His people when he wrote, "For thus says the Lord, 'You were sold for nothing and you will be redeemed without money'" (Isa. 52:3).

Having stated what believers were not redeemed with, Peter declared the means by which God did redeem them—**with precious blood.** He used **blood** as a vivid synonym for sacrificial death involving the shedding of blood. The **blood** was not just any blood but precious because it belonged to **a lamb unblemished and spotless.** Peter's words implicitly picture the immense sacrifice the owner of such a lamb made when he killed his flock's finest, purest, most perfect animal, the very kind of animal God always required for sacrifice (Lev. 22:19; Num. 6:14; 28:3–4; Deut. 15:21; 17:1; cf. Ex. 12:5; Lev. 22:17–25). No sacrificial lamb or any other animal sacrifice could ever really take away sin, as Hebrews 10:1–10 makes clear:

> For the Law, since it has only a shadow of the good things to come and not the very form of things, can never, by the same sacrifices which they offer continually year by year, make perfect those who draw near. Otherwise, would they not have ceased to be offered, because the worshipers, having once been cleansed, would no longer have had consciousness of sins? But in those sacrifices there is a reminder of sins year by year. For it is impossible for the blood of bulls and goats to take away sins. Therefore, when He comes into the world, He says, "Sacrifice and offering You have not desired, but a body You have prepared for

Me; in whole burnt offerings and sacrifices for sin You have taken no pleasure. "Then I said, 'Behold, I have come (in the scroll of the book it is written of Me) to do Your will, O God.'" After saying above, "Sacrifices and offerings and whole burnt offerings and sacrifices for sin You have not desired, nor have You taken pleasure in them" (which are offered according to the Law), then He said, "Behold, I have come to do Your will." He takes away the first in order to establish the second. By this will we have been sanctified through the offering of the body of Jesus Christ once for all. (cf. 9:24–26; 10:11, 14)

Those sacrifices all showed the deadly effects of sin and pictured the idea of an ultimate substitute taking the sinner's place—fulfilled in the sacrifice of Jesus Christ "once for all." That Jesus was absolutely and perfectly **unblemished and spotless** is the clear testimony of Scripture, especially concerning the doctrine of imputation, as contained in 2 Corinthians 5:21, "He made Him who knew no sin to be sin on our behalf, so that we might become the righteousness of God in Him":

Imputation speaks of a legal reckoning. To impute guilt to someone is to assign guilt to that person's account. Likewise, to impute righteousness is to reckon the person righteous. The guilt or righteousness thus imputed is a wholly objective reality; it exists totally apart from the person to whom it is imputed. In other words, a person to whom guilt is imputed is not thereby actually made guilty in the real sense. But he is accounted as guilty in a legal sense. It is a reckoning, not an actual remaking of the person's character.

The guilt of sinners was imputed to Christ. He was not in any sense actually tainted with guilt. He was merely reckoned as guilty before the court of heaven, and the penalty of all that guilt was executed against Him. Sin was imputed, not imparted, to Him.

This is a remarkable statement: "[God] made Him who knew no sin *to be sin* on our behalf." It cannot mean that Christ *became* a sinner. It cannot mean that He committed any sin, that His character was defiled, or that He bore our sin in any sense other than by legal imputation.

Christ had no capacity to sin. He was impeccable. This same verse even says, "[He] knew no sin." He was spotless. He had to be spotless in order to serve as the perfect substitute. He was holy, harmless, undefiled—separate from sinners (Heb. 7:26). He was without sin (Heb. 4:15). If sin had besmirched His character in any sense—if He had become an actual sinner—He would have then been worthy of sin's penalty Himself and thus unqualified to render payment for the sins of others. The perfect Lamb of God could not be other than spotless. So the phrase "[God] made Him ... to be sin" *cannot* mean that Christ was tainted with actual sin.

What it means is simply that the guilt from *our* sins was imputed to Him, reckoned to His account. Many Scriptures teach this concept: "He was pierced through for our transgressions, He was crushed for our iniquities" (Isa. 53:5). "He Himself bore our sins in His body on the cross" (1 Peter 2:24). He bore "the sins of many" (Heb. 9:28).

So in 2 Corinthians 5:21, Paul's simple meaning is that God treated Christ as if He were a sinner. He imputed our guilt to Him and exacted from Him the full penalty for sin—even though Christ Himself knew no sin.

The guilt He bore was not His guilt, but He bore it as if it were His own. God put *our* guilt to Christ's account and made Him pay the penalty for it. All the guilt of all the sins of all who would ever be saved was imputed to Jesus Christ—reckoned to His account as if He were guilty of all of it. Then God poured out the full fury of all His wrath against all of that sin, and Jesus experienced it all. That's what this verse means when it says God made Christ to be sin for us. (John MacArthur, *The Freedom and Power of Forgiveness* [Wheaton, Ill.: Crossway, 1998], 25–26; emphases in original)

Since all sin is a violation of God's holy law and a debt incurred to Him, He is the One to whom the price must be paid. Only the creditor can determine the terms of ransom or redemption. The price was not paid to Satan as some have suggested, as if he had been offended and needed to be compensated for sins against him. All sin is against God, and He sets the terms of redemption. The price He required as payment was the life of His own Son (Acts 20:28; Rom. 3:24–25; Gal. 4:4–5; Eph. 1:7; Col. 1:13–14; Titus 2:13–14).

The blood of Christ is the most precious blood of all because He was the only utterly perfect person who ever lived (cf. John 1:14, 27; Heb. 4:14–15; 7:26–28). The writer of Hebrews captured the essence of Christ as the perfect Mediator and High Priest of the new covenant, made possible by His death as the perfect sacrifice:

But when Christ appeared as a high priest of the good things to come, He entered through the greater and more perfect tabernacle, not made with hands, that is to say, not of this creation; and not through the blood of goats and calves, but through His own blood, He entered the holy place once for all, having obtained eternal redemption. For if the blood of goats and bulls and the ashes of a heifer sprinkling those who have been defiled sanctify for the cleansing of the flesh, how much more will the blood of Christ, who through the eternal Spirit offered Himself without blemish to God, cleanse your conscience from dead works to serve the living God? For this reason He is the mediator of a new covenant, so that, since a death has taken place for the redemption of the transgressions that were committed under the first covenant, those who have been called may receive the promise of the eternal inheritance. (Heb. 9:11–15; cf. 4:15)

In many other passages the New Testament affirms the same truth of the uniqueness of Jesus' atoning death (3:18; John 1:29; 1 Cor. 1:30; Gal. 3:13; Rev. 1:5; cf. 1 Peter 2:4; Rev. 5:6–9; 14:4).

The blood of Christ refers not to the fluid in His body, but to the whole of His redemptive death. Scripture speaks of Christ's blood nearly three times as often as it mentions the cross, and five times more often than it refers to the death of Christ. The word **blood,** therefore, is the chief term the New Testament uses to refer to the atonement.

Peter wrote that election is "unto obedience and sprinkling of the blood of Jesus Christ" (1:2, KJV). The "sprinkling of the blood" is what sealed the new covenant (cf. Heb. 9:1–18). "Without shedding of blood there is no forgiveness" (v. 22). If Christ had not literally shed His blood in sacrifice for believers' sins, they could not have been saved. This is one reason crucifixion was the means God ordained by which Christ should die; it was the most vivid, visible display of life being poured out as the price for sins.

Bloodshed was likewise God's design for nearly all Old Testament sacrifices. They were bled to death rather than clubbed, strangled, suffocated, or burnt. God designed that sacrificial death was to occur with blood loss, because "the life of the flesh is in the blood" (Lev. 17:11).

The literal **blood of Christ** was violently shed at the crucifixion. Those who deny this truth or try to spiritualize the death of Christ are guilty of corrupting the gospel message. Jesus Christ bled and died in the fullest literal sense, and when He rose from the dead, He was literally resurrected. To deny the absolute reality of those truths is to nullify them (cf. 1 Cor. 15:14–17).

The meaning of the crucifixion, however, is not fully expressed in the bleeding alone. There was nothing supernatural in Jesus' blood that sanctified those it touched. Those who flogged Him might have been spattered with blood. Yet that literal application of Jesus' blood did nothing to purge their sins. Had the Lord bled without dying, redemption could not have been accomplished. If the atonement had been stopped before the full wages of sin had been satisfied, Jesus' bloodshed would have been to no avail. If blood per se could redeem sinners, why did Jesus not just bleed and not die? He did not because the "shedding of blood" in Scripture is an expression that means more than just bleeding.

The biblical meaning in this matter is readily apparent. Romans 5:9–10 clarifies the point; those two verses side by side show that to be "justified by His blood" (v. 9) is the same as being "reconciled to God through the death of his Son" (v. 10). The critical element in salvation is the sacrificial death of Christ on sinners' behalf. The shedding of His **blood** was the visible manifestation of His life being poured out in sacrifice, and Scripture consistently uses the term "shedding of blood" as a metonym for atoning death (Heb. 9:22; 12:4; cf. 9:12, 14; 10:19; 11:28;

13:12, 20; Ex. 12:7, 13, 22–23; 23:18; 30:10; 34:25; Lev. 16:27; 17:11; Deut. 12:27; Matt. 26:28; Acts 20:28; Rom. 3:25; 1 Cor. 11:25; Eph. 1:7; 2:13; Col. 1:20; 1 Peter 1:19; 1 John 1:7; Rev. 1:5; 7:14).

So the **blood of Christ** is precious—but as precious as it is, that physical blood alone could not and did not save. Only when it was poured out in death could the penalty of sin be paid (Luke 24:46; Acts 17:3; Rom. 5:8–11; Eph. 2:13–16; Rev. 5:9; 13:8; cf. John 11:50–51).

It is important to note also that though Christ shed His blood, Scripture does not say He bled to death; it teaches rather that He voluntarily yielded up His spirit (John 10:18). Yet even that physical death could not have brought redemption apart from His spiritual death, whereby He was separated from the Father (cf. Matt. 27:46) by bearing the full guilt of all the sins of all who would ever be saved.

Clearly, though Christ shed His literal blood, many references to the blood are not intended to be taken in the literal sense. A strictly literal interpretation cannot, for example, explain such passages as John 6:53–54: "Truly, truly I say to you, unless you eat the flesh of the Son of Man and drink His blood, you have no life in yourselves. He who eats My flesh and drinks My blood has eternal life, and I will raise him up on the last day." It would be equally hard to explain how physical blood is meant in Matthew 27:25 ("His blood shall be on us and on our children"); Acts 5:28 ("[You] intend to bring this man's blood upon us"); 18:6 ("Your blood be on your own heads"); 20:26 ("I am innocent of the blood of all men"); and 1 Corinthians 10:16 ("Is not the cup of blessing . . . a sharing in the blood of Christ?").

Trying to make literal every reference to Christ's blood can lead to serious error. The Roman Catholic doctrine known as transubstantiation, for example, teaches that communion wine is miraculously changed into the actual blood of Christ, and that those who partake of the elements in the mass literally fulfill Jesus' words in John 6:54: "He who eats My flesh and drinks My blood has eternal life, and I will raise him up on the last day."

Some claim that Christ's blood was never truly human. Yet they insist on literalizing every New Testament reference to Jesus' blood. They erroneously teach that the physical blood of Christ was somehow preserved after the crucifixion and carried to heaven, where it is now literally applied to the soul of each Christian at salvation.

Believers are not saved by some mystical heavenly application of Jesus' literal blood. Nothing in Scripture indicates that the literal blood of Christ is preserved in heaven and applied to individual believers. When Peter here said saints are redeemed by the blood, he was not speaking of a bowl of blood in heaven. The apostle meant they are saved by Christ's sacrificial death.

In the same way, when Paul gloried in the Cross (Gal. 6:14), he did not mean the literal wooden beams; he was speaking of all the elements of the redeeming work. Just as the Cross is an expression that includes all of Christ's atoning work, so is the blood. It is not the actual liquid that cleanses believers from sin, but the work of redemption Christ accomplished in pouring His blood out in death.

By Whom Did God Redeem Believers?

For He was foreknown before the foundation of the world, but has appeared in these last times . . . who raised Him from the dead and gave Him glory, (1:20*a*, 21*a*)

In this section Peter more fully describes the uniqueness of the precious Lamb, Jesus Christ. The first aspect of that is His predetermination. That He **was foreknown** (*proegnōsmenou*), literally "he having been foreknown," clearly indicates that God planned to send the Son as the incarnate Redeemer **before the foundation of the world.** The Father did not react to the Fall with a last-minute fix; before the Fall—even before the creation—He predetermined to send His Son as the Savior (Acts 2:23; 4:27–28; 2 Tim. 1:9; Rev. 13:8; cf. Isa. 42:1; Rom. 8:29–30; Eph. 1:5–11). Even Jesus' enemies from among the Jewish rulers, as they stood sneering before the cross, seemed to acknowledge that God had a predetermined Messiah, "He saved others; let Him save Himself if this is the Christ of God, His Chosen One" (Luke 23:35). Sadly for them, those leaders refused to recognize that Jesus was that One chosen to be the sacrifice for sin.

The precious Lamb, secondly, is unique because of His incarnation. The verb rendered **has appeared** (*phanerōthentos*) contains the idea of making something clear or manifest and is an aorist passive, which denotes a historical event—in this context, the Son becoming human (cf. Gal. 4:4–5). In his rich passage on the humility of Christ, Paul summarizes the incarnation:

> Who, although He existed in the form of God, did not regard equality with God a thing to be grasped, but emptied Himself, taking the form of a bond-servant, and being made in the likeness of men. Being found in appearance as a man, He humbled Himself by becoming obedient to the point of death, even death on a cross. (Phil. 2:6–8; cf. John 1:14; Gal. 4:4)

The phrase **in these last times** is a familiar expression referring to the entire period between the birth of Christ and the Second Coming (cf. the synonym "last days" in 2 Tim. 3:1; Heb. 1:2; James 5:3; 2 Peter 3:3; and "last hour" in 1 John 2:18). The Greek for **times** (*chronōn*) refers to a chronological point in God's calendar of events. Years earlier, Peter used a similar expression when he quoted from the Old Testament to describe the Day of Pentecost miracle of the coming of the Holy Spirit: "This is what was spoken of through the prophet Joel: 'And it shall be in the last days,' God says, 'that I will pour forth of My Spirit on all mankind'" (Acts 2:16–17; cf. 1 Tim. 4:1; Heb. 1:2).

The third feature of the Son's uniqueness is His resurrection. God **raised Him from the dead** in unmistakably powerful proof that He was the sacrifice for sin and had accomplished God's redemptive work (Acts 2:24, 32; 3:15; 4:10; 13:33; 17:31; 26:23; Rom. 4:25; 1 Cor. 15:20–26). In his opening salutation to the Romans, Paul concisely summarizes the resurrection's significance: "who was declared the Son of God with power by the resurrection from the dead, according to the Spirit of holiness, Jesus Christ our Lord" (Rom. 1:4).

Fourth, Peter reminds believers that Christ is unique because in ultimate, culminating affirmation, God **gave Him glory.** That phrase points to the ascension (Mark 16:19; Luke 24:50–51; Acts 1:9–11), when Christ returned to the heaven of heavens and the glory He had enjoyed with the Father from all eternity (3:22; Luke 24:26; John 17:4–5; Eph. 1:20–21; cf. Ps. 68:18). Writing of the superiority of Christ, the author of Hebrews referred to His ascension as the reward for His perfect redemptive work: "But we do see Him who was made for a little while lower than the angels, namely, Jesus, because of the suffering of death crowned with glory and honor" (Heb. 2:9; cf. 9:24; 12:2). Philippians 2:9–11 assigns Him absolute lordship over all:

> For this reason also, God highly exalted Him, and bestowed on Him the name which is above every name, so that at the name of Jesus every knee will bow, of those who are in heaven and on earth and under the earth, and that every tongue will confess that Jesus Christ is Lord, to the glory of God the Father.

FOR WHAT DID GOD REDEEM BELIEVERS?

for the sake of you who through Him are believers in God, . . . so that your faith and hope are in God. (1:20*b*, 21*b*)

As if to underscore an already clear truth, Peter reiterated for his readers that Christ's redemptive work was **for the sake of you,** meaning all the redeemed. This emphasis that Jesus died on behalf of the redeemed is further explained in this volume in comments on 2:24 and 3:18 chapters 15 and 19 respectively (cf. Isa. 53:4–6; 2 Cor. 5:21; 8:9; Eph. 1:6).

Since redemption is **through Him** alone (Acts 3:16; 4:12; cf. John 3:36; 10:7, 9; 1 Cor. 1:4; 1 Tim. 2:5; 1 John 5:11–12; 2 John 9–11), there is no other way to God (John 14:6). This marks the exclusivity of the gospel as the only way of redemption. People cannot be **believers in God** apart from acknowledging the death, resurrection, and sovereign lordship of His Son. In fact, all who do not believe the gospel cannot know God at all and are subject to eternal destruction.

> To give relief to you who are afflicted and to us as well when the Lord Jesus will be revealed from heaven with His mighty angels in flaming fire, dealing out retribution to those who do not know God and to those who do not obey the gospel of our Lord Jesus. These will pay the penalty of eternal destruction, away from the presence of the Lord and from the glory of His power. (2 Thess. 1:7–9)

It should also be considered that the phrase **through Him** may not only indicate the *way* to saving belief in God, but the *power* to believe the gospel. In 1 Corinthians 3:5, Paul wrote that he and Apollos were "servants through whom you believed" on the human side; yet, clearly, since all people are helpless, blind, and dead in sin, divine power is required. That is why Paul goes on to say "even as the Lord gave . . . to each one." Christ Himself, by the Holy Spirit, is the agent of believers' salvation. Peter knew this, as some Jewish believers in Jerusalem acknowledged to him years earlier, while agreeing with his teaching, "'Well then, God has granted to the Gentiles also the repentance that leads to life'" (Acts 11:18).

Since redemption **through Him** produces **believers in God,** it is obvious that salvation is appropriated by faith (Mark 1:15; 16:16; John 6:29; 20:31; Acts 11:21; 13:39, 48; 16:31; 20:21; Rom. 3:28; 5:15; 10:9–10, 14–15, 17; Eph. 2:8–9). Saving faith includes both belief **in** the one, true, and living **God** (Heb. 10:39; 11:6) and belief **through** His Son, Jesus Christ (John 6:40). Contained in the phrase **believers in God** is all that is implicit in genuine saving faith.

The end of verse 21 reveals the ultimate, twofold blessing of redemption—**so that** believers **faith and hope** will be **in God. Faith** enables believers to trust God for necessary grace in the midst of life's present circumstances, struggles, and anxieties (5:7; Pss. 5:11; 31:1; 37:5; 56:11; Prov. 29:25; Isa. 26:3; Nah. 1:7; Phil. 4:6), and **hope** enables belief in future grace, to be revealed for them in heavenly glory (see the discussion of 1:4, 5, 13 in chapters 2 and 5 in this volume; cf. Ps. 146:5; Acts 23:6; 24:15; Rom. 5:2; 8:18, 25; Gal. 5:5; Titus 2:13; Heb. 6:11, 19). The psalmist links hope and redemption this way: "But God will redeem my soul from the power of Sheol, for He will receive me" (Ps. 49:15). Believers have an unshakeable hope that one day God will raise them from the grave and welcome them to final glory. The apostle Paul reminded the Romans that believers' sure hope includes redemption of the body: "We ourselves, having the first fruits of the Spirit, even we ourselves groan within ourselves, waiting eagerly for our adoption as sons, the redemption of our body" (Rom. 8:23; cf. Phil. 3:20–21; 1 John 3:2). By faith, saints presently enjoy the redemption of the soul ("the first fruits of the Spirit"), and by hope they anticipate the redemption of the body from all remaining effects of the Fall.

Supernatural Love
(1 Peter 1:22–25)

7

Since you have in obedience to the truth purified your souls for a sincere love of the brethren, fervently love one another from the heart, for you have been born again not of seed which is perishable but imperishable, that is, through the living and enduring word of God. For, "All flesh is like grass, and all its glory like the flower of grass. The grass withers, and the flower falls off, but the word of the Lord endures forever." And this is the word which was preached to you. (1:22–25)

An anecdote from the early 1900s beautifully illustrates how Christians ought to be grateful for what Christ has done for them. While on a three-story scaffold at a construction site one day, a building engineer tripped and fell toward the ground in what appeared to be a fatal plummet. Right below the scaffold, a laborer looked up just as the man fell, realized he was standing exactly where the engineer would land, braced himself, and absorbed the full impact of the other man's fall. The impact slightly injured the engineer but severely hurt the laborer. The brutal collision fractured almost every bone in his body, and after he recovered from those injuries, he was severely disabled.

Years later, a reporter asked the former construction laborer how the engineer had treated him since the accident. The handicapped man told the reporter:"He gave me half of all he owns, including a share of his business. He is constantly concerned about my needs and never lets me want for anything. Almost every day he gives me some token of thanks or remembrance."

Oftentimes believers—unlike the grateful engineer in the story— forget that on Calvary there was a Substitute who caught the full impact of their sinful weight and rescued them as they hurtled toward an eternity in hell. God poured out His wrath on the perfect Sacrifice (1:19; cf. Heb. 4:15; 7:26–27), His sinless Son who "was pierced through for [their] transgressions, He was crushed for [their] iniquities; the chastening for [their] well-being fell upon Him, and by His scourging [they] are healed" (Isa. 53:5; cf. 2 Cor. 5:21; Gal. 1:3–4; Heb. 10:9–10; 1 Peter 2:24). Christ sacrificed Himself for all who believe, and each certainly ought to be consumed with demonstrable gratitude to Him for that love, prompting each to manifest love to Him above what is natural. Beyond that love for the Savior is the mutual love shared with all others who have been rescued from eternal death. The apostle Peter calls it **sincere love of the brethren.**

In this passage, one can pose four basic questions this text answers to explain this supernatural love: When were believers enabled to love? Who are believers to love? How are believers to love? And why are believers to love?

WHEN WERE BELIEVERS ENABLED TO LOVE?

Since you have in obedience to the truth purified your souls (1:22a)

Scripture repeatedly makes it plain that the unconverted person is far from having the ability to demonstrate genuine love (John 5:42; 1 John 2:9, 11; 3:10; 4:20; cf. Job 14:4; Ps. 58:3; John 15:18, 25; Rom. 8:7–8; 1 Cor. 2:14; 2 Cor. 3:5). Jesus told the Pharisees,"Woe to you Pharisees! For you pay tithe of mint and rue and every kind of garden herb, and yet disregard justice and the love of God; but these are the things you should have done without neglecting the others" (Luke 11:42). They were concerned with the minute details of external religion and yet did not (and could not) manifest God's love (cf. John 5:42; 1 John 3:16–17). In contrast, Jesus declared that love unmistakably marks believers: "By this all men will know that you are My disciples, if you have love for one another" (John 13:35; cf. John 14:21; 2 Cor. 5:14; 1 Peter 1:8; 1 John 2:5; 4:12, 19; 5:1).

It was at salvation that believers received the capacity to demonstrate supernatural love (Rom. 5:5). When they evidenced **obedience to the truth** (were saved), they also **purified** their **souls. Purified** (*hāgnikotes*) is a perfect participle that describes a past action with continuing results. Not only did God cleanse Christians' impure past (cf. 4:1–3; Heb. 9:22–23), He also gave them new capabilities for the present and future (2 Cor. 5:17; cf. Rom. 6:3–14; Col. 3:8–10; 2 Peter 1:4–9). Ezekiel looked forward to this spiritual reality when he prophesied of what God would do for believers under the new covenant:

> Then I will sprinkle clean water on you, and you will be clean; I will cleanse you from all your filthiness and from all your idols. Moreover, I will give you a new heart and put a new spirit within you; and I will remove the heart of stone from your flesh and give you a heart of flesh. I will put My Spirit within you and cause you to walk in My statutes, and you will be careful to observe My ordinances. (Ezek. 36:25–27; cf. Jer. 31:31–34; Matt. 26:28; John 3:5; Eph. 5:26; Titus 3:5)

On the surface, **purified** may seem to refer to a human work; on the contrary, it refers to a fully divine work. The prophet Ezekiel made that clear in the passage just cited, and in his letters the apostle Paul also lucidly affirmed that salvation's purifying work is God's:

> For consider your calling, brethren, that there were not many wise according to the flesh, not many mighty, not many noble. . . . But by His doing you are in Christ Jesus, who became to us wisdom from God, and righteousness and sanctification, and redemption, so that, just as it is written, "Let him who boasts, boast in the Lord." (1 Cor. 1:26, 30–31; cf. Ps. 37:39; Prov. 20:9; Rom. 11:6; 1 Cor. 6:11; Eph. 5:25–26; 2 Thess. 2:13; Titus 2:14; 3:5; Heb. 5:9)

In this passage, Peter assumed but did not refer to *faith,* which the New Testament so necessarily associates with salvation (1:9; Acts 14:27; 15:9; 20:21; 26:18; Rom. 3:22, 25–28; 4:5; 5:1; Gal. 2:16; 3:11, 24, 26; Eph. 2:8; Phil. 3:9; 2 Thess. 2:13; 2 Tim. 3:15). But, along with the purging from sin that comes through saving faith (Acts 15:8–9), he did refer to the **obedience to the truth,** an inherent element of the faith that saves (cf. John 3:36; Rom. 10:10; Eph. 2:8–10; Heb. 5:9; 11:1–34). So Peter did not overlook faith in relation to salvation; he merely defined faith. He reiterated for his readers the truth of 1:2, where he affirmed that they were saved "according to the foreknowledge of God the Father, by the sanctifying work of the Spirit, to obey Jesus Christ and be sprinkled with His blood" (see the discussion of that verse in chapter 1 of this volume).

Clearly **obedience** can be a New Testament synonym for *faith*. Other passages affirm this fact. To the Romans Paul wrote, "Do you not know that when you present yourselves to someone as slaves for obedience, you are slaves of the one whom you obey, either of sin resulting in death, or of obedience resulting in righteousness?" (Rom. 6:16; cf. 1:5; 6:17; 15:18; 16:19, 26; 2 Cor. 9:13).

Faith is not a human-initiated work of obedience (Eph. 2:8, "For by grace you have been saved through faith; and that not of yourselves, it is the gift of God"), but if genuinely given by God it will result in believers' regularly obeying the truth (cf. James 1:22–25; 2:14–26; 1 John 2:3–6; 3:7–9, 24) and manifesting God's love to others (cf. 1 John 2:10–11; 3:10–11, 14–17; 4:7–8, 16, 20).

WHO ARE BELIEVERS TO LOVE?

for a sincere love of the brethren, (1:22*b*)

At salvation, believers become members of Christ's body, the church, which then becomes the target for their new, Spirit-empowered capacity for love (Rom. 5:5; 1 Thess. 4:9; 1 John 3:14, 23; cf. John 15:12; Phil. 1:9; 1 John 3:18; 4:7–8; 5:1–2). This **love of the brethren** (*philadelphia*) is to be **sincere** (*anupokriton*, "unhypocritical"). Knowing the danger of hypocrisy, Paul admonished the Romans, "Let love be without hypocrisy" (Rom. 12:9). **Sincere love** is the prevailing standard for believers (Rom. 12:10; 2 Cor. 6:6; 8:8; Phil. 2:1–2; Heb. 13:1; 1 John 3:11, 18), superseding all earthly limitations and considerations (cf. 1 Cor. 10:23–30). God can use the loving unity of believers to attract a lost world and awaken it to its need for salvation (cf. John 13:34–35; 1 Cor. 10:31–33).

HOW ARE BELIEVERS TO LOVE?

fervently love one another from the heart, (1:22*c*)

The well-known New Testament verb *agapaō* expresses the ideal kind of **love,** that which is exercised by the will rather than emotion, not determined by the beauty or desirability of the object, but by the noble intention of the one who loves. **Fervently** (*ektenōs*) is a physiological term meaning to stretch to the furthest limit of a muscle's capacity. Metaphorically, the word means to go all out, to reach the furthest extent of something (Luke 22:44; Acts 12:5; cf. Acts 26:7). That is how Peter used it in 4:8 when he wrote, "Above all, keep fervent in your love for one another, because love covers a multitude of sins." God wants believers' love to stretch way out so it graciously forgives and covers sin among believers (see the full discussion of this verse in chapter 21 of this volume).

Such strong love, however, does not derive from some external, legalistic requirement (cf. Ps. 40:8; Rom. 8:2; Gal. 5:1). On the contrary, Peter told his readers that this love is an attitude compelled from within, **from the heart** (Prov. 4:23; Matt. 22:37–39; Eph. 4:32; 1 Tim. 1:5; cf. Rom. 12:10; 1 Cor. 13:8, 13; Gal. 5:14; 1 Thess. 1:3; Heb. 6:10), because it is a fruit of the indwelling Holy Spirit. Paul told the Galatians that if they lived by that Spirit, they would see His fruit in their lives:

> Walk by the Spirit, and you will not carry out the desire of the flesh.... But the fruit of the Spirit is love, joy, peace, patience, kindness, goodness, faithfulness, gentleness, self-control; against such things there is no law. Now those who belong to Christ Jesus have crucified the flesh with its passions and desires. If we live by the Spirit, let us also walk by the Spirit. (Gal. 5:16, 22–25; cf. Eph. 5:15–21)

WHY SHOULD BELIEVERS LOVE?

for you have been born again not of seed which is perishable but imperishable, that is, through the living and enduring word of God. For, "All flesh is like grass, and all its glory like the flower of grass. The grass withers, and the flower falls off, but the word of the Lord endures forever." And this is the word which was preached to you. (1:23–25)

Believers are to love one another to the fullest extent because it is consistent with new life in Christ. The apostle John wrote, "Whoever believes that Jesus is the Christ is born of God, and whoever loves the Father loves the child born of Him. By this we know that we love the children of God, when we love God and observe His commandments" (1 John 5:1–2; cf. 3:14; 4:7).

It is almost as if Peter anticipated his readers' asking why they should love the way he had commanded them. He therefore told them they should be expected to love that way because they had **been born again.** The perfect tense of the participle *anagegennēmenoi* (**have been born again**) emphasizes that the new birth occurs in the past, with ongoing results in the present. One of those results is that believers will show love for one another.

Paul defined this transformation as a death with subsequent new life in Christ:

> Do you not know that all of us who have been baptized into Christ Jesus have been baptized into His death? Therefore we have been buried with Him through baptism into death, so that as Christ was raised from the dead through the glory of the Father, so we too might walk in newness of life. (Rom. 6:3–4)

The truth of that text is actually a "dry" one. That is, Paul is not speaking of water baptism, but of spiritual immersion into Christ Jesus, *symbolized* by water baptism. Immersion into Christ means believers are placed into His death, by which they die to the old life and God considers them as participating in Christ's resurrection, by which they share new life in Him. Thus the new birth entails a complete, radical, decisive transformation that has to be described in the extreme terms of death and new birth (2 Cor. 5:17). Believers "put on the new self, which in the likeness of God has been created in righteousness and holiness of the truth" (Eph. 4:24; cf. Rom. 6:6; Col. 3:10). Those who are **born again** go from being godless, lawless, and selfish (Rom. 3:9–18; 8:7–8) to manifesting genuine repentance, trust, and love. The Holy Spirit enlightens them to discern spiritual truth (1 Cor. 2:14–15; 2 Cor. 4:6) and empowers them to serve the law of God (truth contained in His Word) rather than the law of sin (Rom. 6:17–18).

The new birth is monergistic; it is a work solely of the Holy Spirit. Sinners do not cooperate in their spiritual births (cf. Eph. 2:1–10) any more than infants cooperate in their natural births. Jesus told Nicodemus, "The wind blows where it wishes and you hear the sound of it, but do not know where it comes from and where it is going; so is everyone who is born of the Spirit" (John 3:8; cf. John 1:12–13; Eph. 2:4–5; Phil. 2:13).

Seed represents the source of life. Everything that comes to life in the created order begins with a seed, the basic life source that initiates plant and animal existence. But nothing in the material world has the capacity to produce spiritual and eternal life. Thus God did **not** effect the new birth using **seed which is perishable.** In contrast to how an earthly father initiates human birth with his corruptible **seed,** God initiates the spiritual birth with an **imperishable** seed. Everything that grows from natural seeds is a sovereign creation of God (Gen. 1:11–12), but it all eventually dies (Isa. 40:8; James 1:10–11). However, sinners born again of God's Spirit gain eternal life. That is because He uses the imperishable seed of **the living and enduring word of God.** Peter's words echoed what James earlier wrote to his readers about the new birth, "In the exercise of His will He brought us forth by the word of truth, so that we would be a kind of first fruits among His creatures" (James 1:18; cf. Rom. 10:17).

To strengthen his point, Peter quoted from Isaiah 40:6, 8, which contains a familiar biblical principle about life's transience (cf. Job

14:1–2; Pss. 39:4; 103:15; Matt. 6:27, 30; James 4:14). **All flesh** refers to all humans and animals, and **grass** refers to the wild grass of the typical Middle Eastern countryside. The phrase **glory like the flower of grass** denotes the beauty of that scenery in which colorful flowers (cf. Matt. 6:28–29) occasionally rise above the grass. So Peter noted that whether something is as common as **grass** or as uniquely lovely as a **flower,** it eventually **withers** or **falls off**—it dies. Human life is brief in this world. People pass away like dry grass under a withering east wind. In their graves, the poor and illiterate of no influence are equal to the wealthy and highly educated of great influence (cf. Job 3:17–19). In Christ, however, whether people are common or uncommon, they will never deteriorate or die spiritually. Instead they are like **the word of the Lord** which **endures forever.**

That saving **word** is the gospel, as Peter's choice of words indicates. He used *rhēma* for **word** (rather than the usual *logos,* the more broad reference to Scripture), which denotes specific statements. **Preached** is *euangelisthen,* from the same root word that means "good news," or "the gospel." He is referring, then, to the particular message of the gospel, that scriptural truth which, when believed, is the **imperishable** seed producing new life that also **endures forever.**

Though believers possess new life in Jesus Christ and the capacity to love in a transcendent, godly manner, the continued presence of their unredeemed flesh (cf. Rom. 7:14–25) causes them to fail to love as they should. Thus, as in all matters of obedience, the New Testament contains a number of other exhortations for believers to genuinely love (John 13:34; 15:12; Rom. 12:10; Phil. 1:9; 1 Thess. 3:12; 4:9; 2 Thess. 1:3; 2 Peter 1:7; 1 John 3:23; 4:7, 21). Those are admonitions for the church to do what it, by God's grace and power, is already capable of doing. The call in this text is for saints to manifest an undying love for fellow believers, which is consistent with an imperishable new life in Jesus Christ by the power of the gospel word which is itself imperishable.

Desiring the Word (1 Peter 2:1–3)

8

Therefore, putting aside all malice and all deceit and hypocrisy and envy and all slander, like newborn babies, long for the pure milk of the word, so that by it you may grow in respect to salvation, if you have tasted the kindness of the Lord. (2:1–3)

Love for and delight in God's Word always marks the truly saved. Jesus said, "If you continue in My word, then you are truly disciples of Mine; and you will know the truth, and the truth will make you free" (John 8:31–32). The apostle Paul echoed those principles when he said, "I joyfully concur with the law of God in the inner man" (Rom. 7:22). The Old Testament saints also expressed a strong desire for the Word of God. Job declared, "I have treasured the words of His mouth more than my necessary food" (Job 23:12). The opening psalm declares that the godly man's "delight is in the law of the Lord, and in His law he meditates day and night" (Ps. 1:2; cf. 19:9–10; 40:8). The prophet Jeremiah cherished God's revelation in a difficult time: "Your words were found and I ate them, and Your words became for me a joy and the delight of my heart" (Jer. 15:16).

The believer's delight in God's Word is the dominant theme of the longest chapter in the Bible, Psalm 119. About midway through the chapter, the psalmist summarizes his delight in and dependence on God's Word:

> O how I love Your law! It is my meditation all the day. Your command-ments make me wiser than my enemies, for they are ever mine. I have more insight than all my teachers, for Your testimonies are my medita-tion. I understand more than the aged, because I have observed Your precepts. I have restrained my feet from every evil way, that I may keep Your word. I have not turned aside from Your ordinances, for You Yourself have taught me. How sweet are Your words to my taste! Yes, sweeter than honey to my mouth! From Your precepts I get under-standing; therefore I hate every false way. (Ps. 119:97–104; cf. vv. 16, 24, 35, 47–48, 72, 92, 111, 113, 127, 159, 167, 174)

Peter wanted Christians to be faithful to that same kind of Spirit-prompted longing for the Word of God. Therefore this passage suggests five perspectives that, if followed, will lead to a stronger, more consistent desire for the Word: believers should remember their life source, they should eliminate their sins, they should admit their need, they should pursue their spiritual growth, and they should survey their blessings.

REMEMBERING THEIR LIFE SOURCE

Therefore, (2:1a)

Therefore refers back to 1:23–25 and "the living and enduring word of God," the "seed which is . . . imperishable"—the gospel that pro-duced the new birth. God's Word was the source of salvation (2 Tim. 3:15) because His transforming grace worked through the Word to create new life (James 1:18; cf. John 20:31; Rom. 10:17). The Word, operating not as a perishable natural seed (cf. 1 Cor. 15:36–37) but as an imperishable divine seed (cf. Luke 8:11; 1 John 3:9), became the source of believers' continued spiritual transformation and growth (Ps 119:105; John 15:3; 17:17; Rom. 15:4; Eph. 5:26; 2 Tim. 3:16–17; cf. Deut. 17:19–20; Josh. 1:8).

Therefore was a concise reminder to Peter's readers to remem-ber that saving power of God's Word in their lives as a basis for ongoing commitment to Scripture as the only power to live the Christian life (cf. Matt. 4:4; Acts 20:32; Rom. 15:4; Gal. 3:3; 4:9; 2 Tim. 3:16–17).

Scripture contains many other reminders and exhortations about its indispensability as the fountain of spiritual life and power (Pss. 19:10; 119:50, 93, 140; Prov. 6:23; 30:5; Matt. 7:24; Luke 11:28; Col. 3:16). God declared through the prophet Isaiah,

For as the rain and the snow come down from heaven, and do not return there without watering the earth and making it bear and sprout, and furnishing seed to the sower and bread to the eater; so will My word be which goes forth from My mouth; it will not return to Me empty, without accomplishing what I desire, and without succeeding in the matter for which I sent it. (Isa. 55:10–11; cf. Heb. 4:12)

Jesus told the disciples, "You are already clean because of the word which I have spoken to you" (John 15:3). God's Word is always as powerful in believers' lives as when they first believed (1 Thess. 2:13; cf. Ps. 19:7–9; Phil. 1:6).

Eliminating Their Sins

putting aside all malice and all deceit and hypocrisy and envy and all slander, (2:1*b*)

Striving to eliminate sins is prerequisite to sustaining the desire for God's Word. Clinging to sins drives one in the opposite direction from the truth that exposes and confronts sin and demands righteousness. Peter used an imperative participle to command his readers to get rid of the sins in their lives. The verb rendered **putting aside** (*apothemenoi*) applied to any kind of rejection, and sometimes referred especially to stripping off soiled garments, which is the analogy Paul had in mind when he admonished the Colossians to "put . . . aside: anger, wrath, malice, slander, and abusive speech from your mouth. Do not lie to one another, since you laid aside the old self with its evil practices" (Col. 3:8–9; cf. Eph. 4:22, 25; Heb. 12:1; James 1:21).

In ancient Christian baptism ceremonies, those being baptized customarily took off and discarded the clothes they wore to the ceremony. Following their baptisms, they put on new robes they received from the church. Exchanging clothes symbolized the salvation reality of laying aside the old life and taking up the new (Rom. 6:3–7; 2 Cor. 5:17; Eph. 4:24). If such a transformation really occurred in someone's life, he should be **putting aside all** (**all** used here three times to emphasize totality) sins that are a hindrance to fully desiring God's Word (Heb. 12:1; cf. 2 Tim. 2:4).

All malice is the first category of sin Peter lists. **Malice** (which in English has the idea of desiring to harm someone else) is an all-inclusive word (*kakia*) for sin referring to general wickedness and baseness. Several other times in the *New American Standard Bible* (NASB) it is translated **malice** (Rom. 1:29; 1 Cor. 5:8; Eph. 4:31; Col. 3:8; Titus 3:3), but it is also rendered "trouble" (Matt. 6:34) and "wickedness" (Acts 8:22; James 1:21).

Second, believers are commanded to eliminate **all deceit,** a term (*dolos*) literally referring to "bait" or a "fishhook." It denotes guile, dishonesty, falsehood, and treachery (2:22; 3:10; cf. Mark 7:22–23; John 1:47; Rom. 1:29). Luke used the same term in Acts 13:10 when citing Paul's rebuke of Elymas the magician for being "full of all *deceit* and fraud" (emphasis added).

Third, Peter lists **hypocrisy** (*hupokrisis*), which originally identified an actor who wore a mask. It refers to spiritual insincerity and pretense (cf. Ezek. 33:31–32; Matt. 15:7–9; 23:23–24; Luke 18:11; 2 Cor. 5:12). The word describes any behavior that is not genuine or consistent with what one really believes or says he believes (Matt. 23:28; Mark 12:15; Luke 12:1; Rom. 12:9; Gal. 2:13; 1 Tim. 4:2; James 3:17).

Envy (*phthonos*) defines the attitude of those who resent others' prosperity (cf. Matt. 27:18; Rom. 1:29; Phil. 1:15; Titus 3:3). It often leads to grudges, bitterness, hatred, and conflict (cf. 1 Cor. 3:3; 1 Tim. 6:4; James 3:16).

Lastly, Peter mentions **all slander** (*katalalias*), an onomatopoeic word designed to sound like the whispers and tattles reported behind someone's back in gossip and backbiting (2 Cor. 12:20). It referred essentially to defamation of character (cf. 2:12; 3:16; James 4:11).

Peter's list of specific sins is not exhaustive but certainly is representative of evil. In fact, the first term, **all malice,** could encompass all the sins so that his readers were called to confession and repentance. This clears the way for an unhindered desire for the truth of God.

ADMITTING THEIR NEED

like newborn babies, long for the pure milk of the word, (2:2a)

Believers need God's truth like a baby needs **milk.** Peter compares the strength of that longing for divine revelation to the singular and dominant desire of **newborn babies** (*artigennēta brephē*) for their mother's milk. Peter could have made his point just with the term *brephē*, but to underscore it he added the modifier *artigennēta*, which literally means "born just now." The two words identify an infant that has just emerged from its mother's womb and is crying for milk from her breast. That sole and desperate hunger for milk is the newborn's first expressed longing designed by God to correspond to their greatest need, and it illustrates how strongly believers ought to desire the Word. It is singular and relentless because life depends on it.

Long for (*epipothēsate*) is an imperative verb that commands believers to strongly desire or crave something. The apostle Paul used the word seven times (Rom. 1:11; 2 Cor. 5:2; 9:14 KJV; Phil. 1:8; 2:26; 1 Thess.

3:6; 2 Tim. 1:4), and in each instance it expresses an intense, recurring, insatiable desire or passion (cf. Pss. 42:1 and 119:174; James 4:5). Its meaning encompasses such things as the strong desire a husband or wife has for a spouse, the strong physical craving that accompanies extreme hunger, the poignant longings one has for a deceased loved one, the intense desire a Christian parent has for a spiritually wayward child to repent and return to obedience, and the strong desires believers have for the salvation of an unbelieving family member or close friend. Those definitions each illustrate the kind of strong, consuming desire Peter wanted his readers to have for Scripture. None is stronger, however, than the desire a baby has for milk.

Peter compares the object of their craving with **pure milk.** **Pure** (*adolos*) means unadulterated or uncontaminated and often referred to farm products such as grain, wine, vegetable oil, or in this instance **milk.** Believers are to crave what is unmixed and pure, that provides real sustenance, namely, **the pure milk of the word. Of the word** translates *logikos;* however that rendering is not the usual translation of the term. In Romans 12:1 the NASB uses "spiritual" to translate *logikos.* In that verse other reliable English Bible versions render *logikos* "reasonable" (cf. KJV; NKJV), a fact which demonstrates that one cannot be overly narrow concerning the word's meaning. Originally, *logikos* meant "belonging to speech," or "belonging to reason," which conveyed a sense of rationality and reasonability. If that meaning were applied to Peter's use of the word, translators would have rendered his phrase "pure rational milk," or "pure reasonable milk." But the NASB translators here chose to render *logikos,* **of the word,** because that adequately conveys Peter's intent to refer his readers to Scripture. The rabbis traditionally referred to God's law as milk and Psalms 19:8–9 and 119:140 say God's Word is pure and clean. Therefore the translation **pure milk of the word** is a legitimate, fair option that describes the Word as the source of **pure** spiritual **milk** for believers.

The broader context of verse 2 further supports the NASB rendering of *logikos.* Peter concludes chapter 1 with a focus on "the living and enduring word of God," which is the source of believers' new life. Therefore his reference to spiritual **milk** contextually relates back to the Word of God. Such milk is thus synonymous with Scripture.

It is notable what Peter did not command. He did not charge believers to read the Word, study the Word, meditate on the Word, teach the Word, preach the Word, search the Word, or memorize the Word. All of those things are essential, and other passages do command believers to perform them (cf. Josh. 1:8; Ps. 119:11; Acts 17:11; 1 Tim. 4:11, 13; 2 Tim. 2:15; 4:2). However, Peter focused on the more foundational element—

which believers need before they will pursue any of the other things—a deep, continuous longing for the Word of truth (cf. 2 Thess. 2:10b).

Whether believers are recent converts or more mature in the faith, craving the Word of God (cf. Neh. 8:1–3; Ps. 119:97, 103, 159, 167; Jer. 15:16; Acts 17:11) is always essential to spiritual nourishment and growth (Job 23:12). Jesus affirmed this when He told Satan in the wilderness, "It is written, 'Man shall not live on bread alone, but on every word that proceeds out of the mouth of God'" (Matt. 4:4; cf. Deut. 8:3; Luke 4:4). In view of postmodern culture's relentless output of informational junk food through radio, television, films, the Internet, computer games, books, periodicals, and even so-called Christian pulpits—all of which causes spiritual malnourishment and dulls appetites for genuine spiritual food—believers must commit to regular nourishment from God's Word.

PURSUING THEIR SPIRITUAL GROWTH

so that by it you may grow in respect to salvation, (2:2b)

It is always sad to see a human being who is malnourished, weak, and retarded in development. But far sadder is seeing believers who are spiritually malnourished and underdeveloped. All believers should be motivated by the opportunity to grow strong and mature in Christ, enjoying greater blessing and usefulness. **May grow** (*auxēthēte*) is a passive verb, literally meaning "it may grow you." Peter used the same verb at the close of his second letter when he commanded believers to "grow in the grace and knowledge of our Lord and Savior Jesus Christ" (2 Peter 3:18; cf. Acts 20:32; 1 Tim. 4:6). It is by the intake of the truth that the Holy Spirit grows and matures believers (cf. 2 Cor. 3:18).

In respect to salvation is the obvious objective of believers' spiritual growth. The Word will grow them into the full, final expression of the sanctification aspect of their salvation, as Paul commanded the Philippians,

> So then, my beloved, just as you have always obeyed, not as in my presence only, but now much more in my absence, work out your salvation with fear and trembling; for it is God who is at work in you, both to will and to work for His good pleasure. (Phil. 2:12–13; cf. John 8:31–32; 2 Cor. 3:18; Col. 1:21–23; Heb. 3:14; James 1:25)

Peter's exhortation for believers to **grow** through the Word strongly implies the necessity of discontent with the present condition of spiritual development. It also recalls what Paul said about his dissatisfaction with the status quo in his life:

> But whatever things were gain to me, those things I have counted as loss for the sake of Christ. More than that, I count all things to be loss in view of the surpassing value of knowing Christ Jesus my Lord, for whom I have suffered the loss of all things, and count them but rubbish so that I may gain Christ, and may be found in Him, not having a righteousness of my own derived from the Law, but that which is through faith in Christ, the righteousness which comes from God on the basis of faith, that I may know Him and the power of His resurrection and the fellowship of His sufferings, being conformed to His death; in order that I may attain to the resurrection from the dead. Not that I have already obtained it or have already become perfect, but I press on so that I may lay hold of that for which also I was laid hold of by Christ Jesus. Brethren, I do not regard myself as having laid hold of it yet; but one thing I do: forgetting what lies behind and reaching forward to what lies ahead, I press on toward the goal for the prize of the upward call of God in Christ Jesus. (Phil. 3:7–14)

Motivation for genuine spiritual growth arises out of a righteous sense of discontent, coupled with a sincere desire to be satisfied with nothing but the Word of God.

SURVEYING THEIR BLESSINGS

if you have tasted the kindness of the Lord. (2:3)

Peter's fifth perspective or motivation for desiring the Word of God echoes the psalmist's words, "O taste and see that the Lord is good" (Ps. 34:8). **If** is a first-class conditional participle introducing the facts or conditions necessary for a proposition to be true. Since his readers had **tasted** or experienced **the kindness**—goodness and grace—**of the Lord** in their conversion, they already knew how blessed and wonderful it was. Therefore, they should have desired more of that goodness through feeding on His Word. Believers ought to regularly survey the blessings of their salvation, remembering the many times God has answered their prayers (cf. Pss. 40:1; 116:1; 138:3; Jer. 33:3; Matt. 7:7; John 15:7; 1 John 5:14–15), and all the times He has touched their lives with His kindness and mercy (cf. Pss. 17:7; 26:3; 36:7; 103:11; 106:1; 117:2; 118:29; 138:2; Lam. 3:22–23; Luke 1:50; Gal. 6:16; Eph. 2:4). The prophet Jeremiah wrote, "Your words were found and I ate them, and Your words became for me a joy and the delight of my heart; for I have been called by Your name, O Lord God of hosts" (Jer. 15:16).

Peter's simple analogy comparing a newborn baby craving for its mother's milk with a believer of any maturity level passionately longing for the Word of God concludes the apostle's series of exhortations that began at 1:13. First, as a result of their salvation, Christians are to respond to God by pursuing holiness (1:13–21). Second, believers must respond to others in the church by loving them as brothers and sisters in Christ (1:22–25). Finally, believers must respond to their essential need for the Word by continually desiring it (2:1–3). With the psalmist all should affirm, "Your word is very pure, therefore Your servant loves it. I am small and despised, yet I do not forget Your precepts. Your righteousness is an everlasting righteousness, and Your law is truth" (Ps. 119:140–142).

Spiritual Privileges— Part 1: Union with Christ and Access to God (1 Peter 2:4–5)

9

And coming to Him as to a living stone which has been rejected by men, but is choice and precious in the sight of God, you also, as living stones, are being built up as a spiritual house for a holy priesthood, to offer up spiritual sacrifices acceptable to God through Jesus Christ. (2:4–5)

The dictionary defines privilege as "a right or immunity granted as a peculiar benefit, advantage, or favor," which may be "attached specifically to a position or an office." It is a blessing or freedom enjoyed by some people, but which most people cannot take advantage of. Christians are a special class of people who enjoy unique and eternal spiritual favors—granted by God—because of their position in Christ. In this portion of his first letter, Peter continually examines the kaleidoscopic array of Christian privilege and rearranges the same basic truths into multiple images so that his readers might see the multifaceted glory of what it means to be children of God.

Many believers view the Christian life more from the standpoint of spiritual duty rather than spiritual privilege. They tend to be preoccupied with the temporal pressures of what they view as obligations and do not cherish the lasting privileges God has given them to enjoy. They often think of those as blessings reserved for heaven, to be appreciated only in the presence of God and Christ in that place of perfect joy, peace, harmony, unity, rest, knowledge, and wisdom. Since there will be no sickness, pain, or death, heaven appears to be the realm where everything is privilege and nothing is duty. However, the privileges of heaven will not exclude duty but will combine perfectly with it in an eternity of worshiping, honoring, serving, and exalting the Lord. So spiritual duty and spiritual privilege are not mutually exclusive for believers, either in this life or in the life to come. In this passage, the apostle emphasizes the richness of the privileges believers already have in Christ.

THE INITIATION OF SPIRITUAL PRIVILEGES

And coming to Him as to a living stone which has been rejected by men, but is choice and precious in the sight of God, (2:4)

It is by **coming to** Christ that believers enter the realm of spiritual privilege. Jesus Himself, with Peter and the other apostles as eyewitnesses, called people to abandon the turmoil of their sin and come to Him in faith and experience true soul rest. "Come to Me, all who are weary and heavy-laden, and I will give you rest. Take My yoke upon you and learn from Me, for I am gentle and humble in heart, and you will find rest for your souls" (Matt. 11:28–29). The once troubled soul is at peace. In John 6:35 He told the multitude, "I am the bread of life; he who comes to Me will not hunger, and he who believes in Me will never thirst" (cf. vv. 37, 44, 65; 7:37–38). The apostle Paul affirmed to the Ephesians that in Christ alone are all spiritual blessings found: "Blessed be the God and Father of our Lord Jesus Christ, who has blessed us with every spiritual blessing in the heavenly places in Christ" (Eph. 1:3; cf. vv. 4–14).

The compound verb **coming** (*proserchomenoi*), however, conveys more than a mere drawing close to Christ for salvation. The preposition *pros* is a prefix to the normal verb *erchomai* and adds intensity, denoting a drawing near to Christ in intimate, abiding, personal fellowship. The writer of Hebrews uses this same term a number of times to denote a conscious coming into God's presence with the intent to remain (4:16; 7:25; 10:22). For Peter, the word implied the movement of the entire inner person into the experience of intimate and ongoing communion with Jesus Christ.

Peter then used the metaphor of **a living stone** to identify the One to whom believers come—Jesus Christ—and to launch his discussion of spiritual privilege. **Stone** (*lithos*) sometimes refers to a carved precious stone, but usually it means "building stone." The Old Testament designates God as the only rock (Deut. 32:3–4, 31), the foundation and strength of His people. In the New Testament, Jesus Christ is the rock (2:8; 1 Cor. 10:4) and the **stone** on which the church rests. Here Peter's image is of a stone that was perfectly designed, shaped, and hewn out to become the cornerstone of the church, not merely a stone but **a living stone.** That living stone is Christ because He lives forever, having risen from the dead (Rom. 6:9). Not only is He alive, but He also gives life to all who trust in Him (cf. 1:3, 23; John 5:21, 25; 6:51–53; 1 Cor. 15:45; Col. 2:13; 1 John 4:9; 5:11–13). The absence of a definite article before **living stone** emphasizes the **living** quality and divine character of Jesus Christ.

Even though Christ is the source of all spiritual privileges, He **has been rejected by men.** That phrase primarily refers to the Jewish leaders and the Jewish people who followed them in demanding Christ's crucifixion. But Peter's words also encompass everyone who has rejected Christ since that time. **Has been rejected** (*apodedokimasmenon*) means "rejected having been examined or tested." Because the Jewish leaders were looking for the Messiah, when Jesus claimed to be the Christ (Matt. 26:63–64; John 1:49–51; 4:25–26; cf. Matt. 16:13–20; Luke 4:14–21) they examined His claim. Based on their blind hearts and false standards (Matt. 12:2, 10, 38; 15:1–2; 16:1; Mark 12:13–34; John 8:12–27), they concluded that He did not measure up, so they rejected Him (John 19:7, 12, 15; cf. 7:41–52; 12:37–38). Contempt and hatred characterized their rejection (Matt. 26:57–68; 27:20–25, 39–43; Mark 12:12; Luke 6:11; 13:14; John 8:59; 10:31, 39; cf. Luke 4:28–30); it was unthinkable to them that Jesus could possibly be the cornerstone of God's kingdom (cf. Ps. 118:22). They viewed Him as one who foolishly denounced their religious system (cf. Matt. 23:1–36; Mark 8:13–21), was too weak and humble to overthrow the occupying Romans and secure the Jews' national freedom, and was willing to die ignominiously on a cross (Matt. 17:22–23; 20:17–19; Mark 9:30–32; Luke 18:31–34). He simply did not measure up to any of the Jewish establishment's expectations.

Even though unbelievers have rejected Jesus Christ, He **is choice and precious in the sight of God.** The Father measured Him by the standards of divine perfection and declared, "This is My beloved Son, in whom I am well-pleased" (Matt. 3:17). God elected and ordained Christ (Deut. 18:15–16; Isa. 42:1; Jer. 23:5–6; Mic. 5:2; Acts 2:23; Gal. 4:4; Eph. 1:22; Heb. 3:1–2; 5:4–5; cf. Gen. 3:15; Num. 24:17; Ps. 45:6–7), as Peter's use of **choice** (*eklekton*) indicates. God also considered Jesus **precious** (*entimon*), which means "costly, highly prized, rare" (cf. 1:19; Ps. 45:2), the perfect, living cornerstone (Isa. 28:16; 1 Cor. 3:11; Eph. 2:20).

One of the major themes of Peter's preaching in the book of Acts is God's attestation of Christ's perfection. In Acts 2:22, he identified Him this way: "Jesus the Nazarene, a man attested to you by God with miracles and wonders and signs which God performed through Him in your midst." Later in Acts he made these declarations: "This Jesus God raised up again" (2:32; cf. 4:10; 5:30); "He is the stone which was rejected by you, the builders, but which became the chief corner stone" (4:11). As a trustworthy eyewitness, Peter was convinced of Christ's extraordinary status: "You know of Jesus of Nazareth," he told those gathered in Cornelius's house, "how God anointed Him with the Holy Spirit and with power, and how He went about doing good and healing all who were oppressed by the devil, for God was with Him. We are witnesses of all the things He did both in the land of the Jews and in Jerusalem" (10:38–39). It is to that unique **living stone** that everyone must go to receive the spiritual privileges that accompany salvation (cf. Matt. 11:28; John 1:12; 2 Cor. 5:17).

THE PRIVILEGE OF UNION WITH CHRIST

you also, as living stones, (2:5a)

When sinners come in faith to Christ, the "living stone," they too become **living stones;** when someone believes in Christ he shares His life (cf. John 17:21, 23; 2 Cor. 3:18; Eph. 4:15–16; 1 John 3:2). To be **living stones** means that believers have the eternal life of Christ. They are united with Him, which is their first spiritual privilege. They do not just worship Him, obey Him, and pray to Him; they are united with Him as stones in a spiritual building of which He is the cornerstone. Christians become partakers of the divine nature: "For you have died and your life is hidden with Christ in God. When Christ, who is our life, is revealed, then you also will be revealed with Him in glory" (Col. 3:3–4; cf. Gal. 2:20). In addition, Paul told the Ephesians,

> So then you are no longer strangers and aliens, but you are fellow citizens with the saints, and are of God's household, having been built on the foundation of the apostles and prophets, Christ Jesus Himself being the corner stone, in whom the whole building, being fitted together, is growing into a holy temple in the Lord, in whom you also are being built together into a dwelling of God in the Spirit. (Eph. 2:19–22; cf. 1 Cor. 3:9)

The foundation of this spiritual building ("household") is the apostles' doctrine (cf. Acts 2:42), the Scripture, which by the Holy Spirit they faithfully received and taught (cf. John 14:26; 15:26–27; 16:13; 2 Tim. 3:16; 2 Peter 1:19–21; 3:1–2, 16).

Believers, in their union with Christ, have spiritual resources to meet their every need. That is why Paul could pray on behalf of the Ephesians, "Now to Him who is able to do far more abundantly beyond all that we ask or think, according to the power that works within us" (Eph. 3:20; cf. Gal. 2:20; Col. 1:29). And it is the reason he could tell the Romans, "I will not presume to speak of anything except what Christ has accomplished through me, resulting in the obedience of the Gentiles by word and deed" (Rom. 15:18). Paul's evangelistic effectiveness resulted from the power of Christ working through him (cf. Acts 13:46–48; 1 Cor. 2:1–5; 1 Tim. 2:7; 2 Tim. 4:17). The power of Christ energizes all spiritual service by believers (cf. 1 Cor. 1:30; Phil. 4:13; 2 Tim. 2:21) and is resident in them because of their union with Him (John 15:4–11). Those who trust Christ for salvation become themselves **living stones** like their Savior and Lord and are privileged to access the spiritual power that resides in Him.

THE PRIVILEGE OF ACCESS TO GOD AS PRIESTS

are being built up as a spiritual house for a holy priesthood, (2:5b)

The vast world of unredeemed people has no access to God. He does not admit unbelievers into His fellowship (cf. Prov. 12:2; Matt. 7:21–23; Col. 1:21; Rev. 22:14–15); in fact, the Bible says they are far off (cf. Acts 2:39; Eph. 2:13). On the other hand, those who know God through Christ have the privilege of full admission into His presence (Ps. 65:4; John 10:9; Rom. 5:2; Eph. 2:18; 3:12; Heb. 4:16; 10:19–22).

As a believing Jew, the apostle Peter realized the New Testament economy was different from the Old in terms of God's presence with believers (John 1:17–18; Heb. 8:7–13). In the old economy, God's temple, representing His presence (1 Kings 8:10–11; 2 Chron. 5:13; 7:2–3), was a temporal, material house (Luke 21:5; John 2:20); but in the new, believers are **being built up as a spiritual house** that supersedes any material building (Eph. 2:20–22; Heb. 3:6). They constitute God's spiritual temple (cf. Acts 17:24; 1 Cor. 6:19–20; 2 Cor. 6:16), which Paul called "the household of God, which is the church of the living God" (1 Tim. 3:15). The writer of Hebrews further identifies the **spiritual house** in this fashion: "Christ was faithful as a Son over His house—whose house we are" (Heb. 3:6). So believers have access to God "as living stones," and they commune with Him as His spiritual dwelling.

Believers also function as **a holy priesthood.** Unfortunately, many people associate "priesthood" with the unbiblical model found in the Roman Catholic Church. But when the Bible speaks about believers being "priests," it does not refer to the Catholic system, nor to the old covenant priesthood in which only a single tribe of priests could officially serve God in sacred ceremonies. In the Old Testament only the high priest could actually go into the Holy of Holies once a year (Lev. 16:2, 29–34; Heb. 9:1–10, 25). Anyone who presumptuously crossed over into the priestly function without fully meeting the requirements and qualifications of the priesthood suffered severe judgment. For example, the rebellious Korah and his cohorts wrongly and sinfully had an ambition to be priests, and God destroyed them (Num. 16:1–40). When King Saul usurped Samuel's priestly function at Gilgal, God removed the kingdom from him (1 Sam. 13:8–14). When Uzzah unwisely touched the ark of God, the action cost him his life (2 Sam. 6:6–7). King Uzziah usurped the role of the priests and incurred God's deadly punishment (2 Chron. 26:16–21).

However, under the new covenant, such limitations do not exist, since all believers are **a holy priesthood** (cf. 2:9). Three Old Testament passages offer significant parallels to the characteristics of believers' priesthood. Exodus 28–29 lays out God's commands regarding the priesthood, such as the standards and principles for the office, as well as the functions of the office. Leviticus 8–9 describes the inauguration of men into the priestly office. Malachi 2 contrasts an apostate priesthood to the legitimate, God-ordained priesthood. From those passages flow six basic characteristics of the Old Testament priesthood that have great relevance to New Testament believers' spiritual privileges as priests.

Exodus 28 first of all reveals that God sovereignly chose the priests. He commanded Moses, "Then bring near to yourself Aaron your brother, and his sons with him, from among the sons of Israel, to minister as priest to Me—Aaron, Nadab and Abihu, Eleazar and Ithamar, Aaron's sons" (28:1). Likewise, the New Testament priesthood of believers is an elect privilege. Jesus told His disciples, "You did not choose Me but I chose you, and appointed you that you would go and bear fruit, and that your fruit would remain" (John 15:16). Christians have this priesthood only because God chose them from before the foundation of the world (Acts 13:48; Rom. 8:29–33; Eph. 1:3–6; 1 Thess. 1:3–4; 2 Thess. 2:13; 2 Tim. 1:9; cf. John 6:44; 15:16).

God chose Aaron and his sons for the Old Testament priesthood even though they were from the tribe of Levi, one of the least respected of Israel's twelve tribes because it was cursed (Gen. 49:5–7). God chose the priests from among a tribe known for its sinful violence. His choice operates by the same principle under the new covenant:

> For consider your calling, brethren, that there were not many wise according to the flesh, not many mighty, not many noble; but God has chosen the foolish things of the world to shame the wise, and God has

chosen the weak things of the world to shame the things which are strong, and the base things of the world and the despised God has chosen, the things that are not, so that He may nullify the things that are, so that no man may boast before God. (1 Cor. 1:26–29; cf. Mark 2:17; Luke 5:32; Heb. 7:28; James 2:5)

God chose the first priests from among particularly imperfect, cursed sinners—the tribe of Levi; and He still chooses His spiritual priesthood from among the ignoble, weak, and despised—ordinary sinners.

The second characteristic of the Old Testament priesthood is that God cleansed them from sin before they embarked on their duties. Leviticus 8:6–36 says,

> Then Moses had Aaron and his sons come near and washed them with water. He put the tunic on him and girded him with the sash, and clothed him with the robe and put the ephod on him; and he girded him with the artistic band of the ephod, with which he tied it to him. He then placed the breastpiece on him, and in the breastpiece he put the Urim and the Thummim. He also placed the turban on his head, and on the turban, at its front, he placed the golden plate, the holy crown, just as the Lord had commanded Moses. Moses then took the anointing oil and anointed the tabernacle and all that was in it, and consecrated them. He sprinkled some of it on the altar seven times and anointed the altar and all its utensils, and the basin and its stand, to consecrate them. Then he poured some of the anointing oil on Aaron's head and anointed him, to consecrate him. Next Moses had Aaron's sons come near and clothed them with tunics, and girded them with sashes and bound caps on them, just as the Lord had commanded Moses. Then he brought the bull of the sin offering, and Aaron and his sons laid their hands on the head of the bull of the sin offering. Next Moses slaughtered it and took the blood and with his finger put some of it around on the horns of the altar, and purified the altar. Then he poured out the rest of the blood at the base of the altar and consecrated it, to make atonement for it. He also took all the fat that was on the entrails and the lobe of the liver, and the two kidneys and their fat; and Moses offered it up in smoke on the altar. But the bull and its hide and its flesh and its refuse he burned in the fire outside the camp, just as the Lord had commanded Moses. Then he presented the ram of the burnt offering, and Aaron and his sons laid their hands on the head of the ram. Moses slaughtered it and sprinkled the blood around on the altar. When he had cut the ram into its pieces, Moses offered up the head and the pieces and the suet in smoke. After he had washed the entrails and the legs with water, Moses offered up the whole ram in smoke on the altar. It was a burnt offering for a soothing aroma; it was an offering by fire to the Lord, just as the Lord had commanded Moses. Then he presented the second ram, the ram of ordination, and Aaron and his sons laid their hands on the head of the ram. Moses slaughtered it

and took some of its blood and put it on the lobe of Aaron's right ear, and on the thumb of his right hand and on the big toe of his right foot. He also had Aaron's sons come near; and Moses put some of the blood on the lobe of their right ear, and on the thumb of their right hand and on the big toe of their right foot. Moses then sprinkled the rest of the blood around on the altar. He took the fat, and the fat tail, and all the fat that was on the entrails, and the lobe of the liver and the two kidneys and their fat and the right thigh. From the basket of unleavened bread that was before the Lord, he took one unleavened cake and one cake of bread mixed with oil and one wafer, and placed them on the portions of fat and on the right thigh. He then put all these on the hands of Aaron and on the hands of his sons and presented them as a wave offering before the Lord. Then Moses took them from their hands and offered them up in smoke on the altar with the burnt offering. They were an ordination offering for a soothing aroma; it was an offering by fire to the Lord. Moses also took the breast and presented it for a wave offering before the Lord; it was Moses' portion of the ram of ordination, just as the Lord had commanded Moses. So Moses took some of the anointing oil and some of the blood which was on the altar and sprinkled it on Aaron, on his garments, on his sons, and on the garments of his sons with him; and he consecrated Aaron, his garments, and his sons, and the garments of his sons with him. Then Moses said to Aaron and to his sons, "Boil the flesh at the doorway of the tent of meeting, and eat it there together with the bread which is in the basket of the ordination offering, just as I commanded, saying, 'Aaron and his sons shall eat it.' The remainder of the flesh and of the bread you shall burn in the fire. You shall not go outside the doorway of the tent of meeting for seven days, until the day that the period of your ordination is fulfilled; for he will ordain you through seven days. The Lord has commanded to do as has been done this day, to make atonement on your behalf. At the doorway of the tent of meeting, moreover, you shall remain day and night for seven days and keep the charge of the Lord, so that you will not die, for so I have been commanded." Thus Aaron and his sons did all the things which the Lord had commanded through Moses.

Every part of the cleansing ceremony—the washings (v. 6), the sin offering (vv. 14–17), the burnt offering (vv. 18–21), the consecration and wave offerings (vv. 22–29)—indicated the same thing: no one, not even a man from the tribe of Levi or the family of Aaron, could enter the priesthood unless God had completely cleansed him from sin.

In like fashion, when He washed His disciples' feet in the Upper Room, Jesus told Peter and the others, "If I do not wash you, you have no part with Me" (John 13:8). Paul later provided additional insight into Christ's cleansing work: "[He] gave Himself for us to redeem us from every lawless deed, and to purify for Himself a people for His own possession, zealous for good deeds. . . . He saved us, not on the basis of deeds which we have done in righteousness, but according to His mercy, by the washing of regeneration and renewing by the Holy Spirit" (Titus 2:14; 3:5). Jesus cleansed His people by His blood (Mark 14:24; Acts 20:28; Rom. 3:25; 5:9; Eph. 1:7; 2:13; Heb. 9:11–15; 1 John 1:7; Rev. 1:5) and by His Spirit (John 3:5; Eph. 1:13–14; cf. Matt. 3:11; Acts 11:16) so they could become His priests.

Third, God clothed the priests for service. Exodus 28 gives a detailed account of the priests' garments, the purpose of which verses 40–43 summarize:

> For Aaron's sons you shall make tunics; you shall also make sashes for them, and you shall make caps for them, for glory and for beauty. You shall put them on Aaron your brother and on his sons with him; and you shall anoint them and ordain them and consecrate them, that they may serve Me as priests. You shall make for them linen breeches to cover their bare flesh; they shall reach from the loins even to the thighs. They shall be on Aaron and on his sons when they enter the tent of meeting, or when they approach the altar to minister in the holy place, so that they do not incur guilt and die. It shall be a statute forever to him and to his descendants after him. (cf. Lev. 8:7–9)

The "linen breeches," or undergarments, symbolized sexual purity, and the other special garments symbolized the priests' unique call to righteousness, virtue, and godliness. God set them apart and wanted them to appear distinct from the people so everyone would know they uniquely belonged to Him (cf. Ps. 132:9, 16).

Believers today are also priests whom God has clothed in righteousness (cf. Ps. 24:5; Isa. 61:10; Rom. 4:5, 11, 22). Paul told the Corinthians, "By His doing you are in Christ Jesus, who became to us wisdom from God, and righteousness and sanctification, and redemption" (1 Cor. 1:30; cf. Rom. 14:17; 2 Cor. 5:21; Phil. 3:9).

Fourth, God through Moses anointed the Levitical priests for service. "So Moses took some of the anointing oil and some of the blood which was on the altar and sprinkled it on Aaron, on his garments, on his sons, and on the garments of his sons with him; and he consecrated Aaron, his garments, and his sons, and the garments of his sons with him" (Lev. 8:30; cf. v. 12). That anointing identified God's power and presence as resting on the priesthood; it symbolized empowerment from the Holy Spirit (cf. Ex. 30:23–25, 29; 40:13–15; 1 Sam. 16:13). In similar fashion, new covenant believers are priests who have received a divine anointing (cf. John 7:38–39; 14:26; 16:13; Acts 1:5, 8; Rom. 15:13; 1 Cor. 12:13; Titus 3:5–6). The apostle John reminded the recipients of his first letter, "But you have an anointing from the Holy One, and you all know" (1 John

2:20; cf. v. 27). God has anointed His own with the power and authority of the Holy Spirit's indwelling presence.

Because God had granted them His special authority, Israel's priests had privileges none of the other people had: they could go where no one else was allowed to go and do things no one else was permitted to do. Christians today have the similar but far greater spiritual advantage of entering God's holy presence at any time, a privilege that unbelievers never have.

A fifth characteristic of the priesthood is that God prepared its members for service. Following the ceremonies described earlier in Leviticus 8, Moses commanded Aaron and his sons, "You shall not go outside the doorway of the tent of meeting for seven days, until the day that the period of your ordination is fulfilled; for he will ordain you through seven days" (v. 33). Although outwardly everything was in order by the conclusion of Leviticus 8, before Aaron and his sons could function as priests (cf. Lev. 9:2–4, 22–23), God required them to spend a time of heart preparation (cf. Ezra 7:10; Ps. 10:17), represented by the seven days.

Paul's life illustrates for New Testament believers the principle of priestly preparation:

> But when God, who had set me apart even from my mother's womb and called me through His grace, was pleased to reveal His Son in me so that I might preach Him among the Gentiles, I did not immediately consult with flesh and blood, nor did I go up to Jerusalem to those who were apostles before me; but I went away to Arabia, and returned once more to Damascus. (Gal. 1:15–17; cf. Heb. 10:22)

After his conversion, Paul possessed all the requirements to be an exemplary spiritual priest, yet he went away for a long time of heart preparation. Ministry must not be entered into prematurely or naively (cf. the principle in 1 Tim. 3:6; 5:22). This suggests the need for preparation before service. This heart preparedness is expressed in the call to self-sacrifice in Luke 9:23–24 and Romans 12:1–2.

Sixth, God called the priests to obedience. Leviticus 10:1–3 graphically illustrates the consequences of disobedience:

> Now Nadab and Abihu, the sons of Aaron, took their respective firepans, and after putting fire in them, placed incense on it and offered strange fire before the Lord, which He had not commanded them. And fire came out from the presence of the Lord and consumed them, and they died before the Lord. Then Moses said to Aaron, "It is what the Lord spoke, saying, 'By those who come near Me I will be treated as holy, and before all the people I will be honored.'" So Aaron, therefore, kept silent.

Perhaps Nadab and Abihu used fire that was somehow unacceptable because it did not come from the sacred place ordained by God (Lev. 16:12–13). Or maybe they used incense that was not made according to the divine recipe (Ex. 30:34–38). Or they might simply have become drunk in celebrating their ordination to the priesthood (cf. Lev. 10:9–11). Whatever the case, God was greatly displeased with their conduct and destroyed them, thereby sending to all subsequent priests the sobering message that He expects full obedience from them (cf. 1 Sam. 15:22; Matt. 7:21; John 8:31; Acts 5:29). In 1:14 Peter admonished his readers concerning their call to obedience:"As obedient children, do not be conformed to the former lusts which were yours in your ignorance."

Obedient priests will have a high regard for the Word of God (Pss. 1:2; 119:42, 97, 161–162; Jer. 15:16; Titus 1:9), a genuine walk with God (Eph. 5:8–10; Col. 4:5–6; James 1:25), and an impact on sinners as messengers of the Lord (2 Cor. 5:18–21). The prophet Malachi emphasized these traits as he looked back to the early days of the priesthood:

> True instruction was in his mouth and unrighteousness was not found on his lips; he walked with Me in peace and uprightness, and he turned many back from iniquity. For the lips of a priest should preserve knowledge, and men should seek instruction from his mouth; for he is the messenger of the Lord of hosts. (Mal. 2:6–7; cf. Deut. 33:10)

Malachi's model for the faithful priest (cf. Mal. 2:5) was likely Aaron himself, who presented a stark contrast to the sinful priesthood of Malachi's day (Mal. 2:1–3) and provided a sound rationale for the prophet's rebuke of those apostates (v. 4; cf. Num. 25:7–13 and the example of Aaron's grandson, Phineas, the zealous priest who turned away the wrath of God from the people and received His covenant of peace). Malachi's portrait of the godly priest also serves as an excellent parallel for Christians (cf. Acts 1:8; Col. 2:6; 1 John 2:6; Jude 3), who are privileged to be messengers of divine truth as new covenant priests.

The Privilege of Access to God Through Spiritual Sacrifices

to offer up spiritual sacrifices acceptable to God through Jesus Christ. (2:5*c*)

The primary function of the Old Testament priests, as they ministered in the tabernacle and then the temple, was to offer animal sacrifices to God (Ex. 29:10–19; 2 Chron. 35:11). But when Christ inaugurated the new covenant, animal sacrifices were no longer necessary (Heb. 8:13; 9:11–15; 10:1–18). Now the only sacrifices remaining for the priesthood of believers **to offer up,** according to Peter, are **spiritual sacrifices.** R. C. H. Lenski, in his commentary, effectively summarizes the difference between the old and new sacrifices:

> The main task of the Old Testament priests was the offering of material, animal sacrifices, all of which pointed to Christ's great sacrifice to come. These are no longer needed since Christ offered his all-sufficient sacrifice once for all. Now there remain for God's holy priesthood only the sacrifices of praise and thanksgiving, seeing that all the treasures of God's grace are now poured out upon us through Christ. Thus Peter writes regarding all his readers: "to offer up spiritual sacrifices acceptable to God through Jesus Christ," [*anenegkai*], aorist, derived from [*anapherein*], to carry or bring up on the altar of their hearts. The aorist infinitive is effective: actually to bring. "Spiritual sacrifices" matches "spiritual house," the adjectives are placed chiastically, the repetition emphasizes the fact that everything in the relation of the readers to God through Christ is now altogether spiritual. (*The Interpretation of the Epistles of St. Peter, St. John and St. Jude* [reprint; Minneapolis: Augsburg, 1966], 90)

Obviously the Old Testament priests were to offer sacrifices that met God's requirements. The animals they offered were to be the best— blameless, spotless, and without defect (Ex. 12:5; Lev. 9:2–3; 22:19; Num. 6:14; Deut. 15:21; 17:1). They also were to offer the animal sacrifices and use incense consistent with God's requirements. (Failure to strictly follow the divine requirements cost Nadab and Abihu their lives.) New Testament priests have a corresponding responsibility. Even though they enjoy the privilege of unrestricted access to God's presence (Heb. 10:19–22), Christians still have the serious responsibility of offering spiritual sacrifices that are **acceptable to God through Jesus Christ.** Christ alone is the mediator (John 14:6; Acts 4:12; 1 Tim. 2:5–6), the One who gives believers true access to the Father (Heb. 4:14–16; 9:11–15).

During His Upper Room Discourse, Jesus told His disciples, "Whatever you ask in My name, that will I do, so that the Father may be glorified in the Son. If you ask Me anything in My name, I will do it" (John 14:13–14). Whatever His followers ask, consistent with His person, will, and kingdom plan, He will accomplish it. Likewise, whatever spiritual offerings new covenant priests present to God must be consistent with the person and work of Christ (1:15–16; 2:21–22; 1 John 2:6). They must conform to the design and method His Word reveals. All such offerings must be pure acts of sacrifice, deriving from pure motives, and focusing on the pure goal of honoring God. The New Testament sets forth seven basic, acceptable spiritual sacrifices for Christians: their bodies, their praise, their good works, their possessions, their converts, their love, and their prayers.

The apostle Paul's familiar and practical exhortation to the Romans says,

> Therefore I urge you, brethren, by the mercies of God, to present your bodies a living and holy sacrifice, acceptable to God, which is your spiritual service of worship. And do not be conformed to this world, but be transformed by the renewing of your mind, so that you may prove what the will of God is, that which is good and acceptable and perfect. (Rom. 12:1–2)

God-honoring spiritual sacrifice begins when believers offer God all their human faculties, including their minds and every part of their bodies. The unregenerate yield the members of their bodies to sin, but the redeemed yield their members as instruments of righteousness (Rom. 6:13). In Romans 12:1, Paul emphasizes that God wants the believer's body to be "a living . . . sacrifice," not a dead one. Like Abraham was willing to do with Isaac in Genesis 22:1–19, it is only when saints offer God everything they are in life, everything they possess, and everything they hope for that they truly present Him with a living sacrifice. That is the total commitment He requires of spiritual priests.

A second spiritual sacrifice that is acceptable to God is praise, or worship. "Through Him then, let us continually offer up a sacrifice of praise to God, that is, the fruit of lips that give thanks to His name" (Heb. 13:15). Offering praise to God involves much more than merely mouthing the words "Praise the Lord." It more completely entails gratefully declaring God's attributes (e.g., Pss. 83:18; 86:5, 10; 90:2; 92:15; 99:9; 102:26–27; 117:1–2; 119:68; 139:1–7; 145:1–9; Isa. 44:6; Rom. 11:33; 1 Tim. 1:17) and His works (e.g., Ex. 15:1–18, 20–21; Judg. 5:1–31; 1 Sam. 2:1–10; 2 Sam. 22:1–51; 1 Chron. 16:7–36; 29:10–15; Pss. 8:1–9; 19:1, 4; 30:1–7; 33:1–22; 66:1–20; 96:1–13; 103–107; 111:1–10; 121:1–8; 135–136; 145:10; 148–150).

Hebrews 13 commends a third and fourth acceptable sacrifice: "Do not neglect _doing good_ and _sharing_" (v. 16, emphases added)."Doing good" involves doing what is righteous and what honors God (cf. 2 Cor. 9:8; Titus 3:8; James 3:17). Any good work—whether it is reproof that restores a brother, loving and helpful action toward someone, studying God's Word, listening to the Word preached, or speaking a righteous word —is a spiritual sacrifice in Christ's name that glorifies God (2:12; Matt. 5:16; Col. 1:10; 3:17; Heb. 13:21; cf. 2 Thess. 3:13).

"Sharing," or generosity, is a specific good work the writer of

Hebrews names. It involves sacrificially giving up one's resources to meet someone else's need (Mark 12:42–44; Acts 2:45; 4:36–37; 2 Cor. 8:1–4; 9:6–7; cf. Luke 12:33; Phil. 2:30). The apostle Paul illustrated for the Philippians many of the aspects of genuine sharing and commended them for their example of true sacrificial generosity to him:

> But I rejoiced in the Lord greatly, that now at last you have revived your concern for me; indeed, you were concerned before, but you lacked opportunity. Not that I speak from want, for I have learned to be content in whatever circumstances I am. I know how to get along with humble means, and I also know how to live in prosperity; in any and every circumstance I have learned the secret of being filled and going hungry, both of having abundance and suffering need. I can do all things through Him who strengthens me. Nevertheless, you have done well to share with me in my affliction. You yourselves also know, Philippians, that at the first preaching of the gospel, after I left Macedonia, no church shared with me in the matter of giving and receiving but you alone; for even in Thessalonica you sent a gift more than once for my needs. Not that I seek the gift itself, but I seek for the profit which increases to your account. But I have received everything in full and have an abundance; I am amply supplied, having received from Epaphroditus what you have sent, a fragrant aroma, an acceptable sacrifice, well-pleasing to God. And my God will supply all your needs according to His riches in glory in Christ Jesus. (Phil. 4:10–19)

Fifth, converts—reconciled sinners—constitute another sacrifice offered to God. Paul described this spiritual sacrifice to the Romans:

> But I have written very boldly to you on some points so as to remind you again, because of the grace that was given me from God, to be a minister of Christ Jesus to the Gentiles, ministering as a priest the gospel of God, so that my offering of the Gentiles may become acceptable, sanctified by the Holy Spirit. (Rom. 15:15–16)

He saw the souls of those God had enabled him to influence savingly for Christ as **spiritual sacrifices acceptable to God.**

Christ's sacrificial death, stemming from His love for sinners, suggests a sixth spiritual sacrifice for believers—their own sacrificial love for one another (4:8; Matt. 22:37–39; Mark 12:33; John 13:34–35; Rom. 12:10; 1 Cor. 10:24; 13:4–7; Gal. 5:13; 1 Thess. 4:9; Heb. 6:10; 2 Peter 1:7; 1 John 4:7, 21; 5:1). Paul encouraged the Ephesians: "Therefore be imitators of God, as beloved children; and walk in love, just as Christ also loved you and gave Himself up for us, an offering and a sacrifice to God as a fragrant aroma" (Eph. 5:1–2). Love demonstrated in selfless humility toward one another is well pleasing to God.

Finally, the New Testament portrays prayers as suitable spiritual sacrifices (4:7; Matt. 6:6; Mark 1:35; Eph. 6:18; Phil. 4:6; 1 Tim. 2:1–2, 8; James 5:16). The apostle John, at the beginning of his vision of the seventh seal, identified the saints' prayers as offerings:

> Another angel came and stood at the altar, holding a golden censer; and much incense was given to him, so that he might add it to the prayers of all the saints on the golden altar which was before the throne. And the smoke of the incense, with the prayers of the saints, went up before God out of the angel's hand. (Rev. 8:3–4; cf. Luke 1:8–10)

Those offerings, supported by divinely supplied incense, demonstrate that God honors the properly offered prayers of believers. Prayer is often overlooked or undervalued as a spiritual sacrifice, but the ancient church had a high view of it. The church father Chrysostom, archbishop of Constantinople in the early fifth century, declared this about prayer's necessity:

> The potency of prayer hath subdued the strength of fire; it had bridled the rage of lions, hushed anarchy to rest, extinguished wars, appeased the elements, expelled demons, burst the chains of death, expanded the gates of heaven, assuaged diseases, repelled frauds, rescued cities from destruction, stayed the sun in its course, and arrested the progress of the thunderbolt. Prayer is an all-efficient panoply, a treasure undiminished, a mine which is never exhausted, a sky unobscured by clouds, a heaven unruffled by the storm. It is the root, the fountain, the mother of a thousand blessings. (Cited in E. M. Bounds, *Purpose in Prayer* [Chicago: Moody, n.d.], 19.)

Believers' spiritual privileges begin the moment the Holy Spirit draws them into a saving union with Jesus Christ. They then have access to the very presence of God as priests who are privileged to offer up a variety of spiritual sacrifices, which are really just the essential characteristics of the Christian life. One of the primary functions in the church's mission to advance God's kingdom is to stimulate its members to fulfill their priestly duties. That fulfillment, above any external representations, is the divine measure of the church's success.

Spiritual Privileges— Part 2: Security in Christ, Affection for Christ, Election by Christ, and Dominion with Christ (1 Peter 2:6–9*b*)

10

For this is contained in Scripture: "Behold, I lay in Zion a choice stone, a precious corner stone, and he who believes in Him will not be disappointed." This precious value, then, is for you who believe; but for those who disbelieve, "The stone which the builders rejected, this became the very corner stone," and, "A stone of stumbling and a rock of offense"; for they stumble because they are disobedient to the word, and to this doom they were also appointed. But you are a chosen race, a royal priesthood, (2:6–9*b*)

A university student once told a pastor, "I have decided I don't believe in God."

"All right," the pastor replied, "could you please describe for me the God you don't believe in."

The student proceeded to sketch a caricature of God, a portrait of one who was completely unfair and lacking in essential goodness.

The pastor said to him, "Well, we're in the same boat. I don't believe in that God either."

Unfortunately, not all believers would make as astute a response as the pastor did. Some people, including professed believers, view humanity's general sin-plagued circumstances and, without a true understanding of sin, conclude that God is less than good, caring, or capable. But when one consistently views things from a biblical perspective, it is clear and convincing that God is indeed good, gracious, merciful, and benevolent. That is the God the Bible portrays, as the psalmist wrote, "The goodness of God endureth continually" (Ps. 52:1, KJV; cf. Nahum 1:7). The original Saxon meaning of the word *God* was "the good," indicating that centuries ago God's name was synonymous with goodness.

God remains the infinite, inexhaustible source of all goodness, visible in the beauties of creation and experienced in His mercy toward sinners (cf. James 1:17). His ultimate and most generous goodness is the gift of redemption from sin, which culminates with eternal life. The apostle Peter wanted his readers to continue to focus on God's goodness, which has granted all spiritual privileges. In 2:4–5 he affirmed the first two privileges as union with Christ and access to Christ—fellowship expressed through believers being made a holy priesthood that offers spiritual sacrifices. In verses 6–9*b* the apostle presents four more spiritual privileges for believers to ponder: security in Christ, affection for Christ, election by Christ, and dominion with Christ.

SECURITY IN CHRIST

For this is contained in Scripture: "Behold, I lay in Zion a choice stone, a precious corner stone, and he who believes in Him will not be disappointed." (2:6)

Peter adds to the list of spiritual privileges by introducing Isaiah 28:16 with the phrase **this is contained in Scripture,** testifying to the inspiration and authority of the prophetic book. That verse is an important messianic statement (cf. Paul's reference to it in Rom. 9:33) that promised when Christ came He would be the cornerstone of God's new spiritual house, which is made up of believers (cf. Matt. 21:42; Acts 4:11; Eph. 2:19–22).

God, through the prophet, called His people to **behold** or view Messiah as the special stone that the Father Himself laid **in Zion**—Israel, and more specifically the mountain in Jerusalem (cf. 2 Sam. 5:7; 1 Kings 8:1; Pss. 48:2; 51:18; 102:21; Isa. 2:3; 4:3; 10:12; 24:23; 30:19; 52:2; Jer. 26:18; Amos 1:2; Mic. 3:12; Zeph. 3:16; Zech. 1:17). Messiah will come to that city to establish His spiritual kingdom among those who believe in Him. Christ did come to Israel, to Jerusalem, and though He was rejected and postponed His earthly rule until the future Millennium (Rev. 20:1–7), He did establish His spiritual rule over the hearts of all who believe in Him (cf. Luke 17:20–21). Figuratively, **Zion** can refer to the new covenant as Sinai does to the old covenant (cf. Gal. 4:24–25), or to heavenly blessings as Sinai does to judgment (cf. Heb. 12:18–23).

Christ is uniquely fitted for His task and thus He is **a choice stone,** God's chosen One. Peter's believing Jewish readers would have remembered that during the building of Solomon's temple, the workers prepared the stones in advance and brought them to the site (1 Kings 6:7). With the help of a careful blueprint of the temple, the craftsmen cut and shaped each stone to its perfect size and determined the exact place each was to fit. With only minor adjustments on site, those temple stones were set precisely together like parts of a large puzzle. That description is analogous to God's choosing Christ as the foundation on which to build His spiritual temple (cf. John 10:16; 1 Cor. 3:9, 16–17; 1 Tim. 3:15; Heb. 3:6) made up of believers in the Messiah Jesus, divinely prepared (elect) from before the creation of the world (2 Tim. 1:9; Rev. 13:8; 17:8).

Christ is not only a living and choice stone, but he is also **a precious corner stone.** The Greek word translated **precious** (*entimon*) means "unequaled in value," "costly," or "irreplaceable." Christ is irreplaceable because He is the cornerstone, the most important stone in any building. The word translated **corner stone** (*akrogōniaios*) denotes a chief cornerstone and describes the stone that sets all the proper angles for the building. It is like the building's plumb line in that it sets the horizontal and vertical lines of the rest of the building; it also establishes the precise symmetry of the entire edifice. To ensure the perfect precision of God's spiritual house, the main cornerstone had to be flawless. The only one who could set all the angles of God's house was the living, perfectly prepared cornerstone, Jesus Christ (Matt. 21:42; 1 Cor. 3:11; Eph. 1:22; Col. 1:18; cf. John 1:14; Phil. 2:9; Col. 1:15; Heb. 1:3; 7:26–28; 8:6).

From this reality issues one of the great privileges for all who believe: when they place their trust in Christ they **will not be disappointed.** The word rendered **disappointed** (*kataischunthē*) denotes being deceived in some confidence, or placing hope in someone and having that hope dashed. Those who sincerely believe in Christ as Lord and Savior will never know any disappointment from Him (Rom. 10:11–13; cf. Jer. 17:7–8). Instead they will be forever secure in Him (John 10:3–4, 14, 27–28; Rom. 8:16; Eph. 1:13–14; Phil. 1:6; 2 Tim. 1:12; James 1:12; 1 John 5:20; cf. Heb. 4:15–16).

Because Jesus Christ is the perfect, exact, precise One on whom God has built His church, all the lines coming from Him in every direction complete the perfect temple of God. No one is ever out of alignment. No one ever falls from the structure. It all fits exactly and permanently together (cf. Eph. 4:16). So here is one analogy that fittingly illustrates believers' security.

The prophet Isaiah, centuries before Christ's incarnation, declared that Israel could have supreme confidence in the security God provided:

> "Fear not, for you will not be put to shame; and do not feel humiliated, for you will not be disgraced; but you will forget the shame of your youth, and the reproach of your widowhood you will remember no more. For your husband is your Maker, whose name is the Lord of hosts; and your Redeemer is the Holy One of Israel, who is called the God of all the earth. . . . For the mountains may be removed and the hills may shake, but My lovingkindness will not be removed from you, and My covenant of peace will not be shaken," says the Lord who has compassion on you. (Isa. 54:4–5, 10; cf. 50:7; 54:1–3)

The apostle Paul expressed the same kind of confidence to the Romans. In view of believers' election (Rom. 8:28–30), he posed a series of rhetorical questions (vv. 31–35) and summarized his answer to those questions with this majestic, poetic expression of praise to God for believers' security:

> But in all these things we overwhelmingly conquer through Him who loved us. For I am convinced that neither death, nor life, nor angels, nor principalities, nor things present, nor things to come, nor powers, nor height, nor depth, nor any other created thing, will be able to separate us from the love of God, which is in Christ Jesus our Lord. (vv. 37–39)

The nineteenth-century church historian and hymnologist John Mason Neale's translation of the words of a seventh-century Latin hymn majestically and succinctly summarizes the essence of verse 6:

> Christ is made the sure foundation, Christ the head and cornerstone, chosen of the Lord and precious, binding all the Church in one, holy Zion's help forever, and her confidence alone.

AFFECTION FOR CHRIST

This precious value, then, is for you who believe; but for those who disbelieve, "The stone which the builders rejected, this became the very corner stone," and, "A stone of stumbling and a rock of offense"; for they stumble because they are disobedient to the word, and to this doom they were also appointed. (2:7–8)

Because of the **precious value** believers place in Jesus Christ, they possess a genuine affection for Him, which is in itself another spiritual privilege. This benefit is the joy of loving Jesus. He told the Jews, "If God were your Father, you would love Me" (John 8:42). In the Upper Room Discourse, He told the apostles, "He who has My commandments and keeps them is the one who loves Me; and he who loves Me will be loved by My Father, and I will love him and will disclose Myself to him" (John 14:21; cf. vv. 23–24). Later in the Discourse Jesus told them, "For the Father Himself loves you, because you have loved Me and have believed that I came forth from the Father" (16:27). Believing in Christ and loving Him are therefore inseparable privileges (1 Cor. 8:3; 1 Peter 1:8; 1 John 5:1).

Only those **who believe** manifest a surpassing love for Christ (cf. Matt. 10:37; 2 Cor. 5:14). In utter contrast to that, however, **those who disbelieve** (such as the unbelieving Jewish leaders) do not and will not love Christ. Quoting Psalm 118:22, Peter asserted that the Jews were **the builders** who **rejected** Christ (**the stone**). As discussed in the previous chapter of this volume, the Jews examined but did not accept the One who **became the very corner stone** (cf. 2:4). To them Jesus was worthless as God's cornerstone because He did not fit their preconceived idea of what the Messiah needed to be like (cf. Matt. 13:54–57; Luke 4:20–30; 6:6–11). Such rejection was tragic but not surprising, as Peter indicated when he quoted Isaiah 8:14–15 (NKJV), which predicted that Messiah would be considered **"A stone of stumbling and a rock of offense"** to most of the Jews, as Isaiah himself was (v. 12). **A stone of stumbling** was any stone that people could trip over as they moved down a road, and **a rock of offense** was the rock bed they could be crushed against after they fell over the other stone. In Peter's symbolism, the Jews threw away the true cornerstone, then wound up falling over it to be finally crushed in judgment by the same rock (Luke 20:17–18; cf. Matt. 13:41).

Verse 8 makes clear that those who reject Christ **stumble** and suffer divine judgment **because they are disobedient to the word.** Unbelievers receive the exact judgment their sinful choice demands— **to this doom they were also appointed**—because they do not believe and obey the gospel. God does not actively destine people to unbelief; but He does appoint judgment (**doom**) on every unbeliever (John 3:18, 36; 8:24; 2 Thess. 1:6–9; Heb. 3:19; 4:11). God judges unbelievers as a consequence of their lack of love for Him, their disobedience to His Word, and their refusal to believe in Him. Paul told the Corinthians, "If anyone does not love the Lord, he is to be accursed" (1 Cor. 16:22).

ELECTION BY CHRIST

But you are a chosen race, (2:9a)

To underscore the contrasting eternal destinies of unbelievers and believers, Peter began this verse with a strong adversative, **but.** Unlike unbelievers who, because of their rejection of Christ, are destined for eternal destruction, believers **are a chosen race.** They are a spiritual people elect by God Himself.

The apostle again drew his terminology from an Old Testament passage:

> For you are a holy people to the Lord your God; the Lord your God has chosen you to be a people for His own possession out of all the peoples who are on the face of the earth. The Lord did not set His love on you nor choose you because you were more in number than any of the peoples, for you were the fewest of all peoples, but because the Lord loved you and kept the oath which He swore to your forefathers, the Lord brought you out by a mighty hand and redeemed you from the house of slavery, from the hand of Pharaoh king of Egypt. Know therefore that the Lord your God, He is God, the faithful God, who keeps His covenant and His lovingkindness to a thousandth generation with those who love Him and keep His commandments. (Deut. 7:6–9)

He identifies those who believe in Christ as **chosen,** just as God had chosen Israel for a special purpose within His redemptive plan (cf. Isa. 43:21). As discussed in chapter 1 of this volume, it is crucial for Christians to understand that their salvation is based on the sovereign, electing purposes of God. Scripture explicitly and implicitly makes that unmistakable (John 15:16; Acts 13:48; Rom. 9:13–16; 11:5; 1 Cor. 1:9; Eph. 1:3–5; 1 Thess. 1:4; 2 Thess. 2:13–14; 2 Tim. 1:9; 2:10; Rev. 13:8; 17:8; 20:15); and election is the great privilege from which all other spiritual privileges derive.

Scripture suggests at least five superlatives related to God's sovereign choice to save certain sinners. First, election is absolutely the solitary decision of God, thus it is the most pride-crushing truth in God's Word. It devastates humans' pride since nothing in their salvation derives from any merit in them—it is all of God (cf. Jonah 2:9; John 1:12–13; Eph. 2:8–9). Second, because election is totally by divine grace, it is the most God exalting doctrine (cf. Rom. 9:23; Eph. 1:6–7; 2:7; 2 Thess. 2:13). Third, election is the most holiness-promoting doctrine. Because God set His love on believers before the world began, they should be consumed with gratitude and a passion to obey Him no matter what (cf. Deut. 11:13; Josh. 24:24; Rom. 6:17; 7:25). Fourth, because God's election is eternal and unchangeable, it is the most strength-giving doctrine in the Bible. Therefore it affords believers genuine peace no matter what circumstances they face (cf. Ps. 85:8; John 14:27; 1 Cor. 14:33; Eph. 2:14–15; Col. 1:20; 3:15; 2 Thess. 3:16). Finally, election is the most joy-producing spiritual privilege because it is the surest hope believers have in the midst of a sinful world (cf. 1:21; Eph. 4:4; Col. 1:5, 23; 1 Thess. 5:8; Heb. 7:19).

DOMINION WITH CHRIST

a royal priesthood, (2:9*b*)

Peter employed a remarkable symbol when he combined in one metaphor references to royalty and the priesthood. The concept of **a royal priesthood** comes from Exodus 19:6, where God through Moses told Israel, "You shall be to Me a kingdom of priests and a holy nation." The sad fact is, however, that Israel forfeited her privilege of priestly dominion because of her apostasy and rejection of the Messiah (cf. John 12:37–48; Rom. 10:16–21; 11:7–10; Heb. 3:16–19). But all those who believe in Jesus as Messiah and trust in Him alone for salvation receive the privilege of becoming royal priests (Rev. 5:10).

Two primary elements constitute the image of the **royal priesthood.** First, the priests serve the King by having access to His holy presence, into which they come offering spiritual sacrifices to Him (see the previous chapter of this volume), and second, the priests rule with the King in His kingdom.

Basileion (**royal**) generally describes a royal residence or palace (cf. Luke 7:25), but it can also refer to a sovereignty or monarchy. Peter used the term here to convey the general idea of royalty. The spiritual house he mentioned in verse 5 turns out to be a royal house, the dominion of a royal family. Believers are a ruling priesthood, literally "a royal house of priests." The apostle John wrote, "Blessed and holy is the one who has a part in the first resurrection; over these the second death has no power, but they will be priests of God and of Christ and will reign with Him for a thousand years" (Rev. 20:6; cf. Luke 22:29–30; Rev. 3:21).

The only one who can establish such a royal house is Jesus Christ. He is both King (Isa. 9:7; Zech. 9:9; Matt. 2:2; Luke 1:33; John 1:49; 12:12–15; 18:36–37; 19:19; Rev. 19:16) and Priest (Ps. 110:4; Heb. 4:15). The writer of Hebrews sets forth the uniqueness of Christ's royal priesthood:

> For it is evident that our Lord was descended from Judah, a tribe with reference to which Moses spoke nothing concerning priests. And this is clearer still, if another priest arises according to the likeness of Melchizedek, who has become such not on the basis of a law of physical requirement, but according to the power of an indestructible life. For it is attested of Him, "You are a priest forever according to the order of Melchizedek." (Heb. 7:14–17; cf. Ps. 110:4; Heb. 5:6; 6:20)

Melchizedek was the Old Testament model for the royal priest (Gen. 14:18–20) and he foreshadowed Christ, the ultimate and perfect royal priest. Like Melchizedek, He did not inherit the priesthood through the priestly line; rather God appointed Him as the sinless royal priest who transcended the Levitical system (Heb. 3:1–2; 5:4–5; 7:11, 14, 16; 8:1–2, 6), fulfilled the old covenant law (Ps. 40:7–8; Matt. 5:17–18; Heb. 10:11–14), and offered Himself as the new covenant sacrifice for sin (Matt. 20:28; John 1:29; Heb. 2:17; 7:27; 9:25–26; 10:12). Because salvation unites believers with Christ, they too become royal priests.

Christians' privilege to rule with Christ includes some practical implications:

> Does any one of you, when he has a case against his neighbor, dare to go to law before the unrighteous and not before the saints? Or do you not know that the saints will judge the world? If the world is judged by you, are you not competent to constitute the smallest law courts? Do you not know that we will judge angels? How much more matters of this life? So if you have law courts dealing with matters of this life, do you appoint them as judges who are of no account in the church? (1 Cor. 6:1–4)

Since believers will rule with Christ in His kingdom, they must be sufficiently qualified—without secular assistance or oversight—to settle relatively small earthly disputes between themselves. Paul further said they will have dominion over those heavenly realms God assigns to them. No one, not even an angel, can stand between them and God.

All this is cause for unleashing a doxology. As believers contemplate all their spiritual privileges, from union with Christ to security in Him to dominion with Him, they ought to be transported into unbounded praise and worship. Anything less betrays sinful indifference to these great privileges.

Spiritual Privileges— Part 3: Separation to Christ, Possession by Christ, Illumination in Christ, Compassion from Christ, and Proclamation of Christ (1 Peter 2:9c–10)

11

a holy nation, a people for God's own possession, so that you may proclaim the excellencies of Him who has called you out of darkness into His marvelous light; for you once were not a people, but now you are the people of God; you had not received mercy, but now you have received mercy. (2:9c–10)

The Gospel narratives repeatedly emphasize the cost of following Jesus Christ. In Luke 9:23–26, Jesus declared to all who would be His disciples,

> If anyone wishes to come after Me, he must deny himself, and take up his cross daily and follow Me. For whoever wishes to save his life will lose it, but whoever loses his life for My sake, he is the one who will save it. For what is a man profited if he gains the whole world, and loses or forfeits himself? For whoever is ashamed of Me and My words, the Son of Man will be ashamed of him when He comes in His glory, and the glory of the Father and of the holy angels. (cf. Matt. 5:19–20; 7:13–14, 21; John 6:53–58, 60)

The regenerate understand there are sacrifices and costs involved in living the Christian life. Jesus gave two analogies of discipleship that illustrate the necessity of assessing the cost:

Whoever does not carry his own cross and come after Me cannot be
My disciple. For which one of you, when he wants to build a tower, does
not first sit down and calculate the cost to see if he has enough to complete it? Otherwise, when he has laid a foundation and is not able to
finish, all who observe it begin to ridicule him, saying, "This man began
to build and was not able to finish." Or what king, when he sets out to
meet another king in battle, will not first sit down and consider
whether he is strong enough with ten thousand men to encounter the
one coming against him with twenty thousand? Or else, while the other
is still far away, he sends a delegation and asks for terms of peace. So
then, none of you can be My disciple who does not give up all his own
possessions. (Luke 14:27–33)

Various other passages in the epistles also emphasize the cost of discipleship (5:8–9; Rom. 12:1–2; 1 Cor. 9:24–27; Eph. 6:10–18; Phil. 3:7–14;
1 Tim. 6:11–12; 2 Tim. 2:1–10; Heb. 12:1–2, 7–11; James 1:21–25; 1 John
2:15–17; cf. Rom. 13:11–14; Gal. 6:1–2; Eph. 5:15–21).

However in 2:4–10 the apostle Peter looks not at the cost and
duty of following Christ but at the rich kaleidoscope of spiritual privileges He gives to those who have embraced that cost. Peter holds the
jewels of redemption to the light of God's grace and reveals wonderful
patterns of spiritual blessings that belong to all who are in Christ. The
theme of spiritual privilege, from union with Christ to dominion with
him, is a familiar New Testament emphasis. In Romans 9:22 Paul wrote
that God wanted to demonstrate His wrath and display His power, thus
He patiently endured the vessels of wrath (unbelievers). Verse 23 then
explains the reason for God's approach: "He did so to make known the
riches of His glory upon vessels of mercy, which he prepared beforehand
for glory." God wanted to pour out on believers the riches of His glory
(2 Cor. 4:6; cf. Eph. 1:12; Phil. 2:11), all the privileges that accompany salvation. Such spiritual riches are promised both now and in the future (cf.
Rom. 11:12; Eph. 1:7–8; 2:7; 3:8, 16; Phil. 4:19).

As Peter concluded his survey of the glories of believers' spiritual
privileges, he listed five additional advantages Christians possess: separation to Christ, possession by Christ, illumination in Christ, compassion
from Christ, and proclamation of Christ.

SEPARATION TO CHRIST

a holy nation (2:9c)

As noted in previous chapters of this volume, Peter continued to
refer to the Old Testament in support of the privileges God has granted

believers. Here he alludes to Exodus 19:6 ("you shall be to Me . . . a holy nation") when he declares that believers are separated to Christ as **a holy nation.** The word **nation** translates *ethnos,* which means "people," as an ethnic group (Luke 7:5; 23:2; John 11:48, 50–52; Acts 2:5; 10:22; Rev. 5:9). **Holy** (*hagios*) means "separate" or "set apart." It was common in the Old Testament to call God's covenant people a holy nation (cf. Lev. 19:2; 20:26; Deut. 7:6; Isa. 62:12). However, because of sin and unbelief Israel forfeited (Deut. 4:27; 28:64; Ezek. 16:59; Hos. 9:17; Zech. 7:14; Rom. 11:17, 20) her great privilege (Gen. 12:2–3; Deut. 33:29; Rom. 3:1–2; 9:4–5) of being God's unique people. But what was a tragedy for Israel became a blessing for believing Gentiles (cf. Rom. 9–11). Israel will not enjoy again the privilege of being God's holy people until the nation finally turns in faith to the Messiah (cf. Ezek. 36:25–31; Rom. 11:24, 26).

God sets apart believers primarily to have a relationship with Him, and service to Him flows out of that relationship. Various Scripture references indicate that at the new birth believers are set apart to God from the condemnation of sin and the world (cf. Ps. 4:3; Rom. 6:4–6; 1 Cor. 6:11; 2 Cor. 5:17; 6:17; 2 Tim. 2:21; Heb. 2:11). Years earlier at the Jerusalem Council, Peter said this:

> Brethren, you know that in the early days God made a choice among you, that by my mouth the Gentiles would hear the word of the gospel and believe. And God, who knows the heart, testified to them giving them the Holy Spirit, just as He also did to us; and He made no distinction between us and them, cleansing their hearts by faith. (Acts 15:7–9; cf. Heb. 10:10, 14)

Thus sanctification (cleansing from sin) is inherently bound up in salvation (cf. 1 Cor. 1:30). And sanctification entails two important aspects: Christians' position before God and their progressive, practical pattern of holy living. That is why earlier in his letter Peter could pronounce his readers holy (1:1–2) and yet in 1:16 urge them to be holy. In the positional aspect of sanctification, God recognizes believers as separated from the penalty of sin, but in the progressive and practical aspect of sanctification, He through the Holy Spirit assists them in living more and more holy lives, thus working out the reality of their position in their conduct (cf. Rom. 6:4; 8:1–2; Gal. 5:16–23; Eph. 4:20–24; Phil. 2:12–13; 1 Thess. 4:3).

The Acts narrative in several places reinforces the truth that sanctification is inseparable from justification. Paul told the Ephesian elders, "And now I commend you to God and to the word of His grace, which is able to build you up and to give you the inheritance among all those who are sanctified" (Acts 20:32). The apostle identified the saved by the phrase "all those who are sanctified." Likewise in his defense before Agrippa, Paul rehearsed part of what God had told him at his conversion on the Damascus Road, that He was sending him to the Gentiles "to open their eyes so that they may turn from darkness to light and from the dominion of Satan to God, that they may receive forgiveness of sins and an inheritance among those who have been sanctified by faith in Me" (Acts 26:18). There again "sanctified" was used to describe all those whom God had forgiven and given heavenly inheritance.

Positional sanctification makes Christians **a holy nation** before God because His own righteousness is imputed to them. And practically, they are progressing in holiness by the work of the Spirit (cf. 2 Cor. 3:18).

Possession by Christ

a people for God's own possession, (2:9*d*)

At Sinai God promised the Israelites, "If you will indeed obey My voice and keep My covenant, then you shall by My own possession among all the peoples" (Ex. 19:5; cf. Deut. 7:6–7; 14:2; 26:18; Mal. 3:17). Again, that foreshadowed the truth of Peter's statement that Christians are now **a people for God's own possession.**

The Greek term rendered **possession** (*peripoiēsis*) means "to purchase," "to acquire for a price" (cf. Eph. 1:14). Believers belong to God because He bought them at the ultimate price (1:18–19; cf. 1 Cor. 6:20; 7:23; Heb. 13:12; Rev. 5:9). As Paul reminded Titus, that price was "Christ Jesus, who gave Himself for us [Christians] to redeem us from every lawless deed, and to purify for Himself a people for His own possession" (Titus 2:13–14; cf. Acts 20:28; 1 Cor. 6:20).

God sovereignly elected all who believe, and by Christ's sacrifice on the cross paid the price to redeem them (2:24; 3:18; Rom. 3:25–26; 5:8–11; Col. 1:20–22; 1 Tim. 2:6; 1 John 4:10), and the Holy Spirit brought them to new life through conviction of sin and faith in the Savior. Therefore all believers belong to the God who redeemed them.

One of the stanzas of George Wade Robinson's nineteenth-century gospel song, "I Am His and He Is Mine," expresses this privilege well:

> His forever, only His—Who the Lord and me shall part? Ah, with what a rest of bliss Christ can fill the loving heart! Heav'n and earth may fade and flee, first-born light in gloom decline, but while God and I shall be, I am His and He is mine.

ILLUMINATION IN CHRIST

who has called you out of darkness into His marvelous light;
(2:9*f*)

Throughout history, the unregenerate world has faced two kinds of darkness: intellectual and moral. Intellectual darkness is ignorance—the inability to see and know the truth, whereas moral darkness is immorality—the inability to see and do what is right (Ps. 58:3; Jer. 17:9; Rom. 8:7–8; 1 Cor. 2:14; Eph. 4:17–19). The **darkness** Peter refers to here is the second type—the sinful state of unbelievers who are trapped in the spiritual darkness of Satan (Eph. 2:1–2; 2 Tim. 2:25–26; 1 John 5:19), the prince of darkness. Such moral darkness is pervasive in its scope and profound in its depth (Ps. 143:2; Eccl. 7:20; Isa. 53:6; Rom. 3:9–12). Unbelievers are children born in the darkness. They not only *walk* in the darkness, they *love* the darkness. According to Jesus,

> This is the judgment, that the Light has come into the world, and men loved the darkness rather than the Light, for their deeds were evil. For everyone who does evil hates the Light, and does not come to the Light for fear that his deeds will be exposed. (John 3:19–20)

However, Peter reminded his readers that Christ had sovereignly, powerfully, and effectually **called** them **out of darkness.** Almost always in the epistles when *kaleō* (**called**) or the related words *klēsis* and *klētos* appear they indicate God's effectual call to salvation (e.g., 1:15; 2:21; 5:10; Rom. 1:6–7; 8:28, 30; 9:24; 1 Cor. 1:9, 24; Gal. 1:6, 15; Eph. 4:4; 2 Tim. 1:9; 2 Peter 1:3; Jude 1). That saving call is a recurring theme, close to the apostle's heart in this letter (cf. 1:1, 15; 2:21; 3:9; 5:10).

The positive side of Christ's calling sinners **out of darkness** is that they are also thereby called **into His marvelous light.** Paul expressed this spiritual privilege to the Colossians: "For He rescued us from the domain of darkness, and transferred us to the kingdom of His beloved Son" (Col. 1:13). When believers receive Christ's light, He illuminates their minds so they can discern the truth, and He changes their souls so they are able to apply it (cf. Ps. 119:105, 130; 1 Cor. 2:15–16; 2 Cor. 4:4; 2 Peter 1:19). They receive both the intellectual light of God's truth and the righteous desires to obey it, neither of which they had before conversion.

COMPASSION FROM CHRIST

for you once were not a people, but now you are the people of God; you had not received mercy, but now you have received mercy. (2:10)

Peter drew an analogy from the prophet Hosea when he introduced the next spiritual privilege for believers, compassion from Christ:

> Then she conceived again and gave birth to a daughter. And the Lord said to him, "Name her Lo-ruhamah, for I will no longer have compassion on the house of Israel, that I would ever forgive them. But I will have compassion on the house of Judah and deliver them by the Lord their God, and will not deliver them by bow, sword, battle, horses or horsemen." When she had weaned Lo-ruhamah, she conceived and gave birth to a son. And the Lord said, "Name him Lo-ammi, for you are not My people and I am not your God." Yet the number of the sons of Israel will be like the sand of the sea, which cannot be measured or numbered; and in the place where it is said to them, "You are not My people," it will be said to them, "You are the sons of the living God." (Hos. 1:6–10)

According to that passage, there was coming a time when the Jews would no longer receive God's compassion. This was directly fulfilled in the judgment that came on the Northern Kingdom at the hands of the Assyrians (722 B.C.). But there will also be a future time (v. 10), during the Millennium, when He will have compassion on "the sons of Israel" and Judah in saving uncounted numbers of them (cf. Isa. 61:4–6; Jer. 16:14–15; Ezek. 37:20–22; Rom. 11:26–27).

In principle, Peter applied to the church—particularly to its Gentile members—the prophet's words concerning the Jews (cf. Hos. 2:23; Rom. 9:22–26). As unbelievers, the Gentiles knew no compassion from Christ—they **once were not a people.** But now they had become the **people of God,** because they had **received** His **mercy. Mercy** is synonymous with compassion and essentially involves God's sympathy with sinners' misery and His withholding from them the just punishment for their sins.

Scripture discusses two kinds of divine mercy. First there is God's general mercy (cf. Ps. 145:9; Lam. 3:22), which is evident in His providential to all creation (Pss. 36:7; 65:9–13; Matt. 5:44–45; Acts 14:14–17; 17:23–28; cf. Rom. 1:20). Common mercy displays God's patient pity and forbearing compassion toward sinners (3:20; Pss. 86:15; 103:8; 2 Peter 3:9; cf. Luke 13:6–9) because He had every right, in view of their sin, to destroy them all. Instead, at the present time He mercifully chooses not to unleash all the disastrous consequences that humanity's sinfulness deserves (cf. Gen. 9:8–11). But eventually God's general mercy will expire and people will feel the full consequences of sin (Matt. 24:4–22; Rev. 6:7–8; 8:7–9:19; 14:14–19; 16:1–21; 18:1–24; 19:17–21; 20:7–15; cf. Gen. 6:3; Isa. 27:11; Jer. 44:22).

Second, there is the divine, saving mercy displayed toward the elect, which is the **mercy** Peter referred to. They receive not only God's common mercy in this life, but also His saving mercy for the life to come (Dan. 7:18; John 14:2; 2 Tim. 4:8; Rev. 2:7; 7:16–17; 21:1–7). The elect, although no more inherently deserving than anyone else, receive God's forgiveness for their sins and His deliverance from eternal condemnation—all according to His sovereign and loving purposes (Rom. 8:28–30; Eph. 1:4; 2 Tim. 1:9; Titus 1:2; cf. Ps. 65:4; Rom. 9:15–16; James 2:5).

Christ's compassion, or **mercy,** for believers is a spiritual privilege that beggars language (cf. Pss. 57:10; 59:16–17; 103:11; 136:1–9). It rescues believers from judgment in hell and grants them an eternal inheritance in heaven (1:4; Ps. 37:18; Acts 20:32; 26:18; Eph. 1:11, 14, 18; Col. 1:12; 3:24; Heb. 9:15), which is why Paul called God "the Father of mercies" (2 Cor. 1:3; cf. Rom. 9:23; Titus 3:5). The words of one writer appropriately express how all Christians should feel toward such divine compassion:

> When all Thy mercies, O my God,
> My rising soul surveys,
> Transported with the view I'm lost,
> In wonder, love, and praise.

PROCLAMATION OF CHRIST

so that you may proclaim the excellencies of Him (2:9e)

Finally, God has provided His kaleidoscope of spiritual privileges for believers for one overarching purpose: that they **may proclaim the excellencies of** Christ. There is no higher privilege than to be a herald for the gospel.

Proclaim (*exangeilēte*) is from a Greek word that appears only here in the New Testament. It means "to publish", or "advertise" and to do so in the sense of telling something otherwise unknown. That which is generally unknown and which Peter encourages believers to publicize is **the excellencies of** Christ, the Savior. **Excellencies** (*aretas*) can imply the ability to perform powerful, heroic deeds. Contrary to what it might indicate in English, the term refers more to those kinds of actions than to some intrinsic royal attributes or qualities. Christians have the distinct privilege of telling the world that Christ has the power to accomplish the extraordinary work of redemption (Acts 1:8; 2:22; 4:20; 5:31–32; Rev. 15:3; cf. Pss. 66:3, 5, 16; 71:17; 73:28; 77:12, 14; 104:24; 107:22; 111:6–7; 118:17; 119:46; 145:4; John 5:36; 10:25 regarding God's amazing acts).

For God to choose undeserving sinners as His representatives and use them to gather other sinners to Himself is a privilege beyond all expectation. It caused Paul to write:

> I thank Christ Jesus our Lord, who has strengthened me, because He considered me faithful, putting me into service, even though I was formerly a blasphemer and a persecutor and a violent aggressor. Yet I was shown mercy because I acted ignorantly in unbelief; and the grace of our Lord was more than abundant, with the faith and love which are found in Christ Jesus. It is a trustworthy statement, deserving full acceptance, that Christ Jesus came into the world to save sinners, among whom I am foremost of all. Yet for this reason I found mercy, so that in me as the foremost, Jesus Christ might demonstrate His perfect patience as an example for those who would believe in Him for eternal life. Now to the King eternal, immortal, invisible, the only God, be honor and glory forever and ever. Amen. (1 Tim. 1:12–17)

Godly Living
(1 Peter 2:11–12)

12

Beloved, I urge you as aliens and strangers to abstain from fleshly lusts which wage war against the soul. Keep your behavior excellent among the Gentiles, so that in the thing in which they slander you as evildoers, they may because of your good deeds, as they observe them, glorify God in the day of visitation. (2:11–12)

In one important respect, today's culture is similar to that of Peter's time—unbelievers from all quarters constantly attack and criticize Christianity. Such opponents of the gospel are often vocal in their criticism and many have succeeded in capturing the major economic, social, and educational institutions of Western society. Christian apologist Wilbur M. Smith at the end of World War II correctly observed that the world has opposed Christianity ever since Jesus' day and believers should not expect things to be different today:

> At first one would think that a religion which exalts and seeks to follow the only perfect and righteous man who has ever lived on this earth, who never harmed anyone, whose words delivered from superstition and fear, whose works redeemed from pain, and demons, and death, and hunger, whose life was as a great shaft of light shot into the murky

darkness of the Roman world, in that sensual and skeptic century, who died because He loved us, and who always sought to bring men into communion with God, to bestow upon them eternal life and a home in heaven, one would have thought that such a character, and the religion which His life and work on earth established, would have been welcomed with open arms the first moment it was announced, and would, by its very message, the good works which flowed from it, and the hope which it established, never know opposition, or attack, or denunciation, except from the demons of hell, and Satan, who is a liar and murderer from the beginning. But such has not been its history. In fact, the New Testament, itself, from the records of the birth of our Lord down to the end of St. John's vision of the era of anarchy and persecution to come, testifies in the most startling way to the fact that Christ Himself was most viciously and constantly attacked, that His apostles suffered the same opposition, and that it was predicted by these very apostles that Christianity would continue so to suffer, down to the end of this age. (*Therefore, Stand* [Grand Rapids: Baker, 1945], 1)

It is often the scandalous conduct of so-called Christians that provides fuel for the critics' and skeptics' vicious accusations, whereas the godliness of true Christians does the most to silence Christianity's opponents. Commentator Robert Leighton wrote,

When a Christian walks irreprovably, his enemies have no where to fasten their teeth on him, but are forced to gnaw their own malignant tongues. As it secures the godly, thus to stop the lying mouths of foolish men, so it is as painful to them to be thus stopped, as muzzling is to beasts, and it punishes their malice. And this is a wise Christian's way, instead of impatiently fretting at the mistakes or wilful miscensures of men, to keep still on his calm temper of mind, and upright course of life, and silent innocence; this, as a rock, breaks the waves into foam that roar about it. (*Commentary on First Peter* [reprint; Grand Rapids: Kregel, 1972], 195)

The nineteenth-century Scottish preacher Alexander MacLaren commented, "The world takes its notions of God, most of all, from the people who say that they belong to God's family. They read us a great deal more than they read the Bible. They see us; they only hear about Jesus Christ" (*First and Second Peter and First John* [New York: Eaton and Maines, 1910], 105). In the Sermon on the Mount, Jesus told all who would seriously follow Him, "Let your light shine before men in such a way that they may see your good works, and glorify your Father who is in heaven" (Matt. 5:16). That is the essence of what Peter in this passage exhorted his readers to do: live godly lives, which is the single most effective foundation for making the gospel attractive and believable.

The recipients of the apostle's letter needed some motivation to persevere in their evangelism in the midst of the stressful and difficult trials and persecutions they were encountering. Peter called his readers to fortify their testimonies with two crucial aspects of righteous living: a personal, godly discipline that is inward and private, and a personal, godly deportment that is outward and public.

GODLY INNER DISCIPLINE

Beloved, I urge you as aliens and strangers to abstain from fleshly lusts which wage war against the soul. (2:11)

Peter began his exhortation by addressing his readers as **beloved,** which implied that they, as objects of God's immeasurable love, had a duty to obey the One who loved them. On that basis he could **urge** (*parakaleō,* "to beseech" [KJV] or "to encourage," as in Rom. 12:1) them to reciprocate God's love by living for Him.

Peter further identified his audience **as aliens and strangers,** which reminded them that they were not truly members of the world's society. Paul wrote, "For our citizenship is in heaven, from which also we eagerly wait for a Savior, the Lord Jesus Christ" (Phil. 3:20). As spiritual **aliens,** believers must shun the things of this world (1 John 2:15–17; cf. Mark 4:19; John 12:25; 15:19; Rom. 12:2; Col. 2:8, 20; James 1:27; 1 John 5:4). **Aliens** (*paroikous*) literally means "alongside the house." The word came to denote any person who lives in a country not his own and is therefore a foreigner. The term fits Christians who do not belong to this world's system but live alongside those who do.

Peter also used the term **strangers** (*parepidēmous*), which is a synonym for **aliens.** It refers to a visitor (the KJV renders the word "pilgrims") who travels through a country and perhaps makes a brief stay there. The writer of Hebrews reminded believers: "For here we do not have a lasting city, but we are seeking the city which is to come" (13:14; cf. 11:13–16).

Since Christians are not part of the world, they must **abstain from fleshly lusts** (cf. Rom. 8:5–9, 12–13; 13:14; Gal. 5:13, 16–17). Even though regeneration produces a new disposition with holy longings, that new life force remains incarcerated within the old, unredeemed human flesh, precipitating an ongoing battle between the spirit and the flesh. Nevertheless, believers are no longer slaves of unrighteousness, and sin is not their master—they are free from its dominant and exclusive power. The command to **abstain** signifies that saints have the ability by the new life and the indwelling Spirit to restrain the lustful flesh, even in a postmodern culture dominated by sensuality, immorality, and moral relativism.

The term **fleshly lusts** is not limited to sexual immorality, but rather encompasses the evils of humanity's sinful nature. The apostle Paul warned the Galatians, "Now the deeds of the flesh are evident, which are: immorality, impurity, sensuality, idolatry, sorcery, enmities, strife, jealousy, outbursts of anger, disputes, dissensions, factions, envying, drunkenness, carousing, and things like these" (Gal. 5:19–21). When they see Christ, believers' unredeemed humanness will be redeemed (cf. Rom. 8:23).

Peter, by use of the phrase **which wage war against the soul,** intensified his discussion of **fleshly lusts.** In the Greek, **which** indicates that it is the character of such lusts and cravings to **wage war** against the new heart God has created within the **soul** of every believer. Even Paul found himself in the midst of intense struggle that every Christian experiences:

> For we know that the Law is spiritual, but I am of flesh, sold into bondage to sin. For what I am doing, I do not understand; for I am not practicing what I would like to do, but I am doing the very thing I hate. But if I do the very thing I do not want to do, I agree with the Law, confessing that the Law is good. So now, no longer am I the one doing it, but sin which dwells in me. For I know that nothing good dwells in me, that is, in my flesh; for the willing is present in me, but the doing of the good is not. For the good that I want, I do not do, but I practice the very evil that I do not want. But if I am doing the very thing I do not want, I am no longer the one doing it, but sin which dwells in me. I find then the principle that evil is present in me, the one who wants to do good. For I joyfully concur with the law of God in the inner man, but I see a different law in the members of my body, waging war against the law of my mind and making me a prisoner of the law of sin which is in my members. (Rom. 7:14–23; cf. Gal. 5:17–18)

Wage war is a strong term that generally means to carry out a long-term military campaign. It implies not just antagonism but a relentless, malicious aggression. Since it takes place in **the soul,** it is a kind of civil war. Joined with the concept of **fleshly lusts,** the image is of an army of lustful terrorists waging an internal search and destroy mission to conquer the soul of the believer.

Prior to conversion, all sinners live under the dominance of fleshly lust:

> And you were dead in your trespasses and sins, in which you formerly walked according to the course of this world, according to the prince of the power of the air, of the spirit that is now working in the sons of disobedience. Among them we too all formerly lived in the lusts of our flesh, indulging the desires of the flesh and of the mind, and were by

nature children of wrath, even as the rest. (Eph. 2:1–3; cf. 4:25–28; 5:8–11; Col. 3:5–11)

Once saved, however, God commands believers to abstain from being driven by lust:

> Do not love the world nor the things in the world. If anyone loves the world, the love of the Father is not in him. For all that is in the world, the lust of the flesh and the lust of the eyes and the boastful pride of life, is not from the Father, but is from the world. The world is passing away, and also its lusts; but the one who does the will of God lives forever. (1 John 2:15–17; cf. 2 Cor. 6:16–7:1)

The key to abstaining from fleshly desires and defeating fleshly temptations lies in walking in the Spirit's power (Gal. 5:16), and exercising a godly discipline (1 Cor. 9:27; 2 Cor. 7:1). The battle is won or lost on the inside, as James reports,

> Let no one say when he is tempted, "I am being tempted by God"; for God cannot be tempted by evil, and He Himself does not tempt anyone. But each one is tempted when he is carried away and enticed by his own lust. Then when lust has conceived, it gives birth to sin; and when sin is accomplished, it brings forth death. (James 1:13–15)

This follows James's call in verse 12 for the same kind of behavior Peter speaks of: "Blessed is a man who perseveres under trial; for once he has been approved, he will receive the crown of life which the Lord has promised to those who love Him."

GODLY OUTWARD DEPORTMENT

Keep your behavior excellent among the Gentiles, so that in the thing in which they slander you as evildoers, they may because of your good deeds, as they observe them, glorify God in the day of visitation. (2:12)

In order to effectively evangelize, Christians' transformed inner lives must be visible to the outside world. Peter thus commanded his readers to **keep** their **behavior** (daily conduct) at a high level. **Excellent** translates a word (*kalēn*) rich and varied in significance, usually meaning "beautiful of outward form." At least six other English words and expressions offer insight into its meaning: lovely, fine, winsome, gracious, fair to look at, and noble. The term connotes the loveliest kind of visible goodness. **Gentiles** (*ethnos*) refers to "nations," or the unsaved world (cf. Luke 2:32; Rom. 2:14; 15:9–12, 16; 1 Cor. 5:1; 12:2, KJV; Gal. 3:8; 1 Thess. 4:5; 3 John 7). If Peter's readers were to witness effectively **among the Gentiles,** it was essential for them to manifest behavior beyond reproach.

In the first century, the label **evildoers** (*kakopoiōn*) brought to mind many of the specific accusations pagans made against Christians—that they rebelled against the Roman government, practiced cannibalism, engaged in incest, engaged in subversive activities that threatened the Empire's economic and social progress, opposed slavery, and practiced atheism by not worshiping Caesar or the Roman gods (cf. Acts 16:18–21; 19:19, 24–27).

In the very **thing in which they slander,** believers must live the opposite way, proving unbelievers wrong and demonstrating the validity of the gospel (Matt. 5:16; Titus 3:8). On the platform of such credibility, personal witness has an impact. Observing the exceptional life of such believers, some will believe, be saved, and **glorify God in the day of visitation.**

Day of visitation is an Old Testament concept (cf. Judg. 13:2–23; Ruth 1:6; 1 Sam. 3:2–21; Pss. 65:9; 106:4; Zech. 10:3) referring to occasions when God visited mankind for either judgment or blessing. The prophet Isaiah wrote of divine visitation for the purpose of judgment: "And what will ye do in the day of visitation, and in the desolation which shall come from far? to whom will ye flee for help? and where will ye leave your glory?" (Isa. 10:3, KJV; cf. 23:17). On the other hand, Exodus 3:2–10 tells of God's visitation to announce Israel's eventual deliverance from Egypt, which would be a blessing for His people. Similarly, Jeremiah prophesied God's visitation to deliver the Jews from Babylon: "For thus says the Lord, 'When seventy years have been completed for Babylon, I will visit you and fulfill My good word to you, to bring you back to this place'" (Jer. 29:10; cf. 27:22). The Old Testament records several other instances in which God visited people for blessing and judgment.

Usually in the New Testament **visitation** indicates blessing and redemption. In the immediate aftermath of John the Baptist's birth, his father Zacharias prophesied, "Blessed be the Lord God of Israel, for He has visited us and accomplished redemption for His people" (Luke 1:68; cf. v. 78; 7:16). On the other hand, concerning the destruction of Jerusalem in A.D. 70, Jesus said, "They will level you to the ground and your children within you, and they will not leave in you one stone upon another, because you did not recognize the time of your visitation" (Luke 19:44). Because the Jews rejected Christ's visitation of salvation, it turned to a visitation of judgment (cf. Matt. 11:20–24; 21:37–43; Rom. 11:17, 20; 1 Thess. 2:14–16).

God's redemption is inherent in Peter's reference to the **day of visitation.** The apostle used the expression to show that because of observation of Christian virtue and good works in the lives of believers, some would be privileged to **glorify God** when He also visited them with salvation.

A stirring twentieth-century example of how godly living can influence the salvation of unbelievers comes from the events in a Japanese prisoner of war camp in the Philippines during World War II. American missionaries Herb and Ruth Clingen and their young son were prisoners of the Japanese for three years. Herb's diary told how his family's captors tortured, murdered, and starved to death many of the camp's other inmates. The prisoners particularly hated and feared the camp commandant, Konishi. Herb described one especially diabolical plan Konishi forced on the Clingens and their fellow inmates near the end of the war:

> Konishi found an inventive way to abuse us even more. He *increased* the food ration but gave us *palay*—unhusked rice. Eating rice with its razor-sharp outer shell would cause intestinal bleeding that would kill us in hours. We had no tools to remove the husks, and doing the job manually—by pounding the grain or rolling it with a heavy stick—consumed more calories than the rice would supply. It was a death sentence for all internees. (Herb and Ruth Clingen, "Song of Deliverance," *Masterpiece* magazine [Spring 1989], 12; emphasis in original)

But divine providence spared the Clingens and others in February 1945 when Allied forces liberated the prison camp. That prevented the commandant from carrying out his plan of shooting and killing all surviving prisoners. Years later the Clingens "learned that Konishi had been found working as a grounds keeper at a Manila golf course. He was put on trial for his war crimes and hanged. Before his execution he professed conversion to Christianity, saying he had been deeply affected by the testimony of the Christian missionaries he had persecuted" ("Song of Deliverance," 13). Effective evangelism flows from the power of a righteous life.

Submission to Civil Authority (1 Peter 2:13–17)

13

Submit yourselves for the Lord's sake to every human institution, whether to a king as the one in authority, or to governors as sent by him for the punishment of evildoers and the praise of those who do right. For such is the will of God that by doing right you may silence the ignorance of foolish men. Act as free men, and do not use your freedom as a covering for evil, but use it as bond-slaves of God. Honor all people, love the brotherhood, fear God, honor the king. (2:13–17)

As citizens of heaven, Christians submit wholly to divine authority, but the potential misapplication of that truth is that they can become indifferent and even disdainful toward the world in which they live, thereby forfeiting many opportunities for positive testimony. Believers' detachment from the world must be balanced by proper respect for and humble submission to all the legitimate institutions of human authority.

Stephen, the first Christian martyr, is a compelling role model of godly submission to the dictates of earthly authority. The New Testament introduces him as "a man full of faith and of the Holy Spirit" (Acts 6:5). Acts 6:8–14 describes the background events leading up to his major confrontation with the Jewish authorities:

And Stephen, full of grace and power, was performing great wonders and signs among the people. But some men from what was called the Synagogue of the Freedmen, including both Cyrenians and Alexandrians, and some from Cilicia and Asia, rose up and argued with Stephen. But they were unable to cope with the wisdom and the Spirit with which he was speaking. Then they secretly induced men to say, "We have heard him speak blasphemous words against Moses and against God." And they stirred up the people, the elders and the scribes, and they came up to him and dragged him away and brought him before the Council. They put forward false witnesses who said, "This man incessantly speaks against this holy place and the Law; for we have heard him say that this Nazarene, Jesus, will destroy this place and alter the customs which Moses handed down to us."

Stephen had an amazing reaction to those unjust, distorted accusations: "All who were sitting in the Council saw his face like the face of an angel" (6:15). He then answered the high priest's terse question, "Are these things so?" (7:1), with a comprehensive, Spirit-inspired, pointed evangelistic message (7:2–53). Stephen's convicting words infuriated the Jewish leaders, but his reaction to their violent rejection of his person and preaching was one of godly submission and humble, unwavering faith:

Now when they heard this, they were cut to the quick, and they began gnashing their teeth at him. But being full of the Holy Spirit, he gazed intently into heaven and saw the glory of God, and Jesus standing at the right hand of God; and he said, "Behold, I see the heavens opened up and the Son of Man standing at the right hand of God." But they cried out with a loud voice, and covered their ears and rushed at him with one impulse. When they had driven him out of the city, they began stoning him; and the witnesses laid aside their robes at the feet of a young man named Saul. They went on stoning Stephen as he called on the Lord and said, "Lord Jesus, receive my spirit!" Then falling on his knees, he cried out with a loud voice, "Lord, do not hold this sin against them!" Having said this, he fell asleep. Saul was in hearty agreement with putting him to death. (Acts 7:54–8:1)

The way Stephen humbly submitted to injustice and persecution undoubtedly made some contribution to Saul of Tarsus's bring transformed from hateful persecutor to faithful apostle of Jesus Christ.

In this passage, full of imperatives, six elements of Christian submission to authority emerge: the command for submission, the motive for submission, the extent of submission, the reason for submission, the attitude of submission, and the application of submission.

THE COMMAND FOR SUBMISSION

submit yourselves (2:13a)

Although they are not ultimately under human authority, God still expects believers to submit to the human institutions He ordained. He wants them to demonstrate godly character qualities (cf. 2 Peter 1:5–7) and a genuine concern for society—a concern that seeks peace (3:11; cf. Ps. 34:14; Matt. 5:9; Rom. 14:19; James 3:18) and desires to prevent trouble and crime (cf. Rom. 12:14–21). To that end Christians will obey all laws and respect all authority, unless called upon to do something God forbids or not do something He commands (Acts 4:19; 5:27–29).

Submit yourselves (*hupotassō*) is a military expression literally meaning "to arrange in formation under the commander." The Old Testament supports the principle of submission to authority (cf. Deut. 17:14–15; 1 Sam. 10:24; 2 Kings 11:12; 1 Chron. 29:24). Proverbs 24:21–22 says, "My son, fear the Lord and the king; do not associate with those who are given to change, for their calamity will rise suddenly, and who knows the ruin that comes from both of them?" Submission to rulers is right because God appoints them; therefore there is no place for supporting "those who are given to change," rebels who might seek to overthrow the government.

Through the prophet Jeremiah, the Holy Spirit declared the following:

> Thus says the Lord of hosts, the God of Israel, to all the exiles whom I have sent into exile from Jerusalem to Babylon, "Build houses and live in them; and plant gardens and eat their produce. Take wives and become the fathers of sons and daughters, and take wives for your sons and give your daughters to husbands, that they may bear sons and daughters; and multiply there and do not decrease. Seek the welfare of the city where I have sent you into exile, and pray to the Lord on its behalf; for in its welfare you will have welfare." For thus says the Lord of hosts, the God of Israel, "Do not let your prophets who are in your midst and your diviners deceive you, and do not listen to the dreams which they dream. For they prophesy falsely to you in My name; I have not sent them," declares the Lord. For thus says the Lord, "When seventy years have been completed for Babylon, I will visit you and fulfill My good word to you, to bring you back to this place. For I know the plans that I have for you," declares the Lord, "plans for welfare and not for calamity to give you a future and a hope. Then you will call upon Me and come and pray to Me, and I will listen to you. You will seek Me and find Me when you search for Me with all your heart. I will be found by you," declares the Lord, "and I will restore your fortunes and will gather

you from all the nations and from all the places where I have driven you," declares the Lord, "and I will bring you back to the place from where I sent you into exile." (Jer. 29:4–14)

Although that passage was primarily a message to the Jews concerning their conduct while captives in Babylon, it has overtones for Christians, who should promote the welfare of their society and government while waiting for their eternal home (cf. John 14:2–3; Heb. 4:9–10; 11:13–16; Rev. 21:1–4).

Nearly a decade before Peter wrote his letter, the apostle Paul had already taught concerning submission to government:

> Every person is to be in subjection to the governing authorities. For there is no authority except from God, and those which exist are established by God. Therefore whoever resists authority has opposed the ordinance of God; and they who have opposed will receive condemnation upon themselves. For rulers are not a cause of fear for good behavior, but for evil. Do you want to have no fear of authority? Do what is good and you will have praise from the same; for it is a minister of God to you for good. But if you do what is evil, be afraid; for it does not bear the sword for nothing; for it is a minister of God, an avenger who brings wrath on the one who practices evil. (Rom. 13:1–4)

Although Peter and Paul both lived in the openly sinful, decadent Roman Empire—a society infamous for evil (homosexuality, infanticide, government corruption, abuse of women, immorality, violence), neither apostle offered any exemption by which believers were free to defy civil authority. Jesus Himself had commanded, "Render to Caesar the things that are Caesar's" (Matt. 22:21).

Throughout history and presently there have been various violations of ordinances, acts of civil disobedience, insurrections, revolutions, and different subversive attempts to overthrow governments—all in the name of Christianity. Scripture nowhere condones such actions. On the contrary, the biblical command is simple—**submit** to civil authority, regardless of its nature (see the discussion of 2:18 in the next chapter of this volume). Even unreasonable, evil, harsh rulers and oppressive systems are far better than anarchy. And all forms of government, from dictatorships to democracies, are filled with evil because they are led by fallen sinners. Still, civil authority is from God, though the individual rulers may be godless.

THE MOTIVE FOR SUBMISSION

for the Lord's sake (2:13b)

Peter stated the motivation for submitting to authority as clearly as he did the basic command to submit. It is **for the Lord's sake,** making it obligatory to submit, as with all divinely inspired commands. Christians obey because they desire to honor the Lord (cf. Ps. 119:12–13, 33; Acts 13:48; 1 Cor. 10:31).

Believers actually obey earthly authority to honor God's sovereign authority (cf. Pss. 2:8; 9:20; 22:28; 46:10; 47:8; 66:7; 72:11; 83:18; 96:10; 113:4). Of God's sovereignty over all human authority, Robert Culver wrote:

> God alone has sovereign rights. . . . Democratic theory is no less unscriptural than divine right monarchy. By whatever means men come to positions of rulership—by dynastic descent, aristocratic family connection, plutocratic material resources, or by democratic election, "there is no power but of God" (Rom. 13:1). Furthermore, civil government is an instrument, not an end. Men are proximate ends, but only God is ultimate end. The state owns neither its citizens nor their properties, minds, bodies, or children. All of these belong to their Creator-God, who has never given to the state rights of eminent domain. (*A Biblical View of Civil Government* [Chicago: Moody, 1974], 47)

Believers also submit in order to imitate Christ's example of obedient submission to His Father. Verse 23 of this chapter reveals the Lord's model behavior: "while being reviled, He did not revile in return; while suffering, He uttered no threats, but kept entrusting Himself to Him who judges righteously." Christ lived under the unjust and unrighteous rule of the Jewish and Roman authorities, yet He never opposed their right to rule. He denounced the sins of the Jewish leaders (Matt. 16:11–12; 23:13–33), but He never sought to overturn their authority. Likewise, Jesus never led demonstrations against Roman slavery and abuse of justice or engaged in any act of civil disobedience. He did not object even when those authorities unjustly tried Him and crucified Him (Matt. 26:62–63; Mark 15:3–5; John 19:8–11). Instead of being preoccupied with political and social reform, Christ always focused on matters pertaining to His kingdom (Matt. 4:17; Mark 1:15; Luke 5:31–32; 19:10; Acts 1:3; cf. Matt. 11:28–30).

God is pleased when unsaved people associate Christians with spiritual virtue, righteousness, love, graciousness, humility, and the gospel of salvation (Phil. 2:14–15; cf. Prov. 4:18) rather than protests against human institutions. Paul also had the single-minded, undivided commitment required for believers as they minister: "When I came to you, brethren, I did not come with superiority of speech or of wisdom, proclaiming to you the testimony of God. For I determined to know nothing among you except Jesus Christ, and Him crucified" (1 Cor. 2:1–2). He would only engage in the spiritual war for the souls of sinners, as explained in the following text:

> For though we walk in the flesh, we do not war according to the flesh, for the weapons of our warfare are not of the flesh, but divinely powerful for the destruction of fortresses. We are destroying speculations and every lofty thing raised up against the knowledge of God, and we are taking every thought captive to the obedience of Christ. (2 Cor. 10:3–5)

The "fortresses" are described as "speculations." The Greek is *logismes,* meaning "ideologies." The real war saints must wage is against the deadly ideas, ungodly ways of thinking, and any religious or philosophical systems "raised up against" the truth of God. All unbiblical systems of thought that hold people captive must be smashed by the Word of truth and captive sinners set free to obey Jesus Christ. When the Lord said, "My kingdom is not of this world" (John 18:36), He defined the sphere of believers' calling and duty—to focus ministry efforts only in matters related to His spiritual and eternal rule.

THE EXTENT OF SUBMISSION

to every human institution, whether to a king as the one in authority, or to governors as sent by him for the punishment of evildoers and the praise of those who do right. (2:13c–14)

In reviewing the foundational and detailed teaching on believers' responsibility to civil authority, one can see three essential purposes for government:

> For rulers are not a cause of fear for good behavior, but for evil. Do you want to have no fear of authority? Do what is good and you will have praise from the same; for it is a minister of God to you for good. But if you do what is evil, be afraid; for it does not bear the sword for nothing; for it is a minister of God, an avenger who brings wrath on the one who practices evil. (Rom. 13:3–4)

Those purposes—the restraint of evil, promotion of the public good, and punishment of wrongdoing—stemming from the overarching truth that God establishes all authority (Rom. 13:1), explain why Peter's command extends **to every human institution.** To maintain peace and order in society, God has ordained them all; thus to limit or make exception to the command to submit to **every** authority would condone disobedience and disrespect for God's plan. (For a more complete, biblical analysis of government's purpose, see chapter 3 of my book, *Why Government Can't Save You* [Nashville: Word, 2000].)

The Greek word *ktisis* ("foundation"), from which **institution** derives, always occurs in the New Testament in connection with God's creative activities (cf. Rom. 1:20, 25; 8:39; 2 Cor. 5:17; Gal. 6:15; Col. 1:15, 23; 2 Peter 3:4). (In fact, the second lexical meaning generally given for *ktisis* is "the act of creating," or "creation.") God has created all the foundations of **human** society—work, family, and the government. Peter designated society human not as to its origin, but as to its function or sphere of operation. The apostle's intent was therefore to command submission **to every human institution** because every one is God ordained. Believers submit to civil authorities, to employers (2:18; Eph. 6:5; Col. 3:22), and in the family (Eph. 5:21–6:2). In the latter two areas, the motive is also for the Lord's sake (Eph. 5:22; 6:1, 5–6; Col. 3:18, 20, 22–24).

That command does not exclude authorities who make bad or unjust decisions. The Old Testament acknowledges the existence of corrupt rulers (cf. Dan. 9:11–12; Mic. 7:2–3) but recognizes God has the prerogative to judge them. Despite the evil that occurs because authorities are fallen and institutions are imperfect, believers must trust that God still exercises sovereign and perfectly wise rule over societies and nations (cf. Gen. 18:25).

Peter elaborates on the extent of believers' submission by noting that it applies to all levels of authority. Breaking authority down to specific categories, he speaks of the highest level of **the one in authority,** the **king.** Obviously this recognizes the legitimacy of one-man rule as a form of God-ordained government. Monarchy, or its parallel, dictatorship, is a form God uses in the world. It was especially a challenge for believers in Peter's time to obey this part of the command because the king (caesar) was a deranged tyrant, the Roman emperor Nero. But even he was divinely ordained for his leadership role of carrying out the fundamental purposes of government. **Governors** is a term referring to a lower level of authority (cf. Luke 2:1–2; 3:1; Acts 7:10), officials under the king who might be **sent by him.**

Peter echoed Paul when he said that ruling officials have been designed by God first **for the punishment of evildoers.** Years earlier, at His betrayal and arrest, Jesus taught Peter the lesson that the responsibility for capital punishment (Gen. 9:5–6) is required for and reserved to government:

Then they came and laid hands on Jesus and seized Him. And behold, one of those who were with Jesus reached and drew out his sword, and struck the slave of the high priest and cut off his ear. Then Jesus said to him, "Put your sword back into its place; for all those who take up the sword shall perish by the sword. Or do you think that I cannot appeal to My Father, and He will at once put at My disposal more than twelve legions of angels?" (Matt. 26:50–53; cf. John 18:10–11)

Jesus was affirming the Roman government's right to use the sword against Peter if he used it on anyone. Only the government has been given that right to bear the sword to punish lawbreakers (Rom. 13:4). Therefore believers must never engage in acts of vigilante justice.

On the other hand, God has appointed civil officials for **the praise of those who do right.** The authorities generally reward good citizenship with fair and favorable treatment (Rom. 13:3; cf. Gen. 39:2–4; 41:37–41; Prov. 14:35; Dan. 1:18–21). The role of government is clear—to create fear that restrains evil, punish those who do wrong, and protect those who do right.

The Reason for Submission

For such is the will of God that by doing right you may silence the ignorance of foolish men. (2:15)

The reason Christians ought to submit to every authority is quite clear and basic—such conduct stops the mouths of the gospel's critics. It is **the will of God** for Christians to engage in **doing right** by respecting authority, so as to **silence the ignorance of foolish men.**

The word rendered **silence** (*phimoun*) means "to restrain, muzzle, or make speechless" (cf. Matt. 22:12, 34; Mark 1:25; 4:39; Luke 4:35). It denotes the gagging or stopping of someone's mouth so as to render that person incapable of response.

The word Peter used for **ignorance** (*agnōsian*) means more than merely a lack of knowledge. If that meaning were all he wanted to convey, he would have used a form of *agnoia*. But *agnōsian* indicates a willful, hostile rejection of the truth (cf. 1 Cor. 15:34). It is a settled lack of spiritual perception that the apostle further characterized as **foolish** (*aphronōn*). That term means "senseless, without reason," and may express a lack of mental sanity.

Integrity, impeccable moral fiber, and purity of life are all effective character tools to muzzle the enemies of Christianity. Paul commanded Titus to tell this to the new believers on Crete:

Remind them to be subject to rulers, to authorities, to be obedient, to be ready for every good deed, to malign no one, to be peaceable, gentle, showing every consideration for all men. For we also once were foolish ourselves, disobedient, deceived, enslaved to various lusts and pleasures, spending our life in malice and envy, hateful, hating one another. (Titus 3:1–3)

Such virtuous conduct and good citizenship is especially necessary for church leaders. One of the qualifications to be an elder is that the man "must have a good reputation with those outside the church, so that he will not fall into reproach and the snare of the devil" (1 Tim. 3:7; cf. Titus 1:6). That kind of unimpeachable testimony, even before those who reject the gospel, silences enemies and enables the saving power of Christ to be manifest.

THE ATTITUDE OF SUBMISSION

Act as free men, and do not use your freedom as a covering for evil, but use it as bondslaves of God. (2:16)

The right attitude is imperative if submissive Christians are to maintain their credibility among unbelievers. They display that right attitude when they **act as free men.** They must realize that, as a result of Christ's redemptive work (cf. 1:18–19), they are free from sin's condemnation (Rom. 6:7, 18; 8:1–2), the Law's penalty (Gal. 3:13), Satan's bondage (cf. Rom. 16:20; Col. 1:13; Heb. 2:14; 1 John 2:13; 4:4), the world's control (cf. 1 Cor. 9:19; Gal. 4:3–5; 5:1; Col. 2:20), and death's power (Rom. 8:38–39; 1 Cor. 15:54–56).

But Peter cautions those who are free in Christ to **not use** that spiritual **freedom as a covering for** the **evil** of not submitting to rulers (cf. 1 Cor. 8:9; 10:32; Gal. 5:13). **Covering** indicates placing a mask or veil over something; **evil** (*kakias*) is a term that means "baseness" and arises from vengeance, bitterness, hostility, and disobedience (Gen. 6:5; 8:21; Prov. 6:14; Isa. 13:11; Matt. 12:35; 15:19; John 3:19–20; 7:7; Rom. 1:29–30; Gal. 1:4).

A truly righteous attitude will cause Christians to use their freedom as **bondslaves of God.** Paul exhorted the Corinthians, "For he who was called in the Lord while a slave, is the Lord's freedman; likewise he who was called while free, is Christ's slave" (1 Cor. 7:22). Their freedom has delivered them from the bondage of serving sin into the privilege of being slaves of righteousness.

Do you not know that when you present yourselves to someone as slaves for obedience, you are slaves of the one whom you obey, either of sin resulting in death, or of obedience resulting in righteousness? But thanks be to God that though you were slaves of sin, you became obedient from the heart to that form of teaching to which you were committed, and having been freed from sin, you became slaves of righteousness. I am speaking in human terms because of the weakness of your flesh. For just as you presented your members as slaves to impurity and to lawlessness, resulting in further lawlessness, so now present your members as slaves to righteousness, resulting in sanctification. For when you were slaves of sin, you were free in regard to righteousness. Therefore what benefit were you then deriving from the things of which you are now ashamed? For the outcome of those things is death. But now having been freed from sin and enslaved to God, you derive your benefit, resulting in sanctification, and the outcome, eternal life. (Rom. 6:16–22)

"Slave" (from the same word as **bondslaves**) defined the lowest level of servitude in the Greco-Roman world, yet for believers it described the joyous freedom to be servants of Christ and do what was right rather than what was wrong (cf. John 15:15; Gal. 5:13; Eph. 6:6; Titus 2:14). Freedom in Christ and citizenship in the kingdom of God in no way permit believers to abuse or disregard the standards of conduct God has established for them on earth.

THE APPLICATION OF SUBMISSION

Honor all people, love the brotherhood, fear God, honor the king. (2:17)

Peter summarized his demand for submission to all authority—his citizenship theology—into four practical, applicatory dimensions of life. First, believers are to **honor all people.** Every person was created in God's image (Gen. 1:26; 9:6*b*; James 3:9*b*; cf. Ps. 100:3*a*) and therefore is due some degree of respect. In the first century, most people viewed slaves as nonpersons with no rights. But Peter told his readers they were not to treat anyone that way (cf. Col. 4:1). Christians are not to discriminate against any class of people because of race, nationality, or economic status (cf. Rom. 2:11; Eph. 6:8–9; James 2:1–9). That does not mean they ignore different levels of authority and social structure or that they engage in a mindless tolerance for everyone's conduct, but it does mean they show proper respect for everyone as individuals made in the image of God.

The second application is that believers **love the brotherhood.**

They are to show the world that they **love** their fellow believers. The apostle John also wrote of this principle a number of times:

> A new commandment I [Christ] give to you, that you love one another, even as I have loved you, that you also love one another. By this all men will know that you are My disciples, if you have love for one another. (John 13:34–35; cf. 15:12)

> This is His commandment, that we believe in the name of His Son Jesus Christ, and love one another, just as He commanded us. (1 John 3:23; cf. 4:7, 21)

> Whoever believes that Jesus is the Christ is born of God, and whoever loves the Father loves the child born of Him. (1 John 5:1)

Third, believers are to **fear God** (Deut. 13:4; Ps. 111:10; Prov. 9:10; Eccl. 12:13; Heb. 12:9, 28; Rev. 15:4), which includes trusting Him in all circumstances (Ps. 36:7; Prov. 3:5; 14:26; 16:20; Isa. 26:4), no matter how difficult they are (cf. 5:7; Ps. 34:22; Prov. 29:25; Nah. 1:7; 2 Cor. 1:10; 2 Tim. 1:12). Christians must worship Him as the sovereign One (Matt. 6:33–34; Rom. 8:28; 11:33) who orchestrates everything according to His perfect will (1 Sam. 2:7–8; Ps. 145:9; Prov. 19:21). Such **fear** also encourages believers to submit to all earthly authorities, because they have the utmost respect for the One who has commanded them to do so.

Finally, believers are to **honor the king,** which brings the issue full circle, back to the basic command of verse 13. This application again echoes Paul's teaching in Romans 13, particularly verse 7, "Render to all what is due them: tax to whom tax is due; custom to whom custom; fear to whom fear; honor to whom honor." As God's agent for carrying out the purposes of government, the monarch, president, premier, or prime minister is worthy of the respect God mandates.

When believers obey the principles of this passage, it gives genuine credibility to their faith. Submission to civil authority is an implementation of what might be called "evangelistic citizenship," along the lines of Jesus' declaration in the Sermon on the Mount:

> You are the light of the world. A city set on a hill cannot be hidden; nor does anyone light a lamp and put it under a basket, but on the lampstand, and it gives light to all who are in the house. Let your light shine before men in such a way that they may see your good works, and glorify your Father who is in heaven. (Matt. 5:14–16)

Submission in the Workplace (1 Peter 2:18–21*a*)

14

Servants, be submissive to your masters with all respect, not only to those who are good and gentle, but also to those who are unreasonable. For this finds favor, if for the sake of conscience toward God a person bears up under sorrows when suffering unjustly. For what credit is there if, when you sin and are harshly treated, you endure it with patience? But if when you do what is right and suffer for it you patiently endure it, this finds favor with God. For you have been called for this purpose, (2:18–21*a*)

Today postmodern culture seems to cling to only one basic moral obligation, the sacred duty to provide equal rights for everyone. No one any longer speaks of sacrifice or privilege—only rights, such as ethnic rights, reproductive rights, immigrant rights, homosexual rights, and workplace rights.

If people do not receive what they think personal freedom should give them, they express their grievances in the form of walkouts, strikes, boycotts, and political rebellions. Such protesters are usually motivated by the belief that everyone is equal in every way and entitled to exactly the same things as everyone else.

In the workplace, employees voice their grievances over a lack of "rights" through work slowdowns, "sick-outs," protests, or all-out strikes that prevent management from conducting business. Management sometimes responds with lockouts or even termination of the striking employees. Job actions on occasion do result in salary increases and improved benefits for employees, or perhaps a compromise agreement that benefits both sides in the long run.

However, the focus on "rights" in the workplace, whatever the results, is incongruous with the Christian life. Believers are to be concerned instead with obedience and submission to God's will. When they obey and submit to their superiors, as He commands, they prove that their real hope is in the world to come. David provides an excellent illustration of the submissive attitude God seeks in the context of serving under someone. Once God chose him to replace Saul as king, Saul sought to kill David. First Samuel describes what underlay Saul's hatred:

> It happened as they were coming, when David returned from killing the Philistine [Goliath], that the women came out of all the cities of Israel, singing and dancing, to meet King Saul, with tambourines, with joy and with musical instruments. The women sang as they played, and said, "Saul has slain his thousands, And David his ten thousands." Then Saul became very angry, for this saying displeased him; and he said, "They have ascribed to David ten thousands, but to me they have ascribed thousands. Now what more can he have but the kingdom?" Saul looked at David with suspicion from that day on. Now it came about on the next day that an evil spirit from God came mightily upon Saul, and he raved in the midst of the house, while David was playing the harp with his hand, as usual; and a spear was in Saul's hand. Saul hurled the spear for he thought, "I will pin David to the wall." But David escaped from his presence twice. (1 Sam. 18:6–11; cf. 19:9–10)

In the face of such hostility, David rested in the divine promise that he would be king. Therefore he did not need to demand his right to rule; neither did he insist on vengeance against King Saul. Nevertheless Saul continued to seek David's life.

> Then Saul took three thousand chosen men from all Israel and went to seek David and his men in front of the Rocks of the Wild Goats. He came to the sheepfolds on the way, where there was a cave; and Saul went in to relieve himself. Now David and his men were sitting in the inner recesses of the cave. The men of David said to him, "Behold, this is the day of which the Lord said to you, 'Behold; I am about to give your enemy into your hand, and you shall do to him as it seems good to you.'" Then David arose and cut off the edge of Saul's robe secretly. It came about afterward that David's conscience bothered him because he had cut off the edge of Saul's robe. So he said to his men,

"Far be it from me because of the Lord that I should do this thing to my lord, the Lord's anointed, to stretch out my hand against him, since he is the Lord's anointed." David persuaded his men with these words and did not allow them to rise up against Saul. And Saul arose, left the cave, and went on his way. Now afterward David arose and went out of the cave and called after Saul, saying, "My lord the king!" And when Saul looked behind him, David bowed with his face to the ground and prostrated himself. David said to Saul, "Why do you listen to the words of men, saying, 'Behold, David seeks to harm you'? Behold, this day your eyes have seen that the Lord had given you today into my hand in the cave, and some said to kill you, but my eye had pity on you; and I said, 'I will not stretch out my hand against my lord, for he is the Lord's anointed.' Now, my father, see! Indeed, see the edge of your robe in my hand! For in that I cut off the edge of your robe and did not kill you, know and perceive that there is no evil or rebellion in my hands, and I have not sinned against you, though you are lying in wait for my life to take it. May the Lord judge between you and me, and may the Lord avenge me on you; but my hand shall not be against you." (1 Sam. 24:2–12)

Unbelievably, from a human standpoint, David again refused to harm Saul, even though he had another opportunity to strike back at the king. First Samuel 26:6–12 chronicles what happened:

Then David said to Ahimelech the Hittite and to Abishai the son of Zeruiah, Joab's brother, saying, "Who will go down with me to Saul in the camp?" And Abishai said, "I will go down with you." So David and Abishai came to the people by night, and behold, Saul lay sleeping inside the circle of the camp with his spear stuck in the ground at his head; and Abner and the people were lying around him. Then Abishai said to David, "Today God has delivered your enemy into your hand; now therefore, please let me strike him with the spear to the ground with one stroke, and I will not strike him the second time." But David said to Abishai, "Do not destroy him, for who can stretch out his hand against the Lord's anointed and be without guilt?" David also said, "As the Lord lives, surely the Lord will strike him, or his day will come that he dies, or he will go down into battle and perish. The Lord forbid that I should stretch out my hand against the Lord's anointed; but now please take the spear that is at his head and the jug of water, and let us go." So David took the spear and the jug of water from beside Saul's head, and they went away, but no one saw or knew it, nor did any awake, for they were all asleep, because a sound sleep from the Lord had fallen on them.

The apostle Paul more specifically articulated the divine principle of granting respect and not seeking retaliation: "Never pay back evil for evil to anyone. Respect what is right in the sight of all men. If possible, so far as it depends on you, be at peace with all men. Never take your own revenge, beloved, but leave room for the wrath of God, for it is written, 'Vengeance is Mine, I will repay,' says the Lord" (Rom. 12:17–19; cf. Luke 6:32–35; 1 Cor. 7:20–21,24). As discussed in the previous chapter of this volume, neither Peter, Paul, nor any of the New Testament writers ever advocated that subordinates should rise up against their superiors.

In this section, Peter moves from politics to work and commands believers who are servants or slaves to submit to their masters. In broader terms, that means Christian employees are to respect and obey their employers. The apostle issued his command as both a mandate and a motive for submission.

THE MANDATE FOR SUBMISSION

Servants, be submissive to your masters with all respect, not only to those who are good and gentle, but also to those who are unreasonable. (2:18)

The workforce in the Roman world consisted of slaves, and the way they were treated was wide-ranging. Some masters loved their slaves as trusted members of the household and treated them like family. But many did not, because there were scant protections—and virtually no rights—for slaves, who were considered property rather than persons. Slaves owned little or nothing and had no legal recourse to which they could appeal when mistreated. For instance, the influential Greek philosopher Aristotle wrote, "A slave is a living tool, and a tool is an inanimate slave" (*Ethics,* 1161*b*). Writing about agriculture, the Roman nobleman Varro asserted that the only thing distinguishing a slave from a beast or a cart was that the slave could talk.

It is safe to say that as the gospel spread throughout the Greco-Roman world most of the converts were slaves. Paul told the Corinthians,

> For consider your calling, brethren, that there were not many wise according to the flesh, not many mighty, not many noble; but God has chosen the foolish things of the world to shame the wise, and God has chosen the weak things of the world to shame the things which are strong, and the base things of the world and the despised God has chosen. (1 Cor. 1:26–28)

That reality is the reason the New Testament addressed much teaching to slaves (1 Cor. 7:20–24; Eph. 6:5–6; Col. 3:22; 1 Tim. 6:1–2; Titus

2:9–10; Philem. 12–16). They made up a large part of the Gentile church and their place in society raised some important issues. First, believing slaves often assumed that since they had become free in Christ (Rom. 6:17–18; 7:6; 1 Cor. 7:22; 12:13; Gal. 3:28; Eph. 6:8; Col. 3:11, 24) they also had a right to freedom from their masters. Second, converted slaves sometimes assumed that certain societal elevation should be theirs because of their spiritual giftedness and leadership in the church. When a slave became a church elder and thus the spiritual overseer of his believing master, the issue of his subordination to that master in the workplace had to be addressed. Under apostolic teaching, the early Christians developed strong and correct convictions on the slavery issues. They did not seek to incite a slave rebellion, but focused on making sure Christian slaves' attitudes were right. Paul's letter to Philemon is inspired testimony to the divine will for a slave, who was a brother in Christ, to fulfill his duty to his master.

Servants (*oiketai*) is from the root meaning "house," and thus is the basic term for household servants (cf. Acts 10:7). Most of those servants served in a home or under an estate owner with duties from being farmers who plowed the owner's field to doctors who cared for his family's medical needs. Peter's basic command to them is **be submissive** (*hupotassomenoi,* a present passive participle with the sense of a present imperative, meaning "to line up under"). Slaves were to be continually submissive to their **masters,** the *despotai* (from which the English word *despots* derives), who had absolute ownership of and complete control over them (cf. 1 Tim. 6:1–2; Titus 2:9).

The submission of servants was to be rendered **with all respect,** that is, without bitterness or negativity, but with an attitude of gracious honor. That was a way to show respect to God Himself and to fulfill Peter's teachings about the fear of God, expressed elsewhere in the letter (1:17 [see the discussion of this verse in chapter 5 of this volume]; 2:17; 3:2; 3:15). God designed the servant-master relationship to ensure safety, care, support, productivity, and the conduct of human enterprise. The earth yields its produce and material wealth to support and enrich mankind through the providence of work relations. This is an institution of God from the Fall onward (Gen. 3:17–19). God has designed a complex of abilities and opportunities, relations and experiences, to allow humans to draw the rich resources out of this planet.

Such a God-fearing attitude is to extend beyond the **good and gentle** masters even **to those who are unreasonable. Good** (*agathois*) means "one who is upright, beneficial, and satisfactory for another's need." **Gentle** (*epieikesin*) refers to "one who is considerate, reasonable, and fair." Therefore **good and gentle** describes a magnanimous, kind, and gracious person, the kind of master to whom it is easy to submit. The kind to whom it is not easy to submit Peter called **unreasonable** (*sko-liois*), a term that literally means "curved" or "crooked," and metaphorically means "perverse" or "dishonest." (The word is transliterated in medical terminology to describe a twisted condition of the spinal column [scoliosis].)

In his letter to the Ephesians, the apostle Paul further stated God's will on this issue:

> Slaves, be obedient to those who are your masters according to the flesh, with fear and trembling, in the sincerity of your heart, as to Christ; not by way of eyeservice, as men-pleasers, but as slaves of Christ, doing the will of God from the heart. With good will render service, as to the Lord, and not to men, knowing that whatever good thing each one does, this he will receive back from the Lord, whether slave or free. And masters, do the same things to them, and give up threatening, knowing that both their Master and yours is in heaven, and there is no partiality with Him. (Eph. 6:5–9)

In the workplace, employees are to submit to employers as if they were serving Christ Himself. Such submissiveness precludes all rebellions, protests, mutinies, strikes, or workplace disobedience of every kind, even if the employer is unreasonable.

The Motive for Submission

For this finds favor, if for the sake of conscience toward God a person bears up under sorrows when suffering unjustly. For what credit is there if, when you sin and are harshly treated, you endure it with patience? But if when you do what is right and suffer for it you patiently endure it, this finds favor with God. For you have been called for this purpose, (2:19–21a)

It should be of little consequence to believers what their circumstances are in the workplace, whether they are chief executive officers or custodians, whether they receive a substantial pay raise or settle for a salary cut so the company can stay solvent. The factor of overarching significance is that they maintain their testimony before the watching world of sinners (cf. Matt. 5:15–16; Mark 4:21; Phil. 2:14–16), and in the workplace that occurs when believers labor with an awareness of God's glory. Such awareness is the motivation not only for godly behavior and submission on the job, but also for trusting in God's sovereignty in every situation. Theologian A. W. Pink wrote,

As [one] sees the apparent defeat of the right, and the triumphing of might and the wrong ... it seems as though Satan were getting the better of the conflict. But as one looks *above,* instead of around, there is plainly visible to the eye of faith a Throne....This then is our confidence —*God is on the Throne. (The Sovereignty of God,* rev. ed. [Edinburgh: Banner of Truth, 1961], 149–50; emphases in the original)

The motivation for believers' submission in the workplace resides in the short phrase, **for this finds favor,** literally,"this is a grace." God is pleased when believers do their work in a humble and submissive way for their superiors (cf. 1 Sam. 15:22; Pss. 26:3; 36:10; James 1:25). It is especially favorable to God when **for the sake of conscience toward God a person** [believer] **bears up under sorrows when suffering unjustly.** Whether it was a slave in Peter's day patiently enduring brutal treatment, or whether it is a modern-day employee not retaliating against an unkind and unjust supervisor, God is pleased. This is what James referred to as a "consider it all joy" experience by which believers are perfected (James 1:2–4). The greater blessing is actually for the one who suffers.

Conscience toward God refers to the aforementioned general awareness of His presence, which again is believers' main motivation for submission in the workplace. The word rendered **bears up under** means "to endure," and the term **sorrows** implies pain, either physical or mental. The Lord wants believers, **when suffering unjustly** in the workplace, not to falter in their witness but humbly and patiently to accept unjust treatment, knowing that God has sovereign control of every circumstance (Pss. 33:11; 103:19; Prov. 16:1, 9; 19:21; Isa. 14:27; 46:9–10; Acts 17:28; Rom. 8:28–30; cf. 1:6–7; 2 Cor. 4:17–18) and promises to bless.

Undoubtedly many recipients of this epistle endured painful and unjust beatings as slaves. Their masters might have deprived them of food, forced them to work unreasonably long hours, or punished them unfairly in a variety of ways. Unlike modern-day employees in Western industrialized countries, those slaves had no one to turn to for redress of grievances—no union representatives, no government boards or ombudsmen to settle disputes, and no way to file civil lawsuits. They just had to endure whatever painful and difficult circumstances their masters imposed on them—and they did so, much to the glory and honor of God (cf. Matt. 5:10; 2 Thess. 1:4–5; James 5:11), which evidenced their heavenly perspective.

Peter pressed his argument with a negative rhetorical question, followed by a positive statement. The implied answer to his question, **For what credit is there if, when you sin and are harshly treated, you endure it with patience?** is, "There is no credit." Believers who sin deserve chastening (cf. Ps. 66:18; Jer. 5:25; Dan. 9:8; Heb. 12:5–11), and they ought to endure it with patience.

On the other hand, Peter offered the positive assertion, **But if when you do what is right and suffer for it you patiently endure it, this finds favor with God.** When the believing slaves did **what** was **right** some still had to **suffer for it,** even to the extent of being **harshly treated** as if they really deserved punishment. This indicates that, among various forms, harsh treatment came physically, by means of repeated, hard blows with the fists or instruments (cf. Mark 14:65). Perhaps some were punished because of their Christian convictions. Again, those who endured such suffering **patiently** found **favor** or grace **with God.** It always pleases Him to see believers faithfully accept and deal with any adversity (cf. 3:14; 4:14, 16; Matt. 5:11–12; 1 Cor. 4:11–13; 2 Cor. 12:9–10; James 1:12).

Peter concluded this section with the amazing statement at the beginning of verse 21, **For you have been called for this purpose. Have been called** refers to the efficacious salvation call (1:15; 5:10; cf. Rom. 8:28, 30; 9:24; 1 Cor. 1:9; Gal. 1:6, 15; Eph. 4:1, 4; Col. 3:15; 2 Thess. 2:14; 2 Tim. 1:9; Heb. 9:15; 2 Peter 1:3). As soon as the Holy Spirit calls people from darkness to light, they become an enemy of the world (John 15:18–19; 1 John 3:13) and a target of unjust and unfair attack as they seek to obey Christ. Paul told Timothy, "Indeed, all who desire to live godly in Christ Jesus will be persecuted" (2 Tim. 3:12; cf. Mark 10:30; John 15:20; 16:33).

It is more important to God that those who are citizens of heaven display a faithful testimony, marked by spiritual integrity, than that they strive to attain all their perceived rights in this world. It is more important to God for believers to uphold the credibility of gospel power than to obtain a raise or promotion in their vocation. It is ultimately far more important to God that believers demonstrate their submission to His sovereignty in every area of life than that they protest against problems at their workplace. Martyn Lloyd-Jones illustrated the value of Christians' submitting to God's **purpose**—the rigor of discipline and trials in everyday life—as follows:

> We are like the school boy who would like to evade certain things, and run away from problems and tests. But we thank God that because he has a larger interest in us and knows what is for our good, he puts us through the disciplines of life—he makes us learn the multiplication table; we are made to struggle with the elements of grammar. Many things that are trials to us are essential that one day we may be found without spot or wrinkle. (*The Miracle of Grace* [reprint; Grand Rapids: Baker, 1986], 39)

Whenever believers encounter trials on the job, they ought to view them as opportunities for spiritual growth and evangelism. The chief reason God allows believers to remain in this world is so He might use them to win the lost and thereby bring glory to His name. Those who suffer with the right attitude will be blessed in this life and honored later in the Lord's presence.

The Suffering Jesus (1 Peter 2:21*b*–25)

15

since Christ also suffered for you, leaving you an example for you to follow in His steps, who committed no sin, nor was any deceit found in His mouth; and while being reviled, He did not revile in return; while suffering, He uttered no threats, but kept entrusting Himself to Him who judges righteously; and He Himself bore our sins in His body on the cross, so that we might die to sin and live to righteousness; for by His wounds you were healed. For you were continually straying like sheep, but now you have returned to the Shepherd and Guardian of your souls. (2:21*b*–25)

If one were to survey a typical cross section of people in Western society about who Jesus was, the answers would undoubtedly include the following accuracies: He was the Christmas child in the Bethlehem manger (Luke 2:15–16); He was the young man from the Nazareth carpenter shop who on one occasion confounded the religious teachers in Jerusalem (Luke 2:45–47); He was a humble and loving teacher (Matt. 5:1–12); He was a compassionate and powerful healer who cured diseases (Matt. 8:14–17) and raised the dead (John 11:1–44); He was a courageous and insightful preacher who stirred the multitudes as He explained God's will (Matt. 7:28–29); and He was the perfect example and the ideal model of manhood (Luke 2:52; cf. Matt. 4:1–11; Phil. 2:7; Heb. 4:15).

Each of the foregoing images of Christ is true and instructive to some extent. But one could affirm all of them and completely miss the point of His life and ministry. One image of the Son of God supersedes all others in significance and is crucial to the purpose of His incarnation. It is that of Jesus as the suffering Servant and the crucified Savior. At the Cross He most clearly displayed His deity and humanity together and completed His redemptive work, the atonement for sin—the reason He came into the world. The apostle Paul summarized the supreme importance of His death and resurrection: "I determined to know nothing among you except Jesus Christ, and Him crucified" (1 Cor. 2:2).

This concluding passage of 1 Peter 2 presents the suffering Messiah and reveals three aspects of His suffering: He was believers' perfect standard for suffering, their perfect substitute in suffering, and became their perfect shepherd through suffering.

Believers' Perfect Standard for Suffering

since Christ also suffered for you, leaving you an example for you to follow in His steps, who committed no sin, nor was any deceit found in His mouth; and while being reviled, He did not revile in return; while suffering, He uttered no threats, but kept entrusting Himself to Him who judges righteously; (2:21b–23)

As discussed in the previous chapter of this volume, Christians have been called to persecution and suffering, whether in the workplace or any other realm of life (2:20–21a). In all forms of suffering, they must look to Christ as their standard, their example. For Him, the path to glory was the path of suffering (Luke 24:25–26), and the pattern is the same for His followers.

Peter's phrase **since Christ also suffered for you** certainly recalls the reality of His efficacious, substitutionary, sin-bearing death— His redemptive suffering (cf. the discussion in the next section of this chapter). His redemptive suffering as the one sacrifice for sin has no parallel in His followers' sufferings. But there are features of His suffering that do provide an example for them to follow in their own sufferings. For instance, in a complete breach of justice and goodness, He was crucified as a criminal (Isa. 53:12; Matt. 27:38) even though He committed no crime (1:19; cf. Isa. 53:9; John 8:46; 2 Cor. 5:21; Heb. 7:26). He was perfectly sinless. Life in this world has always been filled with such unjust treatment of God's faithful (cf. 2 Tim. 3:12). His execution demonstrates that one may be absolutely faithful to God's will and still experience unjust suffering. So Christ's attitude in His death on the cross provides believers with the ultimate example of how to respond to unmerited persecution and punishment (cf. Heb. 12:3–4).

That is clearly Peter's point, because he adds the words **leaving you an example.** Believers will never suffer for others' salvation, including their own. But they will suffer for Christ's sake, and His example is their standard for a God-honoring response. The word translated **example** is *hupogrammon,* which literally means "writing under" and refers to a pattern placed under a sheet of tracing paper so the original images could be duplicated. In ancient times, children learning to write traced over the letters of the alphabet to facilitate their learning to write them. Christ is the **example** or pattern on which believers trace their lives. In so doing, they are following **in His steps.** *Ichnesin* (**steps**) means "footprints" or "tracks." For believers as for Him, the footprints through this world are often along paths of unjust suffering.

In view of the suffering they were enduring (1:6–7; 2:20; 3:14, 17; 4:12–19; 5:9) and would yet endure, Peter wanted his readers to look closely at how their Lord responded to His suffering. Since Christ endured unequalled suffering when He went to the Cross, Peter, to set forth the example, focused on that event as the ultimate experience. The apostle examined Jesus' response to intense suffering through the prophetic words of Isaiah 53, the most significant Old Testament chapter on Messiah's suffering.

Peter first borrowed from Isaiah 53:9 to describe Christ's reaction to unjust treatment. The phrase **who committed no sin, nor was any deceit found in His mouth** is a close parallel to the prophet's words in the second half of that verse, "Because He had done no violence, nor was there any deceit in His mouth." Isaiah used "violence" not in the sense of a single act of violence, but to signify sin, all of which is violence against God and His law. The prophet indicated that the Suffering Servant (the Christ to come) would never violate God's law. The Septuagint translators understood this and used "lawlessness" rather than "violence" to translate the term. Peter chose the word **sin** because under the Holy Spirit's inspiration he knew that was Isaiah's meaning.

Peter further drew from Isaiah, affirming Christ's sinlessness by declaring that there **was** no **deceit found in His mouth.** The heart of man expresses sin most easily and often through the mouth, as the prophet made clear even in documenting his own experience: "Woe is me, for I am ruined! Because I am a man of unclean lips, and I live among a people of unclean lips; for my eyes have seen the King, the Lord of hosts" (Isa. 6:5; cf. Matt. 15:18–19; Luke 6:45; James 1:26; 3:2–12). Jesus' mouth could never utter anything sinful, since there was no sin in Him

(Luke 23:41; John 8:46; 2 Cor. 5:21; Heb. 4:15; 7:26; 1 John 3:5). **Deceit** is from dolos (see the discussion of that word in 2:1, chapter 8 of this volume), which here is used as a general term for sinful corruption.

Peter then describes Christ's exemplary response to such unjust torture by saying **while being reviled, He did not revile in return,** again echoing the prediction of Isaiah 53:7, "He was oppressed and He was afflicted, yet He did not open His mouth; like a lamb that is led to slaughter, and like a sheep that is silent before its shearers, so He did not open His mouth." During the cruel hours preceding His actual crucifixion, Jesus suffered under repeated provocations from His accusers (Matt. 26:57–68; 27:11–14, 26–31; John 18:28–19:11). They tried to push Him to the breaking point with their severe mockery and physical torture but could not (Mark 14:65; Luke 22:63–65). He did not get angry at or retaliate against His accusers (Matt. 26:64; John 18:34–37).

Being reviled is a present participle (*loidoroumenos*) that means to use abusive, vile language over and over against someone, or "to pile abuse on someone." It described an extremely harsh kind of verbal abuse that could be more aggravating than physical abuse. But Jesus patiently and humbly accepted all the verbal abuse hurled at Him (Matt. 26:59–63; 27:12–14; Luke 23:6–10) and did not return abuse to His tormentors. That **He did not revile in return** is all the more remarkable when one considers the just, righteous, powerful, and legitimate threats He could have issued in response (cf. Matt. 26:53). As the sovereign, omnipotent Son of God and the Creator and Sustainer of the universe, Jesus could have blasted His cruel, unbelieving enemies into eternal hell with one word from His mouth (cf. Luke 12:5; Heb. 10:29–31). Eventually, those who never repented and believed in Him would be sent to hell; but for this time He endured with no retaliation—to set an example for believers. **While suffering, He uttered no threats;** instead of giving back threats for the repeated, unjust abuse, He chose to accept the suffering and even ask His Father to forgive those who abused Him (Luke 23:34).

Jesus drew the strength for that amazing response from His complete trust in His Father's ultimate purpose to accomplish justice on His behalf, and against His hateful rejecters. He **kept entrusting Himself to Him who judges righteously.** The verb for **entrusting** (*paredidou*) means "to commit," or "hand over" and is in the imperfect tense signifying repeated past action. With each new wave of abuse, as it came again and again, Jesus was always "handing Himself over" to God for safekeeping. Luke records how that pattern continued until the very end: "'Father, into Your hands I commit My spirit.' Having said this, He breathed His last" (Luke 23:46). Undergirding Jesus' peaceful, resolute acceptance of suffering was an unshakeable confidence in the perfectly righteous plan of **Him who judges righteously** (cf. John 4:34; 15:10; 17:25). He knew

God would vindicate Him according to His perfect, holy justice. Alan Stibbs comments,

> In ... the unique instance of our Lord's passion, when the sinless One suffered as if He were the worst of sinners, and bore the extreme penalty of sin, there is a double sense in which He may have acknowledged God as the righteous Judge. On the one hand, because voluntarily, and in fulfillment of God's will, He was taking the sinner's place and bearing sin, He did not protest at what He had to suffer. Rather He consciously recognized that it was the penalty righteously due to sin. So He handed Himself over to be punished. He recognized that in letting such shame, pain and curse fall upon Him, the righteous God was judging righteously. On the other hand, because He Himself was sinless, He also believed that in due time God, as the righteous Judge, would vindicate Him as righteous, and exalt Him from the grave, and reward Him for what He had willingly endured for others' sake by giving Him the right completely to save them from the penalty and power of their own wrongdoing. (*The Tyndale New Testament Commentaries, The First Epistle of Peter* [Grand Rapids: Eerdmans, 1971], 119)

He is believers' perfect example in suffering for righteousness' sake and sets the standard for them to entrust themselves to God as their righteous Judge (cf. Job 36:3; Pss. 11:7; 31:1; 98:9; 119:172; Jer. 9:24). Though saints are not sinless, they are righteous in Christ and have the promise of God's vindication of them. Such hope undoubtedly prompted Stephen to fix his eyes on the exalted Christ and ask God to forgive his murderers (Acts 7:54–60). Paul wrote,

> For momentary, light affliction is producing for us an eternal weight of glory far beyond all comparison, while we look not at the things which are seen, but at the things which are not seen; for the things which are seen are temporal, but the things which are not seen are eternal. (2 Cor. 4:17–18; cf. Rom. 8:18; 2 Tim. 2:12; Heb. 2:10; James 1:2–4; 1 Peter 1:6–7)

The apostle suggests that the intense but comparatively trifling amount of suffering believers experience in this life will result in an infinitely greater weight (lit., a "heavy mass") of glory in the life to come.

BELIEVERS' PERFECT SUBSTITUTE IN SUFFERING

and He Himself bore our sins in His body on the cross, so that we might die to sin and live to righteousness; for by His wounds you were healed. (2:24)

Peter then moves to the essential reality in the Lord's suffering—His substitutionary death (Mark 10:45; Rom. 5:8; Eph. 5:2; cf. Heb. 2:17). Leon Morris comments,

> Redemption is substitutionary, for it means that Christ paid the price that we could not pay, paid it in our stead, and we go free. Justification interprets our salvation judicially, and as the New Testament sees it Christ took our legal liability, took it in our stead. Reconciliation means the making of people to be at one by the taking away of the cause of hostility. In this case the cause is sin, and Christ removed that cause for us. We could not deal with sin. He could and did, and did it in such a way that it is reckoned to us. Propitiation points us to the removal of the divine wrath, and Christ has done this by bearing the wrath for us. It was our sin which drew it down; it was He who bore it. . . . Was there a price to be paid? He paid it. Was there a victory to be won? He won it. Was there a penalty to be borne? He bore it. Was there a judgment to be faced? He faced it. (*The Cross in the New Testament* [Grand Rapids: Eerdmans, 1965], 405)

Paul, like Peter, placed supreme importance on Christ's substitutionary atonement. To the Galatians he wrote, "Christ redeemed us from the curse of the Law, having become a curse for us—for it is written, 'Cursed is everyone who hangs on a tree'" (Gal. 3:13; cf. 2 Cor. 5:21; 1 Peter 3:18). The significance of Christ's substitution cannot be overstated:

> To put it bluntly and plainly, if Christ is not my Substitute, I still occupy the place of a condemned sinner. If my sins and my guilt are not transferred to Him, if He did not take them upon Himself, then surely they remain with me. If He did not deal with sins, I must face their consequences. If my penalty was not borne by Him, it still hangs over me. (Morris, 410)

Peter explained Christ's sacrifice in believers' behalf with additional allusions to Isaiah's familiar description of Messiah's death (Isa. 53:4–5, 11). **He Himself** (*hos . . . autos*) is an emphatic personalization and stresses that the Son of God voluntarily and without coercion (John 10:15, 17–18) died as the only sufficient sacrifice for the sins of all who would ever believe (cf. John 1:29; 3:16; 1 Tim. 2:5–6; 4:10; Heb. 2:9, 17). The very name *Jesus* indicated that He would "save His people from their sins" (Matt. 1:21). **Bore** is from *anapherō* and means here to carry the massive, heavy weight of sin. That weight of sin is so heavy that Romans 8:22 says "the whole creation groans and suffers" under it. Only Jesus could remove such a massive weight from the elect (cf. Heb. 9:28).

Anyone who understood the Hebrew Scriptures, as Peter did, and experienced the sacrifices in the temple, would have been familiar with the truth of substitutionary death and thus grasped the significance of Christ as the full and final offering for sin.

That Jesus **bore** believers' **sins** means that He suffered the penalty for all the sins of all who would ever be forgiven. In receiving the wrath of God against sin, Christ endured not only death in His body on the cross (John 19:30–37), but the more horrific separation from the Father for a time (Matt. 27:46). Christ took the full punishment for saints' sins, thus satisfying divine justice and freeing God to forgive those who repent and believe (Rom. 3:24–26; 4:3–8; 5:9; 1 Thess. 1:10). Explicit in the pronoun **our** is the specific provision, the actual atonement on behalf of all who would ever believe. Christ's death is efficacious only for the sins of those who believe, who are God's chosen (cf. Matt. 1:21; 20:28; 26:28; John 10:11, 14–18, 24–29; Rev. 5:9; see also the discussion of election in chapter 1 of this volume).

When Christ died, He died **so that** believers **might die to sin and live to righteousness.** This is Peter's way of saying what the apostle Paul says in Romans 6:3–11,

> Or do you not know that all of us who have been baptized into Christ Jesus have been baptized into His death? Therefore we have been buried with Him through baptism into death, so that as Christ was raised from the dead through the glory of the Father, so we too might walk in newness of life. For if we have become united with Him in the likeness of His death, certainly we shall also be in the likeness of His resurrection, knowing this, that our old self was crucified with Him, in order that our body of sin might be done away with, so that we would no longer be slaves to sin; for he who has died is freed from sin. Now if we have died with Christ, we believe that we shall also live with Him, knowing that Christ, having been raised from the dead, is never to die again; death no longer is master over Him. For the death that He died, He died to sin once for all; but the life that He lives, He lives to God. Even so consider yourselves to be dead to sin, but alive to God in Christ Jesus.

Union with Christ in His death and resurrection does not change only believers' standing before God (who declares them righteous, since their sins have been paid for and removed from them), but it also changes their nature—they are not only justified but sanctified, transformed from sinners into saints (2 Cor. 5:17; Titus 3:5; James 1:18).

Apogenomenoi (**might die**) is not the normal word for "die" and is used only here in the New Testament. It means "to be away from, depart, be missing, or cease existing." Christ died for believers to separate them from sin's penalty, so it can never condemn them. The record of their sins, the indictment of guilt that had them headed for hell, was "nailed to the cross" (Col. 2:12–14). Jesus paid their debt to God in full. In that sense, all Christians are freed from sin's penalty. They are also delivered from its dominating power and made able to **live to righteousness** (cf. Rom. 6:16–22).

Peter describes this death to sin and becoming alive to righteousness as a healing: **by His wounds you were healed.** This too is borrowed from the Old Testament prophet when he wrote "by His scourging we are healed" (Isa. 53:5). **Wounds** is a better usage than "scourging" since the latter may give the impression that the beating of Jesus produced salvation. Both Isaiah and Peter meant the **wounds** of Jesus that were part of the execution process. **Wounds** is a general reference—a synonym for all the suffering that brought Him to death. And the healing here is spiritual, not physical. Neither Isaiah nor Peter intended physical healing as the result in these references to Christ's sufferings. Physical healing for all who believe does result from Christ's atoning work, but such healing awaits a future realization in the perfections of heaven. In resurrection glory, believers will experience no sickness, pain, suffering, or death (Rev. 21:1–4; 22:1–3).

In fair consideration of this explanation, it must be admitted that the apostle Matthew seems to relate Jesus' physical healing ministry to Isaiah's prophecy:

> When evening came, they brought to Him many who were demon-possessed; and He cast out the spirits with a word, and healed all who were ill. This was to fulfill what was spoken through Isaiah the prophet: "He Himself took our infirmities and carried away our diseases." (Matt. 8:16–17)

Some say that proves Christians can now claim physical healing in the atonement. However a more accurate understanding of Matthew's narrative (8:16–17) reveals that Jesus healed people to illustrate the physical healing all believers will experience in the glory yet to come.

> Disease and death cannot be permanently removed until sin is permanently removed, and Jesus' supreme work, therefore, was to conquer sin. In the atonement He dealt with sin, death, and sickness; and yet all three of those are still with us. When He died on the cross, Jesus bruised the head of Satan and broke the power of sin, and the person who trusts in the atoning work of Christ is immediately delivered from the penalty of sin and one day will be delivered from the very presence of sin and its consequences. The ultimate fulfillment of Christ's redeeming work is yet future for believers (cf. Rom. 8:22–25; 13:11). Christ died for men's sins, but Christians still fall into sin; He conquered death, but His followers still die; and He overcame pain and sickness, but His

people still suffer and become ill. There is physical healing in the atonement, just as there is total deliverance from sin and death in the atonement; but we still await the fulfillment of that deliverance in the day when the Lord brings the end of suffering, sin, and death.

Those who claim that Christians should never be sick because there is healing in the atonement should also claim that Christians should never die, because Jesus also conquered death in the atonement. The central message of the gospel is deliverance from sin. It is the good news about forgiveness, not health. Christ was made sin, not disease, and He died on the cross for our sin, not our sickness. As Peter makes clear, Christ's wounds heal us from sin, not from disease. "He Himself bore our sins in His body on the cross, that we might die to sin and live to righteousness" (1 Peter 2:24). (John MacArthur, *Matthew 8–15*, MacArthur New Testament Commentary [Chicago: Moody, 1987], 19)

If the atonement's physical healing were fully realized now, no believer would ever be sick or die. But obviously, all do. The Lord's substitutionary sacrifice on behalf of His own heals their souls now and their bodies in the future.

BELIEVERS' PERFECT SHEPHERD THROUGH SUFFERING

For you were continually straying like sheep, but now you have returned to the Shepherd and Guardian of your souls. (2:25)

As he concluded this passage, Peter once more alluded to Isaiah 53, "All of us like sheep have gone astray, each of us has turned to his own way; but the Lord has caused the iniquity of us all to fall on Him" (v. 6). If God had not determined that all believers' sins should fall on Jesus, there would be no shepherd to bring God's flock into the fold.

The phrase **were continually straying like sheep** describes by analogy the wayward, purposeless, dangerous, and helpless wandering of lost sinners, whom Jesus described as "sheep without a shepherd" (Matt. 9:36). The verb rendered **have returned** (*epestraphēte*) carries the connotation of repentance, a turning from sin and in faith a turning toward Jesus Christ. But Peter's readers had trusted in Christ's substitutionary death and turned to Him for salvation. Like the prodigal son in Luke 15:11–32, they had turned away from the misery of their former sinful life (cf. Eph. 2:1–7; 4:17–24; Col. 3:1–7; 1 Thess. 1:2–10) and received new life in Christ (cf. Eph. 5:15–21; Col. 3:8–17; 1 Thess. 2:13–14). All who are saved come under the perfect care, provision, and protection of **the Shepherd and Guardian of** their **souls.**

The analogy of God as shepherd is a familiar and rich theme in Scripture (cf. 5:4; Ps. 23:1; Ezek. 34:23–24; 37:24). Jesus identified Himself as God when He took the divine title and named Himself the "good shepherd" (John 10:11, 14). **Shepherd** is an apt title for the Savior since it conveys His role as feeder, leader, protector, cleanser, and restorer of His flock. And believers as sheep is also an apt analogy because sheep are stupid, gullible (a sheep called the "Judas sheep" in modern times leads the other sheep to slaughter), dirty (the lanolin in sheep's wool collects all kinds of dirt), and defenseless (they have no natural defensive capabilities). (See the discussion of shepherding in chapter 23 of this volume.)

The term **Guardian** (*episkopos*) serves as a synonym, another term describing Jesus' care for His flock. It is the word usually translated "bishop" or "overseer," which along with **Shepherd** also describes the responsibilities of the pastor or elder (cf. 1 Tim. 3:1–7; Titus 1:5–9). Later in this letter, Peter uses both root words when he exhorts elders to "shepherd the flock of God . . . exercising oversight not under compulsion, but voluntarily, according to the will of God" (5:2). By His death and resurrection for His flock, the Lord has become the **Shepherd and Guardian** of their eternal souls. In suffering, He became their example, their substitute, and their shepherd.

Winning an Unsaved Spouse (1 Peter 3:1–7)

16

In the same way, you wives, be submissive to your own husbands so that even if any of them are disobedient to the word, they may be won without a word by the behavior of their wives, as they observe your chaste and respectful behavior. Your adornment must not be merely external—braiding the hair, and wearing gold jewelry, or putting on dresses; but let it be the hidden person of the heart, with the imperishable quality of a gentle and quiet spirit, which is precious in the sight of God. For in this way in former times the holy women also, who hoped in God, used to adorn themselves, being submissive to their own husbands; just as Sarah obeyed Abraham, calling him lord, and you have become her children if you do what is right without being frightened by any fear. You husbands in the same way, live with your wives in an understanding way, as with someone weaker, since she is a woman; and show her honor as a fellow heir of the grace of life, so that your prayers will not be hindered. (3:1–7)

If believers are to maintain an exemplary testimony in this unbelieving world, they must live blamelessly in the four major arenas of God-ordained social interaction that Peter addresses: the society (2:13–17), the workplace (2:18–25), the family (3:1–7), and the church (3:8–9). In relation to the three secular dimensions of life, the apostle commands believers to be witnesses for the positive sake of the gospel (2:9) as well as negatively, to silence the critics of the faith (2:12–15).

This opening section of chapter 3 deals with the third and small-est unit of social structure ordained by God, the family. In the other two categories, submission is required to the civil authority (2:13–14) and to employers (2:18). The issue of submission is also critical in the family, beginning with the wife to her husband. Peter here directs six verses to wives' submission to husbands and one to husbands' serving the needs of wives, a division that may at first glance seem out of balance. But in Peter's day when a wife became a Christian, the potential for difficulty was much greater than it was if the husband first became a believer. In that society when women, who were viewed as inferior to men, became Christians without their husbands also becoming saved, the likelihood of his being embarrassed and shamed by what was viewed as an act of defiance by his wife, was predictable, as was the conflict subsequently generated.

THE WIFE'S RESPONSIBILITY

In the same way, you wives, be submissive to your own husbands so that even if any of them are disobedient to the word, they may be won without a word by the behavior of their wives, as they observe your chaste and respectful behavior. Your adornment must not be merely external—braiding the hair, and wearing gold jewelry, or putting on dresses; but let it be the hidden person of the heart, with the imperishable quality of a gentle and quiet spirit, which is precious in the sight of God. For in this way in former times the holy women also, who hoped in God, used to adorn themselves, being submissive to their own husbands; just as Sarah obeyed Abraham, calling him lord, and you have become her children if you do what is right without being frightened by any fear. (3:1–6)

In first-century Greco-Roman culture, women received little or no respect. As long as they lived in their father's house, they were subject to the Roman law of *patria potestas* ("the father's power"), which granted fathers ultimate life-and-death authority over their children. Husbands had a similar kind of legal authority over their wives. Society regarded women as mere servants who were to stay at home and obey their hus-bands. If a woman decided to obey the gospel, that decision to change religions on her own could result in severe abuse from her unsaved husband. When such conversion did occur, a wife needed to know how to respond to her husband so that she might win him to the gospel. Her essential duty was to be submissive, as in the case of civil and workplace relations.

First, the believing wife has the responsibility to stay with her unbelieving husband. If he wants to maintain the union, she must not divorce him: "A woman who has an unbelieving husband, and he consents to live with her, she must not send her husband away" (1 Cor. 7:13; cf. v. 39; Rom. 7:2–3). Paul went on to say that unsaved spouses benefit from the divine blessings their saved spouses receive from God: "For the unbelieving husband is sanctified through his wife, and the unbelieving wife is sanctified through her believing husband" (1 Cor. 7:14). However, if an unbelieving husband does not want to stay with his believing wife, she does not need to compel him to remain because such an attempt may produce nothing but turmoil, and believers are called to peace: "Yet if the unbelieving one leaves, let him leave; the brother or the sister is not under bondage in such cases, but God has called us to peace" (v. 15). When the bond is broken under such conditions, the believer is free to remarry in the Lord, as in the case of death (v. 39).

That Christian women are spiritually equal to men in Christ is clear from Galatians 3:27–28, "For all of you who were baptized into Christ have clothed yourselves with Christ. There is neither Jew nor Greek, there is neither slave nor free man, there is neither male nor female; for you are all one in Christ Jesus." Still, God has ordained women to have certain obligations to their husbands, which Peter identifies as submission and faithfulness, and modesty.

SHE IS TO BE SUBMISSIVE AND FAITHFUL

In the same way, you wives, be submissive to your own husbands so that even if any of them are disobedient to the word, they may be won without a word by the behavior of their wives, as they observe your chaste and respectful behavior. (3:1–2)

The expression **in the same way** refers back to the two previously mentioned examples of submission: citizens to civil authorities (2:13) and servants to masters (2:18). The same verb (*hupotassō*), rendered **be submissive** and considered in connection with those two references, appears also here and is a present middle form, emphasizing reflexive action ("submitting yourself"). The New Testament usage of this word, meaning "to submit," "be subject to," or "rank under," is common (cf. 2:18; 3:5; 5:5; Luke 2:51; 10:17, 20; Rom. 8:7; 10:3; 13:1, 5; 1 Cor. 14:32, 34;

15:27; 16:16; Eph. 1:22; 5:21, 24; Phil. 3:21; Titus 2:9; 3:1; Heb. 2:5, 8; 12:9; James 4:7). The apostle Paul, under the Spirit's inspiration, also taught that wives are to submit to their husbands' leadership (Eph. 5:22–23; Col. 3:18; Titus 2:4–5). Submission does not imply any moral, intellectual, or spiritual inferiority in the family, workplace, or society in general. But it is God's design for roles necessary to mankind's well-being. Along the same lines, a commanding officer is not necessarily superior in character to the troops under him, but his authority is vital to the proper functioning of the unit. That Peter referred specifically to their **own husbands** (appropriate emphasis added) indicates the intimacy of marriage and points out that he was not commanding women to be servile to all men in every context. Paul also sets forth God's design for authority and submission in men's and women's roles within the church (1 Cor. 11:3, 8–9; 1 Tim. 2:11–14; cf. 1 Cor. 14:34).

Disobedient to the word describes the unbelieving husband's condition as a rejecter of the gospel (cf. 2 Thess. 1:8–9; Heb. 4:2). Amazingly, in spite of the profound enmity of his soul toward the Lord, if his Christian wife will continue to submit to him, she might be the instrument God uses to win him to Christ **without a word.** That expression does not refer to *the* Word of God but to the wife's spoken words. Earlier in the letter, Peter made it clear that Scripture is essential for anyone's salvation: "For you have been born again not of seed which is perishable but imperishable, that is, through the living and enduring word of God" (1:23; cf. Rom. 10:17). Peter's point here is that the wife's godly behavior is the most valuable testimony to open the husband's heart to the gospel. He will need to hear the words of salvation, perhaps from her. But it will be as he is able to **observe** her submission as a faithful wife that she truly commends the gospel to him. How a believer lives in that most intimate relationship helps make the grace of Christ believable (cf. Matt. 5:16).

A lovely, gracious, and submissive attitude is the most effective evangelistic tool believing wives have (cf. Prov. 31:26; Matt. 5:16; Phil. 2:15; Titus 2:3–5). Closely related to that is their responsibility to be **chaste and respectful,** demonstrating their sanctification through Christ by a life composed of irreproachable and pure conduct toward God and her husband. The word **respectful** is *phobos* ("fear"), used in 2:17 to define the required attitude of those who give honor to God Himself (cf. Prov. 24:21). This is precisely what is commanded of the wife in Ephesians 5:22, "Wives, be subject to your own husbands, as to the Lord." That means she shows honor and respect to her husband as to the Lord. This will be further developed and illustrated in the discussion of verse 6, under the next heading.

SHE IS TO BE MODEST

Your adornment must not be merely external—braiding the hair, and wearing gold jewelry, or putting on dresses; but let it be the hidden person of the heart, with the imperishable quality of a gentle and quiet spirit, which is precious in the sight of God. For in this way in former times the holy women also, who hoped in God, used to adorn themselves, being submissive to their own husbands; just as Sarah obeyed Abraham, calling him lord, and you have become her children if you do what is right without being frightened by any fear. (3:3–6)

This text does not prohibit wives from styling their hair, wearing jewelry or lovely clothing, which is why the translators added **merely.** The bride in Song of Solomon was beautifully adorned, e.g., Song of Solomon 1:10; 4:11; 7:1. The point is that this was not to be the preoccupation or main concern in the matter of drawing an unsaved husband to Christ. In the Greco-Roman culture, women were devoted to superficial **adornment,** often wearing the best cosmetics, dying their hair outlandish colors, **braiding** it elaborately, and wearing—especially on their heads—costly jewelry to crown their elegant clothing. But **braiding the hair, and wearing gold jewelry, or putting on dresses** made no contribution to spiritual transformation. Such surface concerns still consume women in the present media dominated culture. Christian women, however, especially those whose husbands are not saved, are still under this mandate.

Long before Peter's time God, through Isaiah the prophet, pronounced judgment on women's obsessive, ostentatious attention to outward adornment:

> Moreover, the Lord said, "Because the daughters of Zion are proud and walk with heads held high and seductive eyes, and go along with mincing steps and tinkle the bangles on their feet, therefore the Lord will afflict the scalp of the daughters of Zion with scabs, and the Lord will make their foreheads bare." In that day the Lord will take away the beauty of their anklets, headbands, crescent ornaments, dangling earrings, bracelets, veils, headdresses, ankle chains, sashes, perfume boxes, amulets, finger rings, nose rings, festal robes, outer tunics, cloaks, money purses, hand mirrors, undergarments, turbans and veils. Now it will come about that instead of sweet perfume there will be putrefaction; instead of a belt, a rope; instead of well-set hair, a plucked-out scalp; instead of fine clothes, a donning of sackcloth; and branding instead of beauty. (Isa. 3:16–24; cf. Jer. 2:32)

Instead of being consumed with their external appearance, Christian wives must be devoted to beautifying **the hidden person of the heart.** (**Person** is the translation of *anthrōpos*, "man," demonstrating the biblical use of the masculine gender to describe even a woman.) They should manifest the inner beauty of spiritual virtue. Paul commanded believing women "to adorn themselves with proper clothing, modestly and discreetly, not with braided hair and gold or pearls or costly garments, but rather by means of good works, as is proper for women making a claim to godliness" (1 Tim. 2:9–10; for commentary on these verses, see John MacArthur, *1 Timothy,* MacArthur New Testament Commentary [Chicago: Moody, 1995], 78–82).

In particular, a believing wife should be characterized not by passing earthly fashions, here today and gone tomorrow, but by literally **the imperishable** (**quality** is implied), translated "incorruptible" in 1:4, KJV where it describes the believer's eternal inheritance in heaven. Christian wives should be devoted, not to temporal beauty, but the lovely adornments of godliness. **Gentle** comes from a word referring to a humble and meek attitude, expressed in patient submissiveness; **quiet** is "still" or "tranquil." Such character in the **spirit** of a believing wife is the true inner beauty that **is precious in the sight of God** and effective in making her not only valuable and attractive to her husband, but demonstrating the beauty and value of regeneration.

It is certainly possible for a woman's appearance to be so unkempt and unadorned as to embarrass and discourage her husband, to whom such indifference in the name of Christ would make the gospel offensive and be just as spiritually detrimental as too much attention given to externals. The Lord is most pleased when a believing woman's modest yet thoughtful and lovely adornment reflects the inner beauty Christ has fashioned in her.

In former times (Old Testament days) many believing women (**holy women**) exemplified these principles of submissive and modest godliness (cf. Ruth 3:11; Prov. 31:10–31). Peter says they **used to adorn themselves, being submissive to their own husbands.** Thus his call for such behavior is not unprecedented, and he specifically cites **Sarah** as an illustration, noting that she **obeyed Abraham,** going so far as to **calling him lord** (master). **Calling him** (*kalousa*) is a present participle, which indicates Sarah's continual attitude of respect toward her husband Abraham—she treated him as her **lord** or master.

When Paul wrote that by faith all saints are children of Abraham, he was saying that all who believe have followed the same path Abraham took. He is the Old Testament model for believing God's Word, and all after him who do the same belong to the same family of faith (Rom. 4:1–16; Gal. 3:7–29). Similarly, all believing wives who follow Sarah's example of submission and modesty **have** in that sense **become her children.** Wives who follow Sarah's pattern have made the commitment to **do what is right** or good, even though they might nevertheless have some serious fears as to where such submission under an unsaved husband could lead. The Greek word for **fear** is *ptoēsis,* a strong word meaning "frightening," or "terrifying." Instead of succumbing to such terrors (cf. Ps. 27:1; Prov. 1:33; 29:25; 2 Tim. 1:7; 1 John 4:18), those who are faithful to submit because it is good and **right** can be used by the Lord in the salvation of their husbands.

THE HUSBAND'S RESPONSIBILITY

You husbands in the same way, live with your wives in an understanding way, as with someone weaker, since she is a woman; and show her honor as a fellow heir of the grace of life, so that your prayers will not be hindered. (3:7)

In the same way refers again to the duty of submission (2:13, 18; 3:1). This time it is the believing husband who submits to serve his wife. **Husbands** obey that duty by adhering to three basic responsibilities in caring for their wives' needs: consideration, chivalry, and companionship.

CONSIDERATION

live with your wives in an understanding way, (3:7*a*)

First, husbands are to **live with** their **wives in an understanding way,** which means they must be considerate. **Understanding** speaks of being sensitive and considering the wife's deepest physical and emotional needs. The word translated **live** (*sunoikountes*) means "dwelling together" and refers to living with someone in intimacy and cherishing them. Believing husbands must constantly nourish and cherish their wives in the bond of intimacy:

> Husbands, love your wives, just as Christ also loved the church and gave Himself up for her, so that He might sanctify her, having cleansed her by the washing of water with the word, that He might present to Himself the church in all her glory, having no spot or wrinkle or any such thing; but that she would be holy and blameless. So husbands ought also to love their own wives as their own bodies. He who loves his own wife loves himself. (Eph. 5:25–28; cf. Prov. 5:18–19; 1 Cor. 7:3–5)

CHIVALRY

as with someone weaker, since she is a woman; (3:7*b*)

A believing husband should also be chivalrous to his wife, realizing she is **someone weaker, since she is a woman.** Just as submission does not imply inherent inferiority for the ones who submit (see the discussion of verse 1 of this passage), so the word **weaker** does not mean the wife is intrinsically weaker in character or intellect than her husband. The word (rendered "weaker vessel" by the King James and New King James translators) also does not mean that women are spiritually inferior to men (cf. Gal. 3:28). It just means that women generally possess less physical strength than men. With that in mind, Christian husbands are the sacrificial providers and protectors of their wives (cf. 1 Sam. 1:4–5; Eph. 5:23, 25–26; Col. 3:19; 1 Tim. 5:8), whether or not the wives are believers.

COMPANIONSHIP

and show her honor as a fellow heir of the grace of life, so that your prayers will not be hindered. (3:7*c*)

Third, the husband is to be a companion for his wife **as a fellow heir** sharing in **the grace of life,** which refers not to eternal life, but to the true and intimate friendship that belongs only to those who are possessors of God's most blessed gift in this life—marriage. Peter labels marriage **the grace of life** because **grace** (*charis*) means "unmerited, undeserved favor" (cf. Rom. 1:5; 3:24; 5:15, 17; 12:3; 15:15; 2 Cor. 8:1; 9:8; Gal. 2:9; Eph. 2:7; 3:2, 7; 4:7; 4:29; 2 Tim. 1:9; Heb. 4:16; James 4:6). Marriage is a divine providence given to man regardless of his attitude toward the Giver. Intimate companionship in marriage, the richest blessing of this life, was a foreign concept to the Greco-Roman culture of Peter's day. Husbands were generally uninterested in friendship with their wives, expecting them to merely maintain the household and bear children. In contrast, the Christian husband is to cultivate all the richness God designed into the grace of marriage by showing **honor** to his wife in loving consideration, chivalry, and companionship. **So that** his **prayers will not be hindered** is the reward God promises to the loving, caring husband (cf. Ps. 66:18; Isa. 59:2; John 9:31; James 4:3). The **prayers** in view may be specifically for the salvation of an unbelieving wife, but nothing in the text limits it to that. The warning is clearly given that if a husband in Christ is not fulfilling his responsibilities toward his wife, God may not answer his prayers. No more serious divine threat could be given to a believer than that—the interruption of all the promises of prayers heard and answered (cf. John 14:13–14). That is severe, cutting off the divine blessing, which shows how critical is Christian husbands' loving care of their partners in this **grace of life.**

The key to having a positive witness to an unsaved spouse is living an exemplary Christian life as a faithful, submissive spouse. That obedience pleases God and provides the testimony that honors Jesus Christ before the unsaved partner.

Living and Loving the Good Life (1 Peter 3:8–12)

17

To sum up, all of you be harmonious, sympathetic, brotherly, kind-hearted, and humble in spirit; not returning evil for evil or insult for insult, but giving a blessing instead; for you were called for the very purpose that you might inherit a blessing. For, "The one who desires life, to love and see good days, must keep his tongue from evil and his lips from speaking deceit. He must turn away from evil and do good; he must seek peace and pursue it. For the eyes of the Lord are toward the righteous, and His ears attend to their prayer, but the face of the Lord is against those who do evil." (3:8–12)

The Declaration of Independence contains the well-known phrase "Life, Liberty, and the Pursuit of Happiness," which its author Thomas Jefferson listed as among the "unalienable rights" God gave to people. For most in today's postmodern society, pursuit of that Jeffersonian ideal means primarily chasing after objects of self-gratification such as money, houses, cars, vacations, fine clothes, gourmet food, the best seats at sporting and entertainment events, and health and fitness. Sometimes this pursuit includes the baser aspects of hedonistic living such as promiscuous sex, frequent alcohol consumption, and the unfettered use of so-called recreational drugs (e.g., marijuana, crack cocaine, ecstasy, and methamphetamines). The sad reality, however, is that such things are merely a temporary rush that falls far short of the genuine good life that really satisfies the heart.

One of the most notorious twentieth-century personifications of the hedonistic life was famed novelist Ernest Hemingway. The author of noted literary works such as *The Sun Also Rises, A Farewell to Arms,* and *The Old Man and the Sea,* Hemingway also became notorious for his avant-garde lifestyle. He had little regard for the teachings of the Bible or traditional systems of morality. He pursued the "good life" with a vengeance. His literary talent brought him fame, prestige, and money, which allowed him to seek pleasure all over the world through hunting and fishing expeditions, celebrity parties and gatherings, heavy drinking, fighting in and reporting on several wars and revolutions, and sleeping with women wherever he went. However none of that ultimately gave Hemingway any lasting or genuine satisfaction. His life ended tragically one day in 1961 when he inflicted himself with a fatal shotgun blast to the head.

Even the pages of Scripture contain examples of men who pursued the good life in all the wrong places. Solomon had incredible wealth in the form of land, palaces, chariots and horses, gold and silver, and many beautiful women. Because he was king over Israel, he also had great power and influence. He seemed to possess everything that constituted the good life. In fact, 2 Chronicles 9:3–4 says that when the Queen of Sheba visited Solomon and observed his immense wealth, power, and imposing presence she was breathless. But toward the end of his life, Solomon was not content and failed to experience life to the fullest. In Ecclesiastes 2:17 he wrote, "So I hated life, for the work which had been done under the sun was grievous to me; because everything is futility and striving after wind." Solomon came to realize that the good life is not found in great accomplishments or much education (Eccl. 1:12–14, 16). Neither did he find it in pleasure (2:3) or material possessions (2:4–11). He finally rendered this sobering conclusion that life was really more oppressive than good:

> Then I looked again at all the acts of oppression which were being done under the sun. And behold I saw the tears of the oppressed and that they had no one to comfort them; and on the side of their oppressors was power, but they had no one to comfort them. So I congratulated the dead who are already dead more than the living who are still living. But better off than both of them is the one who has never existed, who has never seen the evil activity that is done under the sun. (Eccl. 4:1–3)

Believers should love the life God has granted them and enjoy its goodness day by day, but many do not. Peter recognized that believers are not exempt from serious and varied difficulties that steal joy (1:6). As discussed earlier in this volume, believers' faith identifies them as aliens in an aggressively hostile society (2:11), making persecution and suffering an integral part of living in an ungodly environment (2:20–21; 3:14–15, 17; 4:1, 12, 19; 5:10). Still, in spite of the suffering, Peter in this passage addresses the believer as "the one who desires life, to love and see good days" (v. 10) and instructs him on how to realize that desire. Here one can easily discern Peter's four basic admonitions for living and loving the good life, even in the midst of present and menacing trouble: have the right attitude, have the right response, have the right standard, and have the right incentive. The apostle concludes his discussion on the Christian's conduct in an ungodly world, which began in 2:11, starting with the phrase in 3:8*a* **to sum up** (*to de telos*), which actually could be translated by the single word "finally." It does not signal the end of the letter, but the conclusion of the current section. After specific references to civil relationships (2:13–17), workplace relationships (2:18–20), and relationships to unsaved spouses (3:1–7), Peter gives all believers a general exhortation, which will open them to the life of blessing God desires for them to enjoy.

Having the Right Attitude

. . . all of you be harmonious, sympathetic, brotherly, kindhearted, and humble in spirit; (3:8*b*)

Everything begins with the right attitude. Five spiritual virtues constitute this God-honoring perspective.

First, believers are to **be harmonious.** The compound word rendered **harmonious** (*homophrones*) literally means "same think." Believers are to live in harmony together, maintaining a common commitment to the truth that produces an inward unity of heart with one another (cf. Rom. 12:5, 16; 1 Cor. 10:17; 12:12; Gal. 3:28; Phil. 2:1–5). They must not be in conflict with each other, even under severe persecution:

> Only conduct yourselves in a manner worthy of the gospel of Christ, so that whether I come and see you or remain absent, I will hear of you that you are standing firm in one spirit, with one mind striving together for the faith of the gospel; in no way alarmed by your opponents— which is a sign of destruction for them, but of salvation for you, and that too, from God. (Phil. 1:27–28)

Jesus instructed the disciples, "A new commandment I give to you, that you love one another, even as I have loved you, that you also love one another. By this all men will know that you are My disciples, if you have love for one another" (John 13:34–35). In His high priestly prayer, Jesus prayed earnestly for the spiritual unity of all believers (John 17:20–23), which prayer was answered. Believers are all one in Christ (Eph. 4:4–6; cf. 1 Cor. 6:17; 8:6). This spiritual reality should be the basis for the church's visible harmony. The early church was a model of visible oneness (Acts 2:42–47).

Sympathetic, the second factor in experiencing the fullness of Christian life, is virtually a transliteration of *sumpatheis*, which means "sharing the same feeling." Christians are to be united on the truth, but also ready to sympathize with the pain of others, even of those they do not know (cf. Matt. 25:34–40; Heb. 13:3; James 1:27). Like Christ, the sympathetic high priest (Heb. 4:15), they must share in the feelings of others, in their sorrows as well as their joys (Rom. 12:15; 1 Cor. 12:26; 2 Cor. 2:3; Col. 3:12; cf. John 11:35; James 5:11). Believers must not be insensitive, indifferent, and censorious, even toward the lost in their pain of struggling anxiously with the issues of life (cf. Matt. 9:36; Luke 13:34–35; 19:41). Saints must come alongside them with empathy to declare God's saving truth (cf. Acts 8:26–37).

Third, Peter used the term *philadelphoi*, translated here as **brotherly.** The first part of the word stems from the verb *phileō*, "to love," and refers to affection among people who are closely related in some way. Those who demonstrate that affection will do so by unselfish service for one another (Acts 20:35; Rom. 14:19; 15:2; 2 Cor. 11:9; Phil. 4:14–16; 1 Thess. 5:11, 14; 3 John 6). Such service begins in the church among believers and extends out to the world.

Kindhearted translates *eusplagchnoi*, the root of which refers to one's internal organs and is sometimes translated "bowels" or "intestines" (e.g., Acts 1:18). Affections and emotions have a visceral impact, hence this word signifies a powerful kind of feeling (Eph. 4:32; cf. 2 Cor. 7:15; 1 Thess. 2:8). Much like **sympathetic,** the expression calls for being so affected by the pain of others as to feel it deeply, following the kind of tenderhearted compassion God, through His Son, has for sinners (cf. Matt. 23:37; Luke 13:34; 19:41–42; John 11:35).

The final factor in Peter's list for enjoying the goodness of the Christian life, **humble in spirit,** is actually one word in the Greek, *tapeinophrones* ("humble-minded"). Humility is arguably the most essential, all-encompassing virtue of the Christian life (5:5; Matt. 5:3; 18:4; Luke 14:11; 18:14; Eph. 4:1–2; Col. 3:12; James 4:6; cf. Ps. 34:2; Prov. 3:34; 15:33; 22:4). Paul used a form of this Greek word in Philippians 2:3, "Do nothing from selfishness or empty conceit, but with humility of mind regard one another as more important than yourselves." Years earlier Jesus demonstrated the importance of His own example of humility when He said, "Take My yoke upon you and learn from Me, for I am gentle and humble in heart, and you will find rest for your souls" (Matt. 11:29; cf. Phil. 2:5–8).

The joys of their lives in Christ are maximized when believers are united in truth and life with one another, peaceful in disposition, gracious toward those who need the gospel, sensitive to the pains of fallen sinners, sacrificial in loving service to all, compassionate instead of harsh, and above all humble like their Savior.

HAVING THE RIGHT RESPONSE

not returning evil for evil or insult for insult, but giving a blessing instead; for you were called for the very purpose that you might inherit a blessing. (3:9)

A godly approach to life incorporates not only the right action motivated by the right attitude, but the proper reaction when mistreated. **Not returning evil for evil** begins with an imperative present participle expressing a negative command (*mē apodidontes*), which can also mean "stop returning." If a believer is not retaliating to evil with more evil, he must not start; if he is, he must stop (cf. Lev. 19:18; Deut. 32:35–36; Prov. 20:22; 24:29; Rom. 12:19; Heb. 10:30).

Evil is from *kakos*, which denotes the inherent quality of badness, not just bad words or actions. When mistreated by someone with a wicked disposition, believers must not retaliate. Peter echoes what Jesus taught in the Sermon on the Mount:

> You have heard that it was said, "An eye for an eye, and a tooth for a tooth." But I say to you, do not resist an evil person; but whoever slaps you on your right cheek, turn the other to him also. If anyone wants to sue you and take your shirt, let him have your coat also. Whoever forces you to go one mile, go with him two. Give to him who asks of you, and do not turn away from him who wants to borrow from you. You have heard that it was said, "You shall love your neighbor and hate your enemy." But I say to you, love your enemies and pray for those who persecute you, so that you may be sons of your Father who is in heaven. (Matt. 5:38–45*a*; cf. Isa. 53:7; Luke 23:34; Acts 7:60; Rom. 12:14, 17; 1 Cor. 4:12; 1 Thess. 5:15)

And again, as with the right attitude (v. 8), Christ is the example (see discussion of 2:21–23 in chapter 15 of this volume).

Turning to the matter of speech, Peter warned his readers not to return **insult for insult.** The term **insult** (*loidoria*) means "an abusive railing against," "cursing," or "speaking evil of" someone and is the root of the word translated "reviled" in 2:23. To engage in such vengeance is an unacceptable response for believers (Eph. 4:29; Col. 3:8; cf. Prov. 4:24; 19:1; Eccl. 5:6). The apostle Paul sought to have the right verbal response to enemies, "When we are reviled, we bless" (1 Cor. 4:12), and warned other believers not to revile (6:10) or even associate with those who do (5:11). There is one occasion, recorded in Acts 23:1–5, when Paul was guilty of giving a retaliating insult:

> Paul, looking intently at the Council, said, "Brethren, I have lived my life with a perfectly good conscience before God up to this day." The high priest Ananias commanded those standing beside him to strike him on the mouth. Then Paul said to him, "God is going to strike you, you white-washed wall! Do you sit to try me according to the Law, and in violation of the Law order me to be struck?" But the bystanders said, "Do you revile God's high priest?" And Paul said, "I was not aware, brethren, that he was high priest; for it is written, 'You shall not speak evil of a ruler of your people.'"

Rather than retaliating when treated in a hostile way, believers are to respond by **giving a blessing instead.** The term translated **blessing** is the word from which the English word *eulogy* derives. It means to praise or speak well of others (cf. Luke 1:42). Peter's admonition suggests several practical applications.

First, believers can bless people by loving them unconditionally (John 13:34; 15:12; Rom. 12:9–10; Col. 2:2; 3:14; 1 Thess. 4:9; James 2:8; 1 John 3:23; 4:7). Second, they can give a blessing by praying for the salvation of an unbeliever (cf. Matt. 5:44; 1 Tim. 2:1–4) or the sanctification of a fellow believer. Third, believers can bless people by expressing gratitude for them (Rom. 1:8; 1 Cor. 1:4; 2 Cor. 1:11; Phil. 1:3–5; Col. 1:3–6; 2 Thess. 1:3). Finally, and most crucial, believers are to forgive those who persecute them (4:8; Mark 11:25; Luke 17:4; Col. 3:13; cf. Gen. 50:20–21; 2 Sam. 18:5; Prov. 19:11). Jesus perfectly illustrated the motive for such forgiveness in the parable of Matthew 18:21–35,

> Then Peter came and said to Him, "Lord, how often shall my brother sin against me and I forgive him? Up to seven times?" Jesus said to him, "I do not say to you, up to seven times, but up to seventy times seven. For this reason the kingdom of heaven may be compared to a king who wished to settle accounts with his slaves. When he had begun to settle them, one who owed him ten thousand talents was brought to him. But since he did not have the means to repay, his lord commanded him to be sold, along with his wife and children and all that he had, and repay-

ment to be made. So the slave fell to the ground and prostrated himself before him, saying, 'Have patience with me and I will repay you everything.' And the lord of that slave felt compassion and released him and forgave him the debt. But that slave went out and found one of his fellow slaves who owed him a hundred denarii; and he seized him and began to choke him, saying, 'Pay back what you owe.' So his fellow slave fell to the ground and began to plead with him, saying, 'Have patience with me and I will repay you.' But he was unwilling and went and threw him in prison until he should pay back what was owed. So when his fellow slaves saw what had happened, they were deeply grieved and came and reported to their lord all that had happened. Then summoning him, his lord said to him, 'You wicked slave, I forgave you all that debt because you pleaded with me. Should you not also have had mercy on your fellow slave, in the same way that I had mercy on you?' And his lord, moved with anger, handed him over to the torturers until he should repay all that was owed him. My heavenly Father will also do the same to you, if each of you does not forgive his brother from your heart."

It is unthinkable for believers to live by the kind of blatant double standard that the unforgiving servant in the parable displayed. Peter makes that clear by stating that believers have been **called for the very purpose that** they **might inherit** (freely receive) **a blessing** (a gift). The apostle's point is that believers have received the divine, unmerited, and eternal blessing of complete forgiveness of an unpayable debt to a holy God and heavenly life forever with Him (Matt. 1:21; John 10:28; Rom. 5:8–9; 6:23; Gal. 1:4; Eph. 1:7; Col. 1:14; 2:13–14; 1 Thess. 5:9; 1 John 4:9–10), rather than His deserved wrath and vengeance for sin. A believer's freely granting forgiveness to someone who has offended him should be an easy consequence, since both that believer and the offense are so small compared to God's greatness and how He has been offended.

HAVING THE RIGHT STANDARD

For, "The one who desires life, to love and see good days, must keep his tongue from evil and his lips from speaking deceit. He must turn away from evil and do good; he must seek peace and pursue it. (3:10–11)

Robertson McQuilkin wrote the following about a crucial presupposition and conviction all believers must have concerning the nature and use of Scripture:

Since God is the author, the Bible is authoritative. It is absolute in its authority for human thought and behavior. "As the Scripture has said" is a recurring theme throughout the New Testament. In fact, the New Testament contains more than two hundred direct quotations of the Old Testament. In addition, the New Testament has a large and uncertain number of allusions to the Old. New Testament writers, following the example of Jesus Christ, built their theology on the Old Testament. For Christ and the apostles, to quote the Bible was to settle an issue. (*Understanding and Applying the Bible,* rev. ed. [Chicago: Moody, 1983, 1992], 20)

Just as Christ and the apostles lived and ministered by the ultimate standard of Holy Scripture, so also must believers who would enjoy God's gift of life (Prov. 6:23; Matt. 4:4; Rom. 15:4; 2 Tim. 3:16; Heb. 4:12). Peter illustrates that principle here by quoting from a psalm to defend what he just taught.

The word **for** at the beginning of verse 10 connects verses 8 and 9 to Peter's quotes from Psalm 34:12–14, supporting his exhortation that believers must have a right response to hostility. A Christian—described here as **the one who desires life, to love and see good days**—must refrain from speaking anything that comes **from** the underlying **evil** of an immoral disposition.

The **tongue** is often unruly and prone to sin:"And the tongue is a fire, the very world of iniquity; the tongue is set among our members as that which defiles the entire body, and sets on fire the course of our life, and is set on fire by hell" (James 3:6; cf. 1:26; 3:9–10; Ps. 12:3; Prov. 12:18; 15:2, 4).

In addition to refraining from verbal retaliation, believers must stop their **lips from speaking deceit.** They must be absolutely committed to the truth (Ps. 51:6; Prov. 3:3; 23:23; 1 Cor. 13:6; Phil. 4:8; cf. Josh. 24:14; 1 Sam. 12:24) and opposed to all lying, deception, and hypocrisy (Ex. 20:16; Prov. 6:16–19; 10:18; 12:17, 19, 22; Zech. 8:16; Eph. 4:25; Col. 3:9). These matters of speech are controlled, not at the mouth, but on the inside—as Jesus said in Matthew 12:34,"For the mouth speaks out of that which fills the heart."

Verse 11, drawn from Psalm 34:14, contains four straightforward imperative commands. First, believers are to **turn away from evil** (cf. Prov. 3:7; 16:6, 17; Isa. 1:16–17; 1 Thess. 5:22). The verb **turn away** (*ekklinatō*) connotes an intensely strong rejection of what is sinful—in this context, sinful treatment of others, even those who persecute the saints (cf. Matt. 5:44; Rom. 12:14).

Second, Peter commanded his readers to **do good,** what is excellent in quality, what expresses deep-down virtue. That contrasts sharply with the contemporary notion of the good life as "doing one's own thing," whatever feels good (illicit sex, drugs, alcohol, excessive and mindless entertainment) at the expense of obeying God's will. (An examination of several words in the earlier phrase **the one who desires life, to love and see good days** further sharpens the contrast between a worldly view of the good life and a biblical view. **Life** [*zōēn*, rather than *bios*] connotes all the experience and richness of living to the fullest, not merely living as opposed to dying. **Love** [*agapan*] is from the strongest word for that emotion and denotes a strong-willed affection or desire [e.g., Matt. 22:37–39; John 13:34–35; 14:15, 23; 21:15–17; Rom. 5:8; 8:35, 39; 1 Cor. 13:1–4, 8, 13; Eph. 2:4; 5:25; 1 John 3:1, 16]

The third and fourth imperatives appear together in the command for believers to **seek peace and pursue it.** The verbs translated **seek** and **pursue** both convey an intensity and aggressiveness of action. (Implicit in the phrase is the analogy of the hunter vigorously tracking down his prey.) **Peace** (*eirēnēn*) denotes a constant condition of tranquility that produces permanent joy and happiness (cf. Luke 2:14; 8:48; 19:38; John 14:27; 16:33; Rom. 5:1; 8:6; 15:13; Gal. 5:22; Phil. 4:7; Col. 3:15; 2 Thess. 3:16). Christians are to **seek peace** and hunt for it aggressively, even peace with their persecutors and others who do not know Christ (cf. Rom. 12:18; 14:19; 1 Thess. 5:13; 2 Thess. 3:16). They are to be known in the world as peacemakers, those who strive for harmony with others as much as possible without compromising the truth (cf. Matt. 5:9; Rom. 12:18; 14:17, 19; 2 Cor. 13:11; 2 Tim. 2:22; James 3:17).

HAVING THE RIGHT INCENTIVE

For the eyes of the Lord are toward the righteous, and His ears attend to their prayer, but the face of the Lord is against those who do evil." (3:12)

Peter's quote here of Psalm 34:15–16 vividly fixes the reality that ought to motivate believers to live lives pleasing to God. The psalmist's words describe a sovereign, ruling God (Pss. 90:2; 102:25–27; Dan. 4:35; Eph. 3:11) who sees all (Job 28:24; Prov. 5:21), knows all (Ps. 147:5; Rom. 11:33), holds people accountable for their behavior (Gen. 2:16–17; Rom. 1:20), and threatens punishment for disobedience (Ezek. 18:4; Rom. 6:23). But for Peter, the primary issue here is not judgment but God's gracious care for His people.

The eyes of the Lord is a common Old Testament phrase that relates to God's special, caring watchfulness over His people (Prov. 5:21; Zech. 4:10). Sometimes the phrase indicates God's judgmental watchfulness (Amos 9:8; cf. Prov. 15:3), but here the emphasis is on His omniscient awareness of every detail of believers' lives (cf. Ps. 139:1–6).

God is also looking **toward the righteous** so that He can **attend**

to their prayer. The word translated **prayer** (*deēsin*) means "entreaty," "petition," or "supplication," and relates to believers' crying out for God to meet their needs (Ps. 5:2; Matt. 7:7; Phil. 4:6; 1 John 5:14–15). God is always fully aware of everything in the lives of His children. It ought to be a great incentive for believers to live as Peter has outlined, knowing that they can have confidence that the Lord is always watching and waiting, ready to hear and answer their prayers (4:7; Pss. 50:15; 65:2; 138:3; Rom. 8:26; Heb. 4:16).

On the other hand, **the face of the Lord is against those who do evil.** In contrast to **the eyes of the Lord,** which refers to watchfulness, the Old Testament concept **face of the Lord** refers to judgment (cf. Gen. 19:13; Lam. 4:16). His **eyes** represent His all-seeing omniscience, whereas His **face** in this context represents the manifestation of His anger and displeasure (cf. Ps. 76:6–8). God's wrath **is against those who do evil** and those who disobey His Word (cf. Rev. 6:16).

Christians, whether today or in Peter's time, have always had to contend with a hostile world. But they can live humbly, respond to persecution in a Christlike manner, and adhere to God's standard of authority because they have the promise that even in the midst of trying circumstances God is watching over them, protecting them, and ready to extend His blessings.

Securities Against a Hostile World (1 Peter 3:13–17)

18

Who is there to harm you if you prove zealous for what is good? But even if you should suffer for the sake of righteousness, you are blessed. And do not fear their intimidation, and do not be troubled, but sanctify Christ as Lord in your hearts, always being ready to make a defense to everyone who asks you to give an account for the hope that is in you, yet with gentleness and reverence; and keep a good conscience so that in the thing in which you are slandered, those who revile your good behavior in Christ will be put to shame. For it is better, if God should will it so, that you suffer for doing what is right rather than for doing what is wrong. (3:13–17)

Today there is an escalating hostility toward biblical Christianity throughout Western culture. But the roots of that hostility are decades, even centuries, old. Francis Schaeffer provided the following analysis in the 1970s:

> In ancient Israel, when the nation had turned from God and from his truth and commands as given in Scripture, the prophet Jeremiah cried out that there was death in the city. He was speaking not only of physical death in Jerusalem but also a wider death. Because Jewish society

of that day had turned away from what God had given them in the Scripture, there was death in the *polis,* that is, death in the total culture and the total society.

In our era, sociologically, man destroyed the base which gave him the possibility of freedoms without chaos. Humanists have been determined to beat to death the knowledge of God and the knowledge that God has not been silent, but has spoken in the Bible and through Christ—and they have been determined to do this even though the death of values has come with the death of that knowledge.

We see two effects of our loss of meaning and values. The first is degeneracy. Think of New York City's Times Square—Forty-second and Broadway. If one goes to what used to be the lovely Kalverstraat in Amsterdam, one finds that it, too, has become equally squalid! The same is true of lovely old streets in Copenhagen. Pompeii has returned! The marks of ancient Rome scar us: degeneracy, decadence, depravity, a love of violence for violence's sake. The situation is plain. If we look, we see it. If we see it, we are concerned.

But we *must* notice that there is a second result of modern man's loss of meaning and values which is more ominous, and which many people do not see. This second result is that the elite will exist. Society cannot stand chaos. Some group or some person will fill the vacuum. An elite will offer us arbitrary absolutes, and who will stand in its way? (*How Should We then Live?* [Westchester, Ill.: Crossway, 1976], 226-27; emphasis in the original)

Believers in Peter's time lived in the Roman Empire Schaeffer referred to, facing all the same kind of degeneracy and depravity that assaults today's church. But they faced more frequent and overt hostility and persecution than believers in today's culture face. In some parts of the world, however, there is direct persecution of believers, and it is likely that in the coming years Christians everywhere will face increasing hostility, both from civil authorities and from unbelievers at the personal level. This passage speaks to all who would live godly lives in the midst of a hostile, ungodly culture. The apostle Peter gives five principles believers need to embrace to equip and defend themselves against the threats of an unbelieving, hostile world: a passion for goodness, a willingness to suffer—for wrong and for right, a devotion to Christ, a readiness to defend the faith, and a pure conscience.

A PASSION FOR GOODNESS

Who is there to harm you if you prove zealous for what is good? (3:13)

Peter's rhetorical question shows that it is unusual for most people, even those hostile to Christianity, to harm believers who **prove zealous for what is good.** On the other hand, the world has little hesitation attacking with great hostility those charlatans and frauds that enrich themselves at the expense of others. **Good** refers generally to a life characterized by generosity, unselfishness, kindness, and thoughtfulness toward others (cf. Pss. 37:3; 125:4; Prov. 3:27; 11:23; 2 Cor. 9:8; Gal. 6:9–10; Eph. 2:10; Col. 1:10; 1 Thess. 5:15; 1 Tim. 6:18; Titus 1:8; 2:7, 14; 3:14; Heb. 13:16; James 3:13, 17; 3 John 11). Such a lifestyle has a way of restraining the hand of even the most ardent foe of the gospel (cf. 2:12; Matt. 5:16; Rom. 12:20–21).

Prove (*genēsthe*) means "to become" and points to believers' basic character quality, which should be **good** and above reproach (cf. Rom. 13:3; Phil. 2:14–16; 2 Tim. 2:20–22). **Zealous** (*zēlōtēs*) means "intensity" or "enthusiasm" and describes a person with great ardor for a specific cause. In New Testament times, there was a radical political party of Jewish patriots, called the Zealots (from *zēlōtēs*), which pledged to free the Jews from all foreign rule by whatever extreme measures (lying, stealing, assassination) were necessary, even if those efforts resulted in their own deaths. Peter was surely familiar with that group—Simon the Zealot, one of his fellow apostles, had likely been a member (Matt. 10:4; Mark 3:18; Luke 6:15; Acts 1:13)—and he wanted his readers to be zealots for what was noble (cf. 1 Cor. 14:12; 2 Cor. 7:11; Titus 2:14; Rev. 3:19).

Of course, being **zealous for what is good** produces a godly life—the delight and goal of all believers—which leads to pure living and the loss of one's appetite for the world's ungodly attractions.

A WILLINGNESS TO SUFFER—
FOR WRONG AND FOR RIGHT

But even if you should suffer for the sake of righteousness, you are blessed. And do not fear their intimidation, and do not be troubled, . . . For it is better, if God should will it so, that you suffer for doing what is right rather than for doing what is wrong. (3:14, 17)

Having a passion for goodness is certainly not a gilt-edged guarantee against suffering; it may only make it more unlikely or less frequent. Jesus Christ "went about doing good" (Acts 10:38; cf. John 10:32), yet a hostile world eventually killed Him (Matt. 27:22–23; Luke 23:23–25; Acts 2:23; cf. Isa. 53:9). Jesus Himself made it clear that believers cannot presume to escape all suffering if their Lord did not (cf. Matt. 10:24–25; Luke 6:22; John 15:20; Acts 14:22; Phil. 1:29–30; 2 Tim. 3:12; Heb. 12:3–4).

But even if conveys the idea of "perchance" or "contrary to what is expected" and fits with the verb **should suffer** (*paschoite*), which in this Greek verb form (optative) expresses a fourth-class condition implying there is no certainty that suffering will happen, but it might.

Many Christians in the early church, including some of Peter's readers (1:6–7; 2:20; 4:12–16), did **suffer for the sake of righteousness** (Acts 5:40–41; 7:57–60; 8:3–4; 12:1–4; 13:50; 16:20–24; 17:5–9; 26:9–11)— their upright, godly behavior. Likewise, faithful Christians today should not be surprised or afraid if such suffering comes, because that becomes a means by which they **are blessed.** In what ways does suffering for godliness bring blessing? Later in this letter Peter describes some of the ways: "After you have suffered for a little while, the God of all grace, who called you to His eternal glory in Christ, will Himself perfect, confirm, strengthen and establish you" (5:10).

Peter is not the only New Testament writer who expressed the blessing in suffering. James did in his letter: "Consider it all joy, my brethren, when you encounter various trials, knowing that the testing of your faith produces endurance. And let endurance have its perfect result, so that you may be perfect and complete, lacking in nothing" (1:2–4). The blessings of suffering did not escape Paul's observation, either:

> Therefore we do not lose heart, but though our outer man is decaying, yet our inner man is being renewed day by day. For momentary, light affliction is producing for us an eternal weight of glory far beyond all comparison, while we look not at the things which are seen, but at the things which are not seen; for the things which are seen are temporal, but the things which are not seen are eternal. (2 Cor. 4:16–18)

The apostle John was given a promise related to suffering in Revelation 2:10, "'Do not fear what you are about to suffer. Behold, the devil is about to cast some of you into prison, so that you will be tested, and you will have tribulation for ten days. Be faithful until death, and I will give you the crown of life.'"

Blessed (*makarioi*) here does not emphasize the effect— happiness or joy—but the motive for such "privilege" or "honor." Elizabeth, mother of John the Baptist and a relative of Jesus' mother, Mary, said of Mary, "Blessed are you among women" (Luke 1:42). Mary's heart would be pierced with many sorrows (2:35), so Elizabeth's statement was not merely a reference to general happiness. She instead referred to Mary's divinely-endowed favor and privilege of giving birth to Christ (1:26–35).

All believers can have the same sense of privilege by sharing in His sufferings:

> Blessed are those who have been persecuted for the sake of righteousness, for theirs is the kingdom of heaven. Blessed are you when people insult you and persecute you, and falsely say all kinds of evil against you because of Me. Rejoice and be glad, for your reward in heaven is great; for in the same way they persecuted the prophets who were before you. (Matt. 5:10–12; cf. Rev. 14:13)

Peter's admonition for his readers to **not fear their intimidation, and do not be troubled** is an allusion to Isaiah 8:12*b*–13, "And you are not to fear what they fear or be in dread of it. It is the Lord of hosts whom you should regard as holy. And He shall be your fear, and He shall be your dread." The historical setting of those verses is significant. With an impending invasion by Assyria, Ahaz king of Judah faced a crisis. The kings of Israel and Syria had sought to make an alliance with him against the Assyrian forces, but Ahaz had refused. Israel and Syria therefore threatened to invade Judah. Meanwhile Ahaz had allied Judah with Assyria, but the prophet Isaiah warned him against such an ungodly alliance and told him not to be afraid. Ahaz and the people of Judah were not to fear Assyria as Syria and Israel did, but rather they were to fear the Lord by trusting in Him.

Likewise, Peter wrote that Christians must **not fear their intimidation,** literally, that they should "not fear their fear," that is, be intimidated by unbelievers who would persecute them (cf. Ps. 118:6; Prov. 29:25; Matt. 10:28; Luke 12:4–5; Acts 4:23–30). Furthermore they must **not be troubled,** literally "not shaken or stirred up" (cf. 4:16, 19).

In their willingness to suffer, believers must face all circumstances with courage (cf. Josh, 1:7, 9; 10:25; 2 Sam. 10:12; 1 Chron. 28:10, 20; Ezra 10:4; Ps. 31:24; Mark 6:50; 1 Cor. 16:13). Suffering must be viewed as an opportunity to receive spiritual blessings, not as an excuse to compromise the faith before a hostile world. As the seventeenth-century English preacher and writer John Bunyan accepted imprisonment in the Bedford Jail for preaching without a license, and Reformer Martin Luther stood before his enemies and refused to recant his scriptural beliefs, so Christians today must stand firm in the face of suffering. Believers whose minds and affections are set on things above (Col. 3:2–3) will rejoice when they must undergo sufferings because they see through to the blessings to be gained.

Concerning suffering, there are two possibilities. First, believers may **suffer for doing what is right,** accepting that pain as part of God's wise and sovereign plan for blessing their lives. Second, they may

suffer **for doing what is wrong,** receiving the expected discipline of
the Lord for their disobeying His Word (cf. 2:20; 4:15–19). God sometimes
wills that believers suffer for righteousness so they might receive the
blessings that come out of such suffering. It is also God's will that believers endure His beneficial chastisement when they sin (Heb. 12:5–11). Of
the two possibilities that may come, Peter recognizes that the first is
unique because it comes only **if God should will it so.** That is a comforting promise. Paul certainly learned that lesson:

> Because of the surpassing greatness of the revelations, for this reason,
> to keep me from exalting myself, there was given me a thorn in the
> flesh, a messenger of Satan to torment me—to keep me from exalting
> myself! Concerning this I implored the Lord three times that it might
> leave me. And He has said to me, "My grace is sufficient for you, for
> power is perfected in weakness." Most gladly, therefore, I will rather
> boast about my weaknesses, so that the power of Christ may dwell in
> me. Therefore I am well content with weaknesses, with insults, with dis-
> tresses, with persecutions, with difficulties, for Christ's sake; for when I
> am weak, then I am strong. (2 Cor. 12:7–10)

Christians **suffer for the sake of righteousness** when God
wants them to. He never wants us to sin, so that suffering, in one sense, is
not what He wished for them though it has sometimes become His will
for their righteousness (Heb. 12:11).

A Devotion to Christ

but sanctify Christ as Lord in your hearts, (3:15*a*)

Here the apostle again alludes to Isaiah 8:13, "Sanctify the Lord of
hosts" (KJV). When believers **sanctify Christ as Lord in** their **hearts,**
they affirm their submission to His control, instruction, and guidance. In
so doing they also declare and submit to God's sovereign majesty (cf.
Deut. 4:35; 32:4; 1 Kings 8:27; Pss. 90:2; 92:15; 99:9; 145:3, 5; Isa. 43:10; Rom.
8:28; 11:33) and demonstrate that they fear only Him (Josh. 24:22–24; Pss.
22:23; 27:1; 34:9; 111:10; 119:46,63; Prov. 14:26; Matt. 4:10).
Sanctify (*hagiasate*) means "to set apart," or "consecrate." But in
this context it also connotes giving the primary place of adoration, exaltation, and worship to **Christ.** Believers who **sanctify Christ** set Him
apart from all others as the sole object of their love, reverence, loyalty,
and obedience (cf. Rom. 13:14; Phil. 2:5–11; 3:14; Col. 3:4; 2 Peter
1:10–11). They recognize His perfection (Heb. 7:26–28), magnify His
glory (Acts 7:55–56; cf. Rev. 1:12–18), extol His pre-eminence (Col. 1:18),

and submit themselves to His will (Mark 3:35; Rom. 12:2; Eph. 6:6; Heb. 10:36; 1 John 2:17), with the understanding that sometimes that submission includes suffering.

This honoring of Christ as Lord is not external, but **in** the **hearts** of true worshipers—even when they must face unjust suffering. That submission to and trust in the perfect purposes of the sovereign Lord yields courage, boldness, and fortitude to triumph through the most adverse situations.

A READINESS TO DEFEND THE FAITH

always being ready to make a defense to everyone who asks you to give an account for the hope that is in you, yet with gentleness and reverence; (3:15*b*)

It is not just endurance through the blessing of suffering that believers are to submit to; there is also the opportunity to defend the truth when they are being persecuted. Christians must be ready **to make a defense** of the faith. The Greek term for **defense** (*apologia*) is the word from which the English terms *apology* and *apologetics* derive. It often means a formal defense in a judicial courtroom (cf. Acts 25:16; 2 Tim. 4:16), but Paul also used the word informally to denote his ability to answer those who questioned him (Phil. 1:16). **Always** indicates believers' need for constant preparedness and readiness to respond, whether in a formal courtroom or informally, to **everyone who asks** them **to give an account** for why they live and believe the way they do. **Account** is simply *logos*, "word," or "message," and it calls saints to be able at the time someone **asks** (present tense) **to give** the right words in response to questions about the gospel.

The gospel is identified as **the hope that is in** believers. **Hope** is synonymous with the Christian faith because the motive for believers' embracing Jesus Christ as Lord and Savior is their anticipation of escaping hell and entering eternal glory (cf. Acts 26:6; Eph. 1:18; 4:4; Col. 1:23; Heb. 10:23). Thus **hope** becomes the focal point of any rational explanation believers should be able to provide regarding their salvation. (For further insights into the meaning of hope, see the discussion of 1:3 in chapter 2 of this volume.)

The believer's defense of this hope before the unbeliever who asks must be firm and uncompromising, but at the same time conveyed **with gentleness and reverence. Gentleness** refers to meekness or humility, not in the sense of weakness but in the sense of not being dominant or overbearing (cf. Eph. 4:15, "speaking the truth in love"). The Lord

Himself was characterized by this virtue, as was Paul: "Now I, Paul, myself urge you by the meekness and gentleness of Christ" (2 Cor. 10:1*a*).

Reverence expresses devotion to God, a deep regard for His truth, and even respect for the person listening (Col. 4:6; 2 Tim. 2:24–26).

Christians who cannot present a biblically clear explanation of their faith (cf. 1 Thess. 5:19–22; 1 John 2:14) will be insecure when strongly challenged by unbelievers (cf. Eph. 4:14–15). In some cases that insecurity can undermine their assurance of salvation. The world's attacks can overwhelm those who have not "put on the breastplate of faith and love, and as a helmet, the hope of salvation" (1 Thess. 5:8; cf. Eph. 6:10–17).

A PURE CONSCIENCE

and keep a good conscience so that in the thing in which you are slandered, those who revile your good behavior in Christ will be put to shame. (3:16)

The final thing that will allow believers to be secure in a hostile world is a pure **conscience**. The conscience is the divinely-placed internal mechanism that either accuses or excuses a person, acting as a means of conviction or affirmation. As I write elsewhere:

> The conscience is the soul reflecting on itself; both the Greek word *suneidēsis* (**conscience**) and the English word "conscience" have the idea of knowing oneself. According to Roman 2:14, even those without God's written law have an innate moral sense of right and wrong: "For when Gentiles who do not have the Law do instinctively the things of the Law, these, not having the Law, are a law to themselves." The conscience either affirms right behavior or condemns sinful behavior.
> The conscience, however, is not infallible. It is neither the voice of God, nor His moral law, as Colin G. Kruse helpfully observes:

> > The conscience is not to be equated with the voice of God or even the moral law, rather it is a human faculty which adjudicates upon human action by the light of the highest standard a person perceives.
> > Seeing that all of human nature has been affected by sin, both a person's perception of the standard of action required and the function of the conscience itself (as a constituent part of human nature) are also affected by sin. For this reason conscience can never be accorded the position of ultimate judge of one's behavior. It is possible that the conscience may excuse one for that which God will not excuse, and conversely it is equally possible that conscience may condemn a person for that which God allows. The final judgment therefore belongs only to God (cf. 1 Cor. 4:2–5). Nevertheless, to reject the voice of conscience is to court spiritual disaster

(cf. 1 Tim. 1:19). We cannot reject the voice of conscience with impunity, but we can modify the highest standard to which it relates by gaining for ourselves a greater understanding of the truth. (*The Second Epistle of Paul to the Corinthians*, The Tyndale New Testament Commentaries [Grand Rapids: Eerdmans, 1995], 70-71)

Since the conscience holds people to their highest perceived standard, believers need to set that standard to the highest level by submitting to all of God's Word. As they continually fill their minds with the truths of Scripture, believers clarify God's perfect law. Their consciences will then call them to live according to that law.

The conscience functions like a skylight, not like a lamp; it does not produce its own light, but merely lets moral light in. Because of that, the Bible teaches the importance of keeping a clear or good conscience. "The goal of our instruction," Paul wrote to Timothy, "is love from a pure heart and a good conscience and a sincere faith" (1 Tim. 1:5). A few verses later Paul stressed the importance of "keeping faith and a good conscience, which," he warned, "some have rejected and suffered shipwreck in regard to their faith" (v. 19). A necessary qualification for deacons is that they hold "to the mystery of the faith with a clear conscience" (1 Tim. 3:9). Peter commanded believers to "keep a good conscience so that in the thing in which you are slandered, those who revile your good behavior in Christ will be put to shame" (1 Peter 3:16). Both Paul (Acts 23:1; 2 Tim. 1:3) and the writer of Hebrews (Heb. 13:18) testified that they had maintained good consciences.

At salvation, God cleanses the conscience from its lifelong accumulation of guilt, shame, and self-contempt. The writer of Hebrews wrote that "the blood of Christ, who through the eternal Spirit offered Himself without blemish to God, [will] cleanse [the] conscience from dead works to serve the living God" (Heb. 9:14). As a result, believers have their "hearts sprinkled clean from an evil conscience" (Heb. 10:22). The cleansed conscience no longer accuses because of past sins, which are pardoned (Pss. 32:5; 103:12; Prov. 28:13; Mic. 7:18–19; Col. 1:14; 2:13–14; 1 John 1:9) through the blood of Christ (Eph. 1:7; 1 John 1:7; Rev. 1:5).

Believers' must guard the purity of their cleansed consciences, winning the battle for holiness on the inside where conscience works. Paul gained victory at that point, so that he declared to the Sanhedrin, "I have lived my life with a perfectly good conscience before God up to this day" (Acts 23:1), and to the Roman governor Felix, "I also do my best to maintain always a blameless conscience both before God and before men" (Acts 24:16). He wrote to Timothy, "I thank God, whom I serve with a clear conscience" (2 Tim. 1:3). He reminded his young protégé that "the goal of our instruction is love from a pure heart and a good conscience and a sincere faith" (1 Tim. 1:5) and exhorted him to keep "a good conscience, which some have rejected and suffered shipwreck in regard to their faith" (1 Tim. 1:19). As noted above, Paul instructed that deacons must hold "to the mystery of the faith with a clear conscience" (1 Tim. 3:9). Christians must also be careful not to cause other believers to violate their consciences (1 Cor. 8:7–13; 10:24–29). (John MacArthur, *2 Corinthians,* MacArthur New Testament Commentary [Chicago: Moody, 2003], 30–32)

A good conscience is what every Christian must **keep** or, better, maintain.

A clear conscience allows believers to be free from any burden of guilt as they face hostility and criticism from the world (cf. Job 27:6; Rom. 14:22; 1 Tim. 3:9). An impure conscience, however, cannot be comfortable (cf. Gen. 42:21; 2 Sam. 24:10; Acts 2:37) and is unable to withstand the stress originating from difficult trials and persecutions. Regarding **the thing in which** they **are slandered,** believers ought to be able to agree with the apostle Paul, who declared, "I also do my best to maintain always a blameless conscience both before God and before men" (Acts 24:16; cf. 2 Cor. 1:12). (For a more in-depth discussion of the conscience, see John MacArthur, *The Vanishing Conscience* [Dallas: Word, 1994], especially chaps. 2, 3, 10, and appendixes 2 and 3.)

Slandered believers who maintain **good behavior in Christ** will have their consciences at rest, untroubled by guilt, and their godly lives will prove any criticisms from unbelievers to be false. **Slandered** (*katalaleisthe*) is an onomatopoetic word (one whose pronunciation suggests its meaning) that describes "evil speaking" or "verbal abuse." **Revile** means "to threaten," "to insult," or "to mistreat." A pure conscience can withstand and deflect whatever abusive, insulting speech the world hurls at it (cf. 1 Cor. 4:12). Those who engage in such sinful mistreatment of obedient believers (Pss. 42:10; 74:10; Matt. 27:29, 31, 41, 44; Mark 15:32; Luke 23:36; Acts 2:13), with the aim of shaming and defeating them, will themselves **be put to shame** (cf. Gen. 42:8–21).

Adversity is a reality and suffering a spiritual privilege for believers. If they realize "that God causes all things to work together for good to those who love God" (Rom. 8:28), they will be able to accept suffering as part of God's plan for them and equip themselves with His securities against a hostile world. Puritan Thomas Watson wrote,

> Afflictions work for good, as they make way for glory. . . . Not that they merit glory, but they prepare for it. As ploughing prepares the earth for a crop, so afflictions prepare and make us [ready] for glory. The painter lays his gold upon dark colours, so God first lays the dark colours of affliction, and then He lays the golden colour of glory. The vessel is first seasoned before wine is poured into it: the vessels of mercy are first seasoned with affliction, and then the wine of glory is poured in. Thus we see afflictions are not prejudicial, but beneficial, to the saints. (*All Things for Good* [reprint; Edinburgh: Banner of Truth, 1986], 32)

The Triumph of Christ's Suffering (1 Peter 3:18–22)

19

For Christ also died for sins once for all, the just for the unjust, so that He might bring us to God, having been put to death in the flesh, but made alive in the spirit; in which also He went and made proclamation to the spirits now in prison, who once were disobedient, when the patience of God kept waiting in the days of Noah, during the construction of the ark, in which a few, that is, eight persons, were brought safely through the water. Corresponding to that, baptism now saves you—not the removal of dirt from the flesh, but an appeal to God for a good conscience—through the resurrection of Jesus Christ, who is at the right hand of God, having gone into heaven, after angels and authorities and powers had been subjected to Him. (3:18–22)

Peter culminates his section on the unjust suffering of believers with the example of how Christ's unjust suffering achieved God's triumphant purpose. At the heart of the gospel is the fact that Jesus Christ, who was perfectly righteous, died for the utterly unrighteous. He triumphed through that undeserved suffering by, as God had predetermined, providing redemption for the world. In that one event, God had His intentions fulfilled and evil men also had their intentions fulfilled

(Acts 2:23–24; 4:27–28; cf. Gen. 50:19–20). The mystery of divine providence is that God is absolutely sovereign, but His rule and predetermination is never apart from human responsibility. And the evil of man never reduces Him to a secondary cause. God is primary in providentially accomplishing every feature of His eternal will and plan. Christ's perfect example of suffering unjustly and through that accomplishing the glorious saving purpose of God should give believers hope and confidence for the triumph of God's purpose in the midst of their own suffering (cf. Rom. 8:17; 2 Cor. 2:14; Phil. 1:29). To give them a richer understanding of the blessed outcome of the cross's injustice, Peter urged his readers to consider four elements of the Lord's victory: His triumphant sin-bearing, His triumphant sermon, His triumphant salvation, and His triumphant supremacy.

His Triumphant Sin-Bearing

For Christ also died for sins once for all, the just for the unjust, so that He might bring us to God, (3:18*a*)

The conjunctions **also** and **for** point Peter's readers back to the previous passage (3:13–17) and remind them that they ought not to be surprised or discouraged by suffering, since **Christ** triumphed in His suffering even though He **died** an excruciating death, and that of the most horrific kind—crucifixion. In contrast, the author of the letter to the Hebrews reminded his readers who suffered that they had "not yet resisted to the point of shedding blood" (12:4). Most believers will not die as martyrs, but even when they do, that death is the wages of their sin (Rom. 6:23). All people die because they are sinful, which makes even a death for righteousness' sake a just death, in a sense. Man deserves to die; Jesus did not.

Some translations (e.g., KJV, NKJV) of this verse render **died** as "suffered," a reading based on variant Greek manuscripts. But the different translations do not change the meaning: Christ suffered in that He **died for sins.** Sin caused the sinless Christ's death. This is the supreme example of suffering for righteousness' sake (v. 18), and He willingly endured it on behalf of sinners (Isa. 53:4–6, 8–12; Matt. 26:26–28; John 1:29; 10:11, 15; Rom. 5:8–11; 8:32; 1 Cor. 15:3; 2 Cor. 5:15, 18–19; Gal. 1:4; Eph. 2:13–16; Col. 1:20–22; 1 Thess. 1:10; 1 Tim. 2:5–6; Heb. 2:9, 17; 7:27; 9:12, 24–28; 10:10; 13:12; 1 John 1:7; 2:2; 4:10; Rev. 1:5; 5:9). Earlier in this letter, Peter asserted that Christ "committed no sin" (2:22). He never had a single thought, word, or action that did not fully please God; rather His behavior in every respect was perfectly holy (Isa. 53:11; Luke 1:35; 2 Cor. 5:21; Heb. 4:15; 7:26; cf. John 5:30; Heb. 1:9).

So Jesus **died for sins** in that He was "offered once to bear the sins of many" (Heb. 9:28; cf. Rom. 8:3; Heb. 10:5–10). In the Old Testament economy, God required animal sacrifices to symbolize the need to atone for sin by the death of an innocent substitute (Ex. 29:31–33, 36; Lev. 1:4–5; 8:34; 16:2–16; 17:11; 23:26–27; Num. 15:25; 1 Chron. 6:49); the New Testament presents Christ as that perfect sacrifice who fulfilled all the symbols in the reality of atoning for all sinners who would ever believe (John 3:14–15; Rom. 5:6–11; 1 Cor. 5:7; Heb. 9:11–14, 24, 28; 12:24; 13:11–12).

The phrase **once for all** translates the word *hapax*, which means "of perpetual validity, not requiring repetition." For the Jews so familiar with their sacrificial system, that was a new concept. To atone for sin, they had slaughtered millions of animals over the centuries. During their annual Passover celebration, as many as a quarter million sheep would be sacrificed. But Jesus Christ's one sacrificial death ended that insufficient parade of animals to the altar and was sufficient for all *and* for all time (Heb. 1:3; 7:26–27; 9:24–28; 10:10–12), as He took the punishment due the elect and bore it for them, thus fully satisfying God's righteous judgment.

Thus, in Christ's substitutionary death, He suffered **the just for the unjust.** As the perfect offering for sin, He willingly (John 10:15–18) and in accord with the Father's redemptive purpose from before the foundation of the world (Acts 2:23; 4:27–28; 13:27–29; cf. 2 Tim. 1:9; Rev. 13:8) took upon Himself the entire penalty due the unrighteous (2:24). No text says it more concisely than 2 Corinthians 5:21, "He made Him who knew no sin to be sin on our behalf, so that we might become the righteousness of God in Him." Much more can be said about sin and imputation, as is elsewhere (cf. Rom. 3–6), but here Peter directs his statements at the practical, referring to the substitutionary suffering of Jesus as an illustration of how the most extreme affliction and injustice resulted in the singularly supreme triumph of salvation. This should be eminently encouraging to believers who suffer unjustly.

The triumph in Christ's death is expressed in the phrase **that He might bring** [believers] **to God.** The divine tearing of the temple veil from top to bottom (Matt. 27:51) symbolically demonstrated the reality that He had opened the way to God. The heavenly Holy of Holies, the "throne of grace" (Heb. 4:16), was made available for immediate access by all true believers. As royal priests (2:9), all believers are welcomed into God's presence (Heb. 4:16; 10:19–22).

The verb translated **He might bring** (*prosagō*) expresses the specific purpose of Jesus' actions. It often describes someone's being introduced or given access to another. In classical Greek the noun form refers to the one making the introduction. In ancient courts certain officials controlled access to the king. They verified someone's right to see him and then introduced that person to the monarch. Christ now performs that function for believers. Hebrews 6:20 says concerning the inner court of heaven that He "has entered as a forerunner for [believers], having become a high priest forever." Christ entered to bring the elect into communion with God (cf. Ps. 110:4; Heb. 2:17–18; 3:1–2; 4:14–15; 5:4–6; 7:17, 21–22, 25; 8:1–2, 6; 9:13–14).

CHRIST'S TRIUMPHANT SERMON

having been put to death in the flesh, but made alive in the spirit; in which also He went and made proclamation to the spirits now in prison, who once were disobedient, (3:18b–20a)

Some critics have disputed Christ's resurrection from the dead by claiming He never died in the first place. According to such skeptical reasoning, He merely fainted into a semi-coma on the cross, was revived in the coolness of the tomb, unwrapped Himself, and walked out. But the phrase **having been put to death in the flesh** leaves no doubt that on the cross Jesus' physical life ceased. To hasten the deaths of the two thieves at Calvary crucified on either side of Christ, the Roman executioners broke their legs (John 19:31–32). (Crucifixion victims postponed their deaths as long as possible by pushing themselves up on their legs, which allowed them to gasp for another breath.) However, the soldiers did not bother to break Christ's legs because they could see He was already dead. Confirming that reality, one of them pierced His side with a spear, causing blood and water to flow out, a physiological sign He was certainly dead (19:33–37).

The phrase **made alive in the spirit** is a reference to Jesus' eternal inner person. The Greek text omits the definite article, which suggests Peter was not referring to the Holy Spirit, but that the Lord was spiritually alive, contrasting the condition of Christ's **flesh** (body) with that of His **spirit.** His eternal spirit has always been alive, although His earthly body was then dead; but three days later His body was resurrected in a transformed and eternal state.

Some interpreters think the aforementioned phrase describes Jesus' resurrection. But if the apostle had intended to make such a reference he would have used an expression such as, "He was put to death in the flesh but made alive in the *flesh*." The resurrection was not merely a spiritual reality—it was physical (cf. Luke 24:39; John 20:20, 27). Thus Peter's point here must be that though Jesus' body was dead, He remained **alive in** His **spirit** (cf. Luke 23:46).

Although Christ is the One who is eternal life itself (1 John 5:20),

He did experience a kind of spiritual death—defined not as cessation of existence but an experience of separation from God. While on the cross, Jesus was fully conscious as He cried out, "My God, My God, why have You forsaken Me?" (Matt. 27:46). That utterance reflected His temporary and humanly incomprehensible sense of alienation from the Father while God's full wrath and the burden of sinners' iniquities were placed on Him and judged (cf. 2 Cor. 5:21; Gal. 3:10–13; Heb. 9:28). For that brief time, Christ's experience paralleled the condition of unbelievers who live, paradoxically, in spiritual death (separation from God) in this life and face divine judgment in physical death (cf. Dan. 12:2; Matt. 25:41, 46; Mark 9:43–48; John 3:36; Rev. 20:15). In His death for sin and resurrection to eternal glory, Christ conquered death; however, unregenerate sinners die their own deaths for their unrepented sins and go to eternal shame and punishment.

In which also refers to what occurred with His living spirit while His dead physical body lay in the tomb (concerning His burial, see Matt. 27:57–60; John 19:38–42). **He went** (*poreuomai*) denotes going from one place to another (see also v. 22, where the word is used concerning the ascension). When the text says Christ **made proclamation to the spirits now in prison,** it is indicating that He purposefully went to an actual place to make a triumphant announcement to captive beings before He arose on the third day.

The verb rendered **made proclamation** (*kērussō*) means that Christ "preached" or "heralded" His triumph. In the ancient world, heralds would come to town as representatives of the rulers to make public announcements or precede generals and kings in the processions celebrating military triumphs, announcing victories won in battle. This verb is not saying that Jesus went to preach the gospel, otherwise Peter would likely have used a form of the verb *euangelizō* ("to evangelize"). Christ went to proclaim His victory to the enemy by announcing His triumph over sin (cf. Rom. 5:18–19; 6:5–6), death (cf. Rom. 6:9–10; 1 Cor. 15:54–55), hell, demons, and Satan (cf. Gen. 3:15; Col. 2:15; Heb. 2:14; 1 John 3:8).

Christ directed His proclamation **to the spirits,** not human beings, otherwise he would have used *psuchai* ("souls") instead of *pneumasin*, a word the New Testament never uses to refer to people except when qualified by a genitive (e.g., Heb. 12:23; "the spirits of the righteous").

Ever since the fall of Satan and his demons, there has been an ongoing cosmic conflict between the angelic forces of good and evil (cf. Job 1–2; Dan. 10:13; Zech. 3:1; Eph. 6:16; Rev. 12:3–4; 16:12–14). After the devil's apparent victory in inducing Adam and Eve (and consequently all their descendants) to fall into sin (Gen. 3:1–7; Rom. 5:12–14), God promised to the Evil One himself eventual destruction by Messiah, who would triumph with a crushing victory over him, despite suffering a minor wound from him (Gen. 3:15). Satan therefore sought to prevent this by the genocide of the Jews (cf. Est. 3:1–4:3) and the destruction of the Messianic line itself during the time of Joash (2 Chron. 22:10–12; cf. 23:3, 12–21). When all that failed, he attempted to kill the infant Messiah (Matt. 2:16–18). Thwarted at that, he tried to tempt Christ Himself to abandon His mission (Matt. 4:1–11; Luke 4:1–13). Later, Satan incited the Jewish leaders and their followers to mob action that resulted in the Lord's crucifixion (Mark 15:6–15). The diabolical Jewish leaders even saw to it that Jesus' tomb was guarded lest He exit the grave (Matt. 27:63–66). The demons may have been celebrating their seeming victory in the wake of Christ's death and burial—but only to soon be profoundly and permanently disappointed when the living Christ Himself arrived. The angelic spirits Christ was to address were **now in prison** (*phulakē;* an actual place of imprisonment, not merely a condition).

At the present time believers must struggle against the powers of the unbound demon forces as those forces influence them through the corrupt world system over which Satan has rule. The apostle Paul told the Ephesian church, "Our struggle is not against flesh and blood, but against the rulers, against the powers, against the world forces of this darkness, against the spiritual forces of wickedness in the heavenly places" (Eph. 6:12), which clearly says that the demonic hierarchy is actively and freely conducting its evil work in the world. It was not to such unbound spirits, but to the bound demons that Christ went to announce His triumph.

The book of Revelation calls this **prison** the "bottomless pit," literally the "pit of the abyss." Some analysis of Revelation 9:1–2 provides further understanding of the prison and its captive subjects.

> With his theater of operations now restricted to the earth, and his time running out (cf. 12:12), Satan will now seek to marshal all of his demonic hosts—those already on earth, those cast to earth with him, and those incarcerated in the **bottomless pit** (literally "the pit of the abyss"). *Abussos* (**bottomless**) appears seven times in Revelation, always in reference to the abode of incarcerated demons (cf. 9:2, 11; 11:7; 17:8). Satan himself will be held prisoner there during the Millennium, chained and locked up with the other demonic prisoners (20:1, 3).
>
> Scripture teaches that God has sovereignly chosen to incarcerate certain demons in that **pit** of punishment. Second Peter 2:4 says that "God did not spare angels when then sinned, but cast them into hell and committed them to pits of darkness, reserved for judgment." The phrase "cast them into hell" is a participle derived from the Greek noun *Tartarus*. Just as Jesus used a term for hell derived from the Jewish vernacular (*Gehenna;* cf. Matt. 5:22), so Peter chose a term from

Greek mythology with which his readers would be familiar. Tartarus was the name used in Greek literature for the place where the worst sinners, those who had offended the gods personally, went after death and were punished. The place where God keeps demons imprisoned is actually different from the imaginary place of Greek mythology. Yet the use of the term *Tartarus* does seem to convey the idea that because of the heinousness of their sin, God has imprisoned certain fallen angels in such a place of severest torment and isolation. They remain in that place, awaiting their sentencing to final punishment in the eternal lake of fire (Rev. 20:10, 13–14).

The demons incarcerated in the abyss are undoubtedly the most wicked, vile, and perverted of all the fallen angels. Jude describes some of them as "angels who did not keep their own domain, but abandoned their proper abode," noting that God "has kept [them] in eternal bonds under darkness for the judgment of the great day, just as Sodom and Gomorrah and the cities around them, since they in the same way as these indulged in gross immorality and went after strange flesh, are exhibited as an example in undergoing the punishment of eternal fire" (Jude 6–7). That passage describes certain fallen angels who left the angelic domain to indulge in sexual sin with humans, just as the men of Sodom and Gomorrah attempted to engage in perverted sex with angels (Gen. 19:1, 4–5).

Peter reveals when this angelic sin occurred:

> For Christ also died for sins once for all, the just for the unjust, so that He might bring us to God, having been put to death in the flesh, but made alive in the spirit; in which also He went and made proclamation to the spirits now in prison, who once were disobedient, when the patience of God kept waiting in the days of Noah, during the construction of the ark, in which a few, that is, eight persons, were brought safely through the water. (1 Peter 3:18–20).

The "spirits now in prison" in the abyss are those "who once were disobedient . . . in the days of Noah." They are the demons who cohabited with human women in Satan's failed attempt to corrupt the human race . . . (Gen. 6:1–4). That demons still fear being sent to the abyss is evident from the fact that some pled with Jesus not to send them there (Luke 8:31). That suggests that other demons have been incarcerated there since the events of Genesis 6. The demons released by Satan at the fifth trumpet may not include those who sinned in Noah's day (cf. Jude 6), since they are said to be in "eternal bonds" (Jude 6) until the final day when they are sent to the eternal lake of fire (20:10; Jude 7). Other demons imprisoned in the abyss may be the ones released. So the pit is the preliminary place of incarceration for demons from which some are to be released under this judgment. (John MacArthur, *Revelation 1–11*, MacArthur New Testament Commentary [Chicago: Moody, 1999], 257–58)

Peter further identifies the demons to whom Christ preached His triumphant sermon as those who **once were disobedient.** As the reason that God bound them permanently in the place of imprisonment, that **disobedience** is specifically related to something that happened in the time of Noah.

What was that disobedience that had such severe and permanent results? Peter's readers must have been familiar with the specific sin committed by the imprisoned demons because the apostle did not elaborate on it. Genesis 6:1–4 gives the account of this demonic disobedience:

> Now it came about, when men began to multiply on the face of the land, and daughters were born to them, that the sons of God saw that the daughters of men were beautiful; and they took wives for themselves, whomever they chose. Then the Lord said, "My Spirit shall not strive with man forever, because he also is flesh; nevertheless his days shall be one hundred and twenty years." The Nephilim were on the earth in those days, and also afterward, when the sons of God came in to the daughters of men, and they bore children to them. Those were the mighty men who were of old, men of renown.

Satan and his angels had already rebelled and been thrown out of heaven and eternally fixed in a state of unmixed wickedness. Satan had been successful in the Garden and his demonic force had been at work motivating corruption in the world.

The Genesis 6 account was perhaps the most heinous effort they made related to the God-ordained provision of marriage (v. 1). The demons mounted an attack on marriage and procreation that wickedly influenced subsequent generations.

"The sons of God" are juxtaposed against "the daughters of men." The contrast is between supernatural beings and women. "Sons of God" cannot be men, or they would be called "sons of men." Neither can they be righteous men of a righteous line of people, or Sethites (as some suggest), because that does not contrast with "daughters of men," as if all women were unrighteous or all righteous "sons of God" were men only.

The oldest interpretation, the traditional Jewish view of ancient rabbis and modern Jewish commentators, as well as of the church fathers, is that "the sons of God" were demons, or fallen angels. The context of judgment in the Flood precludes holy angels from being in view (see Gordon J. Wenham, *Genesis 1-15,* Word Biblical Commentary [Waco, Tex.: Word, 1987], 1:139).

The phrase "sons of God" (Heb., *bene haelohim*) always refers to angels in its other Old Testament uses (cf. Job 1:6; 2:1; 38:7; Pss. 29:1; 89:6). The term is always used of those brought directly into being by

God—not those who are procreated through human birth, such as Sethites, nobles, kings, or aristocracy. Heavenly spirits are being contrasted with earthly women. These, then, are fallen angels who acted perversely, over-stepping the boundaries of their realm. They defied God by leaving their spirit world to enter the human realm (as Satan had entered the animal world in Eden). This is the first biblical record of demon-possession, demons indwelling people.

Those wicked spirits were drawn to females, whom they saw as "beautiful" in some perverse and lascivious way. They are "the daughters" mentioned in 6:1 (not a special class of women), whom the demons took for wives. The Hebrew is *Laqach,* which describes marriage transactions (Gen. 4:19; 11:29; 12:19; 20:2–3; 25:1), not rape or fornication.

That certainly raises the question: How can spirit beings marry women? It is possible only if they dwell in human bodies, as angels can and have done (cf. Gen. 18:1–2, 8; 19:1, 5; Heb. 13:2). Those demons entered men's bodies (a phenomenon frequently encountered by Christ and the apostles in the Gospel record), as is clear from the children who were born from those unions (Gen. 6:4). Though the children were human, there was a pervasive influence on them from the demons.

> Then the Lord saw that the wickedness of man was great on the earth, and that every intent of the thoughts of his heart was only evil continually. The Lord was sorry that He had made man on the earth, and He was grieved in His heart. The Lord said, "I will blot out man whom I have created from the face of the land, from man to animals to creeping things and to birds of the sky; for I am sorry that I have made them." (Gen. 6:5–7)

That the people were open to demons shows the evil of man at the time. Those wicked, demon-possessed men then produced a generation that was nothing but corrupt inside and out, needing to be destroyed.

> Now the earth was corrupt in the sight of God, and the earth was filled with violence. God looked on the earth, and behold, it was corrupt; for all flesh had corrupted their way upon the earth. Then God said to Noah, "The end of all flesh has come before Me; for the earth is filled with violence because of them; and behold, I am about to destroy them with the earth. (Gen. 6:11–13)

The original temptation in the Garden may help explain the demonic strategy:

Now the serpent was more crafty than any beast of the field which the Lord God had made. And he said to the woman, "Indeed, has God said, 'You shall not eat from any tree of the garden'?" The woman said to the serpent, "From the fruit of the trees of the garden we may eat; but from the fruit of the tree which is in the middle of the garden, God has said, 'You shall not eat from it or touch it, or you will die.'" The serpent said to the woman, "You surely will not die! For God knows that in the day you eat from it your eyes will be opened, and you will be like God, knowing good and evil." When the woman saw that the tree was good for food, and that it was a delight to the eyes, and that the tree was desirable to make one wise, she took from its fruit and ate; and she gave also to her husband with her, and he ate. (Gen. 3:1–6)

Satan's plan in Eden was to convince Eve that she could become like God. She and Adam could be exalted to a higher life, escaping even the few limitations they experienced. If that was attractive—becoming more "supernatural"—before sin and death reigned, how attractive would it be after? Genesis 4 and 5 record that death reigned through all of creation and, with it, pain and sorrow (eight times in chapter 5 the phrase "he died" appears). It would be consistent with Satan's strategy to promise a supernatural elevation, a transcendent experience, communion with the spirits, and even victory over death and eternal life, through a perverse marital union.

Satan has always promised that if man is open to the spirit world, he can circumvent judgment and gain immortality. That insidious promise has a familiar ring to it. Certain false religions since then, beginning as early as the Babylonian mystery religions with their pagan fertility rites, have promised some magical way for humans to attain a higher level of existence (immortality or even godhood), with out-of-the-ordinary sexual relations playing a key part in the process.

But in spite of Satan's involvement and promise, the offspring of the Genesis 6 unions, though demonized, were only human beings and therefore targets for the divine judgment about to occur. When God drowned the world 120 years later, they would all perish because they were all "flesh" (Gen. 6:3). They were nothing other than depraved, demon-dominated people.

Genesis 6:4 adds: "The Nephilim were on the earth in those days, and also afterward, when the sons of God came in to the daughters of men, and they bore children to them. Those were the mighty men who were of old, men of renown." "Nephilim" transliterates a Hebrew word meaning "the falling ones" or those of great power that crushes people. The text says they were on the earth already when the embodied demons went after the women. The term is used in one other place, Numbers 13:30-33, where it describes not a race of people, since none survived the

Flood, but people in the land of Canaan who were powerful conquerors threatening Israel. When the faithless spies who went into Canaan wanted to stop Israel from going to battle, they described the people as Nephilim, borrowing the ancient transliteration to make their point, because the word was familiarly used to describe frightening enemies.

The phrase "and also afterward" makes the purpose of the Nephilim's mention clear. After the "sons of God" and "daughters of men" married, they proliferated children who were like the Nephilim— "mighty men who were of old, men of renown." Out of those unions came an abundance of infamous, powerful warriors, who like the Nephilim were heroes in a dangerous way—attaining power, reputation, and inducing fear in ancient times by being fierce and deadly. All of those offspring, along with the earlier Nephilim, were drowned, with the rest of the world (Genesis 7:23–24).

What seals this interpretation is the text here by Peter. The Lord proclaimed His triumph over Satan, sin, death and hell to the very worst of demons, who disobeyed God in the worst manner in the days of Noah before the Flood. The fallen angels' long effort to demonize people, hinder the redemptive purpose of God, and prevent the "seed" of the woman (Gen. 3:15) from crushing Satan's head and sending the demons into the lake of fire (Matt. 25:41; Rev. 19:20; 20:10, 14, 15) was ultimately foiled at the Cross.

In his second letter, Peter also briefly refers to the bound demons' sin:

> For if God did not spare angels when they sinned, but cast them into hell and committed them to pits of darkness, reserved for judgment; and did not spare the ancient world, but preserved Noah, a preacher of righteousness, with seven others, when He brought a flood upon the world of the ungodly; and if He condemned the cities of Sodom and Gomorrah to destruction by reducing them to ashes, having made them an example to those who would live ungodly lives thereafter. (2 Peter 2:4–6)

The perversion that brought the Flood is linked to the perversion that brought the fire and brimstone on Sodom and Gomorrah (Gen. 18–19). Jude makes the same parallel:

> And angels who did not keep their own domain, but abandoned their proper abode, He has kept in eternal bonds under darkness for the judgment of the great day, just as Sodom and Gomorrah and the cities around them, since they in the same way as these indulged in gross immorality and went after strange flesh, are exhibited as an example in undergoing the punishment of eternal fire. (vv. 6–7)

Those wicked spirits were sent to the abyss because they over-stepped the boundaries of God's tolerance. They filled the earth with their wretchedness to such an extent that not even 120 years of Noah's preaching convinced anyone beyond his family to repent, believe in God, and escape His judgment. Since that time, the demons who com-mitted such heinous sins had been bound and imprisoned when Jesus died at Calvary. Perhaps by then they thought He had lost the upper hand over them, but such was not the case. Instead He appeared in their midst and proclaimed His triumph. Colossians 2:15 declares, "When [God] had disarmed the rulers and authorities, He made a public display of them, having triumphed over them through [Christ]."

Peter's point is riveting and dramatic—believers will suffer "for the sake of righteousness" (3:14), for doing what is right (v. 17). All suffer-ing believers can be encouraged that such is not a disaster but rather the path to spiritual victory. The unequalled example of such triumph is the Lord Himself, who suffered unjustly and through that suffering con-quered sin and the demons of hell (v. 22). God indeed uses unjust perse-cution mightily for His holy purposes.

His Triumphant Salvation

when the patience of God kept waiting in the days of Noah, dur-ing the construction of the ark, in which a few, that is, eight per-sons, were brought safely through the water. Corresponding to that, baptism now saves you—not the removal of dirt from the flesh, but an appeal to God for a good conscience—through the resurrection of Jesus Christ, (3:20b–21)

The biblical account of **when the patience of God kept wait-ing in the days of Noah,** before sending the Flood, Peter saw as an analogy for the triumphant salvation provided through Jesus Christ. God was patient with the corrupt world, as Genesis 6:3 states: "My Spirit shall not strive with man forever, because he also is flesh; nevertheless his days shall be one hundred and twenty years." During that 120-year grace peri-od Noah was "a preacher of righteousness" (2 Peter 2:5) who announced judgment but also offered the way of deliverance. The members of Noah's family were the only **eight persons** on earth to heed the divine warning and escape the coming catastrophe of a worldwide flood. Hence only Noah, his wife, his three sons, and their wives **were brought safely through the water** while the rest of mankind was drowned in God's act of judgment (Gen. 6:9–8:22).

During the grace period, people witnessed **the construction of**

the ark by Noah and his sons. While its purpose was to rescue Noah and his family from the Flood, the ark also was a vivid object lesson to unbelievers of God's impending judgment on the world. The lack of responsiveness to the "sermon of the ark" reveals the profound wickedness in Noah's day: "Then the Lord saw that the wickedness of man was great on the earth, and that every intent of the thoughts of his heart was only evil continually" (Gen. 6:5).

Peter used **corresponding to that,** a phrase containing the word *antitupon,* which means "copy," "counterpart," or "figure pointing to" to make the transition to the salvation in Christ. That word yielded the theological term *antitype,* which in the New Testament describes an earthly expression of a heavenly reality—a symbol or analogy of a spiritual truth (cf. John 3:14–16; Heb. 4:1–10; 8:2, 5). The preservation in the ark of those who believed God is analogous to the salvation believers have in Christ.

Some commentators believe the Flood is the antitype because *antitupon* (v. 21) and *hudatos* (**water,** v. 20) are both neuter nouns. But it is better to view the antitype in the broader sense of Noah and his family's total experience with the ark. God preserved them from the flood waters while the rest of mankind perished. Noah and his children are a genuine type of the salvation in Jesus Christ, which preserves believers safely through God's judgment on sinners.

Certain theological traditions misinterpret Peter's statement **baptism now saves you** to refer to spiritual salvation by water baptism (i.e., baptismal regeneration). But **baptism** (from *baptizō*) simply means "to immerse," and not just in water. Peter here uses **baptism** to refer to a figurative immersion into Christ as the ark of safety that will sail over the holocaust of judgment on the wicked. Noah and his family were immersed not just in water, but in the world under divine judgment. All the while they were protected by being in the ark. God preserved them in the midst of His judgment, which is what He also does for all those who trust in Christ. God's final judgment will bring fire and fury on the world, destroying the entire universe (cf. 2 Peter 3:10–12); but the people of God will be protected and taken into the eternal new heavens and new earth (v. 13).

Peter made clear that he did not want readers to think he was referring to water **baptism** when he specifically said **not the removal of dirt from the flesh.** (For a more complete discussion of baptism and regeneration, see John MacArthur, *Acts 1–12,* MacArthur New Testament Commentary [Chicago: Moody, 1994], 73–75.) That he was actually referring to a spiritual reality when he wrote **baptism now saves** is also clear from the phrase, **an appeal to God for a good conscience— through the resurrection of Jesus Christ.** The only baptism that saves people is dry—the spiritual one into the *death* as well as the resurrection of Christ—of those who appeal to God to place them into the spiritual ark of salvation safety (cf. Rom. 10:9–10).

Just as the Flood immersed all people in the judgment of God, yet some passed through safely, so also His final judgment will involve everyone, but those who are in Christ will pass through securely. The experience of Noah's family in the Flood is also analogous to the experience of everyone who receives salvation. Just as they died to their previous world when they entered the ark and subsequently experienced a resurrection of sorts when they exited the ark to a new post-Flood world, so all Christians die to their old world when they enter the body of Christ (Rom. 7:4–6; Gal. 2:19–20; Eph. 4:20–24). They subsequently enjoy newness of life that culminates one day with the resurrection to eternal life. Paul instructed the Romans:

> Or do you not know that all of us who have been baptized into Christ Jesus have been baptized into His death? Therefore we have been buried with Him through baptism into death, so that as Christ was raised from the dead through the glory of the Father, so we too might walk in newness of life. (Rom. 6:3–4; cf. 1 Cor. 6:17; 10:2; 12:13; Gal. 3:27; Eph. 4:5)

Therefore, God provides salvation because a sinner, by faith, is immersed into Christ's death and resurrection and becomes His own through that spiritual union. Salvation does not occur by means of any rite, including water baptism (**the removal of dirt from the flesh**), **but** by **an appeal to God for a good conscience. Appeal** (*eperōtēma*) is a technical term that was used in making contracts. Here it refers to agreeing to meet certain divinely-required conditions before God places one into the ark of safety (Christ). Anyone who would be saved must first come to God with a desire to obtain a **good** (cleansed) **conscience** and a willingness to meet the conditions (repentance and faith) necessary to obtain it. By appealing to God for a good conscience, that is, a conscience free from accusation and condemnation (cf. Rom. 2:15), the unregenerate show that they are tired of the sin that dominates them and desire to be delivered from its burden of guilt and the threat of hell (cf. Luke 18:13–14; Acts 2:37–38). They crave the spiritual cleansing that comes through Christ's shed blood (3:18; cf. 1:18–19; 2:24; Heb. 9:14; 10:22). Therefore they repent of their sins and plead for God's forgiveness and the removal of the guilt that plagues their consciences, all of which is available through trusting in the atoning sacrifice of Christ. Water baptism does not save; it is the Holy Spirit's baptizing the sinner safely into Jesus Christ—the elect's only ark of salvation—that forever rescues the sinner from hell and brings him securely to heaven. This is the ultimate triumph of Christ's suffering for them, and the pledge of triumph in their own unjust suffering.

HIS TRIUMPHANT SUPREMACY

who is at the right hand of God, having gone into heaven, after angels and authorities and powers had been subjected to Him. (3:22)

Peter concludes this passage with a glorious final note concerning Jesus Christ's triumphant suffering. Both the Old and New Testaments affirm **the right hand** as a place of prestige and power (Gen. 48:18; 1 Chron. 6:39; Pss. 16:8; 45:9; 80:17; 110:1; Mark 16:19; Acts 2:33; 5:31; Rom. 8:34; Eph. 1:20; Heb. 12:2). **The right hand of God** is the preeminent place of honor and authority for all eternity (Ex. 15:6; Deut. 33:2; Pss. 16:11; 18:35; 45:4; 48:10; 89:13; 98:1; 118:15–16; Matt. 26:64; Acts 7:55–56; Col. 3:1; Heb. 1:3; 8:1; Rev. 5:7; cf. Rev. 2:1). That is where Christ went after He finished His work of redemption, and that is where He rules from today.

After describing Jesus' humility, suffering, and death, the apostle Paul confidently asserted:

> For this reason also, God highly exalted Him, and bestowed on Him the name which is above every name, so that at the name of Jesus every knee will bow, of those who are in heaven and on earth and under the earth, and that every tongue will confess that Jesus Christ is Lord, to the glory of God the Father. (Phil. 2:9–11)

The author of Hebrews referred to Christ's position of supremacy several times, beginning early in the letter:

> And He is the radiance of His glory and the exact representation of His nature, and upholds all things by the word of His power. When He had made purification of sins, He sat down at the right hand of the Majesty on high, having become as much better than the angels, as He has inherited a more excellent name than they. For to which of the angels did He ever say, "You are My Son, today I have begotten You"? And again, "I will be a Father to Him and He shall be a Son to Me"? And when He again brings the firstborn into the world, He says, "And let all the angels of God worship Him." (Heb. 1:3–6; cf. Acts 5:31; 7:55–56; Rom. 8:34; Heb. 10:12; 12:2)

Having gone into heaven is a reference to Christ's ascension, which Luke describes in the opening chapter of Acts:

> He was lifted up while they were looking on, and a cloud received Him out of their sight. And as they were gazing intently into the sky while He was going, behold, two men in white clothing stood beside them. They also said, "Men of Galilee, why do you stand looking into the sky? This Jesus, who has been taken up from you into heaven, will come in just the same way as you have watched Him go into heaven." (Acts 1:9–11)

When He ascended to heaven, "Jesus . . . entered as a forerunner for [believers], having become a high priest forever according to the order of Melchizedek" (Heb. 6:20). From that position as heavenly high priest, Christ continuously intercedes for believers (Heb. 7:25; 9:24).

Christ assumed His position of supremacy over **angels and authorities and powers** (angelic beings, including Satan and his demons; see Gen. 19:1; 28:12; Pss. 78:49; 148:2; Matt. 4:11; 13:41; 25:31; Luke 2:15; 15:10; Rom. 8:38; Eph. 3:10; 6:12; Col. 1:16; 2:18; Jude 6; Rev. 5:11; 8:2) **after** they **had been subjected to Him** by the Cross, which fact He proclaimed to the demons in prison. It shows again that He was not preaching to demons a message of salvation, since demons cannot be saved, but are damned forever: "For assuredly He does not give help to angels, but He gives help to the descendant of Abraham" (Heb. 2:16).

Peter's concluding statement to this passage and chapter emphasizes again that the Cross and the Resurrection are what subjected the fallen and rebellious angelic hosts to Jesus Christ, and saved souls from eternal judgment—the greatest triumph ever of the suffering of a righteous person. It also echoes Paul's words to the Ephesians:

> In accordance with the working of the strength of [God's] might which He brought about in Christ, when He raised Him from the dead and seated Him at His right hand in the heavenly places, far above all *rule* and *authority* and *power* and *dominion,* and every name that is named, not only in this age but also in the one to come. (Eph. 1:19–21; emphases added)

The word rendered **had been subjected** (from *hupotassō,* "to line up in rank under") describes the present status of all spiritual beings in relation to Christ. He is supreme over all (Phil. 2:9–11).

Christ's substitutionary death for sinners was an act of grace (Acts 15:11; Rom. 5:15, 17; Eph. 1:7; 2:5, 8–9; Titus 2:11; 3:7; Heb. 2:9)— triumphant, sovereign grace extended to depraved, wicked men and women who actually deserved nothing but eternal judgment from God. In his hymn "And Can It Be," Charles Wesley wrote,

> 'Tis mystery all! Th' Immortal dies!
> Who can explore His strange design?
> In vain the first born seraph tries
> To sound the depths of love Divine!
> 'Tis mercy all! Let earth adore,
> Let angel minds inquire no more.

It was lost human beings for whom Christ died—the lost angels could only listen in dismay to Christ's proclamation of victory. Even the elect angels can only marvel at what they cannot fully understand (cf. 1:12). Believers should be grateful that "while [they] were still helpless, at the right time Christ died for the ungodly" (Rom. 5:6).

Again, how mightily does the Lord God bring triumph out of the persecution of the Savior. And saints can be confident He will do the same in their persecutions. "But thanks be to God, who always leads us in triumph in Christ, and manifests through us the sweet aroma of the knowledge of Him in every place" (2 Cor. 2:14). Eventually they will be at God's right hand in heaven (Rev. 3:21), even ruling over the angels (1 Cor. 6:3).

Believers not only look to Christ as an example of triumph in unjust suffering, they also join fully and forever in that triumph.

Arming Yourself Against Unjust Suffering
(1 Peter 4:1–6)

20

Therefore, since Christ has suffered in the flesh, arm yourselves also with the same purpose, because he who has suffered in the flesh has ceased from sin, so as to live the rest of the time in the flesh no longer for the lusts of men, but for the will of God. For the time already past is sufficient for you to have carried out the desire of the Gentiles, having pursued a course of sensuality, lusts, drunkenness, carousing, drinking parties and abominable idolatries. In all this, they are surprised that you do not run with them into the same excesses of dissipation, and they malign you; but they will give account to Him who is ready to judge the living and the dead. For the gospel has for this purpose been preached even to those who are dead, that though they are judged in the flesh as men, they may live in the spirit according to the will of God. (4:1–6)

Everything from the previous verses (3:8–22), leading up to this passage, has focused on the scattered believers suffering persecution from the world, and even facing the possibility of death. Suffering unjustly for being righteous is also on Peter's mind in 1:6-9; 2:19-23; 4:14-19; 5:6-10. Knowing how to face such trials is critical to Christians' growth and joy.

In this section, Peter calls for believers to be willing to face persecution for righteousness' sake, and even martyrdom for Christ. His call is a call to strength, to resolve, to unwavering firmness like a soldier entering battle.

The key verb in this whole paragraph is the command **arm yourselves,** out of which springs all the motivations to obey the command. The verb, used only here in the New Testament, is from *hoplizō,* an aorist middle imperative, meaning literally, "to arm oneself with weapons" or "to put on as armor." The noun form *hoplon* means "weapons" and is used in six passages eg., John 18:3; 2 Cor. 6:7; 10a. The picture is of preparation for battle.

The apostle Peter provides believers with four perspectives motivating them to be strong when righteousness brings suffering and, perhaps, martyrdom. Believers strengthen their resolve in persecution when they are armed with an understanding of the attitude of Christ, the will of God, the transformation from the past, and the hope of eternal life.

THE ATTITUDE OF CHRIST

Therefore, since Christ has suffered in the flesh, arm yourselves also with the same purpose, because he who has suffered in the flesh has ceased from sin, (4:1)

Therefore obviously points back to what Peter wrote in the preceding passage, that at the Cross Christ endured His greatest suffering, dying under divine judgment as the just for the unjust; yet there He also accomplished for believers His greatest triumph over sin and its condemning power, over the forces of hell, and over the power of death. The cross of Jesus Christ is the ultimate proof that suffering can lead to victory over the forces of evil. **Since Christ has suffered in the flesh,** believers must **arm** themselves **also with the same purpose.** When Jesus **suffered in the flesh,** He died (3:18; cf. Isa. 53:10; Matt. 27:50; Acts 2:23) in fulfilling divine redemption's plan. When He went to the Cross, the Father made Him to be sin and a curse for all who believe; as Paul said: "Christ redeemed us from the curse of the Law, having become a curse for us—for it is written, 'Cursed is everyone who hangs on a tree'" (Gal. 3:13; cf. Deut. 21:23). He came "in the likeness of sinful flesh and as an offering for sin" (Rom. 8:3; cf. 2 Cor. 5:21; 1 Peter 2:24). Therefore He felt the full force of sin's evil unjustly, but in so doing He gained for His saints salvation and for Himself the everlasting honor and praise of all who will live in heaven (cf. Rev. 5:8–14).

The primary weapon Peter calls for in arming believers is **the same purpose** that was manifest through Christ's suffering and death.

That **purpose** ("attitude,""thought," or "principle") is a willingness to die because Christians know death produces the greatest victory (cf. 1 Cor. 15:26, 54–55; 2 Tim. 1:10; Rev. 21:4). Peter himself would have that very opportunity when he faced martyrdom and was faithful unto death (cf. John 21:18–19).

The apostle was not expressing a new concept to his readers. Jesus had taught positively that "if anyone wishes to come after Me, he must deny himself, and take up his cross daily and follow Me" (Luke 9:23), and negatively that "he who does not take his cross and follow after Me is not worthy of Me. He who has found his life will lose it, and he who has lost his life for My sake will find it" (Matt. 10:38–39). Taking up one's cross has no mystical connotation and means more than merely some extra spiritual dedication. When Jesus spoke of taking up the cross, His listeners knew He was talking about being executed on a cross. They knew exactly what He meant—they must confess Jesus as Lord, no matter what—even if it meant to die physically for His sake. The apostle Paul understood well the principle of cross-bearing:

> we are afflicted in every way, but not crushed; perplexed, but not despairing; persecuted, but not forsaken; struck down, but not destroyed; always carrying about in the body the dying of Jesus, so that the life of Jesus also may be manifested in our body. For we who live are constantly being delivered over to death for Jesus' sake, so that the life of Jesus also may be manifested in our mortal flesh. So death works in us, but life in you. (2 Cor. 4:8–12; cf. 1 Cor. 15:31; 2 Tim. 4:6)

Thousands of martyrs throughout church history have been willing to die (cf. Heb. 11:13–16, 35–38) because they armed themselves with **the same purpose** Jesus Christ had—to be faithful to the Father, no matter what, knowing that the cross precedes the crown. The greater the righteous suffering, the greater is the reward. And history's martyrs realized that there is the greatest triumph of all in death, because believers who have died have **ceased from sin.** The perfect tense verb emphasizes a permanent condition free from sin. For Christ it was, of course, eternal. He bore sin's curse only once and for all (Heb. 7:27; 9:12; 10:10, 12, 14). And believers can face death with the same attitude their Lord had, that when it comes they will have entered into an eternal condition of holy perfection, free from all sin's influences and effects (cf. 1 Cor. 15:42–43; 2 Cor. 5:1; Rev. 21:4; 22:14–15).

Jesus is the forerunner who secured complete victory over sin and death. After He died and rose from the tomb, He had a glorified body (Mark 16:9–14; Luke 24:36–43; John 20:19–29; cf. Phil. 3:21) and was freed from the sinful powers (demons and evil men) to which He had voluntarily exposed Himself (Matt. 4:1–11) in His incarnation (John 1:9–11, 14–16; Phil. 2:6–8) and sin-bearing (Isa. 53:4–5; Matt. 20:28; John 1:29; 2 Cor. 5:21; Heb. 2:17; 1 John 2:1–2). Jesus willingly faced death "for the joy set before Him" (Heb. 12:2). Knowing that in His death He would conquer sin forever was a joy that outweighed any suffering He had to endure in this world. The worst that can happen to a believer suffering unjustly is death, and that is actually the best that can happen because it means the final and forever end of sin. If the Christian is armed with the goal of being delivered from sin, and that is accomplished through death, the fearsome threat of death is gone and death even becomes precious (cf. Phil. 1:21; 2 Tim. 4:18).

Christians can be further encouraged when they recall what sin has done to them all their lives on earth. Sin is ever present in their unredeemed flesh and assaults them as long as they live (Ps. 38:18; Rom. 7:5; Heb. 12:1), constantly rising up within them to spread its damaging effects (cf. James 1:14–15). The ever-present conflict with sin causes them to desire more and more to escape it (Rom. 7:18, 23–24; cf. 8:20–22; 2 Tim. 2:19) and realize the hope Paul offered when he affirmed to Titus that "Christ Jesus . . . gave Himself for [believers] to redeem [them] from every lawless deed, and to purify for Himself a people for His own possession" (Titus 2:13–14). And just as Christ rose to newness of life and freedom from sin, God has promised the same for believers after they die: "So also is the resurrection of the dead. It is sown a perishable body, it is raised an imperishable body; it is sown in dishonor, it is raised in glory; it is sown in weakness, it is raised in power" (1 Cor. 15:42–43; cf. vv. 44, 49).

Paul dramatically summarizes the triumph believers have over sin and death in the following climactic words concerning the resurrection:

> But when this perishable will have put on the imperishable, and this mortal will have put on immortality, then will come about the saying that is written, "Death is swallowed up in victory. O death, where is your victory? O death, where is your sting?" The sting of death is sin, and the power of sin is the law; but thanks be to God, who gives us the victory through our Lord Jesus Christ. (1 Cor. 15:54–57)

THE WILL OF GOD

so as to live the rest of the time in the flesh no longer for the lusts of men, but for the will of God. (4:2)

All sin is disobedience to **the will of God.** In that sense all sin is a personal act of rebellion by believers against Him (cf. Ps. 51:4). The New Testament contains many exhortations to obedience that emphasize this. For example, at the conclusion of His Sermon on the Mount, Jesus warned His hearers about disobedience in very personal terms. He called the law "these words of Mine."

> Therefore everyone who hears these words of Mine and acts on them, may be compared to a wise man who built his house on the rock. And the rain fell, and the floods came, and the winds blew and slammed against that house; and yet it did not fall, for it had been founded on the rock. Everyone who hears these words of Mine and does not act on them, will be like a foolish man who built his house on the sand. The rain fell, and the floods came, and the winds blew and slammed against that house; and it fell—and great was its fall. (Matt. 7:24–27)

In the end, condemnation will come on those who did not obey God's will (Matt. 25:41–46; Jude 15)—even those who think they were obedient: "Not everyone who says to Me, 'Lord, Lord,' will enter the kingdom of heaven, but he who does the will of My Father who is in heaven" (Matt. 7:21).

Paul commands believers to "not be conformed to this world, but be transformed by the renewing of [their] mind, so that [they] may prove what the will of God is, that which is good and acceptable and perfect" (Rom. 12:2; cf. Eph. 6:5–6; Col. 4:12). Sin, on the other hand, is an expression of disobedience (cf. Neh. 9:26; 1 John 3:4) and a refusal to do what God has commanded (Pss. 106:24–25; 107:11; cf. Jer. 22:21; 35:14*b*).

The hope of Christians is to cease from sin one day in heaven. Since that is the goal, the purpose for their salvation, it has strong implications for them now, so that they ought **to live the rest of the time in the flesh no longer for the lusts of men.** Since they are headed for holiness in eternity to come, saints are **to live** (*bioō*; a reference to earthly life) the remainder of the time God gives on earth in pursuit of that holiness, no matter the physical cost. They are armed for victory who live for **the will of God,** not the sinful desires of men. Peter calls those desires **lusts,** a strong word (*epithumia*) that means "passionate longing," and in this context connotes an evil desire. He urges believers to shun sin—not to live any longer driven by human lusts (2 Tim. 2:22), which are rooted in their unredeemed flesh (Rom. 7:17–18; Gal. 5:17) and characterized their unregenerate state (Eph. 2:1–3) and life in this world (1 John 2:15–17).

Peter is telling believers to arm themselves with a commitment to do the will of God and abandon their former sins. This is precisely what the apostle Paul calls for in Romans 6:8–12,

> Now if we have died with Christ, we believe that we shall also live with Him, knowing that Christ, having been raised from the dead, is never to die again; death no longer is master over Him. For the death that He

died, He died to sin once for all; but the life that He lives, He lives to God. Even so consider yourselves to be dead to sin, but alive to God in Christ Jesus. Therefore do not let sin reign in your mortal body so that you obey its lusts.

THE TRANSFORMATION FROM THE PAST

For the time already past is sufficient for you to have carried out the desire of the Gentiles, having pursued a course of sensuality, lusts, drunkenness, carousing, drinking parties and abominable idolatries. In all this, they are surprised that you do not run with them into the same excesses of dissipation, and they malign you; but they will give account to Him who is ready to judge the living and the dead. (4:3–5)

This passage is a vivid description of the tragic and devastating life pattern of the unconverted, which ends inexorably in judgment. The verses parallel several of Paul's descriptions of humanity's lost spiritual condition and describe the character and consequences of sin (Rom. 1:18–32; 1 Cor. 6:9–10; Gal. 5:19–21; cf. Eph. 5:3–7; Col. 3:5–10; 2 Tim. 3:1–7). Peter reminds believers to leave all that behind because it belongs to their former life in sin and under judgment. Since they have been delivered from that evil life, their souls are purified (1:22) and **the time** is **already past** for serving sin (Rom. 7:5; 1 Cor. 6:9–11*a*; Eph. 2:1–3). This phrase is literally "the having passed away time" (*parelāluthōs chronos*) meaning chronological time. It is a perfect tense, as are the two following verbs, **have carried out** (from *katergazomai,* "to produce") and **having pursued** (from *poreuomai,* "to conduct one's life"). Each building on the other, these three perfect tense verbs make the point that, for the believer, the sinful past is a closed book and its saga of sin is over. **Sufficient** (*arketos*) in this context means more than simply adequate, but conveys the sense of being more than enough. Peter's readers had had a whole life full of opportunity to sin, and that is more than enough **to have carried out the desire of the Gentiles** (the unconverted peoples) and to have lived to fulfill sinful passions (cf. Eph. 2:1–3). **Desire** (*boulēma*) here conveys the sense of a purposed longing. The hearts of the unsaved determine to follow their passions as part of what Peter earlier called their "futile way of life" (1:18).

That former disposition **pursued a course;** it conducted life's affairs along a specific path of behavior, and Peter described that for his readers with six terms. First, **sensuality** (*aselgeia*) describes those who engage in unbridled, unrestrained vice of all sorts (cf. Rom. 13:13). It could also be translated "debauchery," an excessive indulgence in sensual pleasure. Many unregenerate people live lawlessly, flaunting their vices in open defiance of God's law (cf. Rom. 1:21–32; 2 Cor. 12:21), whereas others are less obvious (cf. 1 Tim. 5:24). **Lusts** (*epithumia*) are the sinful passions that drive people into such indulgence (cf. 1 Thess. 4:5; 1 Tim. 6:9; Jude 18). **Drunkenness** (*oinophlugia*) literally means "wine bubbling up" and refers to habitual intoxication. This term can also refer to the effects of narcotic use. **Carousing** (*kōmos*) refers to participating in wild parties or orgies. In one extrabiblical Greek source, the term described a band of drunken people that sang loudly and staggered wildly through the streets, causing a major public disturbance. The apostle completed his list of terms with two more expressions that fit this picture of uncontrolled conduct, **drinking parties and abominable idolatries.** *Potos* (**drinking parties**) were sessions people engaged in just for the sake of becoming inebriated. **Abominable idolatries** denotes the immoral, debauched worship of false gods (such as Dionysius or Bacchus, the Greek god of wine) that accompanied **carousing** and **drinking parties.**

When pursuing such a path in their former lives, the apostle's audience had indulged in a sufficient amount of such despicable sins and they were never to return to them. The memory of the pain and misery those deeds caused them was to motivate his readers to diligently avoid such behavior, especially since their new life goal was to enter the holy place where sin would forever cease.

Such sins had been so much a way of life for Peter's readers that when they abandoned them their fellow sinners, still unregenerate, were **surprised** (*xenizō*), meaning "astonished," or "shocked," with the connotation of taking offense or being resentful. Sin was such a normal lifestyle for the unbelievers (cf. Ps. 64:5; John 8:34; 2 Peter 2:14) that they were not only amazed that the Christians' lives had changed so totally (cf. 1 Thess. 1:9), they even resented the fact that the new believers no longer went with them **into the same excesses of dissipation.** That expression vividly pictures a large melee of people madly racing forward, what one commentator described as "a euphoric stampede of pleasure seekers." **Excesses** (*anachusis*) pictures waters coming together and pouring out in excess or overflowing. **Dissipation** (*asotia*) is that state in which a person's mind is so corrupt that he thinks about nothing but evil and how he might indulge his sinful passions. Needless to say, Christians no longer desire such mindless pursuit of the passions that throw people into a state of over-the-top debauchery.

One-time friends become enemies and often **malign** those who **do not run with them into** sinful behavior. **Malign** (*blasphemeō*) literally means "to blaspheme," "to slander or defame someone," or "to speak evil of them." Ancient sources, both Christian and non-Christian, provide ample evidence that it was Christians' reluctance to participate in many conventionally accepted amusements and ungodly civic ceremonies, and their refusal to engage in idolatrous, immoral functions that caused unbelievers to hate and revile them. That led to unjust persecution and suffering for righteousness' sake.

Peter, however, assured his readers that those who slander and persecute believers will **give account to Him who is ready to judge the living and the dead.** Such vicious attackers are amassing a debt to God that they will spend eternity paying back. He **who is ready to judge** will ultimately hold them accountable (cf. Matt. 18:23–34). **The living**—those alive when Peter wrote—**and the dead**—those already dead—will all be judged "so that every mouth may be closed and all the world may become accountable to God" (Rom. 3:19; cf. Matt. 25:31–33, 41–46). The apostle Paul perhaps most graphically described the severity of unbelieving persecutors' judgment:

> For after all it is only just for God to repay with affliction those who afflict you, and to give relief to you who are afflicted and to us as well when the Lord Jesus will be revealed from heaven with His mighty angels in flaming fire, dealing out retribution to those who do not know God and to those who do not obey the gospel of our Lord Jesus. These will pay the penalty of eternal destruction, away from the presence of the Lord and from the glory of His power. (2 Thess. 1:6–9)

God is prepared to administer impartial judgment (1:17), but at the same time, since He has committed all judgment to Jesus Christ (John 5:22–27), the Father will through the agency of His Son judge those who oppose Christians:

> Then I saw a great white throne and Him who sat upon it, from whose presence earth and heaven fled away, and no place was found for them. And I saw the dead, the great and the small, standing before the throne, and books were opened; and another book was opened, which is the book of life; and the dead were judged from the things which were written in the books, according to their deeds. And the sea gave up the dead which were in it, and death and Hades gave up the dead which were in them; and they were judged, every one of them according to their deeds. Then death and Hades were thrown into the lake of fire. This is the second death, the lake of fire. And if anyone's name was not found written in the book of life, he was thrown into the lake of fire. (Rev. 20:11–15)

THE HOPE OF ETERNAL LIFE

For the gospel has for this purpose been preached even to those who are dead, that though they are judged in the flesh as men, they may live in the spirit according to the will of God. (4:6)

Finally, believers are to arm themselves with the genuine hope of the reality of eternal life. God has promised them that through death they will overcome sin, escape final judgment, and enter eternal heaven in holy perfection. Peter thus reminds his readers that **the gospel** (the saving message of Christ) **has for this purpose been preached** (announced) **even to those who are dead** (those who had heard and believed the gospel but had died by the time he wrote). Some who read this letter would have known them and realized that some of the dead saints were martyrs. Though some of the dead believers were **judged in the flesh as men** (physically put to death), they were triumphantly alive **in the spirit according to the will of God** (cf. Heb. 12:23). Peter's point is that believers, even under unjust treatment—including death—should be willing and unafraid to suffer, knowing that all death can do is triumphantly bring their eternal spirits into everlasting life in heaven.

There were questions in the early church about whether believers who died and missed the Lord's return may have missed the promise of glory, especially if they were killed by enemies of Jesus Christ. Paul wrote the famous rapture passage to the Thessalonians to assure them that those who died did not forfeit the promises related to Christ's return:

> But we do not want you to be uninformed, brethren, about those who are asleep, so that you will not grieve as do the rest who have no hope. For if we believe that Jesus died and rose again, even so God will bring with Him those who have fallen asleep in Jesus. For this we say to you by the word of the Lord, that we who are alive and remain until the coming of the Lord, will not precede those who have fallen asleep. For the Lord Himself will descend from heaven with a shout, with the voice of the archangel and with the trumpet of God, and the dead in Christ will rise first. Then we who are alive and remain will be caught up together with them in the clouds to meet the Lord in the air, and so we shall always be with the Lord. Therefore comfort one another with these words. (1 Thess. 4:13–18)

Just as Christ was crucified but was alive in spirit and raised from the dead, believers may suffer physical death but their spirits will remain alive and enter into the promise of eternal life. (See the discussion of 3:18–20 in the previous chapter of this volume.)

No pressure from enemies of the gospel and no unjust persecution by an ungodly world can steal believers' victory; rather, all their suffering for righteousness' sake has a perfecting power, increases their spiritual strength, humbles them, drives them to prayer, enriches their reward, and, in the event the enemies of Christ take their lives, they have reached their ultimate goal and God's eternal purpose—they have forever "ceased from sin."

Paul understood this when he wrote:

> Therefore we do not lose heart, but though our outer man is decaying, yet our inner man is being renewed day by day. For momentary, light affliction is producing for us an eternal weight of glory far beyond all comparison, while we look not at the things which are seen, but at the things which are not seen; for the things which are seen are temporal, but the things which are not seen are eternal. (2 Cor. 4:16–18)

Spiritual Duty in a Hostile World (1 Peter 4:7–11)

21

The end of all things is near; therefore, be of sound judgment and sober spirit for the purpose of prayer. Above all, keep fervent in your love for one another, because love covers a multitude of sins. Be hospitable to one another without complaint. As each one has received a special gift, employ it in serving one another as good stewards of the manifold grace of God. Whoever speaks, is to do so as one who is speaking the utterances of God; whoever serves is to do so as one who is serving by the strength which God supplies; so that in all things God may be glorified through Jesus Christ, to whom belongs the glory and dominion forever and ever. Amen. (4:7–11)

Beginning in the late 1960s and extending through most of the 1970s, the evangelical church in North America experienced a renewal and expansion by means of the so-called Jesus movement. It featured a renewed interest in Bible study, and, as a result, evangelism and discipleship, especially on college and university campuses. New Scripture translations and paraphrases appeared (e.g., *The Living Bible, Good News Bible, New International Version*), and other modern translations gained greater acceptance (e.g., *Revised Standard Version, New American Standard*

Bible, New English Bible). At the same time, evangelical broadcasting, publishing, and music ministries expanded rapidly. Across the continent, many new independent churches appeared and, along with some existing evangelical churches, experienced rapid numerical growth. Some built larger auditoriums and other facilities, and thus to a degree those churches were precursors of today's megachurches.

However, present-day trends in evangelicalism have departed greatly from those biblically driven days of revival and renewal. The seeker-sensitive philosophy of church growth, with its spirit of inclusivism and de-emphasis on doctrinal clarity and love for the truth, has imbibed the world's marketing strategy and developed a kind of pop gospel that currently dominates the ecclesiastical landscape. As it continues to eliminate every bit of offensiveness from its communication and thus loses a grip on the true content of the biblical message, the church increasingly exhibits a self-centeredness grounded in secular psychology, pragmatism, and an eagerness to make unbelieving "experts," in effect, the most influential church consultants. (For a much broader and more in-depth analysis of these phenomena, see John MacArthur, *The Gospel According to Jesus*, revised and expanded ed. [Grand Rapids, Zondervan, 1988, 1994; *The Gospel According to the Apostles* [Nashville: Word, 1993, 2000]; *Why One Way?* [Nashville: W Publishing Group, 2002]; and *Hard to Believe* [Nashville: Thomas Nelson, 2003].)

The pursuit of social and cultural acceptance is a more subtle and insidious threat to the church's spiritual health than is theological liberalism, which is clearly defined and easier to recognize and confront. Worldly evangelicalism pretends to adhere to the truth yet quietly undermines it. It offers a pop-style musical experience, sentimental emotion, attention to self-defined needs, and practical problem-solving techniques (often derived from market surveys) instead of scriptural answers regarding law, sin, forgiveness, and righteousness.

The contemporary church urgently needs spiritual revival, and that will occur only when believers get beyond personal desires and long to think, speak, and live in the ways Scripture outlines. When they do, the church will be more than a crowd; it will become spiritually powerful before a hostile world. To that end, the apostle Peter in this passage instructs Christians concerning three very basic aspects of our duty: the incentive to our spiritual duty, the instructions for our duty, and the intention of our duty.

THE INCENTIVE TO OUR SPIRITUAL DUTY

The end of all things is near; (4:7a)

The word rendered **end** (*telos*) does not necessarily indicate cessation, termination, or chronological conclusion. Rather here it means "consummation," "fulfillment," "a purpose attained," or "a goal achieved." In this context, it refers to Christ's second coming. The **end** in view here is not the consummation of persecution for Peter's readers. Neither did the apostle have in mind an imminent change in government that would result in more benevolent treatment for believers. His reference to the fulfillment **of all things** indicates he is speaking of the Lord's return (cf. Acts 3:21; Col. 3:4; 2 Thess. 1:10; 2 Tim. 4:1, 8; Heb. 9:28; Rev. 20:11–13).

The verb translated **is near** (*ēggiken*) means "approaching." The perfect tense indicates a consummated process with a resulting nearness —the event (Christ's return) is imminent; it could occur at any moment (cf. Matt. 24:37–39; Rom. 13:12; 1 Thess. 5:2; Rev. 16:15; 22:20). Therefore believers are to live with an ongoing attitude of anticipation or expectancy, as a mark of faithfulness. That Peter lived with a sense of this imminence is shown as earlier in this epistle he encouraged his readers that they were protected by God's power "for a salvation ready to be revealed in the last time" (1:5)—"at the revelation of Jesus Christ" (1:7; cf. 1:13; 2:12). Numerous other New Testament references also stress the importance of believers' anticipating the Lord's imminent return (Mark 13:35–37; Luke 12:40; 21:36; 1 Cor. 1:7; 1 Tim. 6:14; Titus 2:13; James 5:7–9).

The Jews who lived during Christ's earthly ministry witnessed the end of the Old Covenant and the inauguration of the New Covenant. The entire Old Testament system of ceremonies, rituals, sacrifices, priests, and offerings terminated with the tearing in two of the temple veil and the opening of the Holy of Holies to everyone (Matt. 27:51; John 19:30; Heb. 10:14–22). In A.D. 70 God punctuated that transition by sending judgment by means of the Roman army under Titus, its general, to destroy Jerusalem and the temple. That fulfilled Jesus' prophecy to the apostles, "Jesus came out from the temple and was going away when His disciples came up to point out the temple buildings to Him. And He said to them, 'Do you not see all these things? Truly I say to you, not one stone here will be left upon another, which will not be torn down' " (Matt. 24:1–2).

The apostle Paul wrote to the Corinthians concerning the split-second suddenness of the rapture of the church, the first event in the sequence leading to Christ's return and earthly rule:

> Behold, I tell you a mystery; we will not all sleep, but we will all be changed, in a moment, in the twinkling of an eye, at the last trumpet; for the trumpet will sound, and the dead will be raised imperishable, and we will be changed. For this perishable must put on the imperishable, and this mortal must put on immortality. (1 Cor. 15:51-53)

At that event God will clothe every Christian in immortality (cf. 5:4; Phil. 3:21; 2 Tim. 4:8) within the fraction of a second it takes light to refract off an eye's pupil. That event is both sudden and a mystery, which indicates He has not yet revealed all its details, including the time.

Concerning the rapture, Paul instructed the Thessalonians,

> For this we say to you by the word of the Lord, that we who are alive and remain until the coming of the Lord, will not precede those who have fallen asleep. For the Lord Himself will descend from heaven with a shout, with the voice of the archangel and with the trumpet of God, and the dead in Christ will rise first. Then we who are alive and remain will be caught up together with them in the clouds to meet the Lord in the air, and so we shall always be with the Lord. (1 Thess. 4:15–17)

"We" indicates the apostle believed Christ's return could happen in his lifetime. Today's church should live with far greater expectancy (cf. James 5:7–8).

The author of Hebrews exhorted his readers to keep meeting together and encouraging one another because the day of Christ's return was "drawing near" (Heb. 10:25). Nearly 2,000 years have elapsed since then, and His return is obviously nearer. Therefore it is even more urgent today that believers not neglect meeting to edify and comfort one another with divine truth (cf. Acts 2:42; Rom. 15:5–7; Heb. 3:13; 10:24–25; 12:26–28).

The apostle John, as he neared the end of his life, was firmly convinced that the return of Christ, with all its attendant events and phenomena, divinely revealed to him in the visions of revelation, could occur very soon. Under the Spirit's inspiration, he testified to that truth and to the blessing of Christians' living in daily anticipation of it (cf. Rev. 1:3; 22:20).

Just prior to His ascension, Jesus told the apostles, "It is not for you to know times or epochs [concerning the establishment of His earthly kingdom] which the Father has fixed by His own authority" (Acts 1:7; cf. Matt. 24:36). Even though God wants believers to focus on the hope of Christ's return, He has chosen not to reveal its exact time. If they knew the specific date of the Lord's return was far off, believers could lose motivation and become complacent or, if they knew it was near, engage in frenzied, panicked activity as the day approached. Imminence eliminates both extremes so all Christians throughout the history of the church can live with biblically balanced expectancy.

Living with the realization that the first feature of the Lord's return, the rapture of the church, **is near,** energizes believers for holy living. John wrote,

> See how great a love the Father has bestowed on us, that we would be called children of God; and such we are. For this reason the world does not know us, because it did not know Him. Beloved, now we are children of God, and it has not appeared as yet what we will be. We know that when He appears, we will be like Him, because we will see Him just as He is. (1 John 3:1–2; cf. 2 Cor. 5:10)

Realizing also that when He returns He will come to judge the ungodly (4:5; cf. 2 Thess. 1:6–9) prompts saints to evangelism, as Paul indicated: "Therefore, knowing the fear of the Lord, we persuade men, but we are made manifest to God; and I hope that we are made manifest also in your consciences" (2 Cor. 5:11).

The early church was already in the last days (1 John 2:18), which had begun with Christ's first coming (Heb. 1:1–2). Paul described to Timothy in detail the spiritual atmosphere of his times, so he would know what to expect as he labored in the church:

> But realize this, that in the last days difficult times will come. For men will be lovers of self, lovers of money, boastful, arrogant, revilers, disobedient to parents, ungrateful, unholy, unloving, irreconcilable, malicious gossips, without self-control, brutal, haters of good, treacherous, reckless, conceited, lovers of pleasure rather than lovers of God, holding to a form of godliness, although they have denied its power; Avoid such men as these. (2 Tim. 3:1–5; cf. 4:3–4; 1 Tim. 4:1–3)

The author of the letter to the Hebrews provided further commentary on the full significance of Christ and the last days:

> now once at the consummation of the ages He has been manifested to put away sin by the sacrifice of Himself. And inasmuch as it is appointed for men to die once and after this comes judgment, so Christ also, having been offered once to bear the sins of many, will appear a second time for salvation without reference to sin, to those who eagerly await Him. (Heb. 9:26–28)

The Lord's first coming provided salvation through His death at Calvary. Through Christ's atoning work, God redeemed believers from the kingdom of darkness, forgave their sins, and placed them into the kingdom of His Son (Col. 1:13–14; cf. Ps. 103:12; Matt. 26:28; Acts 26:18; 1 Cor. 1:30; 2 Cor. 5:19; Eph. 1:7; 2:13; Col. 2:13; Heb. 9:14; 1 John 1:7). Christ came to demonstrate His authority, proclaim His kingdom, and defeat sin and death (cf. Ps. 45:6; Isa. 9:7; Jer. 23:5; Matt. 12:28; 18:3; Mark 1:15; Luke 10:9, 11; 11:20; 17:21; John 18:36; Rom. 14:17; Heb. 1:8; 12:28). The church is now in the final days of that spiritual and inward kingdom. His return and judgment will culminate in His establishing His thousand-year earthly kingdom (cf. Isa. 65:17–25; Ezek. 37:24–25; Hos. 3:5; Zech. 14:16–21; Rev. 20:1–6) prior to the eternal new heavens and new earth where the righteous will forever dwell (cf. Matt. 25:34; John 14:2; Heb. 12:22–24, 28; 2 Peter 1:11; 3:13; Rev. 3:21; 7:16–17; 21:1–4; 22:3–4).

Other New Testament texts support Peter's exhortation here that believers ought to live holy lives, expecting the imminent return of Jesus Christ (cf. 1 Cor. 1:7; 16:22; 2 Peter 3:11–13; 1 John 2:28). Scripture, however, does not call for overzealous eschatological extremism (e.g., date-setting, undue preoccupation with or fascination about unrevealed details, unwise speculation about the relationship of current events to last things, or dropping out from society or shirking responsibility while passively waiting for His return). Jesus taught,

> Be dressed in readiness, and keep your lamps lit. Be like men who are waiting for their master when he returns from the wedding feast, so that they may immediately open the door to him when he comes and knocks. Blessed are those slaves whom the master will find on the alert when he comes; truly I say to you, that he will gird himself to serve, and have them recline at the table, and will come up and wait on them. (Luke 12:35–37)

When He comes back, Christ will serve those who have patiently anticipated that day. But He also warned believers to be alert and prepared for that event (Matt. 24:42–44), because they do not know the precise hour or date of His appearance (cf. 2 Peter 3:10).

The apostle Paul asserted that the characteristic of every true Christian is a desire to please the Lord: "Therefore we also have as our ambition, whether at home or absent, to be pleasing to Him. For we must all appear before the judgment seat of Christ, so that each one may be recompensed for his deeds in the body, according to what he has done, whether good or bad" (2 Cor. 5:9–10). Christians will stand before Christ at that judgment to give an account for their lives. He will not judge them for their sins because His sacrifice on the cross has already cleansed those away. At that judgment the Lord will reward all believers for works that were good, assessing their effectiveness, dedication, devotion, and usefulness in serving Him (cf. 1 Cor. 3:10–15; 4:1–5). A realization of that future reality ought to instill within every believer a desire for constant purity (2 Peter 3:14, 18), as it did for the apostles Paul (Phil. 3:14; 2 Tim. 4:7–8) and John (1 John 3:2–3).

THE INSTRUCTIONS FOR OUR DUTY

therefore, be of sound judgment and sober spirit for the purpose of prayer. Above all, keep fervent in your love for one another, because love covers a multitude of sins. Be hospitable to one another without complaint. As each one has received a special gift, employ it in serving one another as good stewards of the manifold grace of God. Whoever speaks, is to do so as one who is speaking the utterances of God; whoever serves is to do so as one who is serving by the strength which God supplies; (4:7b–11a)

All those demanding commands make it clear that anyone who would truly receive Jesus Christ must first count the high cost of doing so. Following Jesus demands total self-denial and eager submission to His lordship, even if obedience means death. "He was saying to them all, 'If anyone wishes to come after Me, he must deny himself, and take up his cross daily and follow Me'" (Luke 9:23; for more on the cost of discipleship, see John MacArthur, *Hard to Believe* [Nashville: Nelson, 2003]). When evangelizing others, believers need also to encourage them to consider the cost (Matt. 19:21; Luke 9:59–62; 14:26–33; cf. Matt. 13:44–46). However, even though the gospel message is a call to submit to Him, it is a gracious invitation. Jesus said, "Take My yoke upon you. . . . For My yoke is easy and My burden is light" (Matt. 11:29, 30). Discipleship is costly and eternally joyous, but the cost of rejection is infinitely greater and eternally horrific (cf. Ps. 9:17; Prov. 13:15; Isa. 33:14; Matt. 8:12; 13:42; 25:41; Luke 16:23). A life without Christ sooner or later entails crushing guilt, hopeless disappointment, unsolvable problems, and after all that, eternal condemnation. So discipleship is a paradox in that following the Lord is costly but easy (cf. Matt. 11:28–30; 1 John 5:3)—and demanding but rewarding (cf. Rom. 2:7; 8:17–18; Heb. 4:9; 10:35; James 1:12; Rev. 2:10; 3:21; 21:7).

God not only calls disciples to obey His commands, but by the Holy Spirit's power, working graciously through Scripture, He enables them to fulfill those commands (Eph. 5:15–21; Phil. 4:13; Col. 3:16–17; cf. 2 Tim. 1:7–8). Because the postmodern world is so complex, contemporary Christianity often erroneously assumes that solutions to believers' problems and difficulties are also complex. But the basic principles of the Christian life are simple and direct, since God has chosen humble, common people to know His purpose and will (1 Cor. 1:27–28). And because of regeneration, believers long to obey God and be more conformed to the image of Christ (Phil. 3:7–14). Sin does limit their ability to do what is right (Rom. 7:19), but all genuine Christians hate sin and love righteousness (vv. 22–25). The key to handling trials and temptations is developing daily spiritual discipline (cf. Luke 6:40; 16:10–12; 1 Cor. 4:2; 2 Tim. 2:2), which includes cultivating the necessary spiritual disciplines that produce growing faith and courage (cf. Ps. 31:24; 1 Cor. 16:13; Eph. 6:16; Col. 1:23; Heb. 11:1–2; 1 John 5:4–5).

This section contains three basic elements saints need to build godly lives and stand strong and effective in witness to the world: personal holiness, which concerns their relationship to God; mutual love, which concerns their relationship with each other; and spiritual service, which concerns their responsibility to the church.

CONCERNING PERSONAL HOLINESS

therefore, be of sound judgment and sober spirit for the purpose of prayer. (4:7*b*)

It is axiomatic that godly thinking is at the heart of communion with God, since the more one knows a person's mind, the richer the relationship will be (Rom. 12:1–2; Eph. 4:23–24; Phil. 4:8). The word rendered **be of sound judgment** derives from a term that literally means, "be in one's right mind" (*sōphroneō*)—to be under control and not be carried away by an errant view of oneself (Rom. 12:3; cf. Prov. 23:7), or undue emotion, or uncontrolled passion. Mark used it to describe the maniac Jesus freed from the legion of demons (Mark 5:15). The verb also refers to guarding the mind (cf. Prov. 4:23) and keeping it lucid. The Christian mind must be clearly fixed on spiritual priorities and righteous living (Josh. 1:8; Matt. 6:33; Col. 3:2, 16; Titus 2:11–12)—objectives that a self-indulgent, deceptive world, heavily influenced by Satan, constantly seeks to distract from, deflect, and destroy (cf. 1 John 2:15–16). When believers' minds are subject to Christ (2 Cor. 10:5) and His Word (Pss. 1:2; 19:7, 10; 119:97, 103, 105; cf. 2 Tim. 3:15–17) they see matters from an eternal perspective.

Holy living also requires spiritual alertness. **Sober spirit** (*nēphō*), closely related in meaning to **sound judgment,** denotes being spiritually observant. Jesus expressed a similar sentiment when He warned the apostles to "be on the alert" (Matt. 24:42) and to "keep watching" (26:41).

Godly thinking and spiritual alertness are crucial **for the purpose of prayer. Prayer** is the access to all spiritual resources, but believers cannot pray properly if their minds are unstable due to worldly pursuits, ignorance of divine truth, or indifference to divine purposes (cf. 1 Cor. 14:15; Heb. 10:22; 1 John 5:14–15). Saints who seriously study Scripture and discover its profound truths about God experience rich communion with Him (Ps. 42:1; John 14:23; 2 Cor. 13:14; 1 John 1:3), understanding what Paul called "the mind of Christ" (1 Cor. 2:16; cf. Isa.

40:13; 2 Tim. 1:7). This essential element in one's relationship to God is illustrated by the Spirit's relationship to the Father. Paul wrote, "He who searches the hearts knows what the mind of the Spirit is, because He intercedes for the saints according to the will of God" (Rom. 8:27). Because the Holy Spirit and the Father know each other's minds perfectly, there is perfect agreement in the Spirit's intercession.

Holy living comes when believers read and meditate on God's Word daily so as to know the thoughts of God and commune with Him according to His will. Jude calls this "praying in the Holy Spirit" (v. 20).

CONCERNING MUTUAL LOVE

Above all, keep fervent in your love for one another, because love covers a multitude of sins. Be hospitable to one another without complaint. (4:8–9)

Mutual love primarily concerns believers' relationships with each other. **Above all** refers to the supreme importance of that virtue in the Christian life (cf. 1 Cor. 13:13; Phil. 2:2; Col. 3:14), and the participle rendered **keep** collects "sound judgment" and "sober spirit for the purpose of prayer" under the priority of **fervent . . . love for one another.** **Fervent** (*ektenēs*) denotes stretching or straining and pictures a person running with taut muscles, exerting maximum effort. Ancient Greek literature used the word to describe a horse stretching out and running at full speed. Earlier in this letter (1:22), Peter also used its related adverb to describe the intensity and exertion that ought to characterize Christian **love.** Such love is sacrificial, not sentimental, and requires a stretching of believers' every spiritual muscle to love in spite of insult, injury, and misunderstanding from others (Prov. 10:12; Matt. 5:44; Mark 12:33; Rom. 12:14, 20; 1 John 4:11; cf. Rom. 12:15; Gal. 6:10; Eph. 5:2; James 1:27).

It is self-evident that genuine love inherently tends to forgive the offenses of others (cf. Prov. 10:12). But commentators differ on how to interpret the expression **love covers a multitude of sins.** Some say it refers to God's love covering sins, whereas others say it describes believers who are lovingly overlooking each other's transgressions. Since the text offers no explanation, it seems best to understand the phrase here as a general axiom. Whether from God or man, love covers sin.

Love derives from the well-known Greek word *agapē* (cf. 1:8, 22; 2:17; 3:10), which carries a strong volitional significance. Salvation results from the Lord's choosing to love all those who believe: "But God demonstrates His own love toward us, in that while we were yet sinners, Christ died for us" (Rom. 5:8; cf. John 3:16; 1 John 4:19). Christians must follow His example, choosing to love even the unlovely, because "the whole Law and the Prophets" (Matt. 22:40) hinges on doing so (vv. 37–39), as does their witness (John 13:34–35). The command to **be hospitable** (literally, "to love strangers") takes that **love** beyond the circle of Christians' friends to other believers they do not even know (cf. Heb. 13:2).

According to the Mosaic law, the Jews were to extend hospitality to strangers (Ex. 22:21; Deut. 14:29; cf. Gen. 18:1–2). Jesus commended believers who provided food, clothing, and shelter to others (Matt. 25:35–40; cf. Luke 14:12–14). However, the spirit of hospitality extends beyond the tangible acts of providing meals or a place to stay. It includes not just the act, but an unselfish attitude, so that what is done, no matter the sacrifice, is done **without complaint.** Biblical hospitality knows nothing of the "Poor Richard's Almanac" mentality that says fish and guests smell after three days.

Because believers still sin (Rom. 7:18–19; 1 John 1:8; cf. 1 Tim. 1:15), the only thing that will preserve the church's unity is love that forgives and reaches out in kindness to strangers. Love also plays a foundational role in the evangelization of the unsaved. Jesus told the apostles, "By this all men will know that you are My disciples, if you have love for one another" (John 13:35).

CONCERNING SPIRITUAL SERVICE

As each one has received a special gift, employ it in serving one another as good stewards of the manifold grace of God. Whoever speaks, is to do so as one who is speaking the utterances of God; whoever serves is to do so as one who is serving by the strength which God supplies; (4:10–11a)

Every Christian **has received** a **special gift** (spiritual gift), a divine enablement for ministry to the body. Paul wrote, "To each one is given the manifestation of the Spirit for the common good. . . . One and the same Spirit works all these things, distributing to each one individually just as He wills" (1 Cor. 12:7, 11). As each part of the human body has a particular function, so does each member of the body of Christ (cf. 12:14).

The categories from which the Lord draws the components for each believer's gift are given in two Pauline passages:

> For through the grace given to me I say to everyone among you not to think more highly of himself than he ought to think; but to think so as to have sound judgment, as God has allotted to each a measure of

faith. For just as we have many members in one body and all the members do not have the same function, so we, who are many, are one body in Christ, and individually members one of another. Since we have gifts that differ according to the grace given to us, each of us is to exercise them accordingly: if prophecy, according to the proportion of his faith; if service, in his serving; or he who teaches, in his teaching; or he who exhorts, in his exhortation; he who gives, with liberality; he who leads, with diligence; he who shows mercy, with cheerfulness. (Rom. 12:3–8)

Now there are varieties of gifts, but the same Spirit. And there are varieties of ministries, and the same Lord. There are varieties of effects, but the same God who works all things in all persons. But to each one is given the manifestation of the Spirit for the common good. For to one is given the word of wisdom through the Spirit, and to another the word of knowledge according to the same Spirit; to another faith by the same Spirit, and to another gifts of healing by the one Spirit, and to another the effecting of miracles, and to another prophecy, and to another the distinguishing of spirits, to another various kinds of tongues, and to another the interpretation of tongues. But one and the same Spirit works all these things, distributing to each one individually just as He wills. (1 Cor. 12:4–11)

(For complete commentary on these two spiritual gifts passages, see John MacArthur, *Romans 9–16*, MacArthur New Testament Commentary [Chicago: Moody, 1994], 153–78, and MacArthur, *1 Corinthians*, MacArthur New Testament Commentary [Chicago: Moody, 1984], 289–307.)

Each believer's spiritual giftedness is unique, as if each were a spiritual snowflake or fingerprint. It is as if God dips His paint brush into different colors, or categories of gifts, on His spiritual palette and paints each Christian a unique blend of colors. Not only does God grant spiritual gifts and arrange them in different ways (Eph. 4:7), but He also gives believers the necessary faith to exercise them, as He did Paul (cf. Rom. 12:3). Paul summarizes the power of their operation as follows: "Now there are varieties of gifts, but the same Spirit. And there are varieties of ministries, and the same Lord. There are varieties of effects, but the same God who works all things in all persons" (1 Cor. 12:4–6).

Because the Holy Spirit sovereignly superintends the distribution of spiritual gifts (1 Cor. 12:11), believers cannot earn, pray for, or in any manner generate them (cf. Acts 8:20). The term rendered "gift" in Ephesians 4:7 (*dōrea*) emphasizes the freeness of His grace and gifts, whereas *charisma* (**gift**) highlights the gracious aspect of what God has done. In the New Testament, that word refers both to spiritual gifts and salvation (e.g., Rom. 1:11; 6:23; 1 Cor. 1:7; 1 Tim. 4:14; 2 Tim. 1:6).

When believers **employ** their gifts **in serving one another,** they minister in a fashion that mutually benefits the church (cf. 1 Cor.

12:7). Conversely, nonuse of gifts or wrongly depreciating some gifts (and perhaps also those who possess them) adversely affects Christ's Body:

> If the foot says, "Because I am not a hand, I am not a part of the body," it is not for this reason any the less a part of the body. And if the ear says, "Because I am not an eye, I am not a part of the body," it is not for this reason any the less a part of the body. If the whole body were an eye, where would the hearing be? If the whole were hearing, where would the sense of smell be? But now God has placed the members, each one of them, in the body, just as He desired. If they were all one member, where would the body be? But now there are many members, but one body. And the eye cannot say to the hand, "I have no need of you"; or again the head to the feet, "I have no need of you." On the contrary, it is much truer that the members of the body which seem to be weaker are necessary; and those members of the body which we deem less honorable, on these we bestow more abundant honor, and our less presentable members become much more presentable, whereas our more presentable members have no need of it. But God has so composed the body, giving more abundant honor to that member which lacked, so that there may be no division in the body, but that the members may have the same care for one another. (1 Cor. 12:15–25)

The highly visible, up-front gifts (e.g., preaching, teaching, evangelism) are not necessarily the most valuable in every instance. God views all believers' gifts as edifying and their exercise essential to the well-being of the body of Christ. **Good stewards** are those who manage their spiritual gifts wisely and use them obediently (cf. 1 Cor. 4:2; Titus 1:7). Peter's readers were familiar with **stewards** who handled an owner's land, funds, supplies of food, and other resources. The apostle's analogy was obvious, and not using one's gifts weakens the local church because others cannot replace the unique giftedness of those who are not ministering.

The variety of spiritual gifts is expressed in the word **manifold,** which literally means "many colored" or "multi-faceted." Two believers may have the gift of teaching, but each will demonstrate it with a unique blend of grace and faith. That provides for edifying and useful spiritual diversity within the church. One leader's preaching may emphasize the showing of mercy and gentleness, whereas another's may emphasize the discerning of truth, and another's the wisdom in its application.

Since spiritual gifts result from the **grace of God,** the church cannot devise some human scheme for passing them out. Many Christians may not be able to neatly categorize their own gift because of its uniqueness, but they can be available to the Holy Spirit (cf. John 14:26; Rom. 14:17; 15:13; 1 Cor. 2:10, 12–13; 2 Tim. 1:14) and observe how He motivates and uses them in ministry.

The two broad categories of spiritual gifts are speaking gifts or serving gifts. **Whoever speaks** will minister through categories of preaching and teaching, wisdom, knowledge, and discernment. **Whoever serves** will minister through areas such as administration, prayer, mercy, or helps. And those who speak must communicate not human opinion but **the utterances of God,** as revealed only in Scripture (cf. Acts 7:38; Rom. 3:2). Similarly, any serving gift is to be exercised, not by human power, but **by the strength which God supplies** (cf. Phil. 4:13), that is, in dependence on the Holy Spirit.

THE INTENTION OF OUR DUTY

so that in all things God may be glorified through Jesus Christ, to whom belongs the glory and dominion forever and ever. Amen. (4:11*b*)

As is the goal of everything for believers, the purpose of their fulfilling the obligations of Christian duty in the midst of a hostile world is that **God may be glorified.** These final clauses of the passage constitute a doxology—an expression of praise and glory to God (cf. Rom. 11:36; 16:27; Eph. 3:20–21; 1 Tim. 1:17; Jude 25), which Christians can correctly utter only **through Jesus Christ. In all things** refers to **all** matters of Christian responsibility.

Commentators have long discussed whether **to whom** refers to **God** or **Jesus Christ.** It is best to view the designation as a blessed and inspired ambiguity—**the glory and dominion** belong to both God in Christ and Christ in God, **forever and ever** (cf. Pss. 104:31; 113:4; 138:5; Hab. 2:14; Matt. 17:2; John 1:14; 10:30; 2 Cor. 4:6; Col. 1:15; Heb. 1:3; 2 Peter 1:16–18).

Believers should want to glorify God in all they think, say, and do. The apostle Paul said, "Whether, then, you eat or drink or whatever you do, do all to the glory of God" (1 Cor. 10:31). They will more readily obey Paul's exhortation if they are motivated by the certainty and nearness of the Second Coming, resulting in personal holiness, mutual love, and spiritual service within the church.

Peter closed this passage with the familiar **amen,** a term of affirmation that means "so let it be."

J. C. Ryle's observations on holy living still apply to all believers living in a world hostile to Christianity:

> A holy man will follow after spiritual-mindedness. He will endeavor to set his affections entirely on things above, and to hold things on earth with a very loose hand. He will not neglect the business of the life that

now is; but the first place in his mind and thoughts will be given to the life to come. He will aim to live like one whose treasure is in heaven, and to pass through this world like a stranger and pilgrim travelling to his home. (*Holiness* [reprint; Hertfordshire: Evangelical Press, 1987], 37)

The Fiery Trial
(1 Peter 4:12–19)

22

Beloved, do not be surprised at the fiery ordeal among you, which comes upon you for your testing, as though some strange thing were happening to you; but to the degree that you share the sufferings of Christ, keep on rejoicing, so that also at the revelation of His glory you may rejoice with exultation. If you are reviled for the name of Christ, you are blessed, because the Spirit of glory and of God rests on you. Make sure that none of you suffers as a murderer, or thief, or evildoer, or a troublesome meddler; but if anyone suffers as a Christian, he is not to be ashamed, but is to glorify God in this name. For it is time for judgment to begin with the household of God; and if it begins with us first, what will be the outcome for those who do not obey the gospel of God? And if it is with difficulty that the righteous is saved what will become of the godless man and the sinner? Therefore, those also who suffer according to the will of God shall entrust their souls to a faithful Creator in doing what is right. (4:12–19)

For nine days during the summer of A.D. 64, a huge fire raged in the city of Rome. The flames spread rapidly through the city's narrow streets and the many tightly bunched wooden tenements, ordinarily crowded with residents. Because of his well-known desire to refurbish

Rome by whatever means, the populace believed Emperor Nero was responsible for starting the blaze. As the fire destroyed most of the city's districts, he watched gleefully from the Tower of Maecenas. Roman troops prevented people from extinguishing the fire and even started new fires. The disaster thoroughly demoralized the Romans because many lost nearly all their earthly goods and found their civic pride scorched as well. With public resentment toward him at a high level, Nero diverted the focus away from himself and made the Christian community the scapegoat for the fire.

Nero's ploy was a clever one because Christians in the Roman Empire were already the unjust targets of much hatred and slander. Unbelievers falsely reported that Christians consumed human flesh and blood during the Lord's Supper (cf. Mark 14:22–25; 1 Cor. 11:23–26) and that the holy kiss (cf. 5:14; Rom. 16:16; 1 Cor. 16:20; 2 Cor. 13:12; 1 Thess. 5:26) was actually a sign of uncontrolled lust. In addition, the Romans viewed Christianity as a sect of Judaism. With the increasing anti-Semitism of those days, the populace easily adopted an anti-Christian attitude as well. Christianity had also caused stress within families when one spouse (particularly women) believed but the other did not. That generated further resentment toward the saints.

Following the burning of Rome, Nero capitalized on that anti-Christian sentiment and punished the Christians by using them as human torches to light his garden parties, by allowing them to be sewn inside animal skins to be devoured by predatory animals, by crucifying them, and by subjecting them to other heinous, unjust tortures.

The apostle Peter likely wrote this letter just before Nero's persecution began. So, as discussed earlier in this volume (1:6–7; 2:11–12, 19–20; 3:8–9, 14, 17; 4:1), Peter's major recurring theme is how his readers should respond to unjust suffering. Today hostility toward Christians who speak out against the culture's sins and in defense of the exclusivity of the gospel is on the rise. Therefore to endure the present hostility, as well as what might come in the future, believers need to heed this passage's instructions on enduring severe trials. These verses direct believers to expect suffering, exult in suffering, evaluate suffering, and entrust suffering to God. (For a more comprehensive treatment of the entire subject of suffering, see John MacArthur, *The Power of Suffering* [Wheaton, Ill.: Victor, 1995].)

EXPECT SUFFERING

Beloved, do not be surprised at the fiery ordeal among you, which comes upon you for your testing, as though some strange thing were happening to you; (4:12)

Not expecting to be so hatefully persecuted, the believers to whom Peter wrote were understandably surprised, troubled, and confused by their suffering. Perhaps they expected life to be full of blessing, benefits, and divine protection. However, believers' expectation for suffering is bound up in the words of Jesus, who told the apostles, "If the world hates you, you know that it has hated Me before it hated you" (John 15:18); Paul's admonition to Timothy, "All who desire to live godly in Christ Jesus will be persecuted" (2 Tim. 3:12); and the apostle John's warning, "Do not be surprised, brethren, if the world hates you" (1 John 3:13). For Christians, the confrontation with sin and the world often results in suffering, which is part of the promised cost of discipleship (cf. Matt. 10:38–39; 16:24–26; John 12:24–26). Counting the cost is behind Jesus' words that no one builds a tower or enters battle without first calculating that cost (Luke 14:28–32).

Beloved (*agapētos,* cf. 2:11) is a common pastoral word conveying tenderness, compassion, affection, and care (cf. 1 Cor. 4:14; 1 Thess. 2:8). Such love provides a sweet pillow for believers' weary souls to rest on in the midst of trials and persecutions. Severe suffering can tempt them to doubt God's love and allow the same thought to enter their minds that once prompted Job's wife to utter the despicable words: "Do you still hold fast your integrity? Curse God and die!" (Job 2:9). Thus the apostle sought to reassure his readers of his and God's unfailing love.

The phrase **do not be surprised** informs believers to expect that the gospel of Christ will be offensive to many and will produce persecution. The original Greek is *zenizō,* meaning "to be surprised or astonished" by the novelty of something. Believers should never be shocked by persecution. Later in the verse, Peter uses the related noun *zenos,* translated **some strange thing,** but that could also be rendered "a surprising thing," which gives a double emphasis to Peter's point to expect persecution. As saints are obedient to God's Word and effective in proclaiming the gospel, animosity from unbelievers is inevitable. "We are a fragrance of Christ to God among those who are being saved and among those who are perishing; to the one an aroma from death to death, to the other an aroma from life to life. And who is adequate for these things?" (2 Cor. 2:15–16; cf. 4:3; 1 Cor. 1:18). As the time-tested spiritual adages state it, "The sun that melts the wax also hardens the clay," and "The gospel saves and slays" (cf. Rom. 9:15–24). Whether it is hostility toward their exclusive message, their efforts to evangelize, or their godly lifestyle, believers need to remember that hardship is a corollary to biblical faith (Mark 10:30; John 16:33; 1 Thess. 3:4; 2 Tim. 2:3–4; 3:12; cf. Matt. 7:13–14).

While the term rendered **fiery ordeal** (*purōsis*) portrays figuratively a painful experience of persecution, it is also used of a furnace melting down metal to purge it of impurities (cf. Ps. 66:10; Prov. 17:3; see also the discussion of 1:6–7 in chapter 3 of this volume). It may be that Peter is here drawing on his familiarity with Malachi's prophecy:

> "Behold, I am going to send My messenger, and he will clear the way before Me. And the Lord, whom you seek, will suddenly come to His temple; and the messenger of the covenant, in whom you delight, behold, He is coming," says the Lord of hosts. "But who can endure the day of His coming? And who can stand when He appears? For He is like a refiner's fire and like fullers' soap. He will sit as a smelter and purifier of silver, and He will purify the sons of Levi and refine them like gold and silver, so that they may present to the Lord offerings in righteousness." (Mal. 3:1–3)

That text speaks of a purifying fire, in contrast to the consuming fire in 4:1, "'For behold, the day is coming, burning like a furnace; and all the arrogant and every evildoer will be chaff; and the day that is coming will set them ablaze,'" says the Lord of hosts, "'so that it will leave them neither root nor branch.'" Evidence that Peter was thinking of Malachi's words is strengthened by the apostle's reference to "the household of God" (v. 17), where such purifying judgment must come. Peter is saying that the persecution is the Lord refining His temple—His people.

Such mistreatment **which comes upon** believers is also **for** their **testing,** proving the genuineness of their faith (cf. Job 23:10; Rom. 5:3; 2 Cor. 1:10; 2 Tim. 3:11; James 1:3–12). Suffering for righteousness' sake not only refines, but, even before that, reveals whether people are truly believers. Jesus illustrated this truth in the parable of the soils: "Others [seeds] fell on the rocky places, where they did not have much soil; and immediately they sprang up, because they had no depth of soil. But when the sun had risen, they were scorched; and because they had no root, they withered away" (Matt. 13:5–6). The Lord described a shallow, inadequate response to the proclamation of the gospel. Some did not allow the seed of the Word to penetrate the hard soil of their heart, and persecution soon revealed their response to the gospel to be nothing but a superficial, false profession (vv. 20–21).

The verb translated **were happening** (*sumbainontos*) may mean "to fall by chance" and calls for Christians to understand that experiences of unjust suffering for Christ are not accidental, but inevitable because the message of sin, salvation, and judgment offends. In addition, these incidents occur by God's design and reveal whether professing believers' faith is truly regenerate (cf. Job 5:17; Prov. 3:11–12; Heb. 12:5–11; Rev. 3:19).

EXULT IN SUFFERING

but to the degree that you share the sufferings of Christ, keep on rejoicing, so that also at the revelation of His glory you may rejoice with exultation. If you are reviled for the name of Christ, you are blessed, because the Spirit of glory and of God rests on you. (4:13–14)

To the degree is a generous way to translate *katho* ("as," "according to which") and thus to show that Christians' eternal reward is proportionate to their earthly suffering (cf. Rom. 8:18; 2 Cor. 4:16–18; Heb. 11:26; 2 John 8; Rev. 2:10). That is a reasonable relationship since suffering reveals faithfulness to their Lord Jesus Christ, who Himself noted this relationship between suffering and reward, saying,

> Blessed are you when men hate you, and ostracize you, and insult you, and scorn your name as evil, for the sake of the Son of Man. Be glad in that day and leap for joy, for behold, your reward is great in heaven. For in the same way their fathers used to treat the prophets. (Luke 6:22–23)

Peter further enriches the endurance of those who are persecuted by stating that they **share the sufferings of Christ.** That is not in any redemptive sense; neither does it refer only to spiritual union with Him, as Paul describes in Romans 6. But it refers to believers experiencing the same kind of sufferings He endured—suffering for what is right. R. C. H. Lenski rightly elaborates the meaning of Peter's expression:

> The readers [of 1 Peter] are only in fellowship with the sufferings of Christ. This is a thought that is prominent and fully carried out by Paul in Rom. 8:17; II Cor. 1:7; 4:10; Phil. 1:29; 3:10; Col. 1:24. It goes back to Christ's word (John 15:20, 21).
>
> We fellowship Christ's sufferings when we suffer for his name's sake, when the hatred that struck him strikes us because of him. Never is there a thought of fellowshiping in the expiation of Christ's suffering, our suffering also being expiatory. In Matt. 5:12 persecution places us in the company of the persecuted prophets (high exaltation indeed); here it places us in the company of Christ himself, into an even greater communion or [*koinōnia*]. Is that "a strange thing" or to be deemed strange? It is what we should deem proper, natural, to be expected, yea, as Peter says (following Matt. 5:12), a cause for joy. (*The Interpretation of the Epistles of St. Peter, St. John and St. Jude* [reprint; Minneapolis: Augsburg, 1966], 203)

Christ who suffered at the hands of wicked men even though He was without sin (Isa. 53:9; Matt. 26:67; 27:12, 26, 29–31, 39–44; John 10:31, 33; 11:8; Acts 2:23) promised believers it would be their privilege to suffer in the same way when He said, "Remember the word that I said to you, 'A slave is not greater than his master.' If they persecuted Me, they will also persecute you; if they kept My word, they will keep yours also" (John 15:20).

To the degree that believers suffer unjustly, they should, as their Lord did, **keep on rejoicing,** a sentiment completely unacceptable to those who have no hope of heavenly reward, but affirmed by the Lord when He declared,

> Blessed are those who have been persecuted for the sake of righteousness, for theirs is the kingdom of heaven. Blessed are you when people insult you and persecute you, and falsely say all kinds of evil against you because of Me. Rejoice and be glad, for your reward in heaven is great; for in the same way they persecuted the prophets who were before you. (Matt. 5:10–12)

The revelation of His glory will come in "the day that the Son of Man is revealed" (Luke 17:30), which refers to Christ's return. The Lord resumed the full exercise of **His glory** after He ascended to heaven, but He has not yet revealed it on earth for everyone to see (cf. Matt. 24:30; Phil. 2:9–11; Rev. 19:11–16). (Peter, James, and John did get a preview of that glory when they witnessed Christ's transfiguration [Mark 9:2–3; cf. 2 Peter 1:16–18].)

Peter's second use of **rejoice** (*chairō*) in verse 13 is qualified by **exultation** (*agalliaō*), a reference to rapturous joy. When Christ returns, believers will **rejoice with exultation** (cf. the discussion of joy in chapter 3 of this volume), and do so in proportion to their share in His sufferings in this life. Those who share His sufferings will also share His glory (5:1; cf. Matt. 20:20–23). The saints' suffering for righteousness proves them, refines them, and earns for them "an eternal weight of glory" (2 Cor. 4:17) so that the greater their suffering the stronger their hope, and the richer their joy (cf. 2 Cor. 4:16–18; James 1:2).

The name of Christ is the cause of evil hatred directed toward believers (Matt. 10:22; 24:9). In the early days of the church, His **name** first became synonymous with the Savior Himself and all that He represents (cf. Luke 24:47; John 1:12; Acts 2:38; 4:17, 30; 9:15; 19:17). In Peter's sermon before the Sanhedrin, he asserted, "There is salvation in no one else; for there is no other name under heaven that has been given among men by which we must be saved" (Acts 4:12). Later the apostles "went on their way from the presence of the Council, rejoicing that they had been considered worthy to suffer shame for His name" (5:41). In His vision concerning the conversion of Saul of Tarsus and his subsequent preaching as Paul the apostle, Christ told Ananias of Damascus, "I will show him how much he must suffer for My name's sake" (9:16). It is not the **name** "Christ" that offends the ungodly, but rather who He is and what He said and did that causes hostility from them.

That animosity is summed up in the word **reviled** (*oneidizō*), meaning "to denounce," or "to heap insults upon." In the Septuagint it described hostility heaped at God and His people by the godless (Pss. 42:10; 44:16; 74:10, 18; cf. Isa. 51:7; Zeph. 2:8). In the New Testament it refers to the indignities and mistreatments Christ endured from sinners (Matt. 27:44; Mark 15:32; Rom. 15:3). In the first century, unbelievers were often exasperated and infuriated that believers were so frequently speaking of Christ, whose indictment of sinners they despised (cf. Acts 4:17–18; 17:1–7).

However, all the hatred and violence of the world against Christians does not diminish their blessedness. Actually they are more **blessed** for such suffering, not only for the eternal reward they will receive but for the present blessing, **because the Spirit of glory and of God rests on** them. It is not merely because of suffering that the Holy Spirit will rest on believers, as when He came on and departed from an Old Testament prophet, but rather that He, already being in believers permanently (Rom. 8:9; 1 Cor. 6:19–20; 12:13), gives them supernatural relief in the midst of their suffering. Because the Spirit is **God,** divine **glory** defines His nature (cf. Pss. 93:1; 104:1; 138:5). **Glory** recalls the *Shekinah,* which in the Old Testament symbolized God's earthly presence (Ex. 24:16–17; 34:5–8; 40:34–38; Hab. 3:3–4). When the tabernacle and the ark of the covenant were brought to Solomon's newly dedicated temple, "the glory of the Lord filled the house of the Lord" (1 Kings 8:11). As the brilliant cloud of the *Shekinah* rested in the tabernacle and the temple, so the Holy Spirit lives in and ministers to believers today. **Rests** (from the present tense of *anapauō*) means "to give relief, refreshment, intermission from toil" (cf. Matt. 11:28–29; Mark 6:31), and describes one of His ministries. "Refreshment" comes on those believers who suffer for the sake of the Savior and the gospel. The Spirit gives them grace by imparting endurance, understanding, and all the fruit that comes in the panoply of His goodness: "But the fruit of the Spirit is love, joy, peace, patience, kindness, goodness, faithfulness, gentleness, self-control; against such things there is no law" (Gal. 5:22–23).

That kind of refreshment and divine power came upon Stephen, a leader in the Jerusalem church and its first recorded martyr. As he began to defend his faith before the Jewish leaders, they "saw his face like the face of an angel" (Acts 6:15). His demeanor signified serenity, tranquility, and joy—all the fruit of the Spirit—undiminished and even expanded by his suffering and the Holy Comforter's grace to him. The Sanhedrin became enraged as Stephen rehearsed redemptive history to them from the Old Testament, an account that culminated in the atoning work of Jesus the Messiah. Stephen's Spirit-controlled rest was evident as "he gazed intently into heaven and saw the glory of God, and Jesus standing at the right hand of God; and he said, 'Behold, I see the heavens opened up and the Son of Man standing at the right hand of God'" (Acts 7:55–56). As his enemies stoned him to death, Stephen "called on the Lord and said, 'Lord Jesus, receive my spirit!' Then falling on his knees, he cried out with a loud voice, 'Lord, do not hold this sin against them!' Having said this, he fell asleep" (vv. 59–60). Truly the Spirit of glory elevated him above his suffering to sweet relief. That powerful work of the Spirit was the cause of Paul's later testimony in 2 Corinthians 12:9–10, "And He has said to me, 'My grace is sufficient for you, for power is perfected in weakness.' Most gladly, therefore, I will rather boast about my weaknesses, so that the power of Christ may dwell in me. Therefore I am well content with weaknesses, with insults, with distresses, with persecutions, with difficulties, for Christ's sake; for when I am weak, then I am strong."

EVALUATE SUFFERING

Make sure that none of you suffers as a murderer, or thief, or evildoer, or a troublesome meddler; but if anyone suffers as a Christian, he is not to be ashamed, but is to glorify God in this name. For it is time for judgment to begin with the household of God; and if it begins with us first, what will be the outcome for those who do not obey the gospel of God? And if it is with difficulty that the righteous is saved what will become of the godless man and the sinner? (4:15–18)

Not all suffering brings Holy Spirit relief. Trouble stemming from lawless actions obviously does not constitute suffering for righteousness. If any believer is **a murderer, or thief** (capital crimes in the ancient world), he or she has no right to complain about being punished, nor any right to expect the Spirit's graces. The same applies if any should suffer **as** an **evildoer** (*kakopoios*), a more general term that encompasses all crimes without exception (cf. 2:14; 3 John 11).

The surprising inclusion of the term rendered **troublesome meddler** (*allotriepiskopos*), used only here in the New Testament, and at first seemingly minor in comparison to Peter's previous terms, shows that all sins, not just crimes, forfeit the Holy Spirit's comfort and rest. The word literally means, "one who meddles in things alien to his calling," "an agitator," or "troublemaker." Paul's exhortations to the Thessalonians illustrate the word's meaning:

> Make it your ambition to lead a quiet life and attend to your own business and work with your hands, just as we commanded you. (1 Thess. 4:11)

> For we hear that some among you are leading an undisciplined life, doing no work at all, but acting like busybodies. Now such persons we command and exhort in the Lord Jesus Christ to work in quiet fashion and eat their own bread. (2 Thess. 3:11–12)

Christians are never to be troublemakers or agitators in society or in their places of work (cf. 1 Tim. 2:1–3; Titus 3:1–5). They may confront the sins in the lives of other believers, help administer church discipline, challenge unbelievers with the gospel, and exhort fellow saints to greater levels of godliness; but regarding others' private matters that do not concern them, believers should never intrude inappropriately. More specifically, Peter was referring to political activism and civil agitation—disruptive or illegal activity that interferes with the smooth functioning of society and government. Such activity would compel the authorities to mete out punishment (Rom. 13:2–4; for a broader discussion of these issues, see chapter 13 of this volume). It is wrong for believers to view that punishment as persecution for their faith. If they step outside the faith and bring trouble, hostility, resentment, or persecution on themselves, they have no more right to expect Holy Spirit relief than if they were murderers. That Peter here includes *allotriepiskopos* in his list of sins may mean that some disciples, in their zeal for the truth and resentment of paganism, were causing trouble in society for reasons beyond a sincere and legitimate concern for the gospel.

I remember a conversation I once had with a Russian pastor who had suffered greatly under Soviet communism. I asked if he or his fellow Christians ever rebelled against that form of government. He replied that it was all their convictions that if they were ever resented and persecuted by the secular authorities, it would be for the gospel only. The Russian church actually grew strong in that environment, and he wondered how pastors in America could have holy people without their suffering for the gospel.

If anyone suffers as a Christian his suffering qualifies for Holy Spirit blessing. He should not feel **ashamed** (*aischunō*, "dishonored"), but rather because of this benediction of supernatural comfort he **is to glorify God in this name** (Christian). First-century believers referred to one another, such as "brethren" (Acts 1:15–16; 6:3; 9:30; 12:17; 15:13), "saints" (Acts 9:13; Rom. 8:27; 15:25; 1 Cor. 16:1), and those of "the Way" (Acts 9:2; 19:9, 23; 22:4; 24:14, 22). Ironically, however, **Christian** was not a name first assumed by believers themselves; instead, because it was originally a derisive designation given them by the world, it was associated with hatred and persecution (cf. Acts 11:26; 26:28). It has become, and should remain, the dominant and beloved name by which believers are known—those who belong to Christ.

To glorify God in this context means to praise Him for the privilege and honor of suffering for **this name,** because of all He has done, is doing, and will forever do for His saints. Not only does this kind of suffering produce joy over heavenly reward and the blessing of **God,** it also purifies the church. Here Peter's thought returns to the Malachi 3:1–3 imagery (see comments on v. 12, earlier in this chapter). The Lord will purge His temple, His people. It is **time** (*kairos*), designating a decisive, crucial moment—in this context, the season—**for judgment to begin.** The Greek for **judgment** is *krima* and refers to a judicial process that renders a decision on someone's sin. The word identifies a matter for ajudication (cf. 1 Cor. 6:7) and is used especially for divine judgment (cf. Rom. 2:5; 5:16 11:33). Divine judgment on believers is the decision God renders on their sin, which includes chastening and leads to cleansing (cf. 5:9–10) of **the household of God,** but not eternal condemnation:

> Therefore there is now no condemnation for those who are in Christ Jesus (Rom. 8:1).

> But when we are judged, we are disciplined by the Lord so that we will not be condemned along with the world. (1 Cor. 11:32)

Household is Peter's reference to the church; other New Testament verses also make that meaning plain (cf. 2:5; Gal. 6:10; Eph. 2:19; 1 Tim. 3:15; Heb. 3:6; 10:21).

Peter poses the comparative question, **if** [judgment] **begins with** [believers] **first, what will be the outcome for those who do not obey the gospel of God?** The answer is plain: judgment concludes with Christ's final condemnation of the ungodly at the Great White Throne (Rev. 20:11–15; cf. Matt. 7:21–23; 25:44–46). Though God chastens His own people now, His future judgment of the lost will be infinitely more devastating (cf. Dan. 12:2; Matt. 13:41–42, 49–50; 22:11–14; 25:41; Mark 9:44–49; Luke 13:23–28; 16:23–24; Rev. 14:10–11).

It is infinitely better for people to endure suffering with joy now as believers being purified for effective testimony and eternal glory than to later bear eternal torment as unbelievers (cf. Luke 16:19–31). Peter reinforced that point for his readers with a quotation from the Septuagint rendering of Proverbs 11:31, **And if it is with difficulty that the righteous is saved what will become of the godless man and sinner? With difficulty** is the adverb *molis* (related to *molos*, "toil"), which means "hardly" or "scarcely" (see uses in Acts 14:18; 27:7, 8, 16) and reveals the difficulty with which believers are brought to final salvation through the fires of unjust suffering, divine purging, and God-ordained discipline:

> It is for discipline that you endure; God deals with you as with sons; for what son is there whom his father does not discipline? But if you are without discipline, of which all have become partakers, then you are illegitimate children and not sons. (Heb. 12:7–8)

Paul affirmed this necessity in response to his own severe suffering at the hands of the wicked Jews who stoned him at Lystra. Luke gives the account of the suffering and Paul's response in Acts 14:19–22,

> But Jews came from Antioch and Iconium, and having won over the crowds, they stoned Paul and dragged him out of the city, supposing him to be dead. But while the disciples stood around him, he got up and entered the city. The next day he went away with Barnabas to Derbe. After they had preached the gospel to that city and had made many disciples, they returned to Lystra and to Iconium and to Antioch, strengthening the souls of the disciples, encouraging them to continue in the faith, and saying, "Through many tribulations we must enter the kingdom of God."

That was only one incident in a long list of unjust pains that the apostle endured, chronicled especially in 2 Corinthians 1:3–11; 4:7–18; 6:4–11; 7:5; 11:23–33, and culminating in 12:7–10, in which Paul reveals that his suffering was to humble and thereby strengthen him:

> Because of the surpassing greatness of the revelations, for this reason, to keep me from exalting myself, there was given me a thorn in the flesh, a messenger of Satan to torment me—to keep me from exalting myself! Concerning this I implored the Lord three times that it might leave me. And He has said to me, "My grace is sufficient for you, for power is perfected in weakness." Most gladly, therefore, I will rather boast about my weaknesses, so that the power of Christ may dwell in me. Therefore I am well content with weaknesses, with insults, with distresses, with persecutions, with difficulties, for Christ's sake; for when I am weak, then I am strong.

Jesus said believers would have tribulation in this world, including being persecuted even to death (John 16:2–3, 33), and that such suffering would come to them because it came to Him (Matt. 10:24–25) to make "the captain of their suffering perfect through sufferings" (Heb. 2:10, KJV; cf. 1 Peter 1:11). It was hard for Jesus to be the Savior because of the immeasurable pain He endured from exposure to this sinful world and His having to be under the curse of God for all the sins of all who would ever believe. If it was **with** excruciating **difficulty** that He gave Himself to redeem sinners, and **with** painful **difficulty** that the redeemed endure to their final glory, does anyone think **the godless man and the sinner,** who has lived his life without suffering for righteousness' sake (because he is unrighteous), will simply die and go out of existence or be given a place in heaven because God is nothing but loving and forgiving? That is a foolish thought. Peter is saying the ungodly's eternal suffering, compared to the godly's temporal suffering, is far greater. Paul draws the distinction between the earthly sufferings of the saints and the endless punishment of the lost this way:

> [Persecution] is a plain indication of God's righteous judgment so that you will be considered worthy of the kingdom of God, for which indeed you are suffering. For after all it is only just for God to repay with affliction those who afflict you, and to give relief to you who are afflicted and to us as well when the Lord Jesus will be revealed from heaven with His mighty angels in flaming fire, dealing out retribution to those who do not know God and to those who do not obey the gospel of our Lord Jesus. These will pay the penalty of eternal destruction, away from the presence of the Lord and from the glory of His power. (2 Thess. 1:5–9)

ENTRUST SUFFERING TO GOD

Therefore, those also who suffer according to the will of God shall entrust their souls to a faithful Creator in doing what is right. (4:19)

Therefore draws the reader into the obvious duty he has in his suffering. **Those who suffer according to the will of God** receive this encouragement concerning the difficulty of their righteous pain—it is **the will of God** (cf. 3:7; 5:10). Knowing that fact, believers rest **their souls** in God's care and purpose. **Entrust** (*paratithemi*) is a banker's term referring to a deposit for safe keeping. One would be properly concerned about the character and ability of the person given such a trust. Jesus used the same word on the cross when He committed His spirit to His Father (Luke 23:46; cf. the discussion of 2:23 in chapter 15 of this volume). Believers are encouraged further to recall that the One to whom they give their souls is the **faithful Creator.** Only here in the New Testament is God called **Creator.** That is because it was generally understood that the Author of everything, the Designer of all that is, the One who sustains not only His material creation but achieves His purpose for it all, will bring to pass what He wills—only He is completely able and trustworthy **in doing what is right.** Who could be better than the trustworthy Creator who always acts righteously? Because God is faithful in Himself and to His own promises, believers' souls are at rest in His power and purpose (cf. 1:3–5; John 10:27–30; 17:11–12, 15; Rom. 8:35–39; Eph. 1:13–14; Phil. 1:6; 1 Thess. 5:23–24; 2 Tim. 1:12; Jude 24–25).

The psalmist David walked the road that took him from anguish over his persecutors to assurance in his faithful Creator. Psalm 31 is a rich example of a believer entrusting himself to God:

> In You, O Lord, I have taken refuge; let me never be ashamed; in Your righteousness deliver me. Incline Your ear to me, rescue me quickly; be to me a rock of strength, a stronghold to save me. For You are my rock and my fortress; for Your name's sake You will lead me and guide me. You will pull me out of the net which they have secretly laid for me, for You are my strength. Into Your hand I commit my spirit; You have ransomed me, O Lord, God of truth. I hate those who regard vain idols, but I trust in the Lord. I will rejoice and be glad in Your lovingkindness, because You have seen my affliction; You have known the troubles of my soul, and You have not given me over into the hand of the enemy; You have set my feet in a large place. Be gracious to me, O Lord, for I am in distress; my eye is wasted away from grief, my soul and my body also. For my life is spent with sorrow and my years with sighing; my strength has failed because of my iniquity, and my body has wasted away. Because of all my adversaries, I have become a reproach, especially to my neighbors, and an object of dread to my acquaintances; those who see me in the street flee from me. I am forgotten as a dead man, out of mind; I am like a broken vessel. For I have heard the slander of many, terror is on every side; while they took counsel together against me, they schemed to take away my life. But as for me, I trust in You, O Lord, I say, "You are my God." My times are in Your hand; deliver me from the hand of my enemies and from those who persecute me. Make Your face to shine upon Your servant; save me in Your lovingkindness. Let me not be put to shame, O Lord, for I call upon You; let the wicked be put to shame, let them be silent in Sheol. Let the lying lips be mute, which speak arrogantly against the righteous with pride and contempt. How great is Your goodness, which You have stored up for those who fear You, which You have wrought for those who take refuge in You, before the sons of men! You hide them in the secret place of Your presence from the conspiracies of man; You keep them secretly in a shelter from the strife of tongues. Blessed be the Lord, for He has

made marvelous His lovingkindness to me in a besieged city. As for me, I said in my alarm, "I am cut off from before Your eyes"; nevertheless You heard the voice of my supplications when I cried to You. O love the Lord, all you His godly ones! The Lord preserves the faithful and fully recompenses the proud doer. Be strong and let your heart take courage, all you who hope in the Lord.

Shepherding the Flock (1 Peter 5:1-4)

23

Therefore, I exhort the elders among you, as your fellow elder and witness of the sufferings of Christ, and a partaker also of the glory that is to be revealed, shepherd the flock of God among you, exercising oversight not under compulsion, but voluntarily, according to the will of God; and not for sordid gain, but with eagerness; nor yet as lording it over those allotted to your charge, but proving to be examples to the flock. And when the Chief Shepherd appears, you will receive the unfading crown of glory. (5:1–4)

"It is no accident that God has chosen to call us sheep," wrote W. Phillip Keller. "The behavior of sheep and human beings is similar in many ways. . . . Sheep do not 'just take care of themselves' as some might suppose. They require, more than any other class of livestock, endless attention and meticulous care" (*A Shepherd Looks at Psalm 23* [Grand Rapids: Zondervan, 1979], 20–21).

For example, God has created most animals with an uncanny instinct to find their way home. But if sheep stray into unfamiliar territory, they become completely disoriented and cannot find their way back home, as in the Lord's poignant parable of the lost sheep (Luke 15:3–7).

Sheep need a shepherd to guide them, provide for them, protect them, and sometimes also to rescue them from harm.

Sheep spend most of their time eating and drinking. But if they become lost, they are helpless to find adequate food and water. Left to themselves, sheep will indiscriminately eat both healthful and poisonous plants, or overgraze and ruin their own pasture. And they need to be led to water that is not impure and stagnant, not too hot or too cold, and water that is not moving too rapidly. That is why the psalmist refers to "quiet waters" in Psalm 23:2.

Sheep are much in need of other assistance as well. Because their wool secretes a large volume of oily lanolin that permeates their fleece, much dirt, grass, and wind-blown debris clings to it. Since they have no ability to clean themselves, they remain soiled until the shepherd shears them. Between shearings that dirty, sticky accumulation must be cut away from under their tails or they cannot eliminate waste and become sick and even die. Because sheep also are naturally passive and virtually defenseless against predators, and when attacked their only recourse is to flee in panic, the shepherd must be continually on guard to defend and rescue the sheep from attack.

It is not surprising, then, that Jesus likened the disoriented, confused, unclean, and spiritually lost crowds to flocks of sheep without shepherds (Matt. 9:36; Mark 6:34). They could not feed themselves spiritually and had no one to lead and protect them. The prophet Isaiah also compared humanity's lost condition to that of stray sheep, "All of us like sheep have gone astray, each of us has turned to his own way" (Isa. 53:6).

All the preceding imagery about sheep and shepherds was familiar to the people in the first century's primarily agrarian society, but it still needs to be borne in mind if one today is to understand the richness of this passage. Certainly Peter understood the imagery when he called believers **the flock of God** and commanded pastors to **shepherd** them. Since even believers are prone to wandering, taking in what is bad for them, becoming unclean, and are highly vulnerable, defenseless on their own, and often naive, the demand for shepherds who are faithful and responsible is compelling. And when the church is under severe persecution, as it was in Peter's day, it is even more vulnerable and in greater need of strong, godly, effective shepherds. The apostle, writing to the elders of various churches in Asia Minor (1:1) and to church elders of all eras, issues several fundamental and crucial commands concerning shepherding. Those commands may be understood by asking four basic questions of this passage: What are the issues in shepherding? Who must be shepherded? How must shepherding be done? Why should shepherds serve?

WHAT ARE THE ISSUES IN SHEPHERDING?

Therefore, I exhort the elders among you, as your fellow elder and witness of the sufferings of Christ, and a partaker also of the glory that is to be revealed, shepherd (5:1–2*a*)

Therefore refers back to the fact that this epistle's recipients were suffering persecution (4:12–19) and being attacked for righteousness' sake. That reality led Peter to **exhort the elders** to shepherd their troubled, beleaguered sheep. The first and obvious point to note here is that the Holy Spirit affirms that such spiritual leadership and responsibility for the church belongs to **elders.** That is unmistakable and consistent in the New Testament books dealing with the church. The first mention of elders is in Acts 11:30, where the writer Luke identifies them as the leaders of the Jerusalem church. Subsequent references in Acts (14:23; 15:4, 6, 22, 23; 16:4; 20:17; 21:18) continue to make clear their role. In 1 Timothy 5:17 Paul identifies them as those men who rule while laboring "in the word and doctrine" (KJV). Titus 1:5 establishes that elders were to lead every church in every city. The qualifications for such men appear in 1 Timothy 3:1–7 and Titus 1:5–9. (For a detailed treatment of these two passages, see John MacArthur, *1 Timothy*, MacArthur New Testament Commentary [Chicago: Moody, 1995], 91–121; MacArthur, *Titus*, MacArthur New Testament Commentary [Chicago: Moody, 1996], 17–52.)

Exhort (*parakaleō*) means literally "to call alongside," or in the general sense, "to encourage or compel someone in a certain direction." The related noun is often associated with the ministry of the Holy Spirit (cf. John 14:16–17, 26; 15:26; 16:7). Here Peter directs the appeal to **the elders,** who are the Lord's appointed and gifted leaders of the church. There are three New Testament terms used interchangeably to refer to these men: elder (*presbuterion;* cf. 1 Tim. 5:19; 2 John 1; 3 John 1), bishop or overseer (*episkopos;* cf. 2:25; Phil. 1:1; 1 Tim. 3:2; Titus 1:7), and pastor (*poimēn;* cf. Eph. 4:11). *Elder* emphasizes the man's spiritual maturity necessary for such ministry, and in many Protestant churches it is the official title chosen for the office. *Bishop,* or *overseer,* states the general responsibility of guardianship. *Pastor* is the word **shepherd** and expresses the priority duty of feeding or teaching the truth of God's Word.

The Old Testament is filled with references to elders in Israel (e.g., Lev. 4:15; Num. 11:25; Deut. 25:7; 1 Kings 21:11; Ps. 107:32; Prov. 31:23). The New Testament also indicates elders were still important in Jewish society in those days (e.g., Matt. 15:2; 16:21; Luke 9:22; Acts 4:5; 24:1). Each synagogue had its ruling elders who held leadership duties and were responsible for teaching (cf. Neh. 8:4–8; 9:5; Acts 15:21). The early church broadly adopted a similar model (cf. Acts 2:42–47; 6:4), appointing a plurality of godly and gifted men to lead, guard, and feed each local congregation (cf. Titus 1:5). It was their responsibility to proclaim the truth so as to build up the people and protect them against sin and error, while always being the highest examples of godliness to the flock (5:3; 1 Tim. 4:12; Heb. 13:7).

It is significant that Peter used the plural, **elders.** In reference to this ministry, the term always appears in the plural in the New Testament, affirming that the office was designed for a plurality of men. A singular usage of the word in reference to church leaders occurs only in such instances as when the apostle John calls himself "the elder" (2 John 1; 3 John 1) or Peter here calls himself a **fellow elder,** and when instruction is given about an accusation against a specific elder (1 Tim. 5:1, KJV, 19). The plurality of godly leaders, as designed by the Lord, not only provides more ministry care (cf. Ex. 18:13–26) but offers some important safeguards (cf. Prov. 11:14). First, it helps protect the church against error. The apostle Paul told the church at Corinth, "Let two or three prophets speak, and let the others pass judgment. . . . and the spirits of prophets are subject to prophets" (1 Cor. 14:29, 32). No one was to speak or minister independently (cf. 1 Cor. 14:26–33), teaching strictly on his own and not being accountable or subject to the knowledge of other teachers.

A plurality of elders in a local church also preserves it against imbalance. It is common that dominance by one leader results in his evil domineering over the flock, often with an overemphasis on some doctrine or practice that is out of harmony with the rest of Scripture, exposing people to serious doctrinal error and unbiblical practice. There are varieties of offices, gifts, and administrations (Rom. 12:3–8; 1 Cor. 12:4–11), and each believer, including elders, has a unique gift (see the discussion on 4:10–11 in chapter 21 of this volume), and no two gifts are exactly alike. A plurality of godly and gifted elders enriches the church since God does not give all the spiritual abilities to one man. The undue elevation of one man above what is proper (cf. 1 Tim. 3:6; 5:22) is an abuse against which a plurality of elders in the church safeguards.

Finally, a plurality of elders avoids discontinuity in the church. When a man who has been the sole or dominant leader in a church leaves without ever developing fellow elders, there is no one able to replace him, resulting in a major disruption of ministry for that church. In the shepherdless vacuum, committees of sheep struggle to find a shepherd from among those who have no flock or would like a different one. The results are often disappointing and even divisive. So, God designed the church to be shepherded by a plurality of elders (cf. Acts 14:23; Titus 1:5).

The task of the shepherd carries with it an unequalled responsibility before the Lord of the church (Heb. 13:17; cf. 1 Cor. 4:1–5). While it includes the positive elements of spiritual leadership toward maturity and Christlikeness, and spiritual guardianship to protect the flock, its chief objective is the feeding of the flock through the skillful preaching and teaching of divine revelation, which is the source of all those positive elements. Peter received firsthand instruction on the shepherd's foremost responsibility from the risen Lord Himself:

> So when they had finished breakfast, Jesus said to Simon Peter, "Simon, son of John, do you love Me more than these?" He said to Him, "Yes, Lord; You know that I love You." He said to him, "Tend My lambs." He said to him again a second time, "Simon, son of John, do you love Me?" He said to Him, "Yes, Lord; You know that I love You." He said to him, "Shepherd My sheep." He said to him the third time, "Simon, son of John, do you love Me?" Peter was grieved because He said to him the third time, "Do you love Me?" And he said to Him, "Lord, You know all things; You know that I love You." Jesus said to him, "Tend My sheep." (John 21:15–17)

Twice Jesus used the word "tend" *(boskō)*, which could be better translated "to feed." "Shepherd" *(poimainō)* embodies all the aspects of shepherding. The shepherd's task is not to tell people only what they want to hear (2 Tim. 4:3–4), but to edify and strengthen them with the deep truths of solid spiritual food that produces discernment, conviction, consistency, power, and effective testimony to the greatness of the saving work of Christ. No matter what New Testament terminology identifies the shepherd and his task, underneath it all is the primacy of biblical truth. He is to feed the sheep.

In Old Testament times, whenever Israel's spiritual shepherds failed to feed or care for the people, God, through His prophets, rebuked them. Jeremiah declared:

> "Woe to the shepherds who are destroying and scattering the sheep of My pasture!" declares the Lord. Therefore thus says the Lord God of Israel concerning the shepherds who are tending My people: "You have scattered My flock and driven them away, and have not attended to them; behold, I am about to attend to you for the evil of your deeds," declares the Lord. "Then I Myself will gather the remnant of My flock out of all the countries where I have driven them and bring them back to their pasture, and they will be fruitful and multiply. I will also raise up shepherds over them and they will tend them; and they will not be afraid any longer, nor be terrified, nor will any be missing," declares the Lord. (Jer. 23:1–4; cf. Ezek. 34:2–16)

Peter includes some compelling motivation in this exhortation for leaders to **shepherd.** First, the respected apostle humbly identified with them, calling himself a **fellow elder.** Rather than take advantage of their respect for him as an apostle and elevate himself, he empathized with their task as one who understood the challenges and difficulties inherent in shepherding (see again John 21:15–17).

As another motivation, Peter reminded them that he was a **witness of the sufferings of Christ.** That he had seen the suffering and risen Christ affirmed the reality of his apostolic identity (Luke 6:12–16; cf. Acts 1:12–17) and gave him authority. **Witness** (*martus*) has a twofold meaning: one who personally saw and experienced something, and one who testified to what he saw. Because so many who gave testimony to their experiences with Christ were killed, the term *martyred* came to refer to one who was killed for being a Christian witness (cf. Matt. 16:24–25; 24:9; Rev. 6:9; 20:4). In Peter's case, his being a **witness** to the sufferings of Jesus along with his fellow apostles, and being commissioned to proclaim those sufferings, to declare the gospel message (cf. Luke 24:45–48; Acts 22:15), made him a trustworthy source to encourage the elders to their duty. The Lord's redemptive work was a primary focus in Peter's preaching (Acts 2:14–36; 3:12–26; 4:8–12), and a major theme in this letter (1:11, 19; 2:21–24; 3:18; 4:1, 13).

Peter's mention of future glory motivates by anticipation. As one who was **a partaker also of the glory that is to be revealed,** Peter could offer the other elders the genuine hope of an eternal reward for their faithful service. **The glory that is to be revealed** looks at the return of Christ (cf. 1:7–9; 4:7, 12–13; Matt. 24:30; 25:31; Mark 13:26; Luke 21:27; see the discussion of 4:7a in chapter 21 of this volume) when He comes in full expression of His glory to destroy the ungodly, reward His own, and establish His kingdom forever. Peter says he is **a partaker** (*koinōnos*) **also** in that ultimate blessing, indicating that so are the elders. That believers share in eternal glory with their Lord is the essence of their hope (5:10; cf. 2 Cor. 1:1–7; Phil. 3:20–21; Col. 1:27; 3:4; 2 Thess. 2:14; Heb. 2:10; 2 Peter 1:3; 1 John 3:2). And that those shepherds would one day receive that reward from Christ Himself should have been a powerful motivation to all Peter's readers (see the discussion of 4:13 in the previous chapter of this volume and of 1:3–5 and 1:13 in chapters 2 and 5, respectively). Certainly Peter's anticipation was magnified exponentially because he had seen that coming glory at the Transfiguration (cf. Matt. 17:1–8; 2 Peter 1:16–19).

WHO MUST BE SHEPHERDED?

the flock of God among you, (5:2b)

This text clearly states that elders have the most serious, delegated stewardship, to shepherd not their own flock, but **the flock of God.** Jesus Christ came to earth to redeem His church (cf. John 10:11; Eph. 5:25*b*–27). After He ascended back to heaven, He sent His Spirit to empower His church (cf. John 16:5–11; Acts 1:4–9) with the necessary spiritual gifts and gifted men to shepherd the flock to Christlikeness (cf. John 14:26; 15:15–17; Eph. 4:11–12). And the fact that Christ purchased that flock with His own blood (1:18–19; cf. Acts 20:28) emphasizes the church's value to the Lord. In form, the term rendered **flock** here (*poimnion*) is a diminutive, a term of endearment, further stressing the preciousness of the church (cf. John 10:1–5). Commentator R. C. H. Lenski echoes this emphasis:

> "Flock" brings to mind all the shepherd imagery found in the Scriptures: the sheep gentle, defenseless, liable to stray, needing a shepherd, happy, peaceful under his care, pitiful when lost, scattered, etc. This is "God's flock" that was bought at a great price (Acts 20:28), that is exceedingly precious in his sight, a great trust placed into the hands of human shepherds who are to pattern after Yahweh, the Shepherd (Ps. 23:1), and Christ, the Archshepherd (v. 4). What shepherd could have the care of any part of *God's* flock and treat it carelessly! Peter's words are sparing but overflow with tender and serious meaning. (*The Interpretation of the Epistles of St. Peter, St. John and St. Jude* [reprint; Minneapolis: Augsburg, 1966], 218; emphasis in original)

How Must Shepherding Be Done?

exercising oversight not under compulsion, but voluntarily, according to the will of God; and not for sordid gain, but with eagerness; nor yet as lording it over those allotted to your charge, but proving to be examples to the flock. (5:2*c*–3)

To the key question of how elders are to shepherd, Peter provides both positive and negative answers. **Exercising oversight** actually translates a single Greek word, *episkopeō*, which literally means "to have scope over," or "to look upon." The noun is *episkopos* ("bishop," or "overseer"; cf. 1 Tim. 3:1). Its clear connotation here in this first positive answer is that shepherds must watch over the sheep to assess their condition, so as to lead, guard, and feed them.

The second positive way elders exercise oversight is by **proving to be examples to the flock.** Shepherds are to become sufficiently involved in the lives of the flock that they establish a godly pattern for the people to follow. The most important aspect of spiritual leadership and the best test of its effectiveness is the power of an exemplary life (cf. the apostle Paul's application of this in Acts 20:17–38; 2 Cor. 1:12–14; 6:3–13; 11:7–11; 1 Thess. 2:1–10; 2 Thess. 3:7–9; 2 Tim. 1:13–14). Paul even went so far as to exhort his sheep to be imitators of him (1 Cor. 4:16; 11:1; 1 Thess. 1:6; cf. Heb. 13:7).

Biblical spiritual oversight also involves avoiding three perils inherent in the shepherding task. The first danger Peter mentions is shepherding **under compulsion,** rather than as eager, willing servant-leaders who minister **voluntarily.** The obvious point is that the shepherd must be diligent rather than lazy, heart motivated rather than forced to be faithful, and passionate about his privileged duty rather than indifferent. When the heart is fully Christ's and driven by love for Him and for souls, there is much internal compulsion that precludes any need for external motivational pressure.

Along this line, Paul declares, "If I preach the gospel, I have nothing to boast of, for I am under compulsion; for woe is me if I do not preach the gospel" (1 Cor. 9:16). He defined the proper compulsion to ministry when he wrote, "Knowing the fear of the Lord, we persuade men ... the love of Christ controls us" (2 Cor. 5:11, 14). Paul's personal passion is also evident in Romans 1:14–16,

> I am under obligation both to Greeks and to barbarians, both to the wise and to the foolish. So, for my part, I am eager to preach the gospel to you also who are in Rome. For I am not ashamed of the gospel, for it is the power of God for salvation to everyone who believes, to the Jew first and also to the Greek.

This zealous service is **according to the will of God,** just as the Lord wills the unjust suffering that perfects His saints (4:19). Those who shepherd God's people should have no doubt about the diligence and seriousness with which they should fulfill their spiritual ministry of caring for the precious souls who are the Lord's, and they will give an account: "Obey your leaders and submit to them, for they keep watch over your souls as those who will give an account. Let them do this with joy and not with grief, for this would be unprofitable for you" (Heb. 13:17).

The second peril for shepherds to avoid is the temptation to be motivated by money or material benefits. In Acts 20:33–35, Paul manifests the right attitude:

> I have coveted no one's silver or gold or clothes. You yourselves know that these hands ministered to my own needs and to the men who were with me. In everything I showed you that by working hard in this manner you must help the weak and remember the words of the Lord Jesus, that He Himself said, "It is more blessed to give than to receive." (cf. 1 Thess. 2:8–9; 1 Tim. 6:6–11)

The basic scriptural qualifications for an elder also make it clear that he is characterized as a selfless servant committed to sacrifice and not preoccupied with money and materialism (1 Tim. 3:3; Titus 1:7; cf. 2 Tim. 3:1–2). That is not to say, however, that shepherds should not be properly compensated. Paul taught that those who minister the Word have a right to live by that ministry (1 Cor. 9:7–14). In fact, those elders who serve diligently, with greater commitment and excellence in teaching the Word and leading the sheep, should receive greater acknowledgment and more generous remuneration from their congregations (1 Tim. 5:17–18; cf. 1 Thess. 5:12–13).

Sordid gain actually goes beyond just seeking wealth and speaks to the shameful acquisition of it. True shepherds will never use the ministry to steal the sheep's money or acquire it dishonestly, like false prophets always do. Such despicable behavior is typical of false shepherds, the charlatans and heretics who masquerade as the servants of God, to make themselves rich and their victims destitute (Isa. 56:11; Jer. 6:13; 8:10; Mic. 3:11). In his second letter, Peter characterizes false teachers in vivid language: "In their greed they will exploit you with false words; their judgment from long ago is not idle, and their destruction is not asleep" (2:3). True shepherds, instead, will eagerly rejoice at the privilege to serve at all personal costs; as Paul told the Corinthians, "I will most gladly spend and be expended for your souls" (2 Cor. 12:15). Ministry for money and personal gain is a prostitution of the calling of the Lord of the church, as is laziness and indifference toward the people entrusted to elders. No true shepherd should need personal wealth to motivate him, but he should serve **with eagerness** (*prothumōs*, "willingly, freely, eagerly") because of the high calling and privilege (cf. 1 Tim. 1:12–17).

Finally, those called to shepherd can be imperiled by the desire to sinfully dominate others. **Lording it over** (*katakurieuō*) connotes intensity in domineering over people and circumstances (see Diotrephes as an example in 3 John 9–10). Any kind of autocratic, oppressive, and intimidating leadership, with elements of demagoguery—traits that typically characterize the leadership style and methodology of unregenerate men—is a perversion of the overseer's office. In Matthew 20:25–28, the Lord Jesus set the standard:

> But Jesus called them to Himself and said, "You know that the rulers of the Gentiles lord it over them, and their great men exercise authority over them. It is not this way among you, but whoever wishes to become great among you shall be your servant, and whoever wishes to be first among you shall be your slave; just as the Son of Man did not come to be served, but to serve, and to give His life a ransom for many."

As if to further challenge elders with the weight of their responsibility, Peter adds a strong reminder that those who shepherd do not choose their responsibility, or those for whom they are responsible. Every shepherd has a flock **allotted to** his **charge** (*klērōn,* "that which is given to another's care") by the Lord Himself. Christ's teaching in Matthew 18, the first instruction regarding life in the church, emphasizes how precious His children (believers) are and how they are to be treated.

> Whoever receives one such child in My name receives Me; but whoever causes one of these little ones who believe in Me to stumble, it would be better for him to have a heavy millstone hung around his neck, and to be drowned in the depth of the sea. Woe to the world because of its stumbling blocks! For it is inevitable that stumbling blocks come; but woe to that man through whom the stumbling block comes! If your hand or your foot causes you to stumble, cut it off and throw it from you; it is better for you to enter life crippled or lame, than to have two hands or two feet and be cast into the eternal fire. If your eye causes you to stumble, pluck it out and throw it from you. It is better for you to enter life with one eye, than to have two eyes and be cast into the fiery hell. See that you do not despise one of these little ones, for I say to you that their angels in heaven continually see the face of My Father who is in heaven. For the Son of Man has come to save that which was lost. What do you think? If any man has a hundred sheep, and one of them has gone astray, does he not leave the ninety-nine on the mountains and go and search for the one that is straying? If it turns out that he finds it, truly I say to you, he rejoices over it more than over the ninety-nine which have not gone astray. So it is not the will of your Father who is in heaven that one of these little ones perish. (Matt. 18:5–14)

WHY SHOULD SHEPHERDS SERVE?

And when the Chief Shepherd appears, you will receive the unfading crown of glory. (5:4)

Chief Shepherd is one of the most beautiful titles for the Savior in all of Scripture. The shepherd imagery for Messiah first appears in the Old Testament (Zech. 13:7; cf. Ps. 23:1). The gospel of John calls Him the Good Shepherd (10:11; cf. vv. 2, 12, 16, 26–27). The writer of Hebrews calls Christ the Great Shepherd (13:20–21). Earlier in this letter, Peter calls Him the Shepherd and Guardian of souls (2:25).

Appears (*phaneroō*) means "to make manifest," "to make clear," or "to reveal." Here, as in 5:1, the reference is to Christ's revelation at the Second Coming, at which time shepherds **will receive the unfading crown of glory.** In the Greco-Roman world of Peter's day, crowns rather than trophies were the awards for victory at athletic events:

Do you not know that those who run in a race all run, but only one receives the prize? Run in such a way that you may win. Everyone who competes in the games exercises self-control in all things. They then do it to receive a perishable wreath, but we an imperishable. (1 Cor. 9:24–25)

Temporal crowns would eventually rust, fade, or, if made from plants, die quickly. Peter was not looking forward merely to some **unfading** version of an earthly **crown,** but metaphorically to eternal **glory,** which can never fade. The term **unfading** is from the same cognate as the name of the flower (amaranth) that supposedly never faded or lost its bloom. (See again the brief discussion of this term under 1:4, in chapter 2 of this volume.) Peter's phrase can be expressed "the unfading crown that is glory." This is consistent with the use of the genitive case in other mentions of eternal reward. James wrote of the crown that is life (1:12). Paul wrote of the crown that is righteousness (2 Tim. 4:8) and the crown that is rejoicing (1 Thess. 2:19). All those are facets of eternal blessing and all are imperishable.

The reward of eternal glory ought to be all the reason any shepherd needs for desiring to serve faithfully. The theme of future rewards as incentive for Christian service has already been one of Peter's emphases in this letter (1:4–5, 13; 4:13; cf. 4:7). The full expression of a shepherd's eternal, glorious crown will be in proportion to his faithful service on earth (cf. 1 Cor. 9:24–27; 2 Cor. 5:10; 2 Tim. 4:6–8; Rev. 2:10).

Shepherding the flock is a serious, sobering responsibility, and elders are accountable to God for their ministry. James was fully aware of that accountability when he wrote the following warning: "Let not many of you become teachers, my brethren, knowing that as such we will incur a stricter judgment" (3:1; cf. Ezek. 3:17–19; 33:7–9; Acts 20:26–27; 2 Tim. 4:1–2; Heb. 13:17). James was not trying to discourage truly qualified and willing shepherds, but reminded the ambitious of God's high standards for them and of the reward ("judgment") they will receive before the judgment seat of Christ (cf. 1 Cor. 3:9–15; 4:3–5; 2 Cor. 5:9–11). Christ's undershepherds face a daunting task, but faithful oversight brings eternal reward in the form of greater service and joy in the Lord's heaven: "His master said to him, 'Well done, good and faithful slave. You were faithful with a few things, I will put you in charge of many things; enter into the joy of your master'" (Matt. 25:23).

Fundamental Attitudes of a Christian Mind (1 Peter 5:5–14)

24

You younger men, likewise, be subject to your elders; and all of you, clothe yourselves with humility toward one another, for God is opposed to the proud, but gives grace to the humble. Therefore humble yourselves under the mighty hand of God, that He may exalt you at the proper time, casting all your anxiety on Him, because He cares for you. Be of sober spirit, be on the alert. Your adversary, the devil, prowls around like a roaring lion, seeking someone to devour. But resist him, firm in your faith, knowing that the same experiences of suffering are being accomplished by your brethren who are in the world. After you have suffered for a little while, the God of all grace, who called you to His eternal glory in Christ, will Himself perfect, confirm, strengthen and establish you. To Him be dominion forever and ever. Amen. Through Silvanus, our faithful brother (for so I regard him), I have written to you briefly, exhorting and testifying that this is the true grace of God. Stand firm in it! She who is in Babylon, chosen together with you, sends you greetings, and so does my son, Mark. Greet one another with a kiss of love. Peace be to you all who are in Christ. (5:5–14)

The spirit of the times in Western society is one of anti-intellectualism. New Age thinking, a major source of that mindlessness, has influenced religion and philosophy in many ways. In the spirit of Hindu mysticism, New Age philosophy believes everything and nothing at the same time. Distinctions between the natural and supernatural tend to blend together in a fuzzy blur. The emphasis is on mystical experiences rather than rational content.

Over the centuries—especially during the past century—that kind of perspective has found its way gradually but steadily into Christendom. The Roman Catholic Church has always been deeply involved in mysticism, with rituals and ceremonies supplanting biblical worship and the proclamation of the true gospel. Protestant Neoorthodoxy promotes a different kind of anti-intellectualism, what the late Francis Schaeffer called a "leap of faith" into the nonrational realm. The charismatic movement is perhaps the most blatant purveyor of mystical anti-intellectualism and spiritual subjectivism. Add postmodernism, the idea that there is no absolute truth and each person can develop his own view of truth based on intuition and experience, and one has a further concept of the extent to which this anti-intellectualism has pervaded today's world.

The foregoing systems reduce God to a detached, transcendent being, reachable and knowable only through mystical experience or feeling, rather than revealed through propositional truth. The Bible is not viewed as the sole, inspired revelation of God, and it is seen as neither infallible nor authoritative. As a result, divine truth is ignored, moral absolutes of right and wrong disappear, and deception about one's true spiritual condition prevails.

Such mystical mindlessness is the antithesis of how God is to be known. He never intended for His people to relate to Him without applying their minds to His revelation. True fellowship and worship must be based on a clear, precise understanding of biblical truth. Through the psalmist David, God declared, "I will instruct you and teach you in the way which you should go; I will counsel you with My eye upon you. Do not be as the horse or as the mule which have no understanding" (Ps. 32:8–9; cf. 25:8). The prophet Isaiah wrote these familiar words, "'Come now, and let us reason together,' says the Lord" (Isa. 1:18). In Jeremiah, God rebuked His people for their dreadful lack of spiritual understanding: "For My people are foolish, they know Me not; they are stupid children and have no understanding. They are shrewd to do evil, but to do good they do not know" (Jer. 4:22; cf. Hos 4:6).

God has always been concerned that believers use their redeemed minds to search the Scriptures in order to know Him (cf. Matt. 13:23; John 17:17; Acts 17:11; 1 Cor. 14:15; Eph. 4:14; Col. 1:9; 2 Tim. 2:15;

Heb. 5:12–14) and become conformed to the image of His Son. The apostle Paul told the Philippians, "This I pray, that your love may abound still more and more in real knowledge and all discernment, so that you may approve the things that are excellent, in order to be sincere and blameless until the day of Christ" (Phil. 1:9–10). Peter also called believers to use their minds to understand God's truth and apply it to their lives: "Now for this very reason also, applying all diligence, in your faith supply moral excellence, and in your moral excellence, knowledge" (2 Peter 1:5; cf. Rom. 12:1–2; 1 Cor. 2:16; 2 Tim. 1:7, NKJV).

The Lord is also concerned about the condition of the unregenerate mind. Paul wrote to the Romans, "Just as they did not see fit to acknowledge God any longer, God gave them over to a depraved mind, to do those things which are not proper" (Rom. 1:28). "The god of this world has blinded the minds of the unbelieving," he explained to the Corinthians, "so that they might not see the light of the gospel of the glory of Christ" (2 Cor. 4:4). He instructed the Ephesians to "walk no longer just as the Gentiles [unredeemed] also walk, in the futility of their mind" (Eph. 4:17), and reminded the Colossians, "You were formerly alienated and hostile in mind" (Col. 1:21). In Romans 8:5–8, Paul gave perhaps the best summary of the contrast between unregenerate thinking and the regenerate mind:

> For those who are according to the flesh set their minds on the things of the flesh, but those who are according to the Spirit, the things of the Spirit. For the mind set on the flesh is death, but the mind set on the Spirit is life and peace, because the mind set on the flesh is hostile toward God; for it does not subject itself to the law of God, for it is not even able to do so, and those who are in the flesh cannot please God. (cf. 1 Cor. 2:14; 2 Cor. 10:5; Gal. 5:19–25; Eph. 2:1)

If the elect have a careless or superficial approach to the truth of Scripture, their minds cannot be filled with the divine thoughts that should shape and control their conduct (cf. Deut. 6:5; Prov. 15:14; 18:15; 22:17; Matt. 22:37; Eph. 4:23; 5:15–17; Heb. 10:16). It is crucial that believers continually take in the truth, "For as [a man] thinks within himself, so he is" (Prov. 23:7).

All that being said, there is still the danger of assuming that spiritual thinking is simply processing information so as to intellectually understand doctrine, when in contrast, spiritual thinking involves far more. It includes all the attitudes, convictions, and motivations that lead to application of doctrinal truth.

In the final section of this letter, Peter addresses the godly attitudes so necessary to produce a spiritual mind. In a closing litany of exhortations and some final words, the apostle leads his readers to consider essential Christian attitudes—submission, humility, trust, self-control, vigilance, fortitude, hope, worship, faithfulness, and love.

SUBMISSION

You younger men, likewise, be subject to your elders; (5:5*a*)

As he did earlier in the letter (3:1, 7), Peter uses *homoiōs* (**likewise**) as a transition word. In the prior verses, the NASB renders the word "in the same way." In all three usages, the word marks a change of focus from one group to another. In 5:1–4 Peter addressed church leaders; now he turned to the congregation. As shepherds submit to the Chief Shepherd, so the flock submits to their shepherds.

The foundational attitude in the life of the saint must be submission, a relatively familiar theme already in this epistle. In 2:13–20 and 3:1–7 Peter commanded believers to be submissive to employers, civil authorities, and within marriage. No less is required of those under the leadership of the divinely instituted office of pastor in the most important entity on earth—Christ's own church.

Although no one is exempt from Peter's exhortation that everyone is to be submissive to their **elders,** he targets specifically the **younger men.** Though it is not stated in the context why he singled them out, probably he did so because it is so obvious that they generally tend to be the most aggressive and headstrong members of any group. There is no reason to view them as some recognized faction or fixed association in the church. The matter of submission would not likely have been as much of an issue for the women or older people in the church; they were more experienced and more spiritually mature (cf. Ps. 119:100; Prov. 16:31; 20:29).

In calling the young to **be subject** to those over them in the Lord, Peter again used the military term *hupotassō*, "to line up under." He calls everyone in the church to put aside self-promoting pride and willingly and respectfully place themselves under the leadership of their shepherds (cf. 1 Tim. 5:17; Heb. 13:7). Clearly, given the previous context (vv. 1–4), **elders** refers to the spiritual leaders, the shepherds and pastors, not merely to older saints. That the entire church has the obligation to submit to those God has placed in authority over it, is a theme in Paul's letters:

> Now I urge you, brethren (you know the household of Stephanas, that they were the first fruits of Achaia, and that they have devoted themselves for ministry to the saints), that you also be in subjection to such

men and to everyone who helps in the work and labors. (1 Cor. 16:15–16)

But we request of you, brethren, that you appreciate those who diligently labor among you, and have charge over you in the Lord and give you instruction, and that you esteem them very highly in love because of their work. Live in peace with one another. (1 Thess. 5:12–13)

As seen in the broader context, Christians are to be submissive to all in authority, but especially in the church. The process of spiritual growth flourishes among those who have an attitude of submission. An unsubmissive flock, on the other hand, makes the shepherds' ministry difficult and forfeits a critical feature in sanctification: "Obey your leaders and submit to them, for they keep watch over your souls as those who will give an account. Let them do this with joy and not with grief, for this would be unprofitable for you" (Heb. 13:17).

HUMILITY

and all of you, clothe yourselves with humility toward one another, for God is opposed to the proud, but gives grace to the humble. Therefore humble yourselves under the mighty hand of God, that He may exalt you at the proper time, (5:5b–6)

Inseparably linked to and underlying a submissive attitude is a mind given to humility (cf. Ps. 25:9; Dan 10:12; Mic. 6:8; Matt. 5:3–5; Eph. 4:1–2; James 4:10). Because always the truly humble—and only the humble—submit, both of Peter's commands encompass **all** believers.

Clothe (*egkomboomai*) literally means "to tie something on oneself," such as a work apron worn by servants. Here it describes figuratively covering oneself with an attitude of **humility** as one submits to authorities over him. The word for **humility** here is *tapeinophrosunēn*, "lowliness of mind," or "self-abasement." It describes the attitude of one who willingly serves, even in the lowliest of tasks (cf. 1 Cor. 4:1–5; 2 Cor. 4:7; Phil. 2:5–7). Perhaps even more so than today, humility was not an admired trait in the first-century pagan world. People saw it as a characteristic of weakness and cowardice, to be tolerated only in the involuntary submission of slaves.

As Peter wrote this verse, he likely recalled Jesus' tying a towel on Himself and washing the disciples' feet, including his own, as recorded in John 13:3–11 and applied by Jesus in verses 12–17, as follows:

So when He had washed their feet, and taken His garments and reclined at the table again, He said to them, "Do you know what I have done to you? You call Me Teacher and Lord; and you are right, for so I am. If I then, the Lord and the Teacher, washed your feet, you also ought to wash one another's feet. For I gave you an example that you also should do as I did to you. Truly, truly, I say to you, a slave is not greater than his master, nor is one who is sent greater than the one who sent him. If you know these things, you are blessed if you do them." (cf. Ps. 131:1–2; Matt. 25:37–40; Luke 22:24–27; Rom. 12:3, 10, 16; Phil. 2:3–11)

To reinforce his exhortation for humility, Peter quoted from Proverbs 3:34, **God is opposed to the proud, but gives grace to the humble** (cf. James 4:6). Peter's quote differs slightly from the Septuagint by substituting **God** for the Septuagint's "Lord," but the names are obviously synonymous. Without question, that the Lord **is opposed to the proud** (cf. Prov. 6:16–17a; 8:13) is the greatest motivation for saints to adopt the attitude of humility. Pride sets one against God and vice versa. On the other hand, God blesses and **gives grace to the humble** (cf. Job 22:29; Ps. 37:11; Prov. 22:4; 29:23; Matt. 11:29; Luke 10:21; 18:13–14; 1 Cor. 1:28–29; 2 Cor. 4:7–18). The prophet Isaiah stated the principle well, "For thus says the high and exalted One who lives forever, whose name is Holy, 'I dwell on a high and holy place, and also with the contrite and lowly of spirit in order to revive the spirit of the lowly and to revive the heart of the contrite" (Isa. 57:15; cf. 66:2).

The apostle Paul knew the grace that comes to the humble:

Because of the surpassing greatness of the revelations, for this reason, to keep me from exalting myself, there was given me a thorn in the flesh, a messenger of Satan to torment me—to keep me from exalting myself! Concerning this I implored the Lord three times that it might leave me. And He has said to me, "My grace is sufficient for you, for power is perfected in weakness." Most gladly, therefore, I will rather boast about my weaknesses, so that the power of Christ may dwell in me. Therefore I am well content with weaknesses, with insults, with distresses, with persecutions, with difficulties, for Christ's sake; for when I am weak, then I am strong. (2 Cor. 12:7–10)

Based on the above verse from Proverbs that Peter mentioned, this command comes forcefully: **therefore humble yourselves** in submission, not only to avoid divine opposition and to receive divine grace, but because the authority over all believers in the church is none other than **the mighty hand of God.** Or as James stated it, "Humble yourselves in the presence of the Lord" (4:10a).

The **mighty hand of God** is descriptive of God's sovereign power at work in and through the elders of the church, as well as in the life experience of His people (cf. Isa. 48:13; Ezek. 20:33–34; Zeph. 1:4; 2:13; Luke 1:49–51). Whether for deliverance (Ex. 3:19–20; 13:3–16), for testing (Job 30:20–21), or for chastening (Ezek. 20:33–38), God's might is always accomplishing His eternal purposes on behalf of His own (cf. Pss. 57:2; 138:8; Isa. 14:24–27; 46:10; 55:11; Jer. 51:12; Acts 2:23; Rom. 8:28; 9:11, 17; Eph. 3:11; Phil. 2:13). In their time of persecution, suffering, and testing, that assurance would encourage Peter's audience to persevere (cf. Ps. 37:24; Prov. 4:18; Matt. 10:22; 24:13; Rom. 8:30–39; Heb. 12:2–3; James 1:4, 12; Rev. 3:5), knowing that all their suffering is only so that **He may exalt** them **at the proper time** (cf. 5:10). Even as Jesus Christ was born at the appropriate time (Gal. 4:4; Titus 1:3) and died a substitutionary death at the exact time God designed (1 Tim. 2:6), God will **exalt** (*hupsoō*, "to raise or lift up") believers out of their trials, tribulations, and sufferings at His wisely determined time. Some have suggested that this exaltation could be a reference to the final eschatological glory that comes to believers at the Second Coming, the "last time" Peter referred to in 1:5 (cf. 2:12); but the Greek phrase *en kairō* is literally "in time" (cf. Acts 19:23; Rom. 9:9) and is not an eschatological term. It is better to see this as the appointed time when the Lord lifts the humble and submissive believer up out of difficulty.

If the foundational attitude for spiritual growth is submission, humility is, then, the footing to which the foundation is anchored. To become proudly rebellious, fight against the Lord's purposes, or judge His providence as unkind or unfair is to forfeit the sweet grace of His exaltation when the trial has fulfilled its purpose (cf. James 1:2–4). It is the Lord Jesus Himself who promised, "Everyone who exalts himself will be humbled, and he who humbles himself will be exalted" (Luke 14:11).

TRUST

casting all your anxiety on Him, because He cares for you. (5:7)

As believers endure humbly and submissively, they find their strength in the midst of trials, by means of confident trust in God's perfect purpose. The psalmist David is surely Peter's source, since this trust was his, and the apostle must have known his words well: "Cast your burden upon the Lord and He will sustain you; He will never allow the righteous to be shaken" (Ps. 55:22). David's **anxiety** came from attacks by a Judas-like friend (see vv. 12–14), a most difficult trial to bear since it comes from one who is loved and trusted. Peter drew from that text to instruct all believers in all kinds of trouble to follow David's example and give themselves to the Lord's care (cf. 2:23; 4:19).

Casting (from *epiriptō*) means throwing something on something else or someone else. For example, in Luke 19:35 (KJV) it is used of throwing a blanket over an animal. Peter exhorts believers to throw on the Lord **all** their **anxiety,** a word that can include all discontentment, discouragement, despair, questioning, pain, suffering, and whatever other trials they encounter (cf. 2 Sam. 22:3; Pss. 9:10; 13:5; 23:4; 36:7; 37:5; 55:22; Prov. 3:5–6; Isa. 26:4; Nah. 1:7; Matt. 6:25–34; 2 Cor. 1:10; Phil. 4:6–7, 19; Heb. 13:6) because they can trust His love, faithfulness, power, and wisdom.

SELF-CONTROL

Be of sober spirit, (5:8*a*)

This command calls for another basic element of godly thinking, which Peter mentioned already (see earlier discussions on 1:13 and 4:7 in chapters 5 and 21 of this volume). On a physical level, **sober** (*nēphō*) refers to self-control in relation to intoxication. Here, as in its other New Testament usages, however, it has a more metaphorical connotation (cf. 1 Tim. 2:15 KJV; 3:2, 11; Titus 2:2). It includes ordering and balancing life's important issues, which requires the discipline of mind and body that avoids the intoxicating allurements of the world (cf. 2:11; Luke 21:34; Rom. 12:1–2; 13:14; Phil. 4:8; Col. 3:2; 1 Thess. 5:6–8; Titus 2:12; James 1:27; 4:4; 1 John 2:15–16).

VIGILANCE

be on the alert. Your adversary, the devil, prowls around like a roaring lion, seeking someone to devour. (5:8*b*)

The reason Christians must cultivate the preceding attitudes of submission, humility, trust, and self-control is that they face fierce and relentless spiritual opposition from Satan and his demons. Believers must not become indifferent to that reality (cf. Prov. 15:19; Heb. 6:12) or indulgent of sin (1 Cor. 5:6; Heb. 3:13), lest they become victims of the enemy (2 Cor. 2:11; Eph. 6:11; cf. 1 Thess. 3:5). Instead, the realities of spiritual warfare call for vigilance. Peter urges believers to **be on the alert** (*grēgorēsate*), an imperative command that means "be watchful," or, "stay awake." The spiritual forces that assault Christians, not only directly (cf. Gen. 3:1–7; Mark 1:13; 2 Cor. 12:7; 1 Thess. 2:18) but often very subtly

(2 Cor. 11:14), demand that those who love Christ maintain such vigilance. The Lord warned His disciples: "Keep watching and praying that you may not enter into temptation; the spirit is willing, but the flesh is weak" (Matt. 26:41).

Peter identifies Satan as **your adversary, the devil,** the pronoun **your** making that designation a very personal one. Satan is not only the adversary of God and His holy angels, but he is the vicious, relentless enemy of all God's people (cf. Job 1:6–8; 2:1–6; Zech. 3:1). **Adversary** (*antidikos*) was used as a technical term meaning "legal opponent," as well as any kind of enemy who was seriously and aggressively hostile. The term rendered **devil** (*diabolos*) takes this opposition to the level of a "malicious enemy who slanders or attacks." Three times Jesus called him the ruler of this world (John 12:31; 14:30; 16:11; cf. Eph. 2:2), which shows the formidable platform from which he launches his malevolent assaults.

The devil commands the demonic realm and administrates the human, fallen world system. Personally and through his surrogates the demons, who like him never sleep nor rest, Satan untiringly, like a predator in the night of his own evil darkness, hunts to kill. He **prowls around like a roaring lion, seeking someone to devour** (cf. Job 1:6–12; 2:1–7). Peter's imagery of the **roaring lion** derives from the Old Testament (Pss. 7:2; 10:9–10; 17:12; 22:13–21; 35:17; 58:6; 104:21; Ezek. 22:25) and pictures the viciousness of this hunter pursuing his prey. **Devour** has the sense of "to gulp down," emphasizing the final objective, not to wound but to destroy. Peter would not have had, as most believers today do, the experience of seeing lions in a zoo. But he might have seen the gory spectacle of lions slaughtering victims for the entertainment of the Romans. Certainly he knew of such events.

Satan's opposition to God and believers is behind the human enemies of God and His Word. Revelation 12 is the watershed passage that draws the battle lines in the long war with the enemies of God's kingdom (vv. 3–4; cf. Isa. 14:12–16; Ezek. 28:1–19). Those demons who are not bound (see the discussion of 3:19–20 in chapter 19 of this volume) are the sinister, diabolical forces behind the world system. God's children, in their struggle against deception and temptation that come from the world to their flesh, are actually wrestling with and contending with demonic strategies (Eph. 6:11–12; cf. 2 Cor. 10:3–5).

Satan and the demons hide unseen in the spirit world, but do their work through human agents (cf. 1 Tim. 4:1–2; 2 Peter 2:1–22; Jude 3–16). Revelation 12:4 says that "the dragon stood before the woman who was about to give birth, so that when she gave birth he might devour her child." The dragon is Satan, the woman Israel, and the child Christ. The dramatic picture is of Messiah about to come out of Israel, God's chosen people, and Satan poised to devour Him. The Enemy sought to implement that plan through Herod the Great's horrific slaughter of all the male children age two and under in and around Bethlehem (Matt. 2:13–18). He attempted to defeat Christ by giving Him the world's kingdoms without any suffering (Matt. 4:1–11; Luke 4:1–12). Judas Iscariot was also a willing pawn of Satan, used to betray the Lord in an ill-conceived effort to somehow thwart God's plan (Luke 22:3; John 13:27; cf. Matt. 26:47–56). Satan also used the Jewish leaders in an effort to hinder Christ's redemptive mission (cf. Matt. 12:14; 21:46; 22:15–16; 26:1–5; 27:20–23; Luke 6:7; John 5:16; 7:1–13, 32; 8:44, 59; 11:8, 47–48, 53, 57). The enemy continues tirelessly in his efforts to oppose Christ through twisting the saving gospel (cf. Gal. 1:6–9; 1 John 4:1–4) and attempting to ruin God's redemptive plan (cf. Matt. 13:38–39; 2 Cor. 2:11; 4:3–4).

In addition to opposing Jesus Christ directly, Satan over the centuries has sought to destroy the nation of Israel (cf. Est. 3:1–4:3), the people from whom the Messiah would come. In his vision, John was given a look into the future time of tribulation at the end of the age and saw that "the woman fled into the wilderness where she had a place prepared by God, so that there she would be nourished for one thousand two hundred and sixty days" (Rev. 12:6). God will preserve Israel ("the woman") during the last half ("one thousand two hundred and sixty days") of the seven-year Tribulation period, when Satan, through the Antichrist, tries again, unsuccessfully, to destroy the Jews. They will be protected, saved (Zech. 12:10; 13:1; Rom. 11:11–12, 25–29), and given the kingdom promised to them (Zech. 14:4–9, 16–21; Rev. 20:1–6).

Third, Satan's strategy has been to oppose the holy angels: "And there was war in heaven, Michael and his angels waging war with the dragon. The dragon and his angels waged war, and they were not strong enough, and there was no longer a place found for them in heaven" (Rev. 12:7–8). When Satan first fell from heaven, those angels who joined his rebellion accompanied him in warring against Michael, the superangel (cf. Dan. 10:13, 21; 12:1), and his legions of holy angels.

Believers are the fourth target in the demonic strategy of warfare against God and the main focus of Peter's admonition in this passage. The apostle John describes that part of the vision: "So the dragon was enraged with the woman, and went off to make war with the rest of her children, who keep the commandments of God and hold to the testimony of Jesus" (Rev. 12:17). After being expelled from heaven, the devil ("the dragon") and his demons began their assault against "the rest of her children" (believers)—those who obey God's commands and trust in Christ for salvation. Not content with deceiving unbelievers (Rev. 12:9; 2 Cor. 4:3–4) and enslaving them to his world system of ignorance, unbelief, false religion, and sin, Satan also focuses his efforts on opposing the saints.

Satan seeks **to devour** believers in a number of ways. First, God may allow him to attack a believer directly. The story of Job's ordeal and the eventual triumph of his faith illustrates this well. In the New Testament, Peter himself experienced Satan's onslaught (Luke 22:31–34) as the enemy caused him to deny Christ three times (vv. 54–62). The Lord, however, used that incident to make his faith stronger and give him a greater ability to instruct others (cf. John 21:15–22). The apostle Paul also had to contend with assault from a demonic agent who led the attack of false teachers on the Corinthian church (2 Cor. 12:7–10). Some of the members of the church in Smyrna suffered as a result of satanic persecution (Rev. 2:10), and some in Thyatira experienced the painful consequences of demonic teaching in their church (Rev. 2:18–24). The fifth seal reveals the thousands killed by Satan through Antichrist during the Great Tribulation as pleading for divine justice to come speedily against evil enemies (Rev. 6:9–11). Finally, God even uses Satan as the agent of punishment for those who profess to preach Christ but actually lead others astray with false doctrine (1 Tim. 1:18–20), and for those who are unwilling to repent of sin (1 Cor. 5:1–5).

More generally, Satan and his demons constantly mount the attack on individual believers through the ubiquitously sinful and alluring world system. John condensed the spiritual battle down to three points at which believers' fallen humanness is susceptible to temptation:

> Do not love the world nor the things in the world. If anyone loves the world, the love of the Father is not in him. For all that is in the world, the lust of the flesh and the lust of the eyes and the boastful pride of life, is not from the Father, but is from the world. The world is passing away, and also its lusts; but the one who does the will of God lives forever. (1 John 2:15–17; cf. Acts 5:3)

Secondly, Paul recognized that Satan attacks believers in the most intimate realm of human relations—marriage and the family. For that reason Paul charged the Corinthians,

> The husband must fulfill his duty to his wife, and likewise also the wife to her husband. The wife does not have authority over her own body, but the husband does; and likewise also the husband does not have authority over his own body, but the wife does. Stop depriving one another, except by agreement for a time, so that you may devote yourselves to prayer, and come together again so that Satan will not tempt you because of your lack of self-control. (1 Cor. 7:3–5)

When one partner withholds the physical relationship from the other, Satan will tempt the one deprived to sin, thereby hastening attitudes that often bring the destruction of that marriage and family.

Third, believers—both the leaders and the members of the congregation—are vulnerable to Satan's attacks within the church. Paul instructed Timothy to choose well-qualified men as shepherds (1 Tim. 3:1–6), lest they be subject to "the snare of the devil" (v. 7). Satan also seeks to destroy the church's unity, render its spiritual power ineffective, and confuse its purpose (cf. 1 Cor. 1:10–13; 6:1–6; 11:17–34; 14:20–38; Rev. 2–3).

Peter's first line of defense for protection from Satan's strategies is simple and direct—**be on the alert.** If Satan so easily deceived Eve in Eden's perfect environment (Gen. 3:1–13; 1 Tim. 2:14; cf, 2 Cor. 11:3), how much more are redeemed sinners living in a sinful, fallen world susceptible to Satan's craftiness and deception (2 Cor. 11:3).

Contrary to what some teach, Scripture nowhere commands believers to attack the devil or demons with prayers or formulas, or to "bind the devil." Those who foolishly engage in useless efforts to speak to Satan (who is not omnipresent anyway), or to command him, or to dismiss him or other demons are confused and wrong about their powers as Christians. Since the saints are not apostles of Christ, they have no authority over demons (cf. Matt. 10:1; Luke 9:1; 2 Cor. 12:12). Only Christ Himself, by dispatching a powerful holy angel, can bind Satan:

> Then I saw an angel coming down from heaven, holding the key of the abyss and a great chain in his hand. And he laid hold of the dragon, the serpent of old, who is the devil and Satan, and bound him for a thousand years; and he threw him into the abyss, and shut it and sealed it over him, so that he would not deceive the nations any longer, until the thousand years were completed; after these things he must be released for a short time. (Rev. 20:1–3)

Satan has already been defeated by Christ (cf. Rom. 16:20) and, through belief in the truth and prayer, can also be defeated in believers' lives. It is by the Word of God, believed and obeyed, that Christians overcome Satan:

> I am writing to you, little children, because your sins have been forgiven you for His name's sake. I am writing to you, fathers, because you know Him who has been from the beginning. I am writing to you, young men, because you have overcome the evil one. I have written to you, children, because you know the Father. (1 John 2:12–13; cf. 4:4–6)

They will be victorious if they are spiritually **alert** for satanic influence coming through their surroundings and relationships, and assess potential temptations and flee from them (Prov. 1:10–17; 4:14–15; Matt. 18:8–9; 26:41; 1 Cor. 6:18; 10:13–14; 2 Cor. 2:11; 1 Tim. 6:11; 2 Tim. 2:22; James 1:13–16).

FORTITUDE

But resist him, firm in your faith, knowing that the same experiences of suffering are being accomplished by your brethren who are in the world. (5:9)

     Peter commands Christians to have a mind that is resolute and to **resist** Satan by being **firm in** their **faith.** Such resistance causes the devil to "flee from you" (James 4:7). **Resist** means "to take a stand against," and to be **firm** is to make that stand solid (the Greek is _stereos_, from which comes the English _stereo_, meaning "solid," or balanced at both ends). That is done by being solidly fixed on _the_ **faith** (_tē pistei_), which is biblical revelation. It is the whole body of revealed truth contained in Scripture (cf. Gal. 1:23; Eph. 4:5, 13; Phil. 1:27; 1 Tim. 4:1). This is a call to know and believe sound doctrine, to be discerning in distinguishing truth from error, and to be willing to defend the truth and expose error. Jude's call is most appropriate in this connection: "Beloved, while I was making every effort to write you about our common salvation, I felt the necessity to write to you appealing that you contend earnestly for the faith which was once for all handed down to the saints" (Jude 3). It is that "once-for-all" faith which is the inscripturated revelation of God and constitutes the **faith** on which believers stand solidly and from which they continually resist Satan. This strong stand is the result of the faithful leading of shepherds in the church, as Paul indicates in Ephesians 4:11–14,

> And He gave some as apostles, and some as prophets, and some as evangelists, and some as pastors and teachers, for the equipping of the saints for the work of service, to the building up of the body of Christ; until we all attain to the unity of the faith, and of the knowledge of the Son of God, to a mature man, to the measure of the stature which belongs to the fullness of Christ. As a result, we are no longer to be children, tossed here and there by waves and carried about by every wind of doctrine, by the trickery of men, by craftiness in deceitful scheming.

Since Satan is a liar (John 8:44; cf. Gen. 3:1; 2 Thess. 2:9) and a deceiver (Rev. 20:7–8), the only sure way to stand up against him is by faithful obedience to biblical truth. The battle is a spiritual one, in the supernatural realm, as Paul notes:

For though we walk in the flesh, we do not war according to the flesh, for the weapons of our warfare are not of the flesh, but divinely powerful for the destruction of fortresses. We are destroying speculations and every lofty thing raised up against the knowledge of God, and we are taking every thought captive to the obedience of Christ. (2 Cor. 10:3–5)

"Speculations" are satanic ideologies, ideas, theories, religious philosophies, and systems of thought "raised up against the knowledge of God"; that is, they are anti-biblical viewpoints that have people captive as if they were imprisoned in a great fortress. Christians cannot smash those ideas with human ingenuity, but only with biblical truth—"taking every thought captive to the obedience of Christ." Only when someone has the mind of Christ on a matter is he rescued from such ideas.

Peter concludes this section with a word of assurance to his readers as they persevered humbly and submissively, vigilantly and courageously in the midst of many persecutions, sufferings, and trials—they were not alone. He reminded them **that the same experiences of suffering** were **being accomplished by** their **brethren who are in the world.** Believers in other places could empathize with them because every segment of the Christian community has experienced or will experience attack from the Enemy (cf. Heb. 13:3). God allows this form of painful testing to accomplish His perfect work in the lives of His elect (cf. 1:6–7; 4:19; 5:10; Matt. 5:10–12; John 15:18–21; 2 Cor. 1:6–7; James 5:11).

HOPE

After you have suffered for a little while, the God of all grace, who called you to His eternal glory in Christ, will Himself perfect, confirm, strengthen and establish you. (5:10)

Hope provides believers with the settling confidence that after the trouble and difficulty of this life, they can count on God glorifying them in heaven. And during this life, they can count on His continued work of sanctifying them through their suffering (cf. Ps. 33:18; Prov. 10:28; Rom. 4:18–21; 5:5; Gal. 5:5; Titus 1:2; 2:13; Heb. 3:6; 6:19; see also the discussion of 1:3, 13, 21 concerning hope, in chapters 2, 5, and 6 of this volume). For them to fully appreciate that future purpose, believers must realize that it may come only after they **have suffered for a little while** (cf. Rom. 8:18; see also the discussion of 1:6 in chapter 3 of this volume). Christians need not fear suffering, knowing that nothing can separate them from the love of Christ (Rom. 8:31–39).

Peter calls God **the God of all grace,** which is reminiscent of Paul's title the "God of all comfort" (2 Cor. 1:3). God has already promised grace for eternity; here **grace** is provided for the present (cf. 4:10; 5:5; Rom. 12:3; 16:20; 1 Cor. 3:10; 15:10; 2 Cor. 1:12; 9:8; 12:9; Eph. 3:7; 4:7; Phil. 1:7; 2 Tim. 2:1; Heb. 4:16; 12:15; 13:9; James 4:6; 2 Peter 3:18), to strengthen believers and make their Christian character what it ought to be.

The apostle further notes that God has **called** believers (a reference to His effectual, saving call; cf. 1:15; 2:9, 21; 3:9) to **His eternal glory in Christ** (1:4–7; 4:13; 5:1, 4). The glory to which saints are called is described by Paul in Philippians 3:11–14,

> In order that I may attain to the resurrection from the dead. Not that I have already obtained it or have already become perfect, but I press on so that I may lay hold of that for which also I was laid hold of by Christ Jesus. Brethren, I do not regard myself as having laid hold of it yet; but one thing I do: forgetting what lies behind and reaching forward to what lies ahead, I press on toward the goal for the prize of the upward call of God in Christ Jesus.

The apostle John also describes it in 1 John 3:2–3,

> Beloved, now we are children of God, and it has not appeared as yet what we will be. We know that when He appears, we will be like Him, because we will see Him just as He is. And everyone who has this hope fixed on Him purifies himself, just as He is pure.

The saints' glory will be to be made like Jesus Christ (Phil. 3:20–21). Because of that objective, God **will Himself** (personally), in the meantime while they are still here—and even when the devil attacks them— use believers' suffering to mold them into Christ's image (cf. 2 Thess. 3:3). Peter concisely describes the promise of that earthly, sanctifying process of spiritual maturation by God with four nearly synonymous words: **perfect** (to bring to wholeness; cf. Phil. 1:6; Heb. 2:10; 10:1; James 1:4); **confirm** (to set fast; cf. Pss. 90:17; 119:106; Rom. 15:8; 1 Cor. 1:8); **strengthen** (to make sturdy; cf. Luke 22:32; 1 Thess. 3:2; 2 Thess. 2:17; 3:3; James 5:8); and **establish** (to lay as a foundation; cf. Pss. 7:9; 89:2; Isa. 9:7; Rom. 16:25; 1 Thess. 3:13). These terms all connote strength and immovability, which God wants for all believers as they face the spiritual battle (1 Cor. 15:58; 16:13; Eph. 6:10; 2 Tim. 2:1). He sets them firmly on the truth of divine revelation, where they stand in faith and confidence until they realize their eternal glory.

Paul's prayer for the Ephesians is consistent with Peter's promise here:

> So that Christ may dwell in your hearts through faith; and that you, being rooted and grounded in love, may be able to comprehend with

all the saints what is the breadth and length and height and depth, and to know the love of Christ which surpasses knowledge, that you may be filled up to all the fullness of God. (Eph. 3:17–19)

WORSHIP

To Him be dominion forever and ever. Amen. (5:11)

Contemplating all the aforementioned divine grace and over-whelmed by the thought of sanctification and glorification, as well as wanting to illustrate a mindset of worship, Peter bursts out in a short dox-ology rejoicing that God has **dominion** over all things **forever and ever** (cf. 4:11). Though no longer issuing commands in this section of the chapter, the apostle is still framing Christian thinking and a godly dis-position, which submits to spiritual leaders and humbles itself before God so as to be exalted in due time. Such an attitude also casts every care on God; exercises self-control, vigilance, and fortitude in His strength against the Enemy; all the while maintaining hope that the process of suffering will perfect believers on earth and bring them heav-enly reward. In addition to all Peter's exhortations, and in response to the promises attached to them, believers' minds must be constantly filled with an attitude of praise and worship toward God (1:3–4; 2:9; Pss. 50:23; 96:2; 138:5; 148:13; Isa. 24:14; 42:12; 43:21; Heb. 13:15; Jude 25; Rev. 4:10–11).

Dominion (*kratos*) actually signifies strength, and here denotes God's ability to dominate, to have everything in the universe under His sovereign and unassailable control (cf. Ex. 15:11–12; Job 38:1–41:34; Pss. 8:3; 66:7; 89:13; 102:25; 103:19; 136:12; Isa. 48:13; Jer. 23:24; Matt. 19:26; Rom. 9:21). Since He has all wisdom, power, authority, and sovereignty, He is worthy of all the praise and worship saints can render to Him.

FAITHFULNESS

Through Silvanus, our faithful brother (for so I regard him), I have written to you briefly, exhorting and testifying that this is the true grace of God. Stand firm in it! (5:12)

This section constitutes final greetings that illustrate several more attitudes of the Christian mind. Although Peter does not specifi-cally command his readers to exhibit them, they are evident in his refer-ences to other believers.

The loyalty of a fellow servant of Christ was on the apostle's mind as he mentioned **Silvanus,** another name for Silas, who traveled with Paul (Acts 15:40; 16:25) and sometimes appears in his letters (2 Cor. 1:19; 1 Thess. 1:1; 2 Thess. 1:1). Silas was a prophet (Acts 15:32, 40) and Roman citizen (16:37) who for this letter was Peter's amanuensis, or secretary. He recorded the apostle's words and later delivered the letter to its intended recipients (see the discussion in the Introduction). Peter calls him a **faithful brother,** a model of fidelity to the truth and the church, and to Peter himself, as indicated by the personal parenthesis **(for so I regard him).**

Peter also parenthetically injects a summary of his purpose as having **written . . . briefly, exhorting and testifying that this is the true grace of God.** What can he mean by this other than the letter itself, with all its gospel truth coming to his readers and all others who love **the true,** saving, sanctifying, and glorifying **grace of God?** This is a claim to inspiration that in a sense previews Peter's statement in 2 Peter 1:20–21, "But know this first of all, that no prophecy of Scripture is a matter of one's own interpretation, for no prophecy was ever made by an act of human will, but men moved by the Holy Spirit spoke from God." There the apostle affirms Old Testament inspiration. Here he speaks of his first letter as the truth concerning God's salvation. He wrote as an inspired, authoritative author of "the living and enduring word of God" (1:23; cf. 2 Peter 3:2). Because this is true, the apostle exhorts believers to faithfulness to the truth of his letter by exclaiming, **Stand firm in it!** This reiterates the call of 5:9 to remain firm in the faith (cf. Rom. 5:1–2).

LOVE

She who is in Babylon, chosen together with you, sends you greetings, and so does my son, Mark. Greet one another with a kiss of love. Peace be to you all who are in Christ. (5:13–14)

Peter closed the epistle not by commanding the attitude of love, but by personally illustrating it. His love for the believers in the church at Rome, from where he wrote, is seen in the designation **she who is in Babylon,** which is an oblique reference to that church. As noted in the Introduction, **Babylon** is possibly Peter's code word or alias for Rome (cf. Rev. 14:8 where John uses Babylon to represent the entire world system controlled by Antichrist; also see 16:19; 17:5; 18:2, 10, 21). Some commentators suggest Babylon summarized Rome's link to false religions. But it may be better to understand that with persecution intensifying, Peter was careful not to endanger the Roman Christians. Having written this letter from Rome, Peter did not want his manuscript discovered and the church to be persecuted even more. Therefore he made no mention of Rome, leaving any curious and hostile authorities ignorant that this letter originated in their imperial capital.

The believers in Rome demonstrated true love and affection by sending their **greetings,** as did **Mark,** whom Peter called **my son,** a designation indicating he was the apostle's spiritual son (as Timothy was to Paul). This is the John Mark mentioned in Acts 12:12. He was Barnabas's cousin and accompanied Paul and him to Antioch and Cyprus (12:25; 13:4–5). He later deserted them at Perga (13:13), which caused Paul to refuse to take him along on the apostle's second missionary journey (15:36–41). Paul later found John Mark to be useful to him (2 Tim. 4:11). **Mark** was also the author of the gospel that bears his name.

Greet one another with a kiss of love is another obvious indicator of the affection believers should have for each other. The holy kiss—men to men, and women to women—was a customary outward sign of affection among believers in the early church (Rom. 16:16; 1 Cor. 16:20; 2 Cor. 13:12; 1 Thess. 5:26; cf. Luke 7:45; 22:47–48).

Peter closed his letter with the simple statement, **Peace be to you all who are in Christ** (cf. Mark 9:50; Luke 2:14; John 14:27; 20:19, 21, 26; Rom. 1:7; 5:1; 1 Cor. 14:33; 2 Cor. 13:11; Eph. 4:3; Phil. 4:7; Col. 3:15; 2 Thess. 3:16; Heb. 13:20; Rev. 1:4).

There is no shortcut to a Christian mind possessing those godly attitudes and motives Peter outlined. They will be perfected only as believers regularly and faithfully place themselves under the preaching, teaching, and study of God's truth and obediently allow His Word to change their hearts and shape their characters (Luke 11:28; James 1:22–25; cf. Pss. 19:7; 119:105; Prov. 6:23; Mark 4:20; Luke 6:46–48; John 14:21; 17:17; Rom. 15:4; Col. 3:16; 2 Peter 1:2–8; see also commentary on 2:1–3 in chapter 8 of this volume).

Bibliography

Arndt, W. F. and F. W. Gingrich. *A Greek-English Lexicon of the New Testament and Other Early Christian Literature.* Chicago: Univ. of Chicago, 1957.

Bigg, Charles. *A Critical and Exegetical Commentary on the Epistles of St. Peter and St. Jude.* The International Critical Commentary. Reprint. Edinburgh: T. & T. Clark, 1975.

Carson, D. A.; Douglas J. Moo; and Leon Morris. *An Introduction to the New Testament.* Grand Rapids: Zondervan, 1992.

Davids, Peter H. *The First Epistle of Peter.* The New International Commentary on the New Testament. Grand Rapids: Eerdmans, 1990.

Guthrie, Donald. *New Testament Introduction.* Revised Edition. Downers Grove, Ill.: InterVarsity, 1990.

Hiebert, D. Edmond. *First Peter: An Exegetical Commentary.* Chicago: Moody, 1984.

_____. *An Introduction to the Non-Pauline Epistles*. Chicago: Moody, 1962.

Kelly, J. N. D. *A Commentary on the Epistles of Peter and Jude*. Peabody, Mass.: Hendrickson, 1988.

Kistemaker, Simon. *New Testament Commentary: Exposition of James, Epistles of John, Peter, and Jude*. Grand Rapids: Baker, 1995.

Leighton, Robert. *Commentary on First Peter*. Reprint; Grand Rapids: Kregel, 1972.

Lenski, R. C. H. *The Interpretation of the Epistles of St. Peter, St. John and St. Jude*. Reprint. Minneapolis: Augsburg, 1966.

MacArthur, John. *Twelve Ordinary Men*. Nashville: W Publishing, 2002.

Rees, Paul S. *Triumphant in Trouble. Studies in 1 Peter*. Westwood, N.J.: Revell, 1962.

Schreiner, Thomas R. *1, 2 Peter, Jude*. The New American Commentary. Nashville: Broadman & Holman, 2003.

Selwyn, E. G. *The First Epistle of St. Peter*. London: Macmillan, 1961.

Stibbs, Alan M. *The First Epistle of Peter.* The Tyndale New Testament Commentaries. Grand Rapids: Eerdmans, 1971.

Vine, W. E. *An Expository Dictionary of New Testament Words*. 4 volumes. London: Oliphants, 1940. One-volume paperback edition. Chicago: Moody, 1985.

Indexes

Index of Greek Words

zenizō, 249
zenos, 249

zōēn, 193

Index of Scripture

Index of Subjects

Titles in the
MacArthur New Testament Commentary Series

MOODY
PUBLISHERS

THE NAME YOU CAN TRUST®

1-800-678-6928 www.MoodyPublishers.org

SINCE 1894, Moody Publishers has been dedicated to equip and motivate people to advance the cause of Christ by publishing evangelical Christian literature and other media for all ages, around the world. Because we are a ministry of the Moody Bible Institute of Chicago, a portion of the proceeds from the sale of this book go to train the next generation of Christian leaders.

If we may serve you in any way in your spiritual journey toward understanding Christ and the Christian life, please contact us at www.moodypublishers.com.

"All Scripture is God-breathed and is useful for teaching, rebuking, correcting and training in righteousness, so that the man of God may be thoroughly equipped for every good work."
—2 TIMOTHY 3:16, 17

MOODY
PUBLISHERS

THE NAME YOU CAN TRUST®

1 PETER MNTC TEAM

ACQUIRING EDITOR
Greg Thornton

COVER DESIGN
Ragont Design

PRINTING AND BINDING
Quebecor World Book Services

The typeface for the text of this book is
Cheltenham